PENGUIN BOOKS

2615

EMPRESS JOSEPHINE

Ernest John Knapton was born in a Yorkshire village and went with his parents to Canada at the age of six. He was educated in the schools of British Columbia; his less formal training included work in a dynamite factory, a logging camp, a night school for Chinese, and a salmon cannery on the Alaskan border. In 1925, after some years of schoolmastering and graduation from the University of British Columbia, he went to Oxford as a Rhodes scholar. Since then Ernest Knapton has been a teacher and lecturer in history. *Empress Josephine*, his fourth book, was published in 1963; since then he has published, with T. K. Derry, *Europe 1815–1914* (1965), *Europe and the World Since 1914* (1966), and *Europe 1815 to the Present* (1966). He has also written for various magazines and has supplied articles for several encyclopedias.

ERNEST JOHN KNAPTON

Empress Josephine

Penguin Books

BALTIMORE · MARYLAND

Penguin Books Ltd, Harmondsworth, Middlesex, England
Penguin Books Inc., 7110 Ambassador Road, Baltimore, Maryland 21207, U.S.A.
Penguin Books Australia Ltd, Ringwood, Victoria, Australia

First published by Harvard University Press 1963
Published in Great Britain by Oxford University Press 1964
Published in Penguin Books 1969
Copyright © The President and Fellows of Harvard College, 1963

—

Made and printed in Great Britain by
Cox & Wyman Ltd,
London, Reading and Fakenham
Set in Monotype Garamond

TO JOCELYN

Contents

Contents

Letters

Preface

THIS book follows the career of the woman who came to be the Empress Josephine as she moved through one of the great formative periods of modern times. Her life, which biography after biography has sought to recapture, is interesting in itself and on occasion rises to moments of absorbing drama. The creole of Martinique who at sixteen undertook the life of a *vicomtesse* of the *ancien régime* became under the Revolution a widowed victim of the Terror. She sought to rebuild her life during the feverish years of the Directory. Marriage with Napoleon Bonaparte ultimately brought her to the very pinnacle of European fame. In this position Josephine played an imperial role for which in all truth she had been only modestly equipped.

In addition to its drama, what gives principal interest and distinction to her life is the vivid picture it presents of a society in the midst of intense change. The Napoleonic court was dominated by one of the most brilliant soldiers and administrators the modern world has known, a leader who sought along with so much else to consolidate his dynasty and to create a new imperial splendour far greater than any that royalty had been able to provide. Josephine was a central figure in this attempt. To some degree at the Tuileries and Fontainebleau, and much more at Malmaison, she played her unique part. Modern scholarship, the nature of which is suggested in the Bibliographical Essay, has made it possible for us to see her role in a richer, a more complex, and assuredly a more human perspective than was apparent to her earlier biographers. Along such lines this study has been written.

My first acknowledgement must be to Wheaton College for a sabbatical leave in 1959 during which some of the research for this book was undertaken in France and England, and also for assistance from the Faculty Research Fund in preparing my manuscript for publication. I thank most sincerely my colleagues, Professor Curtis Dahl and Dr T. K. Derry, for

9

Preface

their painstaking critiques of the form and substance of what I have written. I owe no less thanks to my friend Dr Geoffrey May, whose acute judgement is equalled only by his invariable willingness to be of assistance. To Professor Crane Brinton of Harvard University I am likewise particularly indebted. I express my thanks to M. Pierre Schommer, Conservateur en Chef of the National Museums of France, for a most interesting conversation with him on the subject of Josephine and also to Mlle Marguerite-Marie Paul, Librarian of the Bibliothèque Thiers in Paris, for her equally valuable help. I gratefully acknowledge the permission accorded by Librairie Plon to quote extracts from the Beauharnais and Tascher de la Pagerie letters edited by Jean Hanoteau in *Le Ménage Beauharnais* (Plon, 1935) and *Les Beauharnais et l'empereur* (Plon, 1936). I thank, finally, my wife, Jocelyn Babbitt Knapton, not merely in conventional terms, but with a gratitude for which the dedication of this book to her can be only a most incomplete expression.

E. J. KNAPTON

Wheaton College
Norton, Massachusetts
March 1963

❧ I ❧

Prologue

PARIS in the spring of 1796 – a tired, uneasy, revolutionary city. Here, on the threshold of a spectacular career, a young French general named Napoleon Bonaparte is about to take as his bride Citizeness Beauharnais, a romantic creole of Martinique. It is a time when the fury of the great revolutionary days has subsided. The guillotine is gone, the tumbrils have ceased to clatter through the cobbled streets, the once crowded prisons are empty, and the invader no longer desecrates the soil of France. After years of terror the shadow of death has lifted.

Everywhere the restless Parisians are moving about, seeking excitement and pleasure. Ridiculously overdressed men and scandalously underdressed women throng the cafés and the theatres. Crowds parade in the Champs-Élysées; young bucks ogle the girls in the gardens of the Palais-Royal; speculators wait for hours in the anterooms of the directors of the Republic, hoping for lucrative posts and fat army contracts. In these anterooms the reigning beauties of the hour – 'government property', as one of the most famous of them was described – develop remarkable skill in arranging that those who seek contracts shall meet the politicians who grant them.

Soldiers are everywhere, for in the course of the revolutionary campaigns France has put almost 800,000 men under arms. Many of them are simple 'citizens' (the term is still new) who have been put into uniform by the *levée en masse*; it is they who truly have saved the Republic. One sees a scattering of officers from the *ancien régime* who have thrown in their lot with the new order. But, above all, Paris is dominated by the freshly experienced officer corps born of the Revolution, men usually risen from the ranks – the Neys, the Bernadottes, the Murats, future marshals of France – who are to give their country its great triumphs. These are the 'new men', often uncouth and arrogant, and always cocksure. They are connoisseurs of victory, veterans of the campaigns in the Austrian Netherlands, the Rhineland, and Savoy, eager for still greater triumphs that will settle accounts once and for all with the armies of Austria.

Rising rapidly among them is Bonaparte. This young general (he is only twenty-six), though commissioned under the *ancien régime* and therefore an authentic product of its military traditions, is truly a child of the new age. He is about to take as his wife a former viscountess whom necessity has led to accept the Revolution. The daughter of a sugar-planter of Martinique, she is a widow, having shared prison with a luckless husband who went to the guillotine only three days before Robespierre fell. After narrowly escaping his fate, she was freed with thousands of others, and for the nearly two years since she has lived by her wits and her charm, grateful for occasional remittances from her mother in Martinique, supporting her two young children as best she can. The former viscountess has stormed the cardboard battlements of Directory society, sharing the very centre of the scene with reigning beauties such as Thérèse Tallien and Juliette Récamier, and living on terms of dubious familiarity with Paul Barras, the leading director.

Now the ardent wooing of the young soldier is sweeping the widow into a second marriage, destined to give her a life of spectacular quality and to make her Empress of the French – a title held by the Austrian Marie Louise and the Spanish Eugénie but by no other Frenchwoman. Six of her children and grandchildren are to wear royal or imperial crowns. She will bring elegance and colour to a ruthless age; she will lose her throne; and she will leave behind her a romantic tradition that is not yet forgotten.

Josephine has attracted to herself something of the perennial interest men find in the career of the great emperor. Today, in the superbly restored château of Malmaison, her salon, her music room, her boudoir, and her bedroom vie with the martially decorated council chamber and the workmanlike library of her husband in conveying the authentic spirit of a dead past. If the great cedar of Marengo, planted to celebrate one of Bonaparte's early victories, recalls the great days of the armies of Italy, the rose gardens Josephine planned and the swans of Malmaison, still gliding over their pools, evoke the charm that for a few brief years a woman brought to a war-filled age. '*Malmaison, c'est Joséphine.*'

What manner of woman was she? In essence Josephine was a relatively simple person, and conflicts of interpretation have arisen less from what she was than from the chaotic nature of her time and from the political passions of the years during which her biographies have been written. Moreover, she led not one life but three. For even as Alexander de Beauharnais brought Josephine from Martinique into the fringes of the sophisticated circles of the *ancien régime* in France, so Napoleon Bonaparte carried her into the full sweep of the revolutionary and imperial epochs. Through Josephine we find ourselves at one of the great turning-points of modern history. The interwoven story of her three lives – a story dramatic in itself – acquires heightened significance for the insight it gives into the spectacular age of which she was a part.

❧ 2 ❧

Bird of the Islands

In June of 1763, on the tiny French island of Martinique, a daughter was born to the wife of a struggling sugar-planter. Within a week of the baby's birth, the mother wrote to her sister-in-law, five thousand miles away in Paris:

Contrary to all our wishes, God has chosen to give me a daughter. My joy has been no less great, since I look upon her as one who redoubles my affection for your brother and for you. Why should we not have a more favourable view of our own sex? I know some who combine so many good qualities that it would seem impossible to find them all in any other person.[1]

This daughter, baptized Marie-Josèphe-Rose de Tascher de la Pagerie, and known to history as the Empress Josephine, was the child of her Martinique environment – a warm, indolent, tropical world whose flavour we can still recapture.

In the larger setting of the Antilles the island of Martinique lies towards the lower end of the long chain extending from Puerto Rico to the coast of South America. It is the chief of the Windward Islands, those *Îles du Vent* whose very name suggests their romantic ocean setting. Europeans first saw Martinique, apparently, when Christopher Columbus landed there in 1502. Nine years earlier, during his first great voyage, he had been told by Caribbean natives about the strange island of Matinino, which they believed to be 'wholly inhabited by women without men', as he noted in his journal. On his homeward voyage in 1493 he had planned, understandably, to visit this remarkable spot, but the promise of favourable winds for Spain had led him to alter his course. Not, therefore, until his fourth and last voyage and after a brisk twenty-one-day crossing from the Canaries was he able to make his landfall on Martinique.

A century later, in 1635, the green island fell within the French orbit when a Norman adventurer, Pierre Belain, Sieur d'Esnambuc, crossed from near-by Saint Christopher and took possession. This D'Esnambuc, founder of French power in the Antilles, had a sister, Adrienne, from whom Josephine's paternal grandmother was descended. The island prospered. Sugar and coffee plantations required slave labour, quickly supplied from the Guinea coast of Africa with such consequences that in 1779 when Martinique was estimated to have but eleven thousand whites and three thousand free Negroes and mulattoes, it had some seventy-one thousand slaves. These were the backbone of the economy. Although the famous *Code Noir* – the Black Code of 1685 – guaranteed them what was then called humane treatment, they endured many hardships and indignities. Amid these tropical surroundings Josephine's family pursued its fortune.

The family of Tascher de la Pagerie into which Josephine was born belonged to the ancient country gentry of France, the *gentils hommes de province*, and had originated in the rich countryside of the Loire valley, not far from Blois. Its history shows the typical, the almost inevitable, genealogical details: the Tascher who in 1142 endowed a medieval abbey; the Tascher who in 1190 went crusading; the Taschers who made fortunate marriages, who held administrative posts, who won further lands, all being suitably rewarded by their grateful sovereigns. We come finally to Gaspard-Joseph Tascher de la Pagerie, who in 1726 sailed to Martinique and settled at Carbet, a few miles north of Fort-Royal, the principal island establishment. He seems not to have prospered; he may even have resorted to something not far from menial employment. A son, Joseph-Gaspard, born in 1735, was Josephine's father.

Some reasonably clear picture emerges of this less than spectacular Joseph-Gaspard. Indolent by nature, he was saved by having good connexions in France. An uncle had risen in the Church to become canon of Blois, *abbé* and viscount of Abbeville, and almoner to the dauphine of France. Through him Joseph-Gaspard and his brother won appointments as pages in the dauphine's household, on the very threshold of the court. Joseph crossed the ocean in 1752 and stayed in France for three years. He would, therefore, have been in attendance at the time of the birth to the dauphine in 1754 of the future Louis XVI. As a stripling in one of the great royal households of France he seems to have learned remarkably little. In any event, when he returned to Martinique he was satisfied to live the life of an obscure sugar-planter and to look for social prestige no further than his commission as *sous-lieutenant* of dragoons in the local militia. Shortly afterwards, in 1761, he was lucky in marrying Mlle Rose-Claire des Vergers de Sannois, a daughter of one of the oldest families in the colony, and born, like him, at Carbet. Through his wife he did well: he acquired a plantation at Trois-Îlets, some miles to the south of Fort-Royal, which was to be his home and furnish his livelihood until he died in 1790.

Joseph-Gaspard's life contained little of mark. His three early years as a royal page, a later visit to Paris with Josephine, and an undistinguished participation in the defence of Martinique against the English were the highlights of his career. He did, to be sure, stand his ground for ten hours when his battery came under fire from the English fleet besieging Martinique in 1762, during the Seven Years' War. For this brief encounter he obtained an annual royal pension of 450 livres. His life was beset with ill health, and his business affairs were seldom far from bankruptcy. 'He means well,' his brother once wrote, 'he loves his family, above all, his children – but he must be pushed.'[2]

Josephine's mother was pictured by her contemporaries as a fine woman of high intelligence who had the characteristic creole unwillingness to give up the life of the islands for any other. 'Creole', we may note, is a term used to designate a person of European origin, French or Spanish, who is born in the islands. Although in later years Madame Tascher exchanged warm letters with her famous daughter, she would never risk the acute discomforts and terrors of the long voyage to visit Josephine in France. When the Empire was proclaimed and a fine house set up for her at Fort-Royal, the seventy-year-old widow refused to accept it, preferring instead the familiar circle and the old ways of her modest establishment at Trois-Îlets. She died in 1807, the mother of an empress, and was duly escorted to her grave by a battalion of troops marching to the sound of cannon.

The precise birth date of the first child of Joseph-Gaspard's marriage was 23 June 1763. Martinique had been captured in 1762, the British having attacked, according to their commander, 'with the most irresistable [*sic*] impetuosity.' As the peace with England had just been signed in February, and Martinique had been restored to the French at the end of March, the future empress was spared by four months the embarrassment of having been born on alien soil. In a curious parallel, Napoleon was to be born on Corsica in 1769 only a year after it had become French. Two sisters, Catherine-Désirée, born in 1764, and Marie-Françoise, born in 1766, gave Josephine the principal companionship of her early childhood. Known affectionately to her family as Yeyette, she customarily signed herself at this time as Marie-Rose. Only later, and at the desire of Napoleon Bonaparte, did she come to use the name of Josephine.

The tropical world of the Antilles made Josephine what she was. Tiny Martinique, some forty miles long and fifteen miles wide, lies in its ocean setting dominated by the volcanic peak of Mount Pelée; in 1902 the volcano was to erupt, bringing awesome death to forty thousand inhabitants and leading to the proposal that the entire island be for ever abandoned. Fort-Royal, renamed Fort-de-France, was then, as now, the principal centre of government and trade. Across the bay from it stood the much smaller settlement of Trois-Îlets, with its stone church and its fifty wooden houses. Near here Josephine's family had its home. The West Indian plantations, properly run and with reasonable luck in the perennial battles with storms and pests, richly rewarded their owners. To exploit their wealth many Frenchmen made the long westward voyage.

The unique social pattern arising from the specialized economy of the sugar islands helps to explain the development and character of Josephine. A planter aristocracy, the *grands blancs*, brought to the island echoes of their French homeland. Younger sons, most of them, and of good family, they included many types: the ambitious, the venturesome, the restless, the elusive, and the impecunious, some doubtless escaping from debtors' prisons and *lettres de cachet* in France. The *grands blancs* provided the members of the sovereign council and some of the entourage of the governor-general – a high noble sent out to the colony from France. In this administrative and aristocratic hierarchy Josephine's family had little status: her father and her uncle rose to no higher than a captain's rank in the island militia.

Family life was centred in the plantation, with its fields of sugar cane planted and tilled by slave labour. The *grands blancs* were managers and directors, perhaps comparable to the white settlers in Kenya in our own time. Life, in its externals, had a certain air of ease and gallantry. Generous hospitality, a richness of dress that on great occasions reflected the latest modes from Europe, a passion for gambling, and a ready resort to duelling were all noted by observers as marks of this island society. The sovereign council at Fort-Royal was once presented with a list of seventeen duellists who had lost their lives in a single year.

The easy tempo of tropical existence and the enormous preponderance of slave labour produced the type of creole society that Josephine herself so well exemplified. Affectionate, indolent, sensitive, usually happy in their surroundings and always hospitable, closely bound by ties of family, the creole women established a way of life far removed from the life of France and in some respects indifferent to it.

This world, however remote, had some impact upon the jaded society of France in the last years of the *ancien régime*. The ornate costumes, the hooped petticoats, the rich brocades, and the fantastic coiffures of French fashionable society had then reached their ultimate point of extravagance and impracticality. Just as Marie Antoinette on occasion sought refuge from this stifling atmosphere in the Arcadian pleasures of the Petit-Trianon, so there developed a somewhat corresponding taste among the fashionable of France for the muslins and cottons, the loose gowns, the lightly-woven shawls, the neat fichus, and the simple hair-styles *à la créole* that were the products or the inspiration of the Indies, West and East.

The plantation where Josephine first lived was about a mile from Trois-Îlets, in relatively flat land close to the sea but hidden from it. One came to it by a forest road crossing a stone bridge over a small river called La Pagerie. Like a medieval manor, here was a little world of its own. Here were the enfolding fields of sugar-cane, coffee plants, and tobacco; here were the huts and kitchen gardens for the slave families, the barns full of stalks used as fuel, the round mill built on heavy pillars with its red tiled roof, the square, tall, brick chimney of the furnace, the *case à farine* where the Negroes prepared cassava, the hospital, the lock-up, and, most important of all, the *sucrerie*. The *sucrerie* was a large stone building measuring 120 by 60 feet, with walls two feet thick within which the stalks were crushed by rollers, the liquid collected, and raw sugar produced. Tamarinds, banana palms, mango, orange, and breadfruit trees brought shade everywhere. Tropical flowers and birds made flashes of colour.

Originally Josephine and her family had lived in a large wooden house that had a courtyard planted with shade trees. The terrible hurricane of 1766, the worst in the history of the island, had swept this house away. Forty-eight ships were sunk off Martinique alone, 440 persons were killed, and even more were injured. Many plantations were destroyed, and others, like that of the Tascher family, were badly damaged. Josephine's father never recovered from this loss. Characteristically he did not attempt to rebuild his house, but moved instead into the *sucrerie*, remodelling it as a home with a low outside gallery and sleeping chambers upstairs.

The easy life of the islands put little emphasis on intellectual pursuits. Planters had but one preoccupation, to make money; having made it, many of them expected to return to France. Despite the reluctance of their wives, they hoped to enjoy their wealth on ancestral soil and claim the social privileges that their birth assured them. 'Every man hurries to grow rich,' as one contemporary put it bluntly, 'in order to escape for ever from a place where men live without distinction, without honour, and without any form of excitement other than that of commercial interest.³ A royal official gave his opinion that those who sought higher education should go to France for it. The rest should be satisfied with reading, writing, and 'the principles of religion and arithmetic', studies that could easily be handled by the local *curés* and schoolmasters. In Martinique there was little that could be called true society, nothing that could be called a salon, and no trace of the ferment associated with the Enlightenment. Not a single book, nor even a newspaper, was published in the French islands before the middle of the eighteenth century, when at last a printing-house was established in Santo Domingo.

This was the tropical, island world, with its easy tempo, its self-indulgence, its warmth of colour, its strong domestic affections, and its absence of intellectual ferment, that moulded Josephine's early years.

Six years before Josephine's birth there had arrived at Martinique Messire François de Beauharnais, governor and lieutenant general of the Windward Islands of America. Assuming his post in 1757, at the critical moment of the war with England, he nevertheless found time for an affair of the heart with Joseph-Gaspard's sister – an affair whose outcome in due course profoundly affected the life of Josephine. The Beauharnais family belonged to the same province of France as did the Tascher de la Pagerie family. Though less ancient, dating from the fifteenth century, it was more prosperous by far. Many members had served in the administrative nobility of France, many had had distinguished careers at sea. One had served for twenty-two years as governor of French Canada and had been associated with Verendrye's discovery of the Rocky Mountains. Another had shared with Iberville in the discovery of the Mississippi River.

This François de Beauharnais had a naval career dating from 1729. By following a policy of sticking close to the port of Rochefort and rarely going to sea, he had reached the high rank of *major des armées navales* and had the title of marquis. His governorship of Martinique was uneventful until January

1759, when a British fleet threatened the island. It chose, however, to sail to Guadeloupe, where it launched a serious assault.
Beauharnais delayed an incredible three months before organizing a relief expedition. He was then unable to do much, partly
because he had sent two of his principal warships to inform his
superiors in France that he was being attacked, and even more,
apparently, because he was distracted by his romantic adventures. Guadeloupe fell to the English, and in the following
year the incompetent Beauharnais was removed from command. The governor of Guadeloupe, who was court-martialled
and condemned to life imprisonment for the surrender, said
later that Beauharnais could not have mismanaged affairs more
effectively if he had deliberately tried to lose the island.

Recalled to France in 1761, Beauharnais suffered no further
censure. Following a pattern that was all too typical of the
ancien régime, he was given the higher rank of fleet commander,
secured a fat yearly pension of 12,000 livres (which compared
most favourably with the niggling 450 livres obtained by
Josephine's father for his services in the same campaign), and
was confirmed in the title of Marquis de la Ferté-Beauharnais.
Few have gained more for doing less.

Though the fortunes of war had been inauspicious, those of
Venus had prospered. A connexion grew up at Martinique between the Beauharnais and Tascher families. To be sure, the
social distance between the all-powerful governor general and
the impoverished, unambitious sugar-planter who wore the
uniform of a lieutenant was at first great. It was reduced when
Beauharnais made the acquaintance of the tall, blonde, twenty-
year-old Marie-Euphémie-Désirée, sister of Joseph-Gaspard
Tascher. Doubtless because of this acquaintance the governor
took an active part in arranging her brother's marriage in 1761
to a member of one of the oldest families in the colony. What
began as friendship (Marie-Euphémie was godmother to
Beauharnais' son Alexander, born in Martinique) soon turned,
despite Beauharnais' age, his military responsibilities, and the
presence of his wife, to infatuation.

His infatuation first took the typically Gallic form of finding
the young woman a wealthy husband among the junior officers

of his own staff. His choice was decidedly curious, for Alexis Renaudin had recently returned from four years' imprisonment in France, under a *lettre de cachet*, suspected of having tried to poison his own father. Soon after Renaudin's wedding to Mademoiselle Tascher took place, the young bride accused her husband of trying to poison *her*. Understandably, a marriage of this sort soon fell apart; Renaudin returned to France and entered at Paris a legal plea for separation, which his wife most earnestly supported. Thus Madame Renaudin was freed from her transient commitment to a preposterous husband. When eventually she learned that the Marquis de Beauharnais was to be recalled to France, she made the long Atlantic crossing before him, awaiting in Paris the opportunity to win him completely away from his wife.

On Martinique, meanwhile, the Marquise de Beauharnais had become the mother on 28 May 1760, of a son, Alexandre-François-Marie. Since this infant was considered too young to accompany his parents when they sailed to France in the following year, he was left at Trois-Îlets in the care of the Tascher family. He remained for over five years. Josephine's birth at Trois-Îlets followed by three years that of Alexander. Thus they were infants together in a tropical setting reminiscent of the island paradise in the Indian Ocean on which the novelist, Bernardin de Saint-Pierre, was to place those saccharine, star-crossed lovers, the hurricane-racked Paul and Virginie.

Sentimental historians have had no difficulty in painting a romantic picture of Josephine's youth. They have pictured her sharing in the storytelling, the songs, and the dances of the Negro servants. They have associated her with the weird witchcraft and prophecies of the tropics. They have had her, with her sisters, climbing the green mountains of Martinique and contemplating her white limbs as she bathed naked in forest pools. All this is possible. Her early life, real or fancied, exuded romanticism to the generations that turned the pages of Rousseau, wept over *Paul et Virginie*, read of the Noble Savage, and pictured those idylls as blossoming in corners of the world far removed from the false glitter of France.

At the distance of nearly two centuries we can still catch

occasional vivid glimpses of the simple pattern of Josephine's girlhood. She saw much more of the Negro women slaves than of the rare visitors to the estate, or of the relatives and friends whom the family in turn visited. From her earliest days she was attended by a nurse, a mulatto slave named Marion, for whom she always kept an affectionate regard. Years later Josephine arranged for Marion's freedom, and in 1807 secured an official warrant from the imperial treasury in Paris conferring upon 'demoiselle Marion, free mulatto of Martinique', an annual income of twelve hundred francs.

At the age of ten, after recovering from a slight attack of smallpox, Josephine was sent with her younger sister, Catherine-Désirée, to be educated at the convent school of the *Dames de la Providence* in Fort-Royal. Such a school gave Josephine a modest education. She learned to read, to write, to sing, to dance, and to embroider. Few women of her time could have been expected to learn much more. Then, after four years, on the death of Catherine-Désirée by malignant fever, Josephine returned to Trois-Îlets to be with her mother. By October of 1777, when she was fourteen years old, her formal schooling was completed.

No story of Josephine is more famous than that of the aged negress of Martinique who prophesied to her youthful listener that after an unhappy marriage and widowhood she would some day wear a crown and become 'more than a queen'. The story, now firmly a part of the island tradition, actually appeared in a royalist newspaper in Paris, *Le Thé*, as early as May 1797, when at least part of the prophecy still awaited fulfilment. Josephine liked to tell the tale after becoming empress. Its obvious significance is that it conveys the pervasive quality of 'magic' and 'prophecy' in the primitive Negro environment of her childhood.

Some later narratives shed light on the Martinique period. A certain Count Montgaillard, for example, an officer in the regiment of Auxerrois, visited Martinique in November of 1777, and afterwards when he assembled his *Souvenirs*, recalled the youthful Mademoiselle Tascher. He pictured her as 'graceful, more fascinating than beautiful, already noteworthy for the suppleness and elegance of her bearing, dancing like a fairy, and amorous as a dove'. She was, he adds, 'of a frivolity, a coquettishness, to say no more, that was astonishing, even in the colonies – capricious and extravagant'. She was, we may remind ourselves, fourteen and had just left the convent.[4]

A General Tercier, who as a young officer served in the Martinique regiment from 1772 to 1782, has left in his memoirs a tantalizingly brief note about Josephine: 'I made the acquaintance,' he wrote, 'of Mlle Tascher de la Pagerie, the celebrated Empress Josephine. I was closely linked with all her family. I often spent several days at the establishment of Madame her mother. She was young then; I was also . . .'[5] At this vital point the memoirs fade out in a row of asterisks, by means of which Tercier can imply and his readers can infer as much or as little as they choose. Some, knowing Josephine's later life, have inferred a great deal.

The even more shadowy figure of a young Englishman appears fleetingly in the memoirs of Mademoiselle Cochelet as 'Mr Williams', and equally imprecisely in those of Mademoiselle Lenormand as 'Mr William de K. . . ., neveu de Lord Lova [Lovat?]'.[6] According to these sources, this William, or Williams, climbed Mount Pelée with Josephine on a May day in 1779, flirted innocently with her for a few hours, and then disappeared for thirty-five years. In the spring of 1814, a veteran soldier, he reappeared most belatedly at Malmaison and asked for an audience, only to be told in truly romantic fashion that the Empress was on her death-bed. Whereupon Mr Williams folded his tent like the Arab and, for a second time, silently stole away from the record of history.

A tradition tells of Josephine's youthful association on Martinique with a distant cousin, Aimée du Buc de Rivery, whose life has evoked some fantastic stories. Her father had a plantation a few miles away at the settlement of Robert. Sent to France for her education, Aimée was returning to Martinique in 1784 when her ship disappeared. The story has grown up that she was captured by Barbary corsairs and taken to Algiers. She was then supposed to have been sent by the Bey of Algiers as a gift to the Sultan Selim III in Constantinople, to have entered his harem, and to have become the mother of Mahmud II. Known as 'la Sultane Validée', she is said to have acquired considerable influence, with no desire to abandon the fantastic position to which fate had brought her.

In contrast to this chronicle of speculation and fiction are the few solid facts concerning Josephine's betrothal and marriage. With them her life now entered a strikingly different phase.

❖ 3 ❖

A Marriage is Arranged

THE lengthy negotiations for the marriage of Josephine, still in Martinique, to an almost unknown suitor in far-away France are a classic example of eighteenth-century French matrimonial procedures. The children of that period were trained to remain silent before their parents, who were wont to act both as man and God, first proposing and then disposing in the matter of their offspring's fates. The Alexander who had left Martinique late in 1765 to return to his family was somewhat less than six years old, and the Josephine whom he left behind was then a little more than two. This infant association, while no doubt richly stimulating to the imagination of a W. S. Gilbert or to the mental processes of a Freudian, establishes for the historian little more than that for a short time the two children shared a few common experiences.

What stands out most obviously is that the patterns of these two lives soon sharply diverged. While Josephine undertook her simple schooling with the *Dames de la Providence* at Fort-Royal, returning from them to the patriarchal life of the sugar plantation at Trois-Îlets, Alexander began to move in the sophisticated world of eighteenth-century France. In 1766, shortly after his arrival, he visited his mother, now definitely separated from her husband, in her château at Blois. When she died the following year, the seven-year-old son returned to Paris. Here he came under the direct care of his devoted god-mother, Madame Renaudin, who, well supplied with funds as a result of her separation from Monsieur Renaudin, lived openly with the Marquis de Beauharnais.

The education of this boy, who would be the first husband of Josephine and would powerfully influence her formative years, was typical of that given to aristocratic youth under the *ancien régime.* Alexander first joined his older brother, François, at the Collège de Plessis in Paris. Then at the age of ten he was put with his brother in the charge of a tutor with whom he was to remain for more than six years and whose influence was to last much longer. This tutor, Patricol, an old teacher of mathematics, was a devotee of Rousseau. His pedantic, crabbed, and smug letters to Madame Renaudin, stamping their writer as a character directly out of an eighteenth-century novel, illuminate the first phase of Alexander's career.

Patricol was responsible for taking the two boys to Heidelberg, so that they might learn German. Here Alexander seems to have developed a certain independence, if not precisely a maturity, of ideas. In 1775 Patricol was offered a post in the family of one of the most distinguished members of the French nobility, Louis-Alexandre, Duke de La Rochefoucauld. It was arranged that the younger Beauharnais should accompany his tutor to the château of La Roche-Guyon, some fifty miles down the Seine from Paris, and later to the great *hôtel* Rochefoucauld in the capital. This same château of La Roche-Guyon would serve, nearly two hundred years later, as the headquarters of Field-Marshal Rommel during the Normandy invasion of 1944. Here Alexander absorbed much of the elegance of a great noble household and rubbed against the liberal ideas of the eighteenth century. The duke was a friend of Adam Smith and Voltaire, of Franklin, Lafayette, and Arthur Young. He had spoken before the *Parlement* of Paris, reminding the king of the rights of the French nation. He was a member of the Academy of Science and had served as president of the Royal Society of Medicine. His reputation was so widespread that four years before the outbreak of the French Revolution the city of New York admitted him to honorary citizenship. Alexander could hardly fail to be affected by these stimulating surroundings.

Other influences were at work. Patricol reported that in these years of adolescence Alexander was falling into dubious company who regaled him with stories of their 'garrison adventures'. 'What astonishes me most,' Patricol wrote, 'and greatly displeases me in the young man is the extreme care which he takes to hide, the ease with which he disguises, the sentiments of his heart . . . For the rest, his work does not go badly.'[1] The statement is prophetic. After he married Josephine Alexander would soon find ample opportunity to hide from his young wife his garrison adventures and to disguise with an outpouring of words the true sentiments of his heart.

Alexander was now sixteen. Through the duke, who was its commander, he won a commission as *sous-lieutenant* in the Sarre infantry regiment. A certain youthful gloating over his new station is easy to understand. By April 1777 he was with his regiment at Rouen, resplendent in his white uniform with silver-grey facings, his sword, and his black three-cornered hat. Army affairs did not occupy all his time. For instance, he wrote to his godmother, asking her to send him the documents connected with his membership in the Freemasonic lodge of Saint-Sophia in Paris, so that he might transfer his affiliation to the Sarre regiment's lodge at Rouen, the Lodge of Purity. While a Freemasonic lodge of the eighteenth century would offer its members a certain type of intellectual sophistication, Alexander was also in hot pursuit of sophistication of another sort. The bright eyes of the ladies of Rouen proved to be only less attractive to him than the bright eyes of the ladies of Dieppe, where his regiment soon went.

For an officer of seventeen, well-born and heir to a substantial fortune, the question of marriage could not long be deferred. During a visit that Alexander made to his father and godmother at Paris in October 1777, such discussion of marriage apparently had taken place and a decision been reached. At all events the old marquis wrote to Josephine's father at Martinique, requesting that Alexander be given the hand of Catherine-Désirée, Joseph-Gaspard's second daughter. While the words of the letter were those of the marquis, the driving force behind them was almost certainly the strong-minded Madame Renaudin. She had good reasons for her plans. Madame Renaudin was a creole with a strong sense of family. A marriage of this sort would unquestionably strengthen her position with the marquis. She had maintained a close cor-

respondence with her relatives in Martinique and had long
pestered her brother to send Yeyette (Josephine) to France for
an education. Now that it was a question of marriage, the second
daughter, rather than the eldest, seemed the most suitable. In
view of Joseph-Gaspard's straitened circumstances, a dowry
would not be stipulated, for Alexander was well provided.

The marquis explained that Alexander could anticipate on
marriage an income of forty thousand livres a year, wealth that
must have impressed deeply the impoverished planter. The
value of eighteenth-century currency as compared with
modern money, or what money will buy, suggests that the
purchasing power of a livre would then have been well above
that of the dollar today. Thus Alexander de Beauharnais could
look forward on his marriage to becoming a really rich man.
This prospect of financial independence goes far to explain his
willingness to accept, sight unseen, a bride from five thousand
miles away whom he had known only in his earliest infancy.

The Marquis de Beauharnais further insisted that his son's
high regard for Madame Renaudin had increased Alexander's
desire to marry one of her nieces. Josephine was mentioned
politely, but only to be put aside. 'I would have much desired,'
wrote Beauharnais, 'that your eldest daughter [Josephine]
were several years younger. She would certainly have had the
preference, since I have been given an equally favourable
picture of her, but I must declare to you that my son, who is
only seventeen and a half, finds that a young lady of fifteen is
of an age too close to his own. There are occasions when sympathetic parents must yield to circumstances.'[2]

To strengthen his request, the marquis also wrote to Josephine's mother and to Josephine's uncle, Robert. Madame
Renaudin added her voice. Promising to take full charge of
the niece, she gave a glowing picture of the unseen swain:
'A pleasant face, a charming bearing, wit, intelligence, and –
which is of inestimable price – all the qualities of heart and
soul united in him; he is beloved by all who surround him.'[3] No
dowry was needed, she reiterated, but, if Joseph-Gaspard wished
to do something, he might promise a small annual income, keeping in his own hands control of the capital involved.

The slow-moving negotiations back and forth across the Atlantic were not to succeed. A week before the marquis had sent his request, and of course unknown to him, young Catherine-Désirée had died of a malignant fever. When Joseph-Gaspard wrote the sad news, knowing the loss it would be to the young suitor, he now proposed that Alexander marry instead his youngest daughter, Marie-Françoise. To be sure, she was only eleven and a half, but she was one, he explained, in whom 'health and gaiety of character are combined with a figure that will soon be interesting'.⁴ Alexander, now in Brittany with his regiment, blandly agreed. This alternative solution, he told Madame Renaudin, 'appears to me quite natural'. And with this casual and chilling acceptance he turned to other matters, going on to discuss as a young soldier the contemporary hazards at sea arising from the war in the New World.⁵

Clearly Madame Renaudin, even more than the Marquis de Beauharnais, was pushing the marriage arrangements. When poor Joseph-Gaspard had announced his readiness to make the risky voyage across the Atlantic with his daughter, she wrote to him as follows: 'Arrive with one of your daughters or with two. Whatever you do will be agreeable to us. Consider it good that we should leave you to be guided by the Providence which knows better than ourselves what is good for us.'⁶

The tragicomedy was not yet over, for Joseph-Gaspard had still further confusions and unhappiness to report. Since the daughter whom he had so freely offered was not yet twelve, there was protest within the family. Neither her mother nor her grandmother had any heart to part with so young a child. Manette herself was greatly upset at the prospect and had for three months suffered a fever in consequence. Hence the father had no alternative but to propose Yeyette, twice passed over in favour of her younger sisters but apparently still worthy of consideration. He now described her as 'well formed for her age, and sufficiently matured in the last six months to pass for eighteen'. She had a sweet character, he explained, played the guitar a little, sang, and had a fortunate disposition for music.⁷

Even before this third offer arrived, Madame Renaudin,

fearing trouble, had decided to delay no longer. She got the Marquis de Beauharnais to send to Martinique an official authorization to have the wedding banns published. A blank was left in this document for the name of the future wife to be inserted, whoever it should turn out to be. 'The one whom you judge most suitable for my son,' he amiably explained to Joseph-Gaspard, 'will be the one whom we desire.'[8]

The intended husband, on hearing of these changes, might justifiably have entered a demurrer. Instead, he took refuge in a philosophical acquiescence which may have owed something to the teachings of Patricol. 'I can see the difficulties,' Alexander told his father, 'which these ladies raise about sending their daughter to France.' Concerning Josephine he made some slight reservation: 'Surely it is not your intention to have me marry this young lady if she and I should have a mutual repugnance for each other.' He was, however, writing to his father and diplomatically put the best face upon the situation. 'I do not doubt,' he assured the marquis, 'after the description which has been given, that she will please me. I hope to be fortunate enough to inspire in her the same feelings that I shall have towards her.'[9] And so it was arranged. The marquis wrote to reassure Joseph-Gaspard, and Madame Renaudin added her own voice. She stressed the need, despite all risks of war, for a speedy departure. She feared, so she wrote in November of 1778, the manoeuvres of members of the Beauharnais family who had other candidates to propose, and she was also concerned about 'the ardour of the young man which might cool were he to be forced to wait too long'.[10]

In a letter which Joseph-Gaspard had written to Madame Renaudin somewhat earlier in the negotiations we can see with some vividness the young Josephine on the eve of her marriage. After leaving the convent school, her father said, she had asked him on several occasions to take her to France. This brief observation shows that Josephine, in this respect hardly the typical creole lady, was someone with a touch of the adventurous and the independent. But her father sought rather to gild the lily with more obvious charms. 'She has a very good skin,' he went on to say, 'good eyes, good arms, and a surprising taste for music. I gave her a teacher for the guitar while she was at the convent, and she made full use of this and has a very pretty voice. It is a pity that she has not the advantage of an education in France.'[11]

Josephine's opinion and feelings appear nowhere in these negotiations, so fateful for her happiness. Nor is there any record of her comment later in life upon what was done now. She accepted, in characteristic eighteenth-century fashion, a conventional marriage arrangement that took little note of the desires of the prospective bride. As her father's letter suggests, she may well have looked forward with genuine anticipation and excitement to the glamour of married life in France. She was proceeding to a household where her father's sister would hold out a welcoming hand. When, years later, she found herself compelled to bring suit for separation against Alexander and in so doing to review the course of their married life, she made no complaint whatever about the way in which her marriage had been arranged. This was one of the 'silent' crises of Josephine's life, 'silent' because there is no clear evidence of what she said or thought then on which to base judgement or interpretation today.

What Alexander de Beauharnais said and thought we do know. Seven years later the other partner in the arrangements told a brother officer, the Marquis de Bouillé, that he had married Josephine because he had been forced to by his father, and that he separated from her as much as a result of this same pressure as of any doubts concerning her fidelity.

The marquis and Madame Renaudin had some reason to desire that this marriage be effected as quickly as possible. During the months of correspondence and negotiation Alexander de Beauharnais had been engaged in amorous adventures about which he was anything but silent. He had rejoined his regiment in Brittany, ultimately finding himself stationed at Conquet, a small village fifteen miles from Brest, overlooking the bleak waters of the Atlantic. 'I am,' he wrote unhappily to his great confidante, Madame Renaudin, 'in the most miserable place possible.'[12] From Brittany he sent his lukewarm yet acquiescent comments upon the progress of the arrangements for his betrothal. The letters of this seventeen-year-old youth to Madame Renaudin, meanwhile, contain some striking reports upon his feminine conquests. Towards the end of August he wrote to his godmother saying that he was planning to visit a near-by country house, his hostess a charming woman whose favours he hoped to win. Her name was Madame de Longpré. A week later came the triumphant news:

Yes, your chevalier has tasted happiness in these parts! He is loved by a charming lady, to whom are addressed the devotions of the whole garrison of Brest . . . I expect to go to her country house after the review, and I propose to pass a charming week there. Her husband, who left three days ago, has told me that he is under orders to spend three weeks away. I hope with all my heart that nothing obliges him to return sooner.[13]

How concentrated Alexander's affections were we may well doubt. Explaining his delay in revisiting Madame Renaudin, he wrote that he was overwhelmed by 'the twin sentiments of love and friendship'. To depart had become difficult. 'Pardon your godson if he finishes this letter so soon, but two pretty faces are in the corner of the room, reproaching him for concerning himself with anything but them, and are playing a thousand tricks upon him. Forgive me, dear godmother, but their lovely eyes are my excuse.'[14]

By the close of October Alexander was ready to return to his family, but not without one last, almost clinical, evaluation of his *vie amoureuse*. He wrote again to Madame Renaudin, telling her that never before had he experienced true love, and that he was in despair at having to leave. 'Up till now,' he said, 'I have always misunderstood my feelings, whether because my emotions were not developed, or because I was attached to people incapable of inspiring a violent passion.' That morning a lackey had delivered a letter from Madame de Longpré, which this incredible youth now forwarded to his godmother. Alexander's last sentence implies the prospective birth of a child to the pair of lovers:

Perhaps [he wrote] it may help you to judge the choice I have made, and serve me as an excuse for not being on the road to Paris, even though under other circumstances I would have sold my very shirt not to be the last to leave Conquet. . . . I am about to take horse in order to go to her brother's estate two leagues from here. The word Juliette may intrigue you; it is the name we have chosen for the one who will be very dear to us.[15]

This letter, surely, is a perfect example of the eighteenth-century fondness for the 'outpouring of the ego'. That an eighteen-year-old army officer of the *ancien régime* should have pursued affairs of the heart is not surprising. That he should have displayed his emotions on paper in this age of Rousseau is perhaps to be expected. What is startling, one must admit, is to find him parading the history of his conquests to none other than his godmother, supposedly responsible for his spiritual well-being. And the young Lothario wrote at the very moment, as he well knew, when she was the arch-mover of negotiations that were to result in the marriage of her precious and precocious godson to her niece.

So unusual indeed are Alexander's letters to his godmother that they cannot altogether be explained in terms of their youthful author's sophistication and cynicism. The boy was, after all, writing to a woman who was his father's mistress, and Madame Renaudin, still legally married to another man, was in no position to lecture her godson about the proprieties. She may have reproved Alexander and urged him to cease and desist. On the other hand, fashionable marriage in the eighteenth century put few impediments in the way of a husband's continuing adventures. Whatever the warmth of Madame Renaudin's feelings towards Josephine, the mistress of the Beauharnais household was about to introduce an inexperienced adolescent girl to a life that she would find dangerously unfamiliar.

If Alexander's letters to Madame Renaudin concerning his amour had illustrated merely the passing fancies of a bachelor on the eve of matrimony, they would merit very little attention. The romantic figure, however, for whom Alexander professed first to have experienced true love, was no passing fancy. She reappeared later in his life, haunted him, and ultimately brought his marriage to disaster.

Marie-Françoise de Longpré, who was born in Martinique eleven years before Alexander, came from a family distantly akin to the Taschers. Josephine, indeed, was accustomed to refer to Madame de Longpré's father as her 'uncle'. Madame de Longpré was married to a naval officer and had two children, the second of whom, Alexandre, born in the summer of 1779, may have been the son of Alexander de Beauharnais. She was one of the many transient and elusive figures whose fortunes were to be intermingled with Josephine's. Her behaviour was unquestionably scandalous, yet her stepdaughter, the Marquise de la Tour du Pin, no doubt wishing to make the best of her relative, pictured her as a good, easy-going woman, although weak in character and indolent in the typical creole fashion. She is also said to have had one most curious habit, always carrying with her a candle, the end of which she nibbled incessantly.

After a holiday at Noisy-le-Grand and at Paris, Beauharnais *fils* rejoined his regiment in July. He was now on the staff of his old mentor, the Duke de La Rochefoucauld, stayed with him in the château at Verteuil, and by August was back once more at Brest. 'I plan to follow exactly the salutary advice which you and my papa have had the goodness to give me,' he wrote in his ineffably complacent fashion to Madame Renaudin, 'even that which requires me to have the least possible acquaintance with the Breton females. What will astonish you is that this last advice will probably be followed with the greatest exactness.'[16] A subsequent letter hardly bears out his pledge. Alexander seems to have hit upon the notion that love-making goes best in the presence of a brass band. Hence he had arranged to have the regimental band provide music for the ladies of the town, so that they could dance with the officers in the moonlight on the parade-ground.

The night was magnificent [he reported]. The moon, which no cloud obscured, gave enough light to distinguish all the residents whom the music had attracted. They proposed to spend the night dancing, but the royal lieutenant, who is not a dancing man, objected to the length of our pleasures and insisted that considerations of order required everyone to return home.[17]

Whatever the cause, military duty or dancing by moonlight, Alexander fell ill. After an agreeable recuperation at a near-by château, in October he returned to his family in Paris. At this very time Josephine with her ailing father was making the stormy crossing of the Atlantic for the rendezvous with her intended husband.

Despite all Madame Renaudin's urgings, Joseph-Gaspard had not been able to leave Martinique until August 1779. He was ill of a liver complaint, and unquestionably money was scarce. Eventually he found passage for himself and Josephine, together with a mulatto servant named Euphemia. More than a suspicion existed at Martinique that this servant could look to easy-going Joseph-Gaspard as her father. Their ship, *Île-de-France*, was escorted because of war conditions by a frigate, the *Pomona*. The crossing was exceptionally long and must have been miserably uncomfortable. Years later in Paris, when Madame Renaudin submitted some of her brother's papers to the authorities in support of his request for a pension, she explained their poor condition by describing how, though kept in a trunk during the passage, they had been flooded by water pouring in upon them. Joseph-Gaspard, moreover, had been desperately ill, so ill that the news sent to the Beauharnais family on the party's arrival at Brest on 12 October gravely alarmed them.

Madame Renaudin and Alexander de Beauharnais set out at once from Paris. They reached Brest on the 28th. Alexander's letter to his father conveys the whole tone of the first rendezvous. To begin with, he reported that Joseph-Gaspard was not so seriously ill as they had feared. Next, he explained several things that had needed attention. Alexander had bought a cabriolet for the trip costing forty louis, paying fifteen in cash and drawing a sight draft on the family banker for the balance. He went on to say that they would leave in a few days but could not be sure of the time required for the trip or the date of their arrival in Paris. At long last, after all this humdrum, came the news of the young lady to whom Alexander had been officially betrothed since the publishing of the banns in April, a fiancée whom he had just seen for the first time. 'Madem-

oiselle de la Pagerie,' Alexander wrote with deadly politeness,
'will perhaps seem less pretty to you than you expect, but I
believe I can assure you that the honesty and sweetness of her
character will surpass whatever people have been able to tell
you about her.'[18] One is almost tempted, with the biographer
Masson, to believe that Alexander was persuading the old
marquis to marry Josephine in his place.

Since Joseph-Gaspard's health quickly improved, the party
set off in a few days, being warned by the doctor to travel by
very easy stages. Before leaving Brest the father took the
precaution of granting his sister power of attorney to act for
him in the wedding if any illness should overcome him. En
route, Madame Renaudin sent the marquis reassuring news.
'Our invalid', as she called him, was very tired, but seemed
better. Josephine would be a dear and tender daughter to the
marquis. She 'has all the feelings that you could wish her to
have toward your son, and I have observed with the greatest
satisfaction that she suits him . . . He is busy, yes, very busy,
with your [prospective] daughter-in-law.'[19] Three days later
another happy missive flew from Madame Renaudin: 'You
will have received a letter from your *chevalier* which confirms
what I clearly observed: things are constantly going better
and better.'[20] One further touch comes in a memorandum of a
much later date, signed by Madame Renaudin and entitled:
'Money which I have disbursed for my brother from his
arrival in Paris until 25 June 1782.' She, apparently, was under-
writing all expenses.

When the group arrived in Paris, the preparations for the
wedding moved forward remarkably fast. A trousseau was
quickly purchased with funds provided by Madame Renaudin,
and the banns were read on 5 December. They were read but
once: a special dispensation from the archbishop of Paris had
obviated the need for second and third readings. On 10 December a marriage contract, which throws significant light on
the position and interests of the various participants, was
sealed 'in the apartment which M. de la Pagerie occupies in
the home of the Dame de Renaudin'.[21] Alexander brought to
the marriage the incomes he had inherited from his mother

and his grandmother, the very substantial annual sum of 40,000 livres derived largely from lands in Santo Domingo and from the family estates in France. Josephine brought the promise of a dowry of 120,000 livres from her father, an amount utterly beyond his ability to provide. The 20,000 livres that he agreed to give at once was actually advanced to him by Madame Renaudin and was used to buy Josephine's trousseau, in all but name a bride-price rather than a dowry. Since he had promised to pay interest at five per cent on the unpaid remainder, he had really committed himself to providing his daughter with a yearly income of 5,000 livres. Josephine brought, in addition, the sum of 15,000 livres representing her effects in Martinique and the gifts of various relatives there. Her aunt, Madame Renaudin, made the most substantial provisions of all by presenting the house at Noisy-le-Grand, which she had bought in 1776 for 33,000 livres and which had furnishings valued at about the same sum. She also pledged to the bride the large sum of 121,149 livres constituting an indebtedness due to her from a nephew of her husband, M. Renaudin.

The marriage was celebrated on 13 December at the parish church of Noisy-le-Grand, outside Paris, Significantly, it took place not in the city parish where the Marquis de Beauharnais resided but in the rural parish of Madame Renaudin's country house, now transferred to the newly-weds. Josephine's father being too ill to attend the wedding, he was represented by a distant cousin, a doctor of the Sorbonne and prior of Sainte-Gauburge, who had been given the legal powers to assent to the marriage in the name of both father and mother. On the occasion of the marriage Alexander assumed the title of *vicomte* (which had not yet legally been confirmed to him) instead of the title *chevalier*, which he had previously used. He was married in the presence of a substantial representation of the Beauharnais clan – his father, his uncle, his brother, and his cousin – as well as his old tutor and several of his regimental colleagues.

Josephine must have been very much alone on that bleak December day. Dominating the proceedings was the imposing presence of the sixty-four-year-old Marquis de Beauharnais, former governor of the Antilles, chevalier of the Order of Saint Louis. Yeyette was marrying 'the high and puissant seigneur, Alexandre-François-Marie, Vicomte de Beauharnais, captain in the infantry regiment of the Sarre'. She had been in Paris less than a month. Though her father's representative, the prior, was distantly related to her, and though a very few other distant male relatives and former Martinique acquaintances were at hand, she could hardly have known them well. Even though Madame Renaudin and other ladies were no doubt present, the childlike inscription, 'M. J. R. Tascher de la Pagerie', is the only feminine signature among the fourteen on the marriage register.[22]

Josephine's mother, writing three months later to Madame Renaudin about the wedding, expressed her own feelings: 'The union is your work; their happiness must be your work also.'[23] The statement of fact cannot be questioned, for throughout all these proceedings is evident the dominant – indeed, the masterful – role of Madame Renaudin. She, much more than either the Marquis de Beauharnais or the nearly bankrupt Monsieur Tascher de la Pagerie, had organized, directed, and concluded every stage. The victory was hers.

✦ 4 ✦

Storm and Stress

JOSEPHINE's first two wedded years were spent chiefly in the Beauharnais *hôtel* in Paris, on the now vanished rue Thevenot. The mansion faced upon stone walls and dark, narrow streets – 'a sort of prison', it has been called – a world removed from the blue seas, the mountains, and the tropical greenery of Trois-Îlets. It stood in that part of Paris lying between what now are the Grands Boulevards and Les Halles, an area where dilapidated survivals of the old, dignified homes of the aristocracy still remain. The building was tall and somewhat grim, yet with elegant staircases and high-ceilinged rooms, not far from the noisy, dirty, bustling centre of eighteenth-century Paris. It was a home dominated by the traditions of the family, the house in which Charles de Beauharnais, for twenty-two years governor of French Canada, had died. The old marquis and Madame Renaudin were the hosts, and Josephine's invalid father stayed with them as their guest. Josephine, likewise, was more truly a guest than she was the châtelaine of the establishment. The ages of Josephine's closest associates, apart from her husband, were sixty-four, forty-five, and forty-one; and we remember that Alexander, an officer in the army and a man of the world, was more often away than at home. No promising beginning, surely, for a sixteen-year-old bride brought up in the warm, easy, indulgent surroundings of her West Indian childhood!

The pattern of Josephine's married life took shape when the last decade of what men soon would call the *ancien régime* began. Talleyrand's famous words, 'He who has not lived in the years preceding 1789 does not know the pleasure of living,' however true they may be in general, are less than precise as a picture of the young bride from Martinique in her new surroundings.

In her case the 'pleasure of living' was marred almost immediately by suggestions of domestic storm and stress.

This young bride was a girl rather than a woman. Alexander, on first meeting her, had not found her beautiful, yet her chestnut brown hair, her hazel eyes, her excellent skin, her graceful arms, her attractive voice, and her general pleasantness of manner had won him to her, so that his early letters breathed a sincere warmth of affection. Josephine lacked the intellectual baggage that was standard equipment among the bluestockings of the *ancien régime*. She had been given no chance as yet to acquire the elegances and artifices of French society. She had not grown into the graceful, sophisticated, dazzling hostess of later years. She was young, she was inexperienced, and she had more than a touch of what writers like to call 'creole indolence'. It was entirely natural for her to feel unsure, frightened, and at times lost in her new surroundings. Absolutely nothing in her early training had provided any equivalent to the rich stimulus Alexander de Beauharnais had found in the household of the Duke de La Rochefoucauld. She came to her debonair young husband a warm-hearted, affectionate girl, not without a mind of her own, and was flung into situations of increasing difficulty, which, as it turned out, she could neither master nor accept.

In her new life, as in Martinique, Josephine had abundant leisure. She possessed money enough to shop for clothes and finery in what was then, as now, the centre of fashion. Her husband gave her jewels: earrings, bracelets, a watch, and a diamond-studded chain. These she carried around and played with, so an unsympathetic report had it, like a child with toys. She had little role, however, in society. The old marquis, contented with the company of Madame Renaudin, had few social ambitions and even fewer intellectual interests. The members of the Beauharnais family living in Paris apparently accepted with little comment the equivocal position of Madame Renaudin, who had obtained a legal separation but not a divorce from her actual husband. Josephine no doubt had the conventional social contacts with Alexander's relatives – his married brother, François; his uncle, Claude-Louis; and his cousin, Claude – yet in sum they meant very little to her.

Not even Josephine's dashing husband brought her much acquaintance with the fine world. Alexander, despite his position, his handsome looks, and his superb dancing, was of a nobility too recent to warrant presentation at court. Josephine's family, to his chagrin, was in this sense better than his own. Alexander, moreover, did not relinquish the connexions he had established before his marriage. Unhappily for Josephine, when he went occasionally to enjoy the stimulus of new ideas at his second home – the Duke de La Rochefoucauld's château of La Roche-Guyon – he left his wife behind.

One striking figure was an exception in this colourless milieu. Alexander had an aunt, Marie-Anne-Françoise Mouchard, Countess de Beauharnais. She was the wife of the brother of the marquis. Known as Aunt Fanny, her substantial ambitions as a hostess and writer had led her to maintain a drawing-room in the rue de Montmartre and later in the rue du Tournon, near the Luxembourg palace. This salon of Aunt Fanny was, surely, one of the curiosities of Paris in the last decade of the *ancien régime*, constituting one aspect of the fashionable world where Josephine now became, if not a full participant, at least a spectator.

Fanny de Beauharnais wrote tirelessly. We can list some thirteen works – one running to three volumes – from her ever-fertile pen. She had composed a pamphlet in 1773 with the ringing title, *To All Thinkers, Hail!* She was the author of a novel, *Blinded by Love*, and, much later, of a poem of high topical interest most explicitly entitled, *To Bonaparte, at the Moment When the French People Vote on the Question*: *Shall Napoleon Be Consul for Life?* It has been suspected that Aunt Fanny did not write all that appeared under her name, and she is now remembered chiefly for the neat epigram about her by Lebrun, which in translation could be given thus:

> Of Chloe, fair and a poet, we may two faults rehearse:
> While she makes up her features, others make up her verse.

On the eve of the French Revolution the salon of Aunt Fanny became one of the most frequented in Paris, as much because of the decline of the more noted gatherings, where death had taken its toll, as because of its intrinsic merits. In the stifling atmosphere of her drawing-room, for Fanny detested fresh air, coughing, it was said, was more common than conversation. One can say little for those attending – they have been described as canaries rather than nightingales. Cubières, Restif de la Bretonne, and Sebastien Mercier, 'the triumvirate of bad taste', were her devotees. A memorable picture has survived of Fanny listening to a reading of her poems, enthroned on her silver-and-blue settee, over-rouged, a chaplet of pink rosebuds tilted on her powdered hair. She was pleased to visit Buffon's museum of natural history wearing a *coiffure à la giraffe*. Cubières called her salon 'the egg of the National Assembly', which we may doubt; wits more truly compared it to the prefecture of police because, running from eight in the evening until five in the morning, it rarely closed.

Josephine's connexion with Fanny de Beauharnais was much more personal than it was scholarly or literary. Aunt Fanny stood as godmother to her second child. A tradition that suggests the pattern of their relationship says that Fanny looked after the two children when Josephine was imprisoned during the Terror. It is too much to believe that the artificially scented literary atmosphere of the rue du Tournon could have meant much to the young Josephine – except possibly to alarm her. Indeed, little evidence shows that she was closely in touch with it. Some women, most notably Madame de Staël, were able to find enormous intellectual stimulation in the Paris of the *ancien régime*. 'Oh for the gutters of the rue du Bac!' exclaims Madame de Staël amid the placid beauties of Switzerland. She, with the powerful advantage of her unusual family training, would have managed somehow to find intellectual stimulation on the surface of the moon – provided only that she had an audience. Josephine's background and disposition were altogether different, and thus the new and strange world of Aunt Fanny's salon struck no responsive note. Yet, only a few years later, when she had separated from her husband, Josephine did flit like a gleaming butterfly through Aunt Fanny's fantastic surroundings.

The blue skies of marriage were quickly clouded for Alexander de Beauharnais by a most painful discovery. He found that his young wife was totally devoid of those intellectual interests to which, from his first acquaintance with Patricol at the age of ten, he had been exposed. He need hardly have been surprised at this deficiency in the equipment of a typical creole daughter of the eighteenth century, for creole ignorance in such matters was proverbial. Many of the *grandes dames* of the West Indies could hardly read or write, and, while Josephine wrote a clear hand, could express herself moderately well, and had some facility with music and dancing, the *Dames de la Providence* would have found it hard to take credit for equipping her with much more. In her letters Josephine often failed to add the correct plural endings to her words, and at a much later date she still spelled phonetically – *trafayé* for *travaillé*, for example. However common such failings, Alexander chose to be disturbed.

Alexander's concern about the lack of intellectual depth that he discovered in his wife appears in a letter he wrote to her from La Roche-Guyon in the May following their wedding. This letter (the very first from Alexander to Josephine that has survived) shows that he had already launched on the dangerous course of trying to improve his wife, and that she at this point had responded with all reasonable willingness. Yet we can also hear a faint note of disagreement and strain. Josephine, apparently, had reproached him for not writing to her:

Rely on my fairness [he answered her very sharply], and do not poison the pleasure which I take in reading what you say by reproaches which my heart does not deserve. . . . I am delighted at the desire to improve yourself which you have shown me. Such a taste, which one can always gratify, brings delights which are always pure, and has the precious advantage of leaving no regrets in the one who heeds it. By persisting in the resolution you have made, you will acquire knowledge that will raise you above the others and, combining wisdom with modesty, will make you an accomplished woman.[1]

How can one characterize this letter other than to say that it shows Alexander de Beauharnais as a pedant and a prig? As the months went by, despite Josephine's intermittent and yet well-intentioned efforts to please him, these disagreements became more marked.

The first real test of separation soon came, when Alexander left for Brest in order to do service with his regiment. On the way he wrote to Josephine, telling her how much he anticipated her letters. 'You know how dear they are to me,' he declared, adding with his inescapable touch of officiousness, 'I do not doubt that you will keep yourself safe from any reproach.'[2] From Brest came a note of disappointment: 'I counted on finding letters from you on my arrival, but I was only half satisfied, for I was given a packet which contained letters from my friends only. Their promptness charmed me, but yours would have flattered me even more.'[3] Whatever concern Alexander may have had, in his next letter he breathed contentment: 'How tender, how pleasing, is the letter just received; the heart that inspired it must be sensitive indeed, and worthy of being loved. So it is. Yes, my heart, I truly love you, I long greatly to see you; and this expected moment, however near it may be, seems all too far away.'[4]

Josephine had told him of her hopes that she was to be a mother. Although these turned out to be false, they naturally enough caused Alexander to write tenderly to her. He vowed his delight in domestic tranquillity, urged her to take harp lessons with the famous Professor Petrini, and, ever alert to the problem of Josephine's literary improvement, suggested that she always send him the rough drafts of her letters so that he could go over them for her. He also wrote at this time to Madame Renaudin, seeking to mobilize her help in his great project, to determine, as he put it, 'what is to be done about my wife's letters'.[5]

Alexander visited Paris briefly in December. Then, after a short turn of duty at Verdun, rather than return to his wife, he went still again to La Roche-Guyon and the La Rochefoucauld entourage. Signs were already appearing of a certain unwillingness on the part of Josephine, whether through indolence or through pride, to be 'moulded' as her husband would have wished. One recalls the initial reluctance of the

Marquis de Beauharnais to request Josephine as a bride for his son, on the grounds that she was too near Alexander's age and therefore not easily bent to her husband's will. Yet on the whole the two seemed content. The news had come that Josephine was unmistakably pregnant, in response to which Alexander wrote to Madame Renaudin, saying that he was trying to rearrange his duties so as to get a leave for August and September. 'My greatest desire,' he explained, 'would be gratified if I could have the means to be present at the accouchement of Madame de Beauharnais. Even though the conditions should be very hard I will certainly take my leave.'[6] He could hardly have offered to do less.

The second year of marriage witnessed Alexander pouring forth his troubles to his old tutor, Patricol, whom he saw at La Roche-Guyon. He had believed at first that he could live happily with his wife. He had subsequently formed a plan to 'commence' (the word should be noted) her education. He formed a determination, as he expressed it, 'to repair by my zeal the fifteen neglected years of her life'. Unfortunately, as he told Patricol, Josephine soon displayed 'such indifference and so little will to learn' that he renounced his plan, convinced that he was wasting his time. The failure led Alexander to change the pattern of his domestic life. He no longer stayed at home in the company of one who had nothing to say, but resumed in part his 'bachelor existence'. This, so he told Patricol, was costing him dearly, for he still preferred 'the happiness of a home and of domestic peace' to 'the tumultuous pleasures of society'. Alexander's hope had been that his wife would now make some efforts to attract him and to acquire those qualities he valued so highly. But what had been the result?

She wants me to occupy myself in society solely with her; she wants to know what I say, what I do, and what I write, and she never thinks to acquire the true means of . . . gaining my confidence – which I keep from her only with regret, and which I would gladly give her at the first indication of her eagerness to become better informed and more agreeable.[7]

In answer to this outburst Patricol gave Alexander some sensible advice. Alexander might well be at fault through impatience and over-eagerness. Patricol therefore suggested that he cease the effort to direct his wife's training single-handed, and that others be mobilized in the struggle to provide Josephine with an education. He was sure that Madame Renaudin could find individuals, Josephine's father among them, who would read poetry, drama, history, and geography with her. During the forthcoming winter Patricol would find someone to take general charge of her studies.

Poor Josephine! What Alexander was unable to accomplish alone, the combined energies of all these might somehow achieve. The effort, moreover, seems to have been made. The defenceless, unschooled *oiseau des îlets* was pushed into borrowing the four volumes of the Abbé Vertot's fluent and imaginative *Roman History* in an attempt to improve herself, yet nothing indicates that she did more than borrow them. After Vertot had written his account of the siege of Malta someone belatedly forwarded him certain relevant historical documents for which he had previously asked. Vertot's famous acknowledgement was, 'The siege of Malta is over.' Josephine, as it turned out, had little need to concern herself about Vertot's historical accuracies or inaccuracies. She abandoned her Roman studies almost as easily as Vertot abandoned his account of the siege of Malta, for she could now summon an unassailable womanly defence against this organized onslaught of the pedagogues. By now she was six months pregnant.

Patricol still did his best to improve the domestic atmosphere. He urged Madame Renaudin to persuade Josephine that 'brusqueness and dictatorialness are two bad ways to attract to her a husband whom she loves'. He guaranteed that Alexander had a tender heart and wished to be loved. After some sensible reflections on matrimony, he concluded hopefully, 'Do everything, Madame, which your zeal and affection dictate, and I have no doubt that we shall succeed, you and I, in re-uniting the two spouses whose happiness is so inseparable from our own.'[8] Sensible and honest words, these, which raise Patricol far above the pedantic level of some of his earlier letters!

Josephine was delivered of a son on 3 September 1781 at the family home on the rue Thevenot. She was now eighteen and Alexander twenty-one. The child, destined some day to be viceroy of Italy and to have three of his children upon royal thrones, was baptized the next day at the church of Saint-Sauveur as Eugène-Rose. Alexander was at home for an event that seemed to strengthen the ties binding the two young parents. Yet 'a taste for liberty and an inflexible will' (these are Josephine's words) soon led her husband on further adventures. On 1 November he left alone on a tour of Italy that occupied him until the following year. Madame Renaudin is said to have encouraged him to go away, for even after the birth of Eugène apparently all had not been harmony in the home.

When Alexander returned in July of 1782 Josephine received him 'with the greatest evidences of joy', and he in turn 'seemed enchanted to find himself with her again'. (These too are Josephine's later words.) About this time the Marquis de Beauharnais moved to a more fashionable residence on the rue Neuve-Saint-Charles, not far from the church of Saint-Philippe du Roule. As Josephine's father now left for Martinique, and as the new home was leased in the name of Alexander de Beauharnais rather than of the old marquis, Josephine was nearer to having a *ménage* of her own than she ever had been before.

In these circumstances Josephine now found herself pregnant for the second time. Unfortunately, the domestic rapprochement was brief. In a few months the restless Alexander was away again, this time on the high seas for Martinique, and with him aboard ship was the Madame de Longpré of his romantic amours in the summer before his marriage.

Why did Alexander thus determine to leave France and his wife for Martinique? Although events can be described, motives, especially at the distance of two hundred years, often elude us. Alexander's decision to go abroad may have been inspired by his domestic troubles. It may have been due to the legitimate ambition of a professional soldier, for since the

American Revolution continued, French forces were needed to meet the English threat to the West Indies. The decision may have been a secret plan arranged by him because of his infatuation for Madame de Longpré.

A more complicated explanation, involving the Tascher de la Pagerie family, is also possible. Like Alexander, Madame de Longpré had relatives who had been involved in the humiliating surrender of Martinique to the English in 1762, and these relatives had been the subject of bitter criticisms from the Taschers. Some local historians of Martinique have claimed that Madame de Longpré, deeply resentful of such criticisms, sought her revenge in wrecking Josephine's marriage, and with this plan in mind took passage for Martinique on the very ship on which she had persuaded Alexander to embark.

Whatever the reasons for his going, Alexander moved quickly. He applied to the Marquis de Bouillé, now appointed as governor of the Windward Islands, for a post as aide-de-camp, submitting a letter from his old mentor, the Duke de La Rochefoucauld. The duke claimed to have known him since infancy and vowed him to be 'a young man full of uprightness and character, having wit and a great desire to learn . . .'[9] Because Bouillé left France hastily without heeding the letter, this project fell through. Alexander, nevertheless, was not rebuffed. Applying for leave from his regiment, he arranged to go to Martinique on his own, planning to offer his services to Bouillé as a simple volunteer. On 6 September, with no farewell to his wife, he left Noisy-le-Grand. Echoes persisting all through their exchange of letters in the next two months show that they had quarrelled again.

During the time that Alexander spent en route from Paris to Brest, and while he subsequently waited impatiently for his ship to sail, he sent Josephine at least eighteen highly revealing, if somewhat repetitive letters. His is a remarkably well-documented departure. Although not one of Josephine's letters has survived, it is clear from Alexander's comments that she wrote on numerous occasions to her husband. By turning the pages of one half of this correspondence we can reconstruct a good deal of the couple's relationship, we can obtain some direct insight into the character of Alexander, and, more important for our purposes, make some revealing inferences about Josephine.

Alexander had left Noisy for Paris late at night and by stealth. In a letter to Josephine he professed, in Werther-like fashion, to lay bare his bleeding heart:

Will you pardon me, *ma chère amie* [Alexander wrote at three o'clock in the morning], for having left you without farewell, for having gone away without warning, for having fled without having told you again, a last time, that I am all yours? Alas! What can you not read in my soul? . . . Love of my wife and love of glory, each rules supreme in my heart. . . . You disapprove of me today; this afflicts me cruelly; but the day will come, *ma tendre amie*, when you will be grateful to me for having courage to make so many sacrifices. . . . Adieu! My heart is, and always will be, yours.[10]

Reaching Brest, Alexander was shocked to find that no letter awaited him. Having quickly composed an indignant protest, he sat down to dinner, during which the courier arrived, bearing the letter from Josephine he awaited, which now melted him to tenderness – of his own peculiar sort. Some indication of Alexander's petulant nature appears in the manner of his response, for though he now hastened to add further paragraphs avowing his satisfaction and relief, he evidently saw no need to cancel those stinging passages, hot with indignation, which he had first composed.

Alexander's letters written to Josephine from Brest – 'this bitch of a town', as he called it – where he awaited the ship that would take him to America, are reminders of a relationship in which Alexander's affection grew to be more and more obviously a pretence. News from his wife would cause him to send her messages avowing his devotion while, when couriers arrived without letters from her, anger and bitter denunciation would pour forth. More than once Alexander vowed never to write again. Yet not only did he write when he had vowed that he would not, in language worthy of W. S. Gilbert's Nanki-Poo he itemized those of his complaints which in the same breath he swore he would not itemize:

I will not, then, say that I love you, whatever pleasure I may find in repeating this to you. I will not say that since my departure I have not received, on the average, even two letters a week from you. I will avoid explaining to you that, for myself, I do much work here, that I have duties to perform and a very extensive correspondence to handle. I will avoid saying that you, assuredly, do not have as much business as I have. You would find it wrong [for me to say all this]. I will say simply, therefore, that I believe my letters have not reached you and that I have been no more fortunate in the case of several of my friends.[11]

In our twentieth century, when letter writing is becoming a lost art, the husband who can count on two letters a week from his wife may feel he has little reason to complain. Not so Alexander. In addition to objecting he frequently showed signs of being carried away by his own eloquence. He concluded:

I am excessively sad and melancholy. The most effective means of driving out the blackness of my spirits, you possess. With your assurance of tenderness I would destroy one part of my suffering and would acquire the strength to rise above the other. Adieu, *ma chère amie*. I have promised not to speak of love. I must then, do no more than move my lips as if to kiss you a thousand times.[12]

Alexander had no doubt persuaded himself that he had good reason for his complaints. Since he kept careful inventory of these letters of the heart, he could argue that he had received only one letter from Josephine in return for every two he sent. He, clearly enough, was fluent and plausible; she was less so. We have to imagine Josephine's replies from Alexander's comments. It appears that in some fashion she managed to answer, and that this girl, whose very syntax had been subjected to Alexander's minutest scrutiny, took what steps she could to defend herself against his attacks.

By mid-October the domestic storms caused by these disagreements had subsided. So calm, indeed, was the atmosphere that Alexander wrote his wife what purported to be an abject apology. He declared that he was angry at himself for his injustice and asked pardon a thousand times. 'Since you assure me of it,' he wrote, still with a suggestion of stiffness,

'I do not doubt that you have written to me regularly, but the contents of my last letter to you will prove that the post has not served you well.'[13] Later he wrote in the tenderest terms about the infant Eugène and about Josephine's unborn child, which, with his typical complacency, he assumed would be another boy. 'Kiss my dear little Eugène with all your heart, and guard his little brother,' he urged in one letter. 'I kiss you, Eugène, and the little Scipio. *Mon Dieu!* When shall I see him?' he wrote in another. 'Think of the little being whom you carry; watch over him, and over your health.' On still another occasion he was concerned about Josephine's physical condition. 'Get well fast,' he wrote, 'so that I may have one sorrow less. So Eugène is well.[8] Tell me how many teeth he has, and kiss him as you would your husband, with the same tenderness...'[14]

This happy atmosphere was soon clouded by Alexander's renewed protests. Trivial reasons, complaints about 'silence', complaints about 'sensitiveness', complaints about the other's 'complaints' were piled one on the other. In one letter Alexander grandiloquently vowed that he looked forward to death: 'Amid the risks of war and of the seas, where I go to seek death, I shall, without sorrow and without regret, see a life taken from me whose moments will have been reckoned only in misfortunes. Adieu!'[15] Having thus contemplated death, the versatile Alexander soon afterwards volunteered advice in the difficult realm of infant training. He was concerned lest Eugène be weaned too early. He was equally concerned lest Eugène be the subject of too much motherly affection. 'You will guard in advance,' the twenty-two-year-old soldier on his way to the wars instructed Josephine, 'against a sentiment ... which is almost universal in your sex and which leads most mothers to spoil their children.'[16]

The long-awaited news of imminent departure reached Alexander on 18 November. Sailing orders had arrived and at last he could embark. A week later his vessel had moved from Brest to a position off the harbour of La Rochelle, where it anchored for another exasperating delay. The waiting dragged on; unhappily, no letters came from his wife; and the least of Alexander's virtues was patience.

The novel written in the form of an exchange of letters and the 'comedy of tears' were both standard forms of late eighteenth-century literature. It may well have been that during his long wait, which in sum came to more than three months, Alexander had found diversion and not a little pleasure in fashioning a *comédie larmoyante* of his own. Even so, a note of genuine indignation is discernible amid the self-pity of his last letter from the French coast.

I hoped to receive further news from you; but I have hoped in vain. . . . The dinghy has just arrived, and there is not a word from you! Is it possible that you refuse this consolation to a poor husband who does nothing but toss back and forth without making any progress towards his destination? . . . Ah, unhappy absence! How many troubles you cause me to foresee! For the rest, if your inconstancy is inevitable do not keep me in ignorance, so that I may never see you again. Adieu! Forgive my letter, but I am furious.[17]

After four days at anchor, Alexander's ship, appropriately named the *Venus*, began on 21 December the month-long crossing that took him and Madame de Longpré to Martinique.

Parting

THE *Venus* sighted the towering mountain summits of Martinique late in January 1783. The crossing had been stormy. As the ship moved into the sparkling, tropical blue waters of the anchorage under the guns of the massive old stone fortress of Saint Louis, the passengers could see from the decks the heavy green foliage of this fragrant, indolent world. The Alexander who was now rowed ashore came as a stranger to an island that, as a boy of five, he had left seventeen years before.

A letter to Josephine gave details of the passage. He had been miserable during the voyage, partly because of the rough weather, partly because he smarted under the feeling of his wife's indifference and neglect. Gradually he got control of himself, deciding that he had no right to sulk and that Josephine may have had reasons for her actions. 'I tried to persuade myself that you loved me a little,' he wrote. 'This illusion gave me some contentment – with it I was happy.' He kept a diary, played lotto, and enjoyed the company aboard the ship, which included, so Alexander reported without elaboration, the Chevalier de Girardin and his niece, Madame de Longpré. These and other passengers made the voyage amusing.[1] In such a letter to his wife the expression 'amusing', particularly with reference to Madame de Longpré, reached, if indeed it did not surpass, the limits of discretion.

Arriving at Fort-Royal, the worldly-wise young officer was astonished at the heedless, easy life of the inhabitants. 'Their morals,' he told Josephine, 'the multitude of coloured people in their indecent costumes, their way of living, their dwellings, the evidences of debauchery – all this has amazed me.'[2] Thus did the cultivated product of the Enlightenment comment upon his first sight of the World of Nature.

Parting

Since no one had been told of his coming to Martinique, Alexander went unannounced to the Tascher de la Pagerie plantation, where he received a warm welcome from Josephine's parents. Joseph-Gaspard had preceded him by several months from France, happy at last in the possession of the cross of the Order of Saint Louis and the promise of a pension. Alexander brought presents from Josephine for the family, most notably her portrait. He had to report to Josephine that her young sister, Manette, was ill of scurvy, and that he had strongly urged the family to make use of inoculation. Despite the cordiality of the welcome given him, one can detect in his letters a sense of shock at the run-down, if not actually impecunious, condition of the Tascher household.

One interesting sidelight on the relations between Josephine and Alexander emerges at this time. He had hoped to arrange a marriage between her sister, Manette, and one of his close officer friends in the Sarre regiment. Now he had to explain to Josephine that such plans could not be realized. Because of her illness the parents did not wish to part with Manette; the family, moreover, had heavy debts and were in no position to arrange for a dowry. It is curious, in the light of Alexander's evident domestic troubles and disappointments, that he should have thus considered a marriage into the same family for one of his brother officers. Perhaps the quarrels between Alexander and Josephine so far were less serious than his letters would suggest. Conceivably Josephine had urged him to seek this arrangement in order to have her sister's companionship in France. The Taschers were a good family, and the plantations of the sugar islands did give an immediate impression of wealth. Alexander may have hoped that a better dowry than Josephine's would be forthcoming now. In all events he seems to have been willing, despite the omens, to encourage his brother officer to undertake a marriage arranged with as little thought for the compatibility or happiness of the participants as his own marriage had been.

The first impression that Alexander, the dashing young officer from France, made at Trois-Îlets was overwhelming. 'Ah, the charming boy!' wrote Josephine's aunt, the Baroness

Tascher, 'God grant that Tascher [her son] may resemble him in every way. I ask nothing more from him and would be the happiest of women.'³ Despite his warm reception, Alexander chose to stay with his relatives only two days, returning quickly to Fort-Royal and to the post he had at last obtained as aide-de-camp to the governor. Here he was soon informed that, since the American war was practically over, little prospect for a campaign now remained. The preliminaries of peace between France, Spain, the American colonies, and Britain were, in point of fact, submitted in the House of Commons on 27 January, a week after Alexander's arrival in Martinique. Should peace come, he wrote to Josephine with epigrammatic neatness, 'I would seek my consolation in the pleasure of seeing you again, and of returning to embrace you; love would indemnify me for being deprived of glory.'⁴

For obvious reasons, Alexander had nothing to say to his wife about certain of his associations at Fort-Royal. The gist of the story is simple. What began there as a gay pursuit of various island beauties quickly turned into an ardent affair with his old amour and recent sea-companion, Madame de Longpré. Towards Josephine, despite her failures to write, Alexander professed to be all tenderness. He urged his wife to learn what she could about the direction of a household. 'You know that on my return we shall have to set up our own,' he wrote, 'and you will not forget how little suited I am to run one.' As usual, Alexander the pedagogue displayed the note of officiousness: 'I recommend you above all to keep busy; this will banish laziness which has always been the first cause of forgetting one's duties ... Adieu, a hundred thousand times adieu!'⁵

By early April, Alexander's old indignation reappeared:

I recall, *ma chère amie*, that you once predicted that if ever you should be untrue to me I would perceive it either by your letters or by your conduct towards me. This moment has surely arrived, for during the three months that I have been here, vessels have arrived from every port and not one brings a single word from you. ... I once promised not to write to you again. Vain promises! They are like those which you made to think of me ... Kiss my

dear son for me. Take care of his future, and may he cause you to
think at least for a moment of a husband who will love you all his
life. Adieu, a hundred times![6]

Josephine, though not writing to her husband, had written
to others, including her Aunt Rosette, an elderly spinster at
Carbet with a reputation for temper. Aunt Rosette had shown
the letter to Alexander, who was outraged that his wife found
time to write to her rather than to him, and, even more, that
this letter contained critical comments about himself. 'You
spoke of me,' he protested tartly to Josephine, 'only to say
that you have overcome those lively feelings that I once was
able to inspire in you. Your tone when it concerns me is more
than indifferent.' He vowed, consequently, that he would
write no more and that Josephine would have to obtain news
of him through his father.[7]

A daughter, Hortense, was born to Josephine in Paris on
10 April 1783. The happy tidings were sent immediately to the
family at Martinique, but, most pointedly, not directly by
Josephine to her husband. We must still account for Josephine's
long silence. Such utter failure to reply to her husband's
letters was something other than the habit of delay she had
demonstrated in earlier months. Explanations based on care-
lessness, petulance, self-indulgence, or even illness ring hollow,
for her correspondence with others continued. Josephine's
conduct at this juncture does become understandable in the
light of what she must have known through island gossip of
Alexander's scandalous actions in Martinique. She was deeply
upset, and, having no other means of coping with the situation,
took refuge in what Socrates called woman's crowning glory –
her silence.

Alexander's letter of 10 May (penned in defiance of his
recent pledge not to write) was a mixture of sentimentality,
indignation, and mock despair. 'They speak of a forthcoming
war against the Emperor [of Austria]. May God grant that it
take place, that I may serve in it, and that I may find there the
end of a life that has become a burden. Adieu!'[8] In June
Alexander had still further grievances to chronicle. An old
valet of her father had just returned from France. Before

leaving, this valet had written to Josephine's maid, offering to take letters to Alexander. The maid had replied most tactlessly that the time was too short to think of letters, seeing that the family was so busy with engagements at balls and suppers. 'I ask you,' demanded Alexander, professing outrage once more, 'what I am to think of all this?'[9] He might well have paused to reflect upon the unreliability of third-hand information handed on by valets and ladies' maids, to remind himself that as recently as April Josephine had been delivered of a daughter, and to consider that news of his scandalous behaviour must by now have reached her.

While engaged in his gay affairs with the ladies of Fort-Royal, Alexander had also made frequent criticisms of his wife. He had spoken very bluntly to Josephine's aunt, the Baroness Tascher, deploring the great inadequacy of Josephine's education and most ungallantly blaming her mother and her grandmother for it. He had, unhappily, done much more than this. At the very time when he was denouncing his wife, he continued to scandalize Fort-Royal by his dissipated behaviour. This irresponsible conduct is clearly revealed in the indignant letters written to France by Josephine's family. 'I would never have thought,' Josephine's mother later wrote to the Marquis de Beauharnais about Alexander, 'that he would have let himself be led around so by Mme de Longpré, his companion on the voyage.'[10] She went on to say that he had neglected his relatives in the country and had lived a dissipated life in the town, enjoying the company of other young ladies besides Madame de Longpré.

Clearly Alexander had now decided to obtain some kind of separation from his wife. In order to make a case against Josephine, he had undertaken to question several of her former slaves about her alleged youthful goings-on. Here, again, he was egged on by Madame de Longpré, who at this time had apparently put into his mind the thought that he could not be the father of Josephine's second child.

Failing in his first effort to put the words he desired into the mouth of simple slaves, Alexander had descended to the level, so her mother indignantly told Josephine, of offering money to

'little Sylvester', a slave who was only five when Josephine
had left Martinique. We have an interesting sidelight on
eighteenth-century methods of punishment in her mother's
report concerning another slave who evidently had been
induced to say what Alexander wanted: 'Your husband twice
gave him fifteen *pistoles* . . . I still have him chained up, but he is
being well fed.'[11]

Amidst all this domestic uproar Alexander fell seriously ill
with 'putrid fever', or typhus. On convalescing, he was taken
into the home of a Madame Turon, described to Josephine by
her mother as 'another of your calumniators'. Here the in-
corrigible convalescent carried on an affair with Madame
Turon behind her husband's back. Josephine's aunt informed
Madame Renaudin of this, adding that the ailing Alexander was
indignant because she had not visited him, or even sent her
servant to inquire of his health. 'I would,' she declared acidly,
'have found myself very much out of place in such society.'[12]
Letters from Josephine's uncle, the Baron Tascher, conveyed
much the same tale, and her father, too, added his story.

Six months had now passed since Alexander's arrival at Martinique. The war was over. On the very eve of his departure for
France he wrote Josephine a staggering letter in language so
violent and for reasons so outrageous as to change the entire
course of their two lives. Having previously contented himself
with single cannon shots, he now let go with a full broadside.
Clearly, this document is a major landmark in the career of
Josephine.

Alexander's letter of 12 July 1783, begins with a savage
attack on 'the abominable conduct' of Josephine in the years
of her girlhood:

If I had written to you in the first moment of my rage, my pen
would have burned the paper and you would have thought from
hearing all my invectives that I had seized a moment of temper or of
jealousy to write to you. But I have known what I am going to say
to you, at least in part, for more than three weeks. Despite, therefore, the despair of my soul, despite the fury which suffocates me,
I shall know how to contain myself; I shall know how to tell you

coldly that in my eyes you are the vilest of creatures, and that my stay in this country has revealed to me your abominable conduct.

Alexander then proceeds to itemize what he claims to have been Josephine's clandestine intrigues with men during her youth in Martinique:

I know in the greatest details about your intrigue with M. de Be. . . ., officer of the Martinique regiment, also about that with M. d'H. . . . who has sailed on board the *Caesar*. I am not unaware, either, of the means you took to gratify your desires or of the people you employed to help you. I know that Brigitte has been given her liberty only to guarantee her silence; I know that Louis, who is since dead, was also in the secret; I know, lastly, the contents of your letters and I shall bring with me one of the presents you made. There is, consequently, no more occasion to pretend, and since I am not ignorant of any details you have no other alternative than to be truthful.

The letter goes on to characterize Josephine, whom Alexander called 'beneath all the sluts in the world', as incapable of repentance and a disgrace to her family:

As for repentance, I do not ask this; you are incapable of it. A person who, on the eve of her departure, could receive her lover in her arms at the time when she knew she was destined for another, has no soul; she is beneath all the sluts in the world. If you had the boldness to take advantage of the slumbers of your mother and grandmother it is not surprising that you would also deceive your father at Santo Domingo. I do justice to them all and look upon only you as guilty. You alone have abused an entire family and carried disgrace and ignominy to another, distant family of which you are unworthy.

This savage résumé of Josephine's alleged girlhood behaviour was followed by an attack upon her newborn daughter, about whom Alexander had written with such tender anticipation only a few months before. He now claimed the infant to be illegitimate:

After so many offences and outrages, what is one to think of the clouds and conflicts which have arisen in our own family? What am I to think of this last infant, born eight months and several days after my return from Italy? I am forced to take her, but I swear by the heavens that she is by another, and that a stranger's blood flows in her veins. She will never know my shame, and I here vow that she will never learn, either in the arrangements for her education or in those of the household, that she owes her life to an adulterer.

The solution for this alleged state of affairs was for Alexander to order Josephine to a convent. On returning to France he would see her only once, and never would he live with her again:

You must know, however, how essential it is for me to avoid a similar catastrophe in the future. Make your arrangements, then; never, never will I allow myself to be abused again; and, as you would be the kind of woman to deceive the public if we were to live under the same roof, have the goodness to go to a convent as soon as you receive my letter. This is my last word, and nothing in the world is capable of making me change.

When I return to Paris I shall see you once only; I wish to have a conversation with you and return you something. But, I repeat, no tears, no protestations! I am already on guard against all your efforts, and my care will always be to arm myself further against vile promises which would be as contemptible as they are false. In spite of all the slanders which your fury will spread about me, you know me, Madame, you know that I am kind and sympathetic; and I know that in your heart you will do me justice. You will persist in denying this, because from your earliest age you have made a habit of falsehood, but you will none the less be inwardly convinced that you are getting only what you deserve.

In conclusion Alexander indicates guardedly the means he had taken to unearth his evidence against Josephine. This evidence, he insists, is decisive:

Probably you do not know the means I have taken to expose so many horrors, but I will tell them only to my father and to your aunt. It will be sufficient for you to know that people are very indiscreet, all the more when they have reason to complain; moreover, you have written; moreover, you have given up the letters of M. de B. . . . to the one who succeeded him; finally, you have employed coloured people whom money can make to talk. Behold the shame with which you and I, as well as your children, are going to be covered, like a punishment from heaven which you have deserved but which should obtain for me your pity and the pity of all decent people!

Adieu, Madame! I will write to you in duplicate, and both will be the last letters you will receive from your desperate and unfortunate husband.

P.S. I leave today for Santo Domingo and I expect to be in Paris in September or in October, if my health does not yield to the fatigue of the voyage in my present frightful condition. I expect that after this letter I shall not find you at my house, and I must warn you that you will find me a tyrant if you do not follow precisely what I have told you.[13]

What are we to make of this outraged letter – this torrent of savage denunciation, which in the gravity of its charges and the violence of its feeling far exceeds anything Alexander had ever written before? His alleged grievances can be simply stated: since coming to Martinique he claims to have uncovered shocking evidence of Josephine's immoral conduct on the very eve of her marriage. Moreover, the news from France of Hortense's birth compels him, on the evidence of dates, to ascribe the infant's paternity to another. Life together is henceforth impossible. Josephine must immediately make arrangements to take up residence in a convent. Like Hamlet to Ophelia, Alexander cries, 'Get thee to a nunnery.'[8]

These elaborate charges of Josephine's infidelity cannot be answered, obviously, in one sentence. At this point one may simply note that not a single piece of corroborative evidence was supplied either by Alexander or by any responsible person in Martinique, and that Josephine's relatives, Tascher and Beauharnais alike, rallied as one in her support. She unhesitatingly submitted the complete text of Alexander's accusing letters as evidence on her *own* behalf when she eventually brought suit against him in Paris. As for the imputation concerning the paternity of Hortense, the dates are against Alexander, to say nothing of his repeated letters of 1782 expressing his delight in looking forward to the infant's birth. Further argument remains unnecessary when one realizes that in 1785 Alexander himself was brought to admit the complete base-lessness of every single one of his charges, inspired, as he then conceded, 'by the passions and anger of youth'.

A final touch of the preposterous is added to this entire episode by the fact that Alexander arranged to have his long tirade against Josephine delivered to Paris by none other than Madame de Longpré. While she seems to have been willing enough to oblige, Madame de Longpré's interest in Alexander was now nearly at an end. Before leaving Martinique, this instigator of so much trouble had forsaken him for Count Arthur Dillon, an Irishman in the service of France who held the post of governor of the island of Saint Christopher. Dillon followed her to Paris, where she established herself in a fine town house on the rue de la Chaise. Two years later, when she married him, the impressive wedding contract bore the signature of Marie Antoinette and Louis XVI. The sequel is illuminating. Dillon, like Alexander, was elected to the Estates-General in 1789, and like him was guillotined during the Reign of Terror. After becoming empress, Josephine showed no bitterness towards the woman who had helped to ruin her first marriage. True to her kindly instincts, she even arranged a pension for Dillon's widow, saying simply in the note accompanying the request, 'This lady is now very infirm.'[14]

The story now moves from the West Indies to France. After a month's crossing, Alexander arrived at Rochefort in September. Before reaching Paris, having learned that Josephine was still with his family, he sent her the following letter, dated 20 October:

On my arrival in France I learned with astonishment through the letters of my father that you were not yet in a convent, as I had ordered you in my letter dated from Martinique. I imagine that you have chosen to await my arrival in order to submit to this necessity, and that this delay is not to be considered as a refusal . . . I am unshakeable in the decision I have taken, and I engage you to tell my father and your aunt that their efforts will be useless and will only add to my sorrow . . .[15]

The last reference is most significant. It is understandable that Josephine's family at Martinique should have rallied to her side. Her uncle, for example, had even offered to go to France to help her. What is really striking is the unwillingness of a single one of Alexander's relatives to come to his support. His father, his uncle, his aunt, his brother, and his sister-in-law – all stood by Josephine. Devoted to her cause, they seem to have struggled for a month to persuade Alexander, albeit unavailingly, to seek a reconciliation with his wife.

Josephine's kindly mother in Martinique attempted a few sympathetic words to the old marquis:

I will do justice to the viscount. He has let himself be carried away without reflecting, without thinking of what he has done. He has good qualities and a good heart . . . So much pettiness is not compatible with an elevated and sympathetic nature. When he last came to the plantation to bid us good-bye I saw that he was troubled and moved. He seemed to be anxious to get away from me speedily, to avoid my presence. His heart was already reproaching him for such mistaken conduct.

These were the words of an understanding woman, conscious of family ties and anxious not to close all doors to reconciliation. Yet, however well meant, they seemed to carry little conviction that the marriage could be saved.

It is hardly possible [she went on] for my daughter to remain with him unless he gives sincere proof of a genuine desire to return, and a perfect forgetting of what has happened . . . O, my poor daughter, all your sorrows are in my breast – they leave me without rest both night and day! Come, mingle your tears with those of a tender mother! All your friends do you justice, they love you always and will console you! Return her, Monsieur, to me and you will give me a new existence![16]

Joseph-Gaspard likewise wrote, begging his daughter to return to her family, where she could forget, as he put it, 'the behaviour of a husband who is not worthy of you'. Josephine however, proved to have other plans. Domestic troubles or no, her life was henceforth to be lived in France.

Avoiding his wife and relatives, Alexander took up residence in the town house of the La Rochefoucaulds and most inconsiderately proceeded to sell the furniture in the Beauharnais home on the rue Saint-Charles, with the consequence that Madame Renaudin and the marquis were obliged to move to the country at Noisy-le-Grand. Pressed, apparently, for funds, Alexander referred to his father a jeweller's bill that demanded payment for what he had bought four years earlier at the time of his wedding. He was determined that the breach with his wife should be decisive.

Josephine at length agreed to accept her husband's stipulation that she enter a convent. Accompanied by Madame Renaudin and Eugène, but leaving her new baby at Noisy-le-Grand, she moved towards the end of November into a house of retreat at the convent of Pentemont, renting at the very modest cost of three hundred livres per year one of the apartments maintained by the order. Josephine 'entered a convent' only in the most literal and limited sense of the expression. Her new home, in a fashionable part of Paris, was a place where women of the very best society, many of them in domestic difficulties similar to hers, could compare notes while finding pleasant company, cheap living, and mutual sympathy.

Within two weeks of her arrival Josephine had started legal proceedings against her husband. However much she may have been encouraged and supported by her relatives in this decision, her prompt action demonstrated a conviction of innocence, a sense of outrage, and a courage worthy of notice in a young woman not yet twenty-one. Her decision was furthered by the complete failure of all family efforts to bring about a reconciliation, and by the unyielding attitude of her husband. Alexander was now chiefly concerned to renew his military career, hoping to secure a captain's commission in the Royal-Champagne cavalry regiment and to become an aide-de-camp to his old patron, the Duke de La Rochefoucauld. He did, nevertheless, continue to show an interest in his infant daughter. The village *curé* at Noisy-le-Grand wrote to Madame Renaudin as follows:

M. le vicomte has come to see Mademoiselle his daughter ... He did not call on me, because of his travelling companions, but sent his apologies. He paid the wet-nurse for two months, gave his daughter jewellery from the fair, and left, seeming very satisfied. It is said that he is amusing himself greatly in Paris.[17]

On a December morning in 1783, at about eleven o'clock, Louis Joron, counsellor of the king and commissioner at the Châtelet in Paris, paid a formal visit to the convent of Pentemont on the rue de Grenelle. He was shown into parlour number three, on the second floor, overlooking the courtyard. Here, according to his official report, he met 'Dame Marie-Rose Tascher de la Pagerie, aged twenty years, creole of Martinique, wife of Alexandre François, Vicomte de Beauharnais'. She had summoned him to make official record of a complaint against her husband.

The documents concerning Josephine's suit for separation can still be seen in the archives at Paris. We can read her long statement, taken down by Joron in his precise, legal hand. On each page there is her signature of approval – 'Tascher de la Pagerie'. We have Alexander's savage letter of 12 July, with the blank spaces carefully ruled over by Joron so that nothing subsequently could be added, and with Josephine's authenticating signature. We have the second letter of 20 October, likewise authenticated. Together, these papers give the simple outline of the failure of four years of married life.[18]

Josephine told how she had been brought by her father to France in 1779 and how, after marrying Alexander, she had lived in the home of the Marquis de Beauharnais. Because of 'the great dissipation' of her husband, his long absences, and his indifference towards her, clouds soon appeared. The birth of a son in 1781 temporarily improved matters, yet shortly afterwards, in November, Alexander went to Italy, not returning until the following July. Although he seemed enchanted to find himself with her again, he soon left for America, knowing that his wife was pregnant. Until the time of the birth of her second child, her husband's letters 'breathed nothing but tenderness and affection', but this news, strangely enough, 'served as a pretext to heap her with unjust reproaches' concerning her early life in Martinique.

Josephine submitted as evidence Alexander's two letters of 1783: 'The said letters contain the most atrocious imputations and, not content with accusing the petitioner of adultery, he treats her with infamy, saying that he has too great a contempt for her ever to live with her again.' Consequently he has ordered her to a convent and threatened her if she refused to go. Although he returned to Paris in October, he would not even visit his wife at the Beauharnais home. Josephine calculated that in their four years of married life her husband had not spent more than ten months in her company. 'It is not possible,' the document continued, 'for the petitioner to suffer patiently so many affronts. To do this would be lacking in what she owed to herself and to her children, and to expose herself to the most terrible fate.' Consequently, she has submitted this complaint, desiring a legal separation 'of body and habitation'.

If any confirmation were needed for what Josephine here described as 'the great dissipation' of her husband, it could be found in the memoirs of a young brother-officer, Louis-Joseph, Marquis de Bouillé. This officer describes Alexander as not striking in appearance, but a remarkable dancer. He was generally graceful and attractive, particularly to women, with whom he had numerous brilliant successes.

This kind of merit, for so it was considered at the time [Bouillé wrote], flattered his self-esteem and occupied him almost exclusively . . . He regaled me almost incessantly with his successes, even submitting the documentary evidence which he kept and classified as another would have done the record of his military glories. He included with his confidences advice about the way to behave with women which certainly was not dictated by good sense or morality and which, illustrated by very striking examples, was bound at this period to impress my inexperienced nature.[19]

The first result of Josephine's complaint was that on 3 February 1784 the *Prévôt* of Paris issued an order authorizing her to stay at Pentemont until a court decision was reached. Alexander, meanwhile, was to provide food and maintenance for his children, wages and food for the servant attending the three-year-old, and money for educational costs hitherto assumed by the petitioner. For some time matters rested thus. Alexander struck back by appealing to the authorities to make his father pay the large arrears due to him as an inheritance from his mother. Because his father had failed to pay these sums, Alexander claimed that he had been obliged to sell his furniture.

While in Pentemont, Josephine had written to a friend, complaining that in her husband's absence she had been without money. This, written in March 1784, is the earliest of her letters that have survived, and money is its theme. When Hortense was born, the improvident Alexander was in Martinique, and Josephine's own father had been unable to send even the costs of baptism. She had been compelled, therefore, to sell some jewellery to find the necessary funds. Now, she explained bitterly, 'M. de Beauharnais must know that I have nothing and need everything, but since money is not my God, this is not what concerns me the most.'[20] Still later she wrote to a creditor, who was pressing her for money, with more complaints about Alexander:

Since his return from Martinique he has rejected nearly all the bills submitted to him, promising to pay them if I would recognize that these bills were correct. I would not have refused if the merchant had actually delivered the merchandise and the worker had done his work; but all these things did not remain in my possession; M. de Beauharnais sold everything as soon as he arrived in Paris. He should know better than anyone what has become of this furniture.[21]

Even further trouble developed early in 1785, when Alexander, whose affection for his children was real, used open force to take his son Eugène away from Josephine. She wrote at once to the *Prévôt* of Paris, asking that the authorities compel Alexander to restore the child. This request brought matters to a head, for the two were required to appear at the Châtelet. A month later, on 5 March 1785 the long conflict terminated in the study of *Maître* Trutat, notary of Paris. An out-of-court settlement made unnecessary the costs, complications, and embarrassments of further legal action.

The victory was all to Josephine. In the preamble to the agreement Alexander made an abject surrender:

The said Vicomte de Beauharnais recognizes that the Vicomtesse, his wife, has pleaded with just cause; that he was wrong to write to the said lady the letters of 12 July and 20 October of which she complains, and which were inspired by the passions and anger of youth. He regrets all the more having given way to these passions because on his return to France the testimony of the public and of her father [-in-law] was all to her advantage . . . He realizes that his conduct would secure for the lady Vicomtesse de Beauharnais the separation which she desires. Seeking to avoid the publicity of a legal plea, he has offered to consent voluntarily to what his wife would have been able to obtain judicially, and his wife, wishing to avoid disagreeable publicity and to give the strongest proof to her two children of her maternal love, has consented . . . to accept the offer which has been made to her.[22]

The terms of the 'amicable agreement' were as follows: Josephine was free to live wherever she chose and to enjoy the revenues from her dowry and whatever else might fall to her. Alexander would further provide her with an annual income of five thousand livres. Hortense was to remain entirely with her mother, Alexander providing one thousand livres annually for her until she was seven, and fifteen hundred livres annually thereafter. Eugène was to go to his father, although remaining until the age of five with his mother and visiting her thereafter during the summers. All his expenses would be assumed by his father. Alexander agreed to give his wife whatever legal powers became necessary and to defray all the costs of the suit.

With this sweeping vindication, the conflicts of five years were at an end. A financial agreement had been reached, arrangements had been made for the two children, and married life together was legally terminated. Josephine was now twenty-one.

❧ 6 ❧

Freedom

JOSEPHINE left the convent of Pentemont late in 1785, as little aware as were the people about her that she moved amid a dying world. Her life was now only four years distant from the opening scenes of the vast drama of the French Revolution. These were the final halcyon days of the *ancien régime*, those days about which Talleyrand wrote so warmly. They were, for all his fine words, times of grave stress, and, to those administering the government, times when financial bankruptcy had become an imminent possibility. Behind the glittering façade of aristocratic society new forces were mobilizing that would in time destroy the world where Josephine played her part and would create another in its place.

During the months when Josephine was entering upon her new freedom a trial rocked French society, brought scandal upon the queen, and pointed ominously to unknown troubles ahead for her and for France. A cardinal of the church, hoping for the favours of Queen Marie Antoinette, had lent himself unwittingly to the intrigues of criminals; he had kept a moon-lit rendezvous in the gardens of Versailles with an adventuress impersonating the queen; and he had arranged secretly with Paris jewellers to purchase the celebrated 'Queen's Necklace' for a million and a half livres. Although the jewellers were led to believe that Marie Antoinette was backing the purchase, the necklace never reached her, falling instead into the hands of conspirators. When the scandal was revealed, the Cardinal de Rohan was arrested at the very instant when he prepared to celebrate Mass before the royal court. The principal conspirators were punished. Rohan was tried before the *Parlement* of Paris and, amid intense excitement, acquitted. The first, ominous shadow had fallen upon the queen. Among all the improbabilities of life, none would have seemed greater than that the young *vicomtesse* now leaving the gates of Pentemont someday would assume a position loftier than that of Marie Antoinette and be the consort of an emperor whose power would be immeasurably stronger than that of Louis XVI.

Still a married woman, meeting the world with the fine title of *vicomtesse*, Josephine was no longer subject to the authority of her husband. The annual income of five thousand livres that Alexander was obliged to pay her, together with an equal amount due from her father and an additional one thousand livres due for the maintenance of her daughter, gave her all told a hypothetical yearly income of eleven thousand livres. For a lady in her circumstances this would be a reasonably comfortable sum, provided only that it materialized.

Josephine's immediate problems were those of her domestic arrangements. The *hôtel* that had been leased on the rue Saint-Charles in Paris was no longer attractive, and in any case Alexander had sold its contents. The country house at near-by Noisy-le-Grand, turned over to Josephine by Madame Renaudin at the time of the wedding, had proved too expensive and had recently been sold. Plans, therefore, were quickly made to leave Paris and rent a much smaller house at Fontainebleau, a congenial centre where Aunt Fanny and various acquaintances now lived. Josephine arranged to have some furniture shipped to her from Martinique. By September she, Madame Renaudin, the marquis, and the two children were installed at Fontainebleau in rented quarters on the rue de Montmorin.

Josephine's life was punctuated by the inevitable minor crises of family existence. A year after she had settled at Fontainebleau, when Eugène reached the age of five, his father took him by pre-arrangement to Paris, putting him in the pension of a M. Verdière on the rue de Seine. The attachment between father and son evident at this time was genuine and lasting. In the following year, on the eager insistence of her father, who had doubtless absorbed some of his new medical notions from his patron, the Duke de La Rochefoucauld,

Hortense was inoculated, though not without anxious misgivings on the part of her mother. Eugène, having trouble with his seven-year molars, was happily exempted from such alarming new treatment. The episode suggests the continued concern of Alexander for his children. He and Josephine, indeed, developed the custom of exchanging weekly letters on the doings of Eugène and Hortense. Although one cannot speak of a true rapprochement, yet they seem to have met occasionally in the society of others, so that the painful wounds of their conflict seem gradually to have been reduced. Grounds for disagreement, however, still existed. Since Alexander was often slow in paying Josephine her allowance, legal arguments and threats of lawsuits over the proper division of their joint property in Martinique arose. Other sources of worry were the growing ill-health of the marquis, now in his seventies, and the painful stomach ailments that began to attack Madame Renaudin.

Although Josephine had triumphantly weathered the storm aroused by her husband's scandalous accusations, she was now approaching a point in her life when new charges were to be made against her by others. The first of such arose from a curious domestic mystery concerning a child, apparently born at Paris in June of 1786 but not baptized until three years later, with the name of Marie-Adélaide d'Antigny, this last name being that of her foster parents. Both Josephine and Madame Renaudin took an active interest in the little girl, arranging for her to have as a trustee the same Monsieur Calmelet who had also assumed some responsibility for Hortense's affairs. When Madame Renaudin died in 1803, she bequeathed 'Adèle' an annual income of three hundred livres. In 1804 Josephine negotiated Adèle's marriage with a Captain Lecomte, bought her a trousseau, and provided her with a farm as a dowry. Gossiping tongues were as quick to speak then as they are now. Although scandal said that Josephine must have been the child's mother, not the slightest evidence has ever been brought forward to prove such an insinuation. What does seem highly probable, however, is that Alexander de Beauharnais was the father in consequence of an affair with someone who remains unknown. Late in the nineteenth century Adèle's grandson declared that family tradition concerning Alexander's paternity was unanimous. Since Alexander took no interest in this child, and since the mother of Adèle, already married, refused to assume any responsibility, Josephine and Madame Renaudin undertook her care. Alexander, apparently, was content to have Josephine assume the responsibility he chose to ignore.

The vast financial problems that threatened France were mirrored on a tiny scale in the little household at Fontainebleau. Its members could no longer count on the general support of Alexander de Beauharnais, who now was engaged in frittering away the substantial fortune that had been his since his marriage. In 1786 the council of state, at long last brought to a mood of economy, reduced the pension of the Marquis de Beauharnais from 12,000 to 2,800 livres annually – a sorry blow to one who, as he wrote bitterly, had once enjoyed an annual income of 150,000 livres. In the following January Josephine was prompted to write to the minister of war, asking that something be done for her father-in-law, but with no apparent result. Another source of trouble came from the properties held by the marquis in the West Indies. Their revenues fell off sharply, so that the funds due to be sent to France arrived most irregularly. Although the easy-going Joseph-Gaspard, who served as agent for the Marquis de Beauharnais in these matters, was bombarded with letters, his incompetence kept him from finding any satisfactory means to stimulate the steadily dwindling revenues. For his own part, he was sorely put to it to find even a portion of the annual 5,000 livres that at the time of her marriage he had promised to his daughter. Despite their difficulties, the family found money in 1787 to buy a house on the rue de France that had both courtyard and garden, keeping it for eight years.

Josephine struggled as best she could with these financial matters. A letter of November 1785, addressed to a government tax collector who demanded payment from her, has a curiously modern ring. After telling him how she had rented an apartment at Pentemont for 300 livres annually, she went on:

Now I receive a demand for a poll tax amounting to the sum of sixty-six livres, fifteen *sols*, three *deniers*. I have the honour to inform you, monsieur, that I am still legally bound to my husband, who makes his residence in Paris, and that I have no more than an amicable separation from him. If, after noting this, you insist on my paying a tax, I venture to submit that I am being taxed at an exorbitant price in relation to my resources . . .[1]

The letter was effective. In the margin appears the endorsement of an official: 'Reduce to thirty livres.'

On another occasion, answering a creditor who was dunning her for payment, Josephine referred to the troubles that she still had with Alexander. Her husband, she said, had tried to get her to acknowledge possession of furniture and jewels some part of which she had never even seen. Apparently, some jewellery had once been ordered by Alexander but had gone into other hands than those of his wife. The furniture he had sold. And now Josephine was asked to acknowledge possession of it all, and the marquis was asked to pay! Truly this was too much, and so she made it clear. Happily, like a harbinger of better times, Josephine's uncle, Baron Tascher, arrived from Martinique in the spring of 1787, bringing her the less than adequate, yet welcome, sum of 2,789 livres from Joseph-Gaspard. 'This makes me hope,' Josephine wrote to her father, 'that you are seriously trying to provide me soon with more considerable sums . . . You know me well enough, dear papa, to be quite sure that were it not for a pressing need of money I would speak of nothing but my fondest sentiments for you.'[2]

Life at Fontainebleau, apart from these recurrent financial difficulties, moved pleasantly. As the family lived in the environs of a royal palace, a fairly wide circle of fashionable and near-fashionable acquaintances was at hand. A Monsieur d'Azy, neighbour to the Beauharnais, called daily to play cards with the old marquis. Josephine came to know the Viscount and Viscountess de Béthisy, an aunt of the viscount having been abbess of Pentemont during her stay there. She also made the acquaintance of no less a personage than Monsieur de Montmorin, governor of the royal establishment at Fontainebleau. Aunt Fanny, now a widow, lived near by, pursuing her literary and social interests as ardently as ever. A mature Josephine, living on the fringes of the court, was in a position to acquire a sophisticated elegance that, in association with her native creole charm, now made her a striking figure in whatever society she entered.

A new and unexpected diversion for Josephine also became possible. Whatever the deficiencies of Louis XVI as a monarch, none could doubt his prowess as a hunter. The king came occasionally to Fontainebleau for the chase, with an army of courtiers in his train. Season upon season, blazing away with gun after gun handed to him by his loaders, and with a page standing close by to enter in the record book the ever-mounting total of game as fast as it fell, Louis amassed between 1775 and 1789 an incredible total of 189,251 game birds brought to the slaughter, in addition to 1,254 deer and uncounted wild boar and hares. Josephine, through her new Fontainebleau connexions, now could follow some of these sanguinary expeditions. In November of 1787, for example, the marquis wrote to Madame Renaudin, temporarily absent in Paris, to report that Josephine recently had followed a royal boar hunt all day and had returned, soaked to the skin. This did not deter her from further trips afield, or from eager anticipation of still more in the future. In this way, as in others, the shy young bride of 1779 was experiencing a transformation.

In the summer of 1788 Josephine left suddenly for Martinique – so suddenly, indeed, as to give rise subsequently to the most hostile conjectures about her reasons. Later, under the Revolution, Josephine was to find herself part of a dissipated society at Paris where she made both warm friends and bitter enemies. Some of these enemies have pushed their tales about Josephine and their condemnations of her back into these earlier years. And so the explanations have been offered that Josephine now went hastily to Martinique to conceal a pregnancy that would have been embarrassing and humiliating for her to admit at Fontainebleau. Would the news of a pregnancy have been any the less embarrassing if aired in the wide circle of her relatives and friends at Martinique? While rumour may flourish, acceptable evidence of any scandalous behaviour is literally non-existent. Rumour apart, many substantial reasons would justify Josephine's visit to Martinique: her one surviving sister and her father were both gravely ill; her mother had long been begging her to return; the money due from her father had been slow in coming; and the income expected by the Marquis de Beauharnais had been steadily dwindling. These, together with an understandable restlessness on Josephine's part, provide, surely, adequate explanation for her sudden departure. Leaving Paris late in June, she went with her daughter Hortense and the ever-faithful mulatto, Euphemia, to Le Havre, and on 2 July the group departed in the packet, *Sultan*. Narrowly avoiding shipwreck at the mouth of the Seine, they crossed the Atlantic safely, reaching Martinique on 11 August 1788. It was the very eve of the French Revolution.

The stay in Martinique lasted for two years. Having been away for nearly ten, Josephine would, naturally enough, be busily occupied with visits to members of her family and with renewing acquaintance among old friends. She travelled by boat, on horseback, and even by hammock, carried in oriental fashion by Negro slaves. Some social occasions presented themselves, and Josephine had to write to Madame Renaudin for her evening dresses. Odd coincidence again appears, for none other than the young Marquis de Las Cases, ultimately to be the companion and memorialist of Napoleon at St Helena, was on naval duty at Martinique in these months and dined with Josephine at the home of her aunt, the Baroness Tascher. Since, however, Josephine's sister Manette continued to be seriously ill, her stay involved as many worries as gay times. Although Josephine had previously urged her family to send Manette to France, where better medical attention was available, they had been unwilling to do so. Under whatever mediocre care was available on the island the younger sister's health grew slowly worse.

Just as unkind rumour in France had tried to make Josephine the mother of the mysterious Marie-Adélaïde, so two years later an occasion arose for the relentless gossipmongers to whisper their further stories. Josephine was purported to be the mother of one Marie-Joséphine Benaguette, a child born supposedly about this time at Martinique, in whom Josephine's mother took a particular interest and for whom when the young woman married in 1808 Josephine provided a dowry of sixty thousand francs. The charge that Josephine during her stay on the island gave birth to this illegitimate child, known familiarly as 'Fifine', needs to be examined.

The only substantiating evidence, if such it can be called, comes from a letter written half a century later, in 1857, to the Emperor Napoleon III by a Monsieur Blanchet of Le Havre, who claimed to be Fifine's son. Declaring that Josephine was his grandmother, Blanchet flatly demanded a pension. Napoleon III properly ignored this letter. It would have passed into the limbo of forgotten things had not the provisional government set up after the fall of the Second Empire found this and other documents in the Tuileries and quickly published them with the intention of blackening the imperial record. The rebuttal did not truly come until 1909. Then the Martinique biographer, R. Pichevin, published a copy of the marriage certificate of Fifine from the French colonial archives in which two facts emerge. The first is that Fifine was born at Martinique on 17 March 1786, a date that would immediately rule out Josephine as a parent. The other is that Fifine's mother is explicitly stated to be Marie-Louise Benaguette, living at the Rivière Salée near the La Pagerie plantation.[3] The constant kindliness of Josephine's mother to her workers and dependents in time of misfortune is well known. We can easily accept, therefore, an explanation for this interest in an unfortunate child that does not require us to accuse Josephine of any scandalous behaviour. One can reasonably infer that the distortions and exaggerations were part of the widespread anti-Beauharnais propaganda that developed in the course of the nineteenth century.

By an odd paradox, Martinique, the scene of Josephine's

innocent childhood days, first exposed her to the terrors of revolution. She had left France in the summer of 1788, on the very eve of the summoning of the Estates-General, of which Alexander de Beauharnais was to be a member. The two years of her absence were the fateful period when an assembly of more than twelve hundred representatives of the people transformed the political and social institutions of France. The work that they sought to complete by peaceful, orderly means was punctuated by recurrent episodes of increasing violence. The fall of the Bastille on 14 July 1789 was only the first of a series of spectacular landmarks in consequence of which reform gave place to the terrifying phenomenon of revolution.

What happened in France was felt overseas. The French West Indies, having an economy based on slavery and with a dominant planter aristocracy, added the storms of their own unrest to the winds of freedom blowing across the ocean. Santo Domingo had quickly demanded and obtained representation in the Constituent Assembly sitting at Paris. Martinique and the other islands followed. In 1790, elected colonial assemblies with political rights for mulattoes were decreed by the legislators in France. Santo Domingo produced posthaste an irregularly elected body that came to be known as the 'Assembly of Saint-Marc'. When this was repudiated by the authorities in France, mulatto riots, followed by even more serious troubles, occurred.

The new question was that of full emancipation for Negroes. Ever since 1788 a *Society of the Friends of Negroes* had worked in France for this end. Among its enlightened supporters were members of the La Rochefoucauld family. When news that its spokesmen in the Constituent Assembly at Paris had demanded the total abolition of slavery reached Martinique, Negro revolts took place. This was the alarming world in which the unpolitical Josephine now moved.

By May of 1790 the island of Martinique was electric with unrest. In the seclusion of Trois-Îlets, to be sure, Josephine found herself and her family in relative security. For those at Fort-Royal, however, and more particularly for her uncle, the Baron Tascher, the situation was menacing. He had become port commander at Fort-Royal where, in attempting to parley with Negro rioters, he was seized and held as a hostage. The insurgents captured one of the forts and from it threatened a general bombardment of the town.

These troubled circumstances gave a powerful impetus to Josephine's plans to leave Martinique. By thus abandoning the small-scale disturbances of the island for the mighty storms that were brewing in France, she was jumping most certainly from the frying pan into the fire. Josephine could not have been expected, however, to realize this. In the steaming, unhealthy climate of Martinique's rainy season, these local dangers would have, to her restless and sensitive nature, seemed all the greater, the distant charms of Paris and its surroundings all the more compelling. Concern for the health of Hortense, who was with her, and a desire to return to her son Eugène brought still further pressure to bear.

In the late summer of 1790 Josephine chanced to be in Fort-Royal with Hortense, staying as guests of the governor. At this moment the Negroes who had seized Fort Bourbon threatened the white population with immediate destruction. In this terrifying situation, Josephine and Hortense welcomed the invitation of the captain of a frigate, the *Sensible*, and fled with all haste to his ship. On their way, as they crossed the broad public square known as the Savane, where Josephine's statue stands today in dilapidated grandeur, a cannon shot from the Negro conquerors of the fort kicked up the dust at their feet.

Josephine and Hortense had no time for gathering even a minimum of luggage, or for good-byes to the family at Trois-Îlets. Aboard ship, as they moved slowly from the anchorage to the open sea, they witnessed the insurgent cannoneers threaten the *Sensible* briefly and unsuccessfully with their fire. In this way Martinique bade a last farewell to its most famous daughter, for Josephine never again returned to the island of her birth.

During the crossing Josephine was obliged to have recourse to the ship's stores to eke out her wardrobe. The seven-year-old Hortense, who became the darling of all aboard, went

round the decks in the costume of a cabin boy and wore shoes
made for her by the crew. By November 1790, having narrowly
escaped shipwreck when the *Sensible* ran aground at Gibraltar,
Josephine found herself on French soil at Toulon. Soon she
would receive the sad news that shortly after the time of her
passage her father, Joseph-Gaspard, had died at Trois-Îlets in
his fifty-fifth year. She would likewise learn that he had died
bankrupt. Almost exactly one year later her only sister, Marie-
Françoise, 'after a long and cruel malady', as her burial certificate stated, died also.

More than ever before – without husband, without father,
and without sister – Josephine found herself alone. She was
returning, to be sure, to the company of Madame Renaudin,
from whose worldly counsels she seems to have learned much.
Even so, she faced the problems of a revolutionary age counting principally upon herself, and leaning on whatever experience and skill life so far had given her. The bird of the
islands, assuming a more striking plumage, was now on the
point of new adventures.

7

Revolution and Terror

WHEN Josephine returned from Martinique to France at the close of 1790, she escaped from revolution in the New World only to encounter it even more dramatically in the Old. The tedious November journey across the French countryside from Toulon to Paris brought her to a capital where violence and terror soon were to dominate the scene. Violence of a sort had first appeared in July 1789, when the Paris mob had burst into the old fortress-prison of the Bastille and paraded the bloody head of its governor on a pike through the streets. Violence recurred in the peasant riots, the haystack-burnings, and the château-burnings of that same summer. Violence was also present in those October days when Louis XVI, escorted by a mob from the gutters of the capital, transferred his court from Versailles to Paris. The lull that fell over the restless country during the year 1790 was no more than a momentary respite – a brief spell of clear weather before the breaking of even greater storms.

Josephine's life to this point is an altogether personal chronicle, the story of an inexperienced girl drawn into an unhappy marriage who frees herself from it as best she can. Her story emerges from the conventional record of baptismal and marriage registers, from family letters and anecdotes, from scattered memoirs and narratives. Whatever unusual quality it possesses comes from the exotic setting of Martinique and from the conflict in personalities of the young husband and wife.

From this domestic scene of modest proportions Josephine now moves into a world of momentous events, lighted by the fires of revolution. As in our own age, the forces of change were sweeping away the great citadels of privilege, and with them also many lesser strongholds, where little people had lived their quiet lives in comfortable obscurity. Josephine, least revolutionary of women, was soon threatened by these new forces, so that if for no other reason than self-defence she was compelled to assume the colouration of a revolutionary. Within three years of her return to France this sheltered child of a West Indian plantation, this viscountess of the *ancien régime*, was to describe herself in a letter to one of the great committees of the Revolution – with what truth one need not ask – as a devotee of republican principles, a *sans-culotte*, and 'a good Jacobin'.

Josephine was now legally separated, though not divorced, from her husband. By virtue of her title and her connexions she was able to make her way and to find an entrée into such parts of the *grand monde* as still flourished. And yet, though one fails to detect anything that could truly be called reconciliation or renewed affection, Alexander de Beauharnais still counted for something in Josephine's life. The two were still linked by their common name, by their mutual affection for their two children, by their correspondence, and, apparently, by their occasional meetings in polite society.

It may come as a surprise to those who have seen Alexander de Beauharnais only in the dissipated and trivial years of his youth to discover that for a few dramatic months he now shot upwards into a career of national prominence, holding the office of president of the Constituent Assembly at a most critical moment in France's history, and later serving at the age of thirty-three as commanding general of the Army of the Rhine. Revolution, which so unexpectedly raised Alexander to the heights, was also to bring him down. It likewise brought deadly peril to Josephine. Arrested in 1794, the two found some sort of reconciliation in the prison of the Carmelites, a grim setting where the guillotine's steel blade that destroyed Alexander missed destroying his wife as well only by the narrow margin of a few days.

During Josephine's absence in Martinique, Alexander de Beauharnais had moved on to the stage of great events. He was selected as a deputy of the nobility from his ancestral home, the electoral division of Blois, to the newly summoned Estates-General of France. The prospect of national bankruptcy had led Louis XVI and his advisers in 1788 to a fateful decision: they would turn for advice and assistance to this ancient assemblage of clergy, noblemen, and commonalty that had not met for 175 years. Alexander was thus able to join with the other deputies to the Estates-General in the magnificent setting of Versailles. With him came his elder brother, François, chosen as a representative of the nobility of Paris. Unlike Alexander, who warmly espoused the cause of reform, François was an uncompromising royalist. When the former on one occasion proposed that the king be deprived of command of the army, François eloquently opposed him, saying that such a proposal was so impossible that it could not be accepted, even if diluted by amendment. From this statement, in order to distinguish him from his brother, François became known as 'Beauharnais without amendment'. Two years later, despairing of the course of events, he emigrated from France and joined the counter-revolutionary army across the Rhine. Alexander stayed behind.

The debonair Alexander's qualifications for his new role of statesman and lawgiver were hardly self-evident. One recalls, however, the distant figure of the old tutor, Patricol, with his pedagogue's interest in the democratic teachings of Rousseau, and remembers also Alexander's close and frequent connexions with the liberal La Rochefoucauld household. The great figures of Mirabeau and Talleyrand likewise remind one that a private life of the most reckless dissipation was not incompatible with statesmanship of a high order. Alexander's brother-officer, the young Marquis de Bouillé, who wrote so candidly of Beauharnais' amorous affairs, had recognized almost in the same breath that there was much more in the viscount than the mere playboy. 'Beneath this air and this habit of frivolousness,' Bouillé wrote, 'M. de Beauharnais possessed energy, a stubbornness of disposition, a depth of intelligence, a longing to win fame, and an overpowering ambition.'[1] These qualities, so Bouillé believed, drove Alexander to win his prominent place in the Constituent Assembly.

Alexander quickly associated himself with the movement for reform, joining such liberal nobles as Lafayette, La Rochefoucauld, and the Duke d'Orléans. Always fluent in expressing himself, he spoke out on the famous night of 4 August, when feudal and manorial privileges were abolished. He could well side with the reformers who required the nobles to surrender their rights, for his landed fortune was by now largely dispersed. The impression he made must have been favourable, for in November 1789, he was made one of the secretaries to the Constituent Assembly.

Much later Alexander's son, Eugène, recalled these great days, after the Assembly had moved with the king from Versailles to Paris. Here the young lad was permitted on occasion to visit the sessions of the Assembly. Warming himself by the stove placed near the centre of the royal riding-school where the deputies met, Eugène could admire his father's oratory, as Alexander, happy in an audience of a thousand listeners, spoke from his position well to the left of the presiding officer. Eugène could likewise harken to the austere counsels of his Uncle François, an enemy of all revolution, as he in turn spoke from the benches of the right.

As a professional soldier, Alexander won a place on the military committee of the Assembly. He was also one of the group that first reported the need for free public education for all French children. In the increasingly radical Parisian world outside the Assembly he joined the Jacobin Club, making some name for himself by his speeches and actually serving for a time in 1791 as its president. He was also for a time president of the Constituent Assembly, and was in the chair on the historic morning of 21 June 1791 when the news came that the king and royal family had fled the Tuileries – no one knew to where. Alexander made the announcement in a phrase that has become historic: '*Messieurs*, the King has fled during the night. Let us proceed to the order of the day.'[2] He then went on to preside efficiently over tumultuous debates, which, with one day's interruption, lasted continuously from the 21st to the 26th – a remarkable endurance feat of over 126 hours. Small wonder that at the end Alexander wrote to his father saying, 'I am exhausted with fatigue.' He added the hope that his work would be useful to the public welfare and to the tranquillity of the realm. At this time Josephine was planning to abandon her life in the Beauharnais home at Fontainebleau for a career of her own in Paris. Alexander closed his letter to his father with a sentence that gives us a momentary glimpse of her – a faint ghost on the distant fringe of great events: 'I embrace my children. Tomorrow I shall try to write to Madame de Beauharnais.'[3]

With the dramatic arrest of the royal family at Varennes and its humiliating return under guard to Paris, the excitement subsided. The name of Beauharnais now took on a new significance. Alexander's son always looked back with pride to these days when his father was, as in his *Memoirs* Eugène wrote with filial exaggeration, '*le premier personnage de la France*'. The pride was understandable, for he, too, was touched by the brief glory of his father. On the streets of Fontainebleau passers-by would point out the young Eugène with the comment, '*Voilà le Dauphin!*'[4]

Alexander had reached the climax of his political career. Although re-elected president of the Assembly, he served only until September 1791, when that body was dissolved. Under the new constitution, none of the previous members were permitted to sit in the forthcoming Legislative Assembly. The obvious move now was for him to return to his professional life as a soldier. By an unusual irony, however, the same Alexander who had shone so brightly in the Assembly was to experience humiliating failure and disaster when he returned from the field of politics to the field of war.

Revolution was gradually engulfing Josephine's little world. Yet people living in the midst of great events cannot always be expected to understand them. The shrewd anecdote in Anatole France's novel, *The Gods Athirst*, is the kind of fiction that rings as true as history. It tells of the good *citoyen* Desmahis pursuing a pretty dressmaker along the streets of Paris in 1793 and being cut off from her by a grim procession. Desmahis knows only frustration; intent on his charming prey, he has no eyes for the central figure of a young, unknown aristocrat with hands bound and locks shorn, standing silently erect in the tumbril, en route to the guillotine.

In these months when blow after blow was being delivered at the whole social order of which Josephine was a part, she still remained at Fontainebleau with her aunt and father-in-law, attempting to pick up the threads of the life she had lived before her visit to Martinique. Her attempt was not successful, for Fontainebleau in 1791 was not what it had been during the *ancien régime*. Eugène, now transferred fully to the control of his father, had left to begin his studies at one of the most famous schools in Paris, the Collège d'Harcourt. Hortense was approaching the age when she, too, would have to be sent off for formal schooling. Josephine, at twenty-eight, was a far different person from the hesitant young wife of the previous decade. It is easy, therefore, to understand why after a year she found that the semi-bucolic life of Fontainebleau began to pall.

By October 1791, Josephine was in Paris, most definitely on her own, renting an apartment on the rue Saint-Dominique, just off the fashionable Boulevard Saint-Germain. Hortense, who was watched over by a kind of servant-governess, Madame Lannoy, was sent to the convent school of the Abbaye-aux-Bois. She stayed there until the following August when, by the orders of the government, all such church schools were closed. In addition to the rapidly fading society of the capital, Josephine had also a new interest in the theatre. Paris at this time saw a remarkable blossoming of dramatic productions of all kinds, a phenomenon that continued unabated into the imperial period. Josephine developed an enthusiasm for the stage that never left her, drawing her to the many performances – occasionally good, usually mediocre – of her time. Some externals of polite life still remained. Flowers bloomed in the well-kept gardens of the Tuileries, and the elegant carriages of a few fashionable ladies still drove through the streets. Yet over all hung the shadow of war and destruction. Even had Josephine desired, she would have found no opportunity to renew closer acquaintance with her now famous husband, for Alexander, on the dissolution of the Constituent Assembly

at the close of September, had quickly left Paris for the pleasant
countryside of Blois, where he served as lieutenant-colonel in
the twenty-first military division. At this very time many young
officers, Napoleon Bonaparte among them, were preparing to
find in the great revolutionary campaigns unlimited oppor-
tunities for victory and fame.

Josephine's circle at Paris was both old and new. It included
Aunt Fanny, just returned from an Italian tour with her lover,
the writer Cubières, and also a Madame Hosten-Lamotte, a
creole from the island of St Lucia who was to share Josephine's
imprisonment in 1794. She also made more splendid acquaintances, notably the Princess Amalia of Hohenzollern-Sigmaringen, who lived with her brother, the Prince de Salm, in
a magnificent *hôtel*, now the palace of the Legion of Honour.
More for social, certainly, than for political reasons, Josephine
also made the acquaintance of many of the 'respectable'
members of the constitutional party – men such as Lafayette,
Montesquieu, Barnave, Mounier, and Chapelier. She also
knew some of those royalists still in Paris, such as Mathieu de
Montmorency and the Baron de Viel-Castel, whose allegiance
to the monarchical cause carried them through the entire
revolutionary and Napoleonic period to their long-delayed
rewards at the time of the Bourbon restoration in 1814. These
connexions are significant, for frequently during the years
when she was empress, Josephine would take what steps she
could to assist any royalists who were seeking to avoid the
censures of her imperial husband.

It is possible also to compile still another kind of list. Gossip,
rumour, and scandal have singled out the names of some who
in these tormented times were believed to have won the
intimate favours of Josephine. Here scholarship falters and
documentation fails. With whatever degree of conviction, the
biographer can do little more than annotate the list of the most
generally accepted candidates; he cannot crown them with the
laurels of victory. First comes one Scipio de Roure, a naval
officer whom Josephine had met on board the *Sensible* when
she was returning from Martinique; then the Chevalier de
Cresnay, a kinsman of the Caulaincourts who later faithfully

served Napoleon; then the Chevalier de Coigny, so ardent a
champion of the Bourbons that Josephine had to intercede with
Napoleon to save him from execution; and, lastly, Charles,
Baron de Viel-Castel, in 1814 one of the agents of the Bourbon
restoration. This royalist pattern is, to say the least, interesting,
and gives some basis for the republican suspicions that soon
caused Josephine to be sent to prison.

Her life, heedless, gay, and inconsequential, was soon transformed by the march of events. In April 1792 France had come
to war with Austria and soon afterwards with Prussia. During
the summer the invading armies of the Duke of Brunswick
moved across the plains of Champagne in the direction of
Paris. Suspicion of the monarchy, already widespread, flared
up first on the 'Day' of 20 June, when crowds broke into the
royal palace. Violence flared even more savagely on 10 August,
when the mobs appeared for a second time and the courtyards
of the Tuileries ran with the blood of the loyal Swiss Guards.
Josephine was in Paris on this terrible day and rushed, understandably, to be near her daughter at the Abbaye-aux-Bois.
In this frenzied atmosphere monarchy was suspended, the
royal family imprisoned, and a convention was quickly summoned in order to give new republican institutions to France.

Two episodes highlighted for Josephine the dangers that
were striking everywhere. The Duke de La Rochefoucauld
had taken a vigorous and enlightened part in the work of the
Constituent Assembly. As a former noble, however, he had
come into disfavour. In September a National Convention had
been summoned to draft a republican constitution for France.
At this very moment La Rochefoucauld was in the country at
Gisors, where a mob, inflamed by the emotions aroused by
the invasion of France, fell upon him and hacked him to pieces.
His nephew, Charles, a boyhood friend of Alexander, was also
murdered. At this same time, too, Alexander's brother came
to the parting of the ways. When Louis XVI and his family
were imprisoned at the Temple in 1792, this François 'without
amendment' tried to organize a plot to release them. The plot
failing, he emigrated, becoming ultimately a major-general in
the army of the Duke de Condé across the Rhine. He had

found safety for himself, but, as in the case of so many today who have escaped from the iron curtains of tyranny, he had unwittingly cast the menace of death over some of his relatives who remained behind.

The most dramatic evidence of the vast transformation that was coming over the old order appeared in December 1792, when the weak-willed and well-intentioned Louis XVI was brought to public trial on the charge of treason. He was found guilty, and in the following month executed in what is now the Place de la Concorde. Josephine's first concern was for the safety of her children. It was all very well for her husband to serve the cause of revolution; she must depend on the world she knew. Hence she sent Eugène and Hortense into the care of her friend, the Princess of Hohenzollern-Sigmaringen, now living near Saint-Pol about fifty miles from Calais. The intention was that from here on the first opportunity they should be sent to England. The high-minded Alexander, however, serving with the armies of the Republic, had other notions. Hearing of the plan, he sent a special courier to forbid emigration, and for a time took Eugène with him, putting the lad to school in Strasbourg, while Hortense he ordered back to Paris. Under these circumstances Josephine's only recourse was to assimilate herself and her children, at least outwardly, to the new patterns of republican virtue. Following the decree of the Convention that all children should learn a trade, Hortense was sent to her governess, Madame Lannoy, to 'learn the trade' of seamstress. Eugène, on his return from Strasbourg, was sent into the country at near-by Croissy, where he was 'apprenticed' to a carpenter. The former *vicomtesse*, her title abandoned, now appeared under the good republican designation of *citoyenne* Beauharnais.

In September 1793 the Convention voted the terrifying Law of Suspects. This measure, surely a classic example of the technique of discovering and punishing guilt by association, ordered the immediate arrest of all 'suspects', and defined them as 'those who by their conduct, their connexions, their remarks, or their writings show themselves the partisans of tyranny . . .' Suspects were further defined as the relatives of any who had emigrated, and as 'those who have been refused certificates of citizenship'.[5] Understandably alarmed, Josephine made the quick decision to leave Paris with her friend, Madame Hosten, and to lease a new residence in the suburban village of Croissy, where republican fanaticism was less rampant than in Paris, and where the indispensable certificate of citizenship probably could more easily be obtained. Her new home was an attractive, indeed an elegant, villa once occupied by Madame Campan, principal lady-in-waiting to Marie Antoinette. From its rooms, decorated in the antique style of Louis XIII, one looked across a green meadow to the quiet waters of the Seine. Near by lay the wooded slopes of Saint-Cloud and the ancient estate of Malmaison, as yet unknown to Josephine. Near by, too, stood the parish church of Rueil where in 1814 Russian imperial guards were to escort Josephine's coffin to burial, and where in 1825 Eugène and Hortense were to erect a magnificent tomb in her memory.

At Croissy, in a process similar to that by which people today acquire identity cards, Josephine presented herself to the local authorities, and on 26 September successfully made her declaration of republicanism. Some months earlier, the aged and ailing former Marquis de Beauharnais had appeared with Madame Renaudin before the authorities at Fontainebleau, where this servant and beneficiary of the Bourbon monarchy had likewise declared himself to be a loyal partisan of the new republican order.

While Josephine thus manoeuvred for safety between Fontainebleau, Paris and Croissy, Alexander had returned to the army. By August 1792, when the monarchy was crumbling, he served as a staff officer in the Army of the Rhine. Few of the old professional officers remained in the reorganized forces of the Republic, and for those aristocrats who did, and could demonstrate their patriotism, promotion came fast. For the soldiers of the new revolutionary generation, among them many future marshals of Napoleon, promotion was equally rapid. Marmont, for example, became general of brigade at twenty-three, Davout at twenty-four, Soult, Grouchy, and

Bonaparte at twenty-five. By March of 1793 Alexander was in command of a division, and by the end of May, still in his early thirties, he held full command of the Army of the Rhine.

Alexander reached this high rank just at the time when the war was going very badly for France. In the Netherlands General Dumouriez, having lost the Battle of Neerwinden, deserted in April to the Austrians. His successor, General Custine, like Dumouriez an officer of the *ancien régime*, was recalled to Paris, despite his efforts to rally the defence. Here in August the Jacobins sent him to the guillotine, as Voltaire doubtless would have said, *pour encourager les autres*. During this same summer the moderate republican leadership in the Convention had been overthrown by the fanatical Jacobins, who were ruthlessly determined to bring the war to a successful conclusion, to transform France, and to weed out and destroy all who stood in their way.

In this atmosphere Alexander de Beauharnais assumed his command. Unhappily, he proved to be no more of a general than his father had been at Martinique. The Prussians had besieged Mainz (earlier captured by the French) in April, and throughout the summer, though he most obviously should have done so, Alexander took no steps to relieve it. Much of his time was spent in composing long dispatches to be published in the official journal, the *Moniteur*; some time he still devoted to affairs of the heart. Mistrusting the political intrigues of the capital, he had quite wisely rejected a proposal made by his friends in the Convention that he return to Paris to become minister of war. When finally Mainz fell to the Prussians at the end of July, Alexander submitted his resignation. 'In these times of revolution,' he wrote sadly to the Convention, 'when treason is becoming so frequent and the ex-nobles always seem to be the leaders in plots to destroy liberty, it is the duty of those who, though stained with this hereditary taint, have liberty and equality graven upon their hearts, to proclaim their own exclusion.'[6] His resignation was formally accepted by the Convention on 21 August – one day after the passing of a decree that forbade anyone of noble birth to hold any military commission whatsoever. A further decree required all officers who had resigned or been dismissed to stay on their estates. In September the Law of Suspects made Alexander liable to immediate arrest.

Alexander now had no choice but to return to the family village of La Ferté, where, as proof of his civic patriotism, he was elected mayor. He occupied himself in attending meetings of the local Jacobin societies and collecting various testimonials to his republicanism. One such letter from the Popular Society of Blois, copied by Josephine at the time of his imprisonment, still lies in the family papers – mute testimony to her efforts to save his life.

For a few unreal weeks existence took on a strangely innocent quality. Alexander wrote to his father asking to have their maid, Marianne, come to La Ferté in order to mark his linen. He explained that Josephine at Paris had two volumes of the novelist, Richardson, which belonged to Madame Renaudin, and that he was arranging to have her return them. 'I would never have thought,' he added, 'that having left a life as active as that of the army, time would go so fast in the quiet of solitude . . . It is true that my brain is not lazy. It tires itself in projects for the good of the Republic, even as my heart overflows in efforts and aspirations for the well-being of my fellow-citizens.'[7]

This benign atmosphere was quickly transformed. In August the great port of Toulon fell to the English fleet. As the guillotine began to operate with increasing speed both at Paris and in the provinces, the First Terror, as it was called, took shape. This Terror struck the very highest. After a despicable two-day trial, in which Marie Antoinette was accused of corrupting the morals of her own son, she was beheaded on 16 October. Along with the famous, the less notable were not spared. Two weeks later, Françoise de Beauharnais, daughter of Aunt Fanny and divorced wife of Alexander's *émigré* brother, François, was arrested under the Law of Suspects and held at the Sainte-Pélagie prison. The dangers were now coming very close to home.

Josephine ran grave risks in writing to the president of the Committee of General Security, attempting to have her sister-

in-law released. This letter to Vadier, dated 17 January 1794
seems, however, even more a defence of her own husband
against anticipated dangers than it is of the imprisoned woman
whom she professed to champion:

> I am convinced that, on reading this memoir, your sense of
> humanity and justice will cause you to consider the situation of a
> woman who is utterly miserable, but only for having been united
> to an enemy of the Republic, to the elder Beauharnais whom you
> have known and who, in the Constituent Assembly, was in oppo-
> sition to Alexander – your colleague and my husband.
> I would have much regret, citizen-representative, if you should
> confuse Alexander in your mind with the elder Beauharnais. I can
> put myself in your place: you are entitled to doubt the patriotism
> of former nobles, but it is within the realm of possibility that among
> these there are ardent friends of Liberty and Equality. Alexander
> has never deviated from these principles: he has constantly kept to
> the line. If he were not a republican he would have neither my
> respect nor my affection.

What Josephine then proceeded to assert about not knowing
other members of her husband's family and having brought
up her children, before the Revolution, as 'republicans', is
quite clearly a desperate falsehood, penned in a time of great
danger. She went on:

> I am an American, and know him [Alexander] alone of his family.
> If I could have seen you, your doubts would have been dispelled.
> My household is a republican household: before the Revolution
> my children were not distinguishable from the *sans-culottes*, and I
> hope they will be worthy of the Republic.
> I write to you frankly, as a genuine *sans-culotte* . . . I do not de-
> mand either favour or grace, but I appeal to your sympathy and
> humanity on behalf of an unfortunate citizeness. If I have been
> misled about her in thus picturing her situation, and if she really
> were and should appear to you a suspect, I beg you to disregard
> what I have said, for like you, I would be inexorable. But do not
> make a mistake about your old colleague [Alexander]. Believe that
> he is worthy of your respect.[8]

No answer came to this and, despite all efforts, early in 1794
the blow fell. Alexander was denounced to the local committee
of the Department of Loire-et-Cher as a suspect, under the

provision of the law which listed as suspects 'all public functionaries suspected or removed from their functions by the National Convention or its commissioners and not reinstated'. In March 1794 he was arrested and conducted to Paris. History has its ironies. Among the seven signatures on the letter from the Committee of General Security ordering his arrest is that of Jacques-Louis David – now revolutionary patriot and artist, but a decade later to be famous as the official painter of the vast canvas depicting the imperial coronation of Napoleon and Josephine. During the conversations when Josephine sat for this painting, would David have remembered his signature upon the document of 1794? Alexander, first held at the prison of the Luxembourg, was transferred in March to the grim prison of the Carmelites.

Within five weeks Josephine was a prisoner beside her husband. Her efforts to find obscurity and acceptance had failed, for she and Madame Hosten were denounced as 'dangerous' in an anonymous letter to the Committee of General Security. This sinister document read as follows:

Note for Paris. The Hosten woman's dwelling, whether in the city or in the country, is a gathering-place for suspected persons, among others someone named Calon, also Vergennes *père* and his older son, the younger having emigrated. Beware of the former viscountess, wife of Alexander de Beauharnais, who has many connexions in the offices of the ministries. This Hosten woman has a dwelling at Croissy and one at Paris, rue Saint-Dominique . . .[9]

On 19 April the Committee, one of the principal organs of revolutionary government, acted under the provisions of the Law of Suspects and ordered the arrest of 'Beauharnais, wife of the *ci-devant* general, rue Dominique no. 953', and authorized the search of all her papers. Her friend, Madame Hosten, was included in the same order. On the following day Josephine's apartment was searched and sealed. Nothing incriminating, as it happened, was found. On the contrary, the agents reported that they came upon 'a multitude of patriotic letters [could some of these have been from Alexander?] which would serve only as praise for the citizeness.'[10] Nevertheless, on 21 April she, like her husband, became a prisoner.

In these late spring and early summer months of 1794, as Josephine and Alexander lay in prison, revolutionary France experienced the Second Terror – an even greater wave of accusations, imprisonments, and executions than the Terror of 1793. The prisons of Paris were crowded with suspects, so that by the end of April more than eight thousand were being held. Many monastic buildings – no longer needed for their original purpose and convenient with their cells, their refectories, their enclosed courtyards, and their heavy stone walls – were pressed into service as jails.

Among these prisons the old convent of the Carmelites on the rue Vaugirard stood out as one of the most sinister. While it may be that the aristocratic inmates of some of the Paris prisons during the Terror lived a relatively easy life, this was anything but true of those held at the Carmelites. The convent had a longer prison history than most, having been taken over by the state in the critical month of August 1792, when foreign invasion seemed to threaten the very life of France. Over two hundred persons, largely priests, had then been held there. During the terrible September massacres of 1792, which in a few days claimed the lives of more than two thousand prisoners in Paris alone, mobs raged through the streets and 'visited' the prisons. The Carmelites had been a place of terror where altogether a hundred and fifteen of the clergy, including the archbishop of Arles and the bishop of Beauvais, had been hacked to pieces. When Josephine entered the prison, the marks of sabres and the ugly bloodstains from these massacres could still be seen on the walls. The cells were dark, vermin-infested, and so damp that the inmates had to wring out their clothing every morning. Some of the women slept fourteen to a room. While prisoners had some freedom to move about and even to receive visitors, they were limited in their circulation to the corridors, where meals were given at long tables, first to the men and then to the women. In these corridors people stumbled amid water-buckets, slop-pails, and all the confusions, filth, and smells of a crowded prison. Here Alexander spent more than four months and Josephine more than three.

One found all types in such prisons. General Hoche was

there, as was Delphine, lovely daughter-in-law of the recently guillotined General Custine. Josephine's cellmate was the Duchess d'Aiguillon. The Prince de Salm, brother of Josephine's good friend, the Princess of Hohenzollern-Sigmaringen, shared imprisonment with the director of marionettes at the little Champs-Élysées theatre. Some of the prisoners were as young as thirteen. Between December 1793 and the following July, when Robespierre fell, the average population of these narrow confines was about two hundred.

Josephine, according to her prison companion, Delphine de Custine, did not bear up well, showing a degree of discouragement that was embarrassing to her companions. She played solitaire, and wept much. But, says Delphine, despite her lack of courage, she was naturally gracious and had charming manners. Josephine was visited occasionally by her children, and tradition tells that the letters brought in by them from outside were kept from the eyes of the jailers by being stuffed under the collar of the family pet, the pug dog, Fortuné. Eugène paid a visit to Tallien, one of the leading Jacobins, asking help for his mother, but with no success. Two letters of this time, ostensibly from Eugène and Hortense but obviously composed by an older hand, have survived. One, written in May, was addressed to the Convention, and asked freedom for their mother, 'against whom no one has been able to bring any other reproach than that of having had the misfortune to belong to a class to which she has proved herself to be alien, since she has been surrounded by none but the best patriots, the most excellent Jacobins'.[11] In June, the twelve-year-old Eugène and the eleven-year-old Hortense addressed an appeal to the Committee of General Security, urging them in equally unchildlike terms to complete the assembling of the documents in their mother's case, certain that such action would 'hasten the moment that would restore her to liberty'. They concluded their letter, again in words that could hardly be their own: 'When one has nothing to fear from a judgement, one burns to have it rendered'.[12]

While Josephine remained in prison, her children savoured the excitements of revolutionary Paris. On 8 June Robespierre, now at the very pinnacle of his power, presided over the elaborate celebration known as the Fête of the Supreme Being. As part of a carefully rehearsed programme, a huge statue of Atheism, made of inflammable materials, had been erected in the gardens of the Tuileries. At the climactic moment, amid patriotic hymns and chants, Robespierre was to set fire to Atheism so that another ingeniously engineered statue – that of Wisdom – could arise triumphantly from its embers. Atheism did indeed burn, but so furiously that only a jet-black and most unsteady Wisdom rose heavenward through the choking clouds of smoke. Poor Hortense had a narrow escape. She was so near to the centre of excitement that her dress was set on fire by flying embers, her chest was burned, and she narrowly escaped the dire fate that Atheism had so justly met.

Was there a last reconciliation between husband and wife? The pair could not have been very close. On the very eve of his death Alexander wrote to Josephine, calling her simply *mon amie*, and speaking only of 'the fraternal affection which binds me to you'. Both, to be sure, must have been drawn together by the common bond of the two children whom they now expected to see for the last time. On the other hand there are suggestions of counter-attractions. The *Memoirs* of General Montgaillard and the utterly vicious *Memoirs* of Barras, the latter written, to be sure, at a time when he had no other thought than to blacken the memory of Josephine, say that in these days of captivity she was swept off her feet by the gallant figure of General Hoche, her fellow prisoner. If there is any truth in the story, the infatuation must have been of remarkably short duration, for Hoche was transferred from the Carmelite prison just four weeks after Josephine had entered. There is more substantiation to the story of Alexander's brief infatuation with the beautiful Delphine de Custine – an episode altogether in keeping with his history and his character. As he left the Carmelites for the Conciergerie – a sinister indication that he was approaching the guillotine – he gave her as a last gesture a ring mounted with an Arab talisman that, according to her brother, Delphine cherished all her life.

In June 1794 the Convention voted the terrible measure

known, from the month in the new revolutionary calendar
that marked its passage, as the Law of Prairial. This law defined
'enemies of the people' in the vaguest terms, denied them any
legal defence, and set their only penalty as death. In the seven
weeks from the passage of the measure to the fall of Robespierre,
the Revolutionary Tribunal at Paris sent 1,366 victims to the
guillotine. One of them was Josephine's husband.

Alexander had assembled in advance a meticulous dossier
to defend himself. This included an elaborate, two-page, folio
statement, put together in six neat columns and chronicling
his services to the state; a list of the various popular societies
of which he had been president (Paris, Blois, Valenciennes,
Strasbourg, Chaumont); a statement as to the care with which
his two children had been educated 'in republican principles';
and a testimonial from the loyal villagers of La Ferté who had
elected him their mayor. None of this material did him the
slightest good. Alexander was subjected to an interrogation
on 21 July, after which he was removed to the Conciergerie.
Here he wrote the long letter to his wife and children that has
become his last memorial.

The text of Alexander's letter was published in what is now
a very rare pamphlet, the *Almanach des prisons*, sold on the
streets of Paris within a few weeks of his death. The way in
which his interrogation had been conducted made it clear to
Alexander, even before his actual trial, that he had no hope of
escaping the guillotine:

. . . I am the victim [he wrote to Josephine] of the rascally calum-
nies of some aristocratic, would-be patriots in this prison. The likelihood that this diabolical conspiracy will follow me to the Revolutionary Tribunal leaves me without hope of seeing you again, my
friend, or of embracing my dear children. I shall not speak of my
regrets; my tender affection for them and the fraternal affection
which binds me to you can leave you in no doubt as to my feelings
as I leave this world.

Alexander did not dwell long on these expressions of 'tender
affection' for his children and 'fraternal affection' for his wife
– all that was left of a marriage begun fifteen years before. His
last words were for his country and his name:

I regret equally having to leave a country which I love, for which I would have willingly given my life a thousand times, which I will be unable to serve, and which will see me depart, believing me to be a bad citizen. This intolerable thought requires me to entrust my reputation to you. Work to redeem it, by showing that a life wholly dedicated to the service of one's country and to the triumph of Liberty and Equality must, in the eyes of the people, repudiate those odious calumniators who themselves belong to the class of suspects.[13]

On 23 July Alexander appeared before the Revolutionary Tribunal. He was included in a group of forty-nine against whom charges were drawn up by the public prosecutor, Fouquier-Tinville. This group, typical of the strange fellowship of revolution and prison, included, in addition to Alexander, a Vice-Admiral Montbazon-Rohan, aged sixty-four; two *curés*; some artisans; a Thomas Ware, aged forty-eight, born in Dublin and now provisional general in the Army of the North; his servant, John Malone; many former nobles; a sailor, aged seventeen; and, without further identification, one Charles Harrop, aged twenty-two, of London. All were charged with being enemies of the people. The particular accusations brought by Fouquier-Tinville against Alexander included some of the typical clichés of the Revolution: he was 'agent of Pitt and Coburg', he was 'accomplice of the treasons of Custine'. Through inaction he was claimed to have deliberately let Mainz fall to the enemy.[14] The group of forty-nine appeared again before the Revolutionary Tribunal on 24 July. Out of the total, forty-six were immediately found guilty, Alexander among them.

They were guillotined on the same day, in what is now the Place de la Nation. Not far away was the old convent of Picpus and near it the common ditch. Into this unmarked grave, with many others, was thrown the poor, decapitated body of the former nobleman, the 'high and puissant seigneur, Alexandre-François-Marie, Vicomte de Beauharnais, captain in the infantry regiment of the Sarre', whom Josephine had married on that bleak December day of 1779. She learned of his death only by finding his name in the daily list of executions printed in a Paris newspaper, and fainted at the news.

❧ 8 ❧

Life, Liberty, and the Pursuit of Happiness

In the last days of the Terror, during which Josephine came within a hair's breadth of destruction, she was saved by the dramatic working of events. Three days after her husband's death, on the ninth day of the revolutionary month of Thermidor, the seemingly all-powerful Robespierre fell. The great Jacobin was brought down by other, lesser Jacobins, fearful that the Terror by means of which he had hoped to inaugurate the Reign of Virtue would destroy them too. On the hot 28th of July – the tenth of Thermidor – Robespierre and his little group of zealots were taken to what is now the Place de la Concorde and there guillotined as many thousands had been before them.

With Robespierre's fall the extreme Terror quickly subsided. The Revolution, to be sure, still continued. The great Committee of Public Safety, the Revolutionary Tribunal, and the other political machinery of these bloodstained years could not at once be put aside, but since new and less fanatical men were at the helm the whole tempo of revolution gradually changed. This 'Thermidorean Reaction', so different from what preceded it, has been compared not inappropriately to the stage of exhaustion in a patient following the crisis of a desperate illness.

What lucky chance was it that had helped Josephine to escape her husband's fate? She seems to have anticipated death. Witness the story which says that soon after Alexander's execution she found that the straw mattress in her own cell was gone. Despite her companion's urging her to regain it, she said there was no need to complain, as she too would soon make the journey to the guillotine. The facts proved to be otherwise, and the explanation of them may lie in a strange tale.

There has been unearthed the mysterious name of one Delperch de la Bussière, a minor actor employed by the Committee of Public Safety, who is said to have made a practice of removing the dossiers of certain favourite prisoners, so that, through the default of documents, their trials would have to be postponed. We are asked to believe more than this – that La Bussière not only stole selected dossiers, he then literally *ate* them, thereby most decisively bringing the machinery of revolutionary justice to a full halt. It has been asserted that in all he caused 1,153 compromising documents and dossiers to disappear. Josephine gave evidence of believing that she owed some debt to La Bussière. Much later, in April of 1803, she paid handsomely for tickets to a benefit performance put on at the Porte Saint-Martin Theatre on behalf of this unusual character. She attended with her husband and sent him a purse of a thousand francs with the notation, 'in grateful remembrance'. Whatever the explanation for the failure of Josephine to come to trial, it is a fact that the folio in the national archives that contains the documents for Alexander's trial does not have those for his wife.

One after another the doors of the prisons swung open. General Hoche, leaving the Conciergerie, soon offered a post on his staff to the youthful Eugène de Beauharnais. On 6 August 1794 an official order signed by Jean Tallien, a member of the Committee of Public Safety, declared that *la citoyenne* Beauharnais was to be released. Josephine had come in contact with Tallien during the preceding year when she had written to him asking for the release from prison of the niece of the aged Marquis de Moulins. She had also sought his help at the time of Alexander's arrest, but without success. Much later Eugène wrote in his *Memoirs* about Josephine's liberation as follows:

My mother was freed some little time after [the death of Alexander]. I would like to name here the man to whose kindness we owed this good deed. It was the deputy, Tallien. I have always been grateful to him for this, and fortunately I have been in a position to give him repeated proofs of what I felt.[1]

Josephine collapsed on hearing the news that she was to be

free. Despite the rigours and strains of the Carmelite prison, her charm had not deserted her. One of the inmates tells of how at this critical moment a crowd of her companions applauded the good news. 'When she came to herself,' the account adds, 'she made her adieux and went forth amid the good wishes and benedictions of the whole establishment.'[2]

A new age was beginning for France. A revolutionary, republican régime was, to be sure, still in the saddle and the so-called 'new men' – the 'Thermidoreans' – were in reality not new at all; they were simply agile revolutionaries who had survived the Terror. Slippery careerists such as Barras, Tallien, and Fouché, names that will recur in the life of Josephine, now took up the reins of power from the grim Robespierrists whom they had overthrown. Gradually the most savage of the revolutionary legislation was repealed. In November the Paris Jacobin Club, with whose aims Josephine had so desperately asserted her sympathies (surely the most bizarre claim she ever made), was closed.

'Revolutionary government' was clearly becoming a thing of the past, so much so that by September of 1795, the surviving deputies of the Convention were able to complete a new constitution for France. Executive power was to be in the hands of a committee of five directors, elected from the legislative body, and legislative power was divided between two elected groups, the Council of Ancients and the Council of Five Hundred. Constitutional developments had, as such, little interest for the unpolitical Josephine, yet it was to be the changing fortunes of politics between the years 1794 and 1799 that made Josephine's new life what it was. The most prominent of the directors, Paul Barras, soon came into close association with her. Moreover, by challenging and overthrowing the authority of the Council of Ancients and the Council of Five Hundred, a certain Napoleon Bonaparte, having made himself master of Josephine, likewise made himself the master of France.

Josephine undertook her new life, not in the arena of politics, but in the neurotic atmosphere of a sick society.

Europeans of the twentieth century who have lived through the fevered aftermath of two world wars can doubtless appreciate the nature of the uprooted, cynically immoral society that followed the austere period of 'republican virtue'. The Revolution had earlier found its heroes in such noble Romans as Brutus, Cicero, and the Gracchi. These ancient shadows of the Roman past were now ignored by the living exponents of a life of dissipation and pleasure.

Groups of foppish young men known as the Gilded Youth (the *Jeunesse dorée*) roamed the streets, wearing fantastically cut clothing with tight trousers, coats with very narrow waists, and huge neckerchiefs concealing the chin, often the mouth, and sometimes the nose. They carried daggers, sword-sticks, and heavy canes, armed with which they would enter cafés and theatres in order briskly to crack open the heads of former Jacobins. Their speech was marked by an affected lisp. The letter 'r' disappeared entirely from the vocabulary of those who vouched for their assertions with the simpering oath, 'paole supême'. In their eccentric manner of conversation a new, single word, 'Sexa?' replaced the conventional question, 'Qu'est-ce que c'est que ça?'

'Pleasure,' wrote a Swiss visitor, 'is the order of the day.' Paris had at least thirty-three public theatres and over two hundred smaller halls for amateur performances. Gambling was all the rage. On the streets the crowds of prostitutes began to operate with what a police report called 'their former audacity'. Above all, the public devoted itself to dancing. This became such a mania that the more than six hundred dancehalls of the capital could not suffice. Dances were held everywhere. With reckless affectation people danced in the former prisons – the Carmelites, for example. The *Bal des Zéphyrs* was held among the very tombs of the cemetery of Saint-Sulpice. 'They would have danced,' writes an outraged historian of a later generation, 'on Noah's Ark. They would have danced on the Raft of the Medusa.'[3] An especially popular entertainment was the *Bal à la Victime* to which only relatives of those who had been guillotined could be invited. As if in preparation for the guillotine, men cut their hair short and women wore theirs high on the head leaving the nape of the neck bare. A narrow scarlet ribbon worn by the ladies seemed to make a blood-red line around the throat, while during the dance the head was jerked back and forth as if ready to fall into the basket of the guillotine.

These gruesome pleasures went on while some Frenchmen waxed fat and others starved. Fortunes were made and then recklessly squandered by the war profiteers, the contractors, and the speculators who had flourished in these years of crisis. This was at a time when a vicious inflation affected France. A bushel of flour which in 1790 would have cost 2 livres now in 1795 cost 225 paper livres. The cost of a pair of shoes in the same time had risen from 5 to 200 livres, and a half-hogshead of wine from 80 to 2,400 livres. While some people begged and shivered in the streets, others gorged themselves at magnificent banquets.

Feminine society in these last months of the Convention and in the new era of the Directory was a strange, hot-house growth. 'Good' society had disappeared. On the streets, in the walks and arcades of the Palais Royal, in the pleasure gardens of Tivoli, in the rustic haunts of the Champs-Élysées, in the theatres, the dance-halls, and the cafés, everywhere paraded the women of this new age, the 'Marvellous Ones' – *les Merveilleuses*. They read little except erotic romances, and talked little except scandal. Their dress was at first ridiculously ornate, with skirts so long and full that they had to be carried looped over one arm. Women wore enormous bonnets which made the face almost invisible, and were prone to festoon themselves with a wild litter of trinkets, fans, satchels, and jewellery. Their faces, first dusted white with rice-powder, were then heavily rouged. It was fashionable, too, to have a small dog on leash, preferably a mongrel, or *carlin*. Josephine had hers – the much-loved Fortuné, with its weasel head and corkscrew tail, that Eugène and Hortense had brought with them when they visited their mother in prison and that later bit Napoleon on his wedding night. For reasons that are not clear it was understood that such dogs were to be led by a ribbon that must be green.

Les Merveilleuses soon discovered the charm of the antique Greek costume, a charm all the more alluring because its exponents could make use of fragile, diaphanous fabrics. After the *sans-culottes* now came the *sans-chemises*. The elements of this costume were a classic diadem on the head, a clinging, gauzelike robe having a belt fastened with large cameos, a very light cashmere shawl, sandals fitted to bare feet, and toes covered with rings. This attire underwent increasingly daring modifications, all intended much less to cover than to reveal the charms of nature – most particularly those intimate charms elegantly described by a contemporary as the twin reservoirs of maternity. The dazzling Madame Tallien was pleased to appear in a diaphanous robe under which she wore flesh-coloured tights spangled with golden stars. Even in Paris, however, it was possible to overdo (or underdo) such matters, for when Josephine's creole friend, Madame Hamelin, undertook to walk from the Luxembourg to the Champs-Élysées, in a costume that left her naked to the waist, she was followed by a jeering mob. Josephine, who soon became a part of this society, achieved a certain distinction by refusing to adopt the wilder vagaries of such fashions.

The leader of this society – 'the sorry queen of a motley court' – was Thérèse de Cabarrus, the lovely daughter of a Spanish banker, once married to a Monsieur de Fontenay and subsequently divorced. During the Revolution she had plunged into a reckless life that led her, after imprisonment under the Terror, to become the mistress and then for a few years the wife of Tallien, one of the most prominent of the victors of Thermidor. One of the directors, Barras, took Madame Tallien for a time as his mistress; she then turned from him to the banker, Ouvrard. Under the Empire she married again to become Countess of Caraman – a title later changed to that of Princess of Chimay. So prominent was Thérèse in these first months of the Directory that she became known, in the blasphemously cynical phrase of the times, as 'Our Lady of Thermidor'. Jean Tallien introduced Thérèse to Josephine and, discovering a mutual affinity, the two women became in some sense the twin rulers of this strange society.

In July of this year Commander of Brigade Napoleon Bonaparte, then anything but a ladies' man, wrote from Paris to his brother Joseph as follows:

Women are everywhere – applauding the plays, walking in the promenades, reading in the bookshops. You will find the lovely creatures even in the professor's study. Here is the only place in the world where they deserve to steer the ship of state; the men are mad about them, think of nothing else, and live only for them. Give a woman six months in Paris, and she knows where her empire is and what is her due.[4]

And in August the moody soldier wrote again:

I hardly care what happens to me. I watch life almost indifferently. ... Everything leads me to face death and destiny without flinching, and if this continues I shall end by not stepping out of the way of a passing carriage. I am sometimes astonished at myself, but such is the abyss to which I have been brought by the moral spectacle of this country and by my familiarity with danger.[5]

Amid this 'moral spectacle' Josephine had to find her way.

In this cynical, disillusioned world of 1795 Josephine appears in a new light. Her problem – starkly simple – was that of survival. The boy, Eugène, now under the wing of General Hoche, was no longer a prime responsibility. After a short service with Hoche he was sent to a school at Saint-Germain – the *Collège irlandais* directed by one Patrick McDermott. Hortense returned to the care of Madame Renaudin and the Marquis de Beauharnais at Fontainebleau. From here she was soon sent to the thriving school, the *Institution nationale de Saint-Germain-en-Laye* founded and directed by Madame Campan, once first *femme de chambre* to Marie Antoinette. Now freer than ever before, mature, sophisticated, and surely a woman of few illusions, Josephine, by the testimony of observers, had developed an elegance, a charm, and a sympathy for others that served her well and kept her from succumbing to the wild extravagances and shrill vulgarities of her surroundings. The writer Frénilly, who knew Josephine in 1795, while conceding her kindliness and charm described her rather acidly as one of those women who are able to stay for fifteen years at the age of thirty – no small achievement, surely, in view of fortune's buffetings. A woman for whom the ties of family had been now sharply broken, for whom religion seems to have offered little consolation or guidance, is it surprising that she should have drifted with the currents of her times?

The charm that Josephine demonstrated in these months did not lack an element of calculation. A member of the Convention, Jean Debry, had taken occasion in a public session to speak well of her late husband. She wrote at once to thank him for 'doing justice to a virtuous republican who had perished, victim to his aristocratic lineage'. Josephine sent Debry a copy of Alexander's last letter:

You will see [she explained] that as he approached the close of a life devoted entirely to the Revolution, and at the moment where a man would have no reason to hide his true feelings, he was happy to expound still further that ardent love of country which has never ceased to be his inspiration.[6]

Josephine ended her letter by urging Debry to continue likewise to serve his country with zeal, and to protect wherever he could innocence and virtue. Sensibly enough, Josephine sought to have friends in court.

Unwilling now to fling herself upon the sympathy and help of the ageing Madame Renaudin at Fontainebleau, Josephine sought her means of support elsewhere. With her husband dead and his estates sequestered she could count on nothing from this source. During the revolutionary years she had been advanced substantial sums by a banker of Dunkirk named Emmery who traded with the Antilles and for years had done business for the Tascher family. Emmery had been a member of the Legislative Assembly in Paris and was imprisoned for a time during the Terror. Besides having this connexion with Josephine's family, he had in some degree, therefore, shared her prison experiences. From 1792 onwards she had practically lived on loans from 'our good friend Emmery', who, as she told her mother in Martinique, 'has fed me for three years'.[7] By 1795 she had come to owe him what she described only as 'considerable sums'. Josephine also wrote several letters to the Hamburg bankers, Matthiessen and Guillem, who had acted as a transfer agent for funds, telling them, too, of her hardships and offering jewellery as a pledge for cash from them. Sometime in 1795 she managed even to make a hasty trip to Hamburg, seeking to expedite the arrival of money.

Several letters to her mother in these anxious months of 1794 and 1795 tell the same story. Since England and France were at war and Martinique had been captured again, communications were difficult. In November, apparently giving news of her troubles for the first time, she wrote as follows:

A person leaving for New England has agreed to forward this letter to you. I shall be very happy to have it bring you the news that your daughter and grandchildren are well. Doubtless you have heard of my misfortune. I have been a widow for four months. For consolation I have only my children, and you, dear mama, for my support. My most eager wish is that someday we may all be united.[8]

In December she wrote again:

As for your poor daughter, she exists, as do her children, but they have the misfortune to have lost their father. I had reasons for being attached to my husband which cause me to regret his loss; my children now have only me for their support, and I cling to life only to make them happy. Even as I do, they owe to M. Emmery of Dunkirk their means of subsistence.[9]

And again in January 1795:

Without the care of my good friend Emmery and his associate I don't know what would have become of me. I know your affection too well to have even the least doubt that you will provide me with the means to live, and that you will recognize and pay off what I owe to M. Emmery.[10]

Again and again the requests went forth to Martinique. Madame Tascher de la Pagerie, widowed and poor, was in no position to do much. Some funds, however, were sent, and with their aid Josephine survived.

Little trace of the timid bird of the islands appears in the hard-driving woman of this new age. In February of 1795 Josephine petitioned the Committee of General Security to have the seals taken from her apartment on the rue Saint-Dominique, so that she could take over her furniture and belongings. The Committee approved, 'as an act of justice', over the signatures of Josephine's good friend, Tallien, and others. In April she organized a 'family council' of close friends, which appointed her as *tutrice* of her children; on the strength of this she went to Fontainebleau and borrowed from Madame Renaudin the sum of fifty thousand livres in inflated assignats in the name of her children, the money coming from the proceeds of the sale of the house at Fontainebleau. In June she ingeniously submitted a formal appeal to the Committee of Public Safety, asking them to supply her with two horses and a carriage in compensation for those horses which Alexander had left behind when he gave up command of the Army of the Rhine. Surprisingly enough, her request was granted, so that she could appear on the streets of Paris with a fine carriage and a pair of seven-year-old black Hungarian horses. Soon afterwards she asked that Alexander's books, silver, and furniture, which had been impounded at La Ferté, be returned to her or, in the event they had been sold, that she be compensated for them. In March 1796 this request, too, was granted. Still later she asked (this time without success) that in return for the loss of a family plantation at Santo Domingo, pillaged by native insurgents, she be indemnified in actual quantities of sugar and coffee – commodities that would have been very profitable on the Paris market. No mean undertakings, these, for a woman whose life had given her little experience in the fine arts of diplomacy, financial bargaining, and backstairs intrigue.

The chance survival of two official passes from the Committee of General Security, granting permission for Josephine to travel from Paris to Fontainebleau, gives us an almost photographic impression of what she then must have looked like. The first, dated '27 messidor an III' (15 July 1795), is as follows:

Age twenty-nine years, height five feet, nose and mouth well-made, eyes orange, hair and eyebrows dark brown, face long, chin somewhat prominent.

The second, dated '5 brumaire an IV' (27 October 1795), reads:

Age twenty-nine years, height five feet, eyes dark, hair chestnut, mouth small, chin round, forehead medium, nose small.[11]

Beauty, and the classification of it, owe much to the beholder. The strange description of the eyes as 'orange' probably represents what we would call hazel – which under varying conditions of light and costume could vary from topaz to green or to blue. We can understand and accept, therefore, the obvious discrepancies in these documents. Josephine alone must be held responsible, however, for understating her age by three years. She doubtless had her reasons, for at this latter date (October) she had just made the acquaintance of an interesting Corsican officer nearly six years younger than herself.

A little more than a year after leaving prison – to be exact, on 17 August 1795 – Josephine had signed a lease on the town house occupied by the *citoyenne* Julie Carreau, estranged wife of the celebrated French actor Talma. For this house, despite her perennial financial troubles, Josephine agreed to pay the large annual rent of four thousand francs in metallic currency. (The franc had replaced the livre in April as the basic monetary unit.) She took possession in October. In this soon to be famous dwelling, Number 6, rue Chantereine, Josephine and Bonaparte were to begin their married life. Here too, in November of 1799, was hatched the conspiracy of Brumaire that made Bonaparte master of France. And a few months later Josephine would leave this home to take up her residence at the Luxembourg and later at the Tuileries as wife of the first consul and first lady of France.

Not a stone now remains of Josephine's house, for it was demolished in 1859 to accommodate the splendid building plans of Napoleon III. Today, in the bustling centre of Paris, not far from the Gare Saint-Lazare, the modern banking and commercial buildings of the present rue de la Victoire rise where it once stood. The establishment exists, therefore, only as a legend, yet one that is vivid and spectacular. In 1795 the scandals connected with the name of Julie Carreau, along with others in the vicinity like her, had helped to give an air of disrepute to this neighbourhood where gallant adventures, so it seems, were easily come by.

An atmosphere of seclusion, impossible in the Paris of today, marked the house of 1795. One approached it through a massive porter's lodge on the rue Chantereine. From this a paved lane, flanked by high buildings opened into a courtyard, on either side of which were a stable and coach-house. In the stable were kept the two fine carriage horses from Hungary, and, with deceptive rusticity, a utilitarian red cow. The main house, in reality a small pavilion, stood in the centre of the open space with a small wooded garden beyond. Several steps led up to a kind of veranda that shielded the principal entrance.

Everything about the interior, in time to be elaborately re-decorated by Josephine's orders, suggested both the fashions of the period and the particular quality of her taste. The house is best pictured, therefore, not as it was when Josephine took it over, but as it appeared after two or three years of her lavish attention, when it was to be the home of General Bonaparte, conqueror of Italy. A small entrance hall, the walls painted with military trophies, was sparsely furnished with a fountain of copper, an oak lowboy, and a tall pine cupboard. In the dining-room, which also served as a *petit salon*, stood a round mahogany drop-leaf table, four mahogany chairs covered in black horse-hair, some serving wagons, and two elegant marble-topped side tables. Glass-doored cupboards fitted into the walls contained an English tea service of Sheffield plate in an Etruscan design, together with vases and dishes. On the walls were eight prints, one, in red chalk, representing *Innocence in the Arms of Justice*. Beyond this was another small *salon*, semicircular in shape. Its marble mantelpiece had gilt-bronze decorations; there was a fine pianoforte by Bernard; sixteen framed prints hung on the walls. This semicircular *salon* had white painted woodwork, green walls, ornaments of griffins' wings, and stucco bas-reliefs of scenes from Roman history. Amid this Roman décor Josephine also managed to include, for whatever reason, a bust of Socrates. Such classic magnificence undoubtedly represented the vogue, yet one is intrigued to think that somewhere the restless ghost of Alexander de Beauharnais could rejoice that sixteen years after he had urged his wife to the reading of Vertot's *Roman History* the artistic fruits were thus manifest.

A narrow staircase curved upwards to the next floor, which was low-ceilinged and insufferably hot in summer. Josephine's bedroom had a kind of awning fitted to the ceiling on which were painted garlanded swans swimming in a sea of pink roses. The chairs were finished in bronze; the bed was covered in blue nankeen tufted with red and yellow; and a fine harp made by Renaud stood in the corner. On the door was painted a head of Diana, goddess of the moon and of various other matters, including fertility in women. An adjacent dressing-room had its walls, and even the doors leading from it, entirely covered with mirrors. After marrying Bonaparte, Josephine had the bedroom decorated in red, white, and blue to represent a soldier's tent. Instead of chairs there were stools covered with cloth and chamois to simulate regimental drums, while the twin beds, finished in bronze, had an artful spring arrangement enabling them to come together or be separated at will. Bonaparte was also provided with a tiny study so dark that reflectors were placed outside the two windows in an attempt to dispel some of the gloom. In the attic above were tiny chambers suitable either for servants or for the occasional visits of Eugène and Hortense.

To run such an establishment Josephine had need of a coachman, a manservant, a cook, a chambermaid, and a personal maid, the last being the faithful and long-suffering Marie Lannoy, whose wages, fixed at six hundred francs a year, Josephine usually kept for herself as a kind of perpetual and ever-expanding loan. Josephine also accepted in addition the larger sums that from time to time Marie somehow managed to scrape together for her impecunious mistress.

In these sophisticated and over-elegant surroundings, to

maintain which she would need resources far beyond her
evident capacity to provide, a new Josephine took up residence
about the end of October 1795. She did so just as the final rump
sessions of the Convention had come to an end and France, at
last freed from the wild fury of the Revolution, entered the
uncertain era of the Directory.

The most obvious means by which Josephine could ensure
her own survival and prosperity in this new world was to turn
to those figures in whose hands influence lay. Tallien, one of the
victors of Thermidor, had helped her to win her freedom; and
through Tallien Josephine had come to be a close friend of
Thérèse Cabarrus. Thérèse was very well connected in government circles – she was the one whom the wits had dubbed
'government property'. Through Thérèse Josephine came
to know some of the bankers, among them Ouvrard, who were
making fortunes out of France's necessities. Through Thérèse
also, Josephine now met Barras – another of the victors of
Thermidor, a dominant power in Paris, and in the light of
history surely one of the most unattractive figures that the
Revolution had produced. Josephine, so much and so inevitably a part of her times, saw him otherwise.

The biographers of Paul Barras have found few redeeming
features in him. Yet in comparison with some of the bloodstained figures of the days of the Terror, savagely destroying
all those who stood in their path, he might well have appeared
to Josephine in a different light. He was, after all, an ex-noble-
man and an ex-officer of the old régime; once in authority he
sought to replace the rough surroundings of the Luxembourg
with something of the elegance of a past era. His venality
would hardly single him out from his immediate fellows. Most
important of all, he was at the very centre of power. Josephine
was in no position to judge too nicely. Only a year before she
had been in prison, daily watching her friends go to their
deaths and momentarily expecting the same fate. Now free,
and alone, she made her way, like thousands of others, as best
she could.

Barras, in his youth an officer in the regiment of Languedoc, had sided enthusiastically with the Revolution, winning election to the Convention and voting without hesitation for the death of Louis XVI. He had made a fine career for himself as a 'deputy on mission' – one of those powerful agents of the central government sent periodically to the provinces to supervise both military and civilian affairs. At the siege of Toulon in 1793 he had come to know and respect Napoleon Bonaparte. Returning to Paris, he became a principal architect of Robespierre's downfall, and thus one of the most prominent figures in France. He had a remarkable instinct for survival. It is an interesting fact that of the five directors elected in the autumn of 1795 Barras received the smallest number of votes, and yet managed to remain a director until 1799 – the only one of the original membership to do so. At the time of the Vendémiaire rising (October 1795) in Paris against the Convention, Barras was the man who was put in charge of the troops and he was responsible for ordering Bonaparte to mount the artillery in the streets, which quickly dispersed the crowds.

By common report, which Josephine did much to encourage and nothing to deny, she now became the mistress of Barras. Her move was certainly one for which the exalted society of the *ancien régime* – to say nothing of the riotously immoral society of her own day – could have given ample precedent. It also provided generous scope for her enemies. A drawing by the English caricaturist, James Gillray – a violent opponent, to be sure, of everything connected with the Revolution and Napoleon – shows Josephine and Madame Tallien dancing naked before this most durable of the directors, while a startled General Bonaparte peers at the scene through a gauze curtain. One of his colleagues, La Revellière, has described Barras as follows:

With a fine carriage and a manly figure, he always had something of that common and brash air found in low society . . . He had a great, a tireless, capacity for intrigue. Falsehood and bottomless dissimulation, joined to other vices, grew stronger over the years. At the Luxembourg he was surrounded by the most dissolute fomenters of anarchy, by lost women, ruined men, 'fixers', speculators, mistresses, and *mignons*. The most infamous debauchery was openly practised in his house . . . Though he always employed the language of a patriot, and even of a *sans-culotte*, he surrounded himself with an extraordinary luxury. He had all the tastes of an opulent, extravagant, magnificent, and dissipated prince.[12]

After November 1795, Barras set up his official residence in the Luxembourg Palace, where apartments had been allotted to each of the five directors. The setting was at first of Spartan simplicity. The years of revolution had worked their hardships, so that on arrival the new leaders of France were hard put to it to assemble even a few kitchen chairs and tables for their business, and were compelled to send out a footman for armfuls of firewood to counteract the bitter, freezing weather. Barras, the possessor of a considerable fortune, soon changed all that. Wearing the official director's costume designed by the artist David – a long, red mantle of richly embroidered fabric with a lace collar, knee breeches and silk stockings, a 'Roman' sword, and a plumed hat – and surrounded by cohorts of women 'more elegant than virtuous', he entertained constantly in a splendid setting of crystal chandeliers, gilt furniture, and red velvet armchairs festooned with gold lace. When he drove abroad the harness of his horses was mounted with solid silver.

Barras also maintained a retreat near the Rond-Point of the Champs-Élysées. This dwelling, 'La Chaumière', romantically designed like a farm-house with a thatched roof, stood amid a setting of poplars and lilacs in what were truly rustic surroundings. Leaders of the new society, Josephine among them, were often invited there to his suppers. Barras had in addition a town house where Josephine sometimes acted as hostess, sending out invitations over her own name. As if this were not enough, the director became a regular visitor to Josephine's country villa at Croissy. It was still hers in the sense that she continued to be obligated for the rent – an impossible burden that Barras willingly assumed. A neighbour, the future chancellor Pasquier, has recorded how on the morning of Barras' arrival at Croissy basket-loads of luxuries – game, fowls, and fruits – would precede him from Paris. Josephine, a 'typical creole' and never a good housekeeper, would send urgently to her neighbours for casseroles, glasses, and plates. Sooner or later Barras and a gay cavalcade of friends would arrive on horseback from the city, and the celebrations would begin.

One little vignette of this unsavoury world occurs in the *Memoirs* of an obscure civil servant, François Besnard. Even after her marriage to Bonaparte in 1796, Josephine evidently did not deny herself the attractions of society in Barras' headquarters at the Luxembourg:

> One day [Besnard writes] I happened to be at the foot of the staircase leading to the apartment of Citizen Barras, when I saw three ladies appear, tripping lightly up the steps. Their beauty, and the elegance of their dress which, according to the mode of the day, veiled but did not disguise their charms, caused me to think of the Three Graces of Antiquity. After they were gone I imagined that I could still see them. Later I found out that they were *mesdames* Tallien, Bonaparte, and Récamier and that they came regularly to adorn the salons of the director. This was a new kind of surprise for me, who took him to be one of the most austere of republicans.[13]

One is surprised indeed that Besnard should have been surprised.

To Josephine, surely, nothing quite like Barras had ever appeared before. Whatever his dissipated qualities, and however transient their relationship, he gave Josephine a prominent place in this strange, vicious society of the Directory. Tiring at length of her, Barras was widely believed to have deliberately arranged her marriage to Bonaparte – a belief that gives him more credit than he deserves. Though not the matchmaker, Barras was, without question, close to both Josephine and Bonaparte. Until his definite breach with Napoleon after the coup of 1799 the generous-hearted Josephine kept on excellent terms with Barras, firing letters at him on a variety of matters – usually concerning jobs and money for others, or, on occasion, money for herself.

❧ 9 ❧

Bonaparte

LESS than a year before that long-distant autumn of 1779 when Josephine with her father had taken ship from Martinique to marry Alexander de Beauharnais, an obscure government official on the Mediterranean island of Corsica had likewise embarked for France. The month was December 1778. With this official was his nine-year-old son, Napoleone Buonaparte, who still used the Italian form of his name, and still spoke only the Corsican-Italian dialect. By virtue of belonging to the island nobility the boy had been given a government scholarship, first to a school at Autun where he could master French, thence to the military academy of Brienne where he would train for a career in the armies of Louis XVI. Boy and girl alike, each an utter stranger to the France where they were being taken, stood on the threshold of extraordinary lives, which after many turns of fortune would unite and find them a common destiny on an imperial throne.

The man who was to give Josephine her place in history came from an island setting strikingly different from that which she had known in Martinique. Each island had its singular beauties. The coastal areas of Corsica, where vineyards and chestnut forests are hemmed in by the blue waters of the Mediterranean, give place inland to a thinly settled countryside that is mountainous, wild, and semi-desert. The towns are small, and the simple life of the inhabitants, most of whom are farmers, shepherds, or vineyard keepers, has suggested to many visitors, not the least of them being James Boswell, the proud, stubborn, half-barbarous existence of the Highlanders of Scotland.

In the middle of the eighteenth century to be a native of Corsica was to wear a badge of honour. The Corsican people, aided by France, had plunged into a struggle to win freedom from the unwelcome rule of the Republic of Genoa. The champion of Corsican independence, Pasquale Paoli, whose name became a household word to lovers of freedom throughout Europe, counted among his many followers the father of Napoleon. Napoleon's elder brother, Joseph, was born in the midst of the struggle and was carried, an infant in the arms of his mother, again great with child, as she loyally shared the rigorous campaigns with her husband. Napoleon himself was born soon after the conflict ended. In 1768 Genoa admitted defeat, ceding Corsica to France for a large cash payment. Many patriots, however, followed Paoli's lead and fought on, refusing to recognize this transfer to French sovereignty. Paoli himself did not actually give up the struggle until the following year when he left Corsica for an English exile. Just two months after Paoli's departure, Napoleon was born on 15 August 1769, at Ajaccio, thereby providing historians with the interesting, if inconclusive, speculation as to what might have been the course of history had his family followed Paoli to England and Bonaparte had been born a British subject.

Napoleon's father, Charles-Marie Buonaparte, was a member of the Corsican nobility – a nobility hardly noted for its elegance or sophistication, and one that was denied formal recognition in France. He had studied at Pisa and Rome, having the degree of doctor of laws. Extravagant and restless, the holder of various administrative posts in Corsica, he owned several houses, vineyards, and mills. He was a writer of poetry. A portrait of him in wig, lace ruff, velvet coat, and gold braid suggests a man very different from the picturesque rustics fighting with Paoli in the Corsican mountains.

Bonaparte's mother, Letizia Ramolino, was of Neapolitan descent; her father was an inspector-general of roads and bridges under the Genoese régime. Letizia was a remarkable character, so poorly educated as to be almost illiterate in the narrow sense of the term, yet dignified and intelligent. Many have described her as strikingly beautiful and, although she never could speak or write French without ridiculous mistakes, she had native ability and solid common sense. Throughout his life Napoleon was invariable in his admiration and respect for her. Letizia, for her part, accepted the meteoric rise of her son with unassailable caution, a quality that may go far to explain the reputation for parsimony unkind critics were quick to give her. 'She had her own version of Newton's law of gravity, and realized too well that what goes up must surely soon come down.'[1] She was to appear and reappear in the lives of Napoleon and Josephine and to outlive her famous son by fifteen years.

Thirteen children were born into the family, only eight of whom survived infancy. Joseph, the eldest to survive, preceded Napoleon by a year and a half. There were three younger brothers: Lucien, Louis (later to marry Josephine's daughter, Hortense), and the baby of the family, Jérôme. The three sisters were Elisa, Pauline, and Caroline. By the time this family of eight was completed Letizia was thirty-four; she had borne altogether thirteen children in less than twenty years; and she might well have had more. Her husband, however, died before fame had come to his second son. Napoleon's meteoric rise was to make possible splendid careers for all the members of his family, yet despite this, or perhaps even because of it, most of them displayed a hostility towards Josephine that grew with the years and continued to be directed towards her Beauharnais descendants throughout the nineteenth century.

When Bonaparte, at the age of nine, arrived with his father in France he left behind the fleeting world of childhood for his lifelong career as a soldier. The contrast is striking between the dedicated career of this strange young Corsican, now moving through the five disciplined years at Brienne to one further year of training at the famous *École Militaire* in Paris, and the easy, fashionable ascent of Alexander de Beauharnais. Bonaparte was poor, and his Corsican nobility – such as it was – gave him no entry into sophisticated society. He was an aspiring professional soldier, an artillerist, a student of mathematics and topography, a lonely reader of Plutarch's *Lives*, of Bossuet's *Universal History*, of Montesquieu's *Spirit of the Laws*, and of Rousseau's *Social Contract*. His commission as second lieutenant in the *Régiment de la Fère* – a crack French regiment – was won in 1785, at the age of sixteen. This new career made him a soldier, but at first little else. In the same year he began his regimental duties, Josephine, having won her 'amicable separation' from Alexander de Beauharnais, had left the convent of Pentemont for a life of independence in Paris.

The moody young Corsican officer found ample time to commit to paper the many reflections arising from his reading. His notebooks were filled with annotations on Plato's *Republic*, on Rollin's *Ancient History*, on Buffon's *Natural History*. In his first year as an officer he composed his *Thoughts on Suicide*. A striking passage in his comments on Rousseau's *Discourse on the Origins of Inequality* reads as follows:

I think that man has never been a wanderer, isolated without connexions, without need of his fellows. I believe on the contrary that having emerged from infancy and arrived at the age of adolescence man felt the need of his fellows, that he became united to a woman and selected a cavern which had to be the centre of his excursions . . . The union was strengthened by custom, and by the tie of children, but it could be broken at will.[2]

There has survived, too, a curious personal document of another sort – Bonaparte's account of what he calls a 'philosophic experience', a chance encounter with a girl in the arcades of the Palais-Royal on a November evening of 1787. His picture of this poorly clad, half-frozen *fille*, who had been brought to Paris from Nantes by an army officer and then abandoned, telling the young lieutenant bitterly of her sordid manner of existence ('one must live'), and then going with Bonaparte to his warm room, is an odd record of what seems to have been a novel episode in the young officer's life.

The French Revolution speeded up and transformed Bonaparte's career. For a time he was in the south of France with his regiment. Then for over a year he enjoyed an extended leave in Corsica visiting his family. Here some local sentiment had turned against France, and Bonaparte was in the unusual position of opposing some of those alongside whom his father fought. Early in 1791 he rejoined his regiment. Some unhappy encounters on the journey may have now prompted him to compose a brief sketch, his *Dialogue on Love*. 'I do more than dispute the existence of Love,' he wrote, 'I consider it to be actually as injurious to society as to the personal happiness of mankind. I believe that it adds to our lot more evil than it does good, and it would be a lucky chance if some kind fairy were to set us free from it.'[3] His scepticism ran deep: the boy of thirteen, he declared, has a friend; at twenty-three he has a mistress; at forty he loves his fortune; at sixty he loves nothing but himself.

Returning to Paris, he watched the mob attack the Tuileries in June 1792 and saw it massacre the Swiss guards in the uprising of the following August. The collapse of the monarchy made him a republican. In June 1793, he brought his almost impoverished family from Corsica to France, establishing them first at Toulon. A little pamphlet he wrote in 1793, *Le Souper de Beaucaire*, stamped him as a Jacobin. When Toulon, tiring of Robespierre's dictatorship at Paris, opened its harbour to the British fleet and defied the Republic, Bonaparte was one of the officers sent to recapture the city. He made his plans, brilliantly. 'From that date,' Las Cases wrote at St Helena, 'history took him up, never to let him go. Then began his immortality.'[4] Toulon fell in December 1793, and Bonaparte, a marked man, became general of brigade. Throughout the following year he was in the south of France, involved in plans for an invasion of Piedmont. On the fall of Robespierre he became suspect and was imprisoned for ten days in the Mediterranean town of Antibes. His release after this brief imprisonment, which curiously parallels that of Josephine, meant that his position in the new régime following the Jacobin ascendancy was secure.

During the opening months of 1795 Napoleon came close to marriage with Désirée Clary. In the previous August his older brother, Joseph, had taken as his bride Julie Clary, daughter of a wealthy banker and silk merchant of Marseilles. Joseph and his wife then hoped that Julie's sister, the graceful, sensitive, seventeen-year-old Désirée-Eugénie, would in turn wed Napoleon – and this despite the expressed view of Monsieur Clary that one Bonaparte in the family was enough. Désirée, it seems, was more in love with Napoleon than he with her. In April, nevertheless, they made some tender pledge to each other. How nearly the young general escaped marriage we can only guess; he told Bertrand at St Helena that on one occasion he found Désirée hiding under his bed. 'Take care of your life,' she wrote to him when he left for Paris, 'in order to preserve that of your Désirée, who could not live without you. Keep the vow that you have made to me, even as I shall keep mine to you.'⁵ Désirée never destroyed the first drafts of these affectionate letters written to the man whom she did not marry. She was to become ultimately the wife of a marshal of France and go on to reign as queen of Sweden; she was to have many adventures and to live to be eighty-three; yet on her death these papers were still in her possession. And throughout her life she detested Josephine.

The Bonaparte who now came to Paris in May was a tormented man. In a military sense he had prospered. Only twenty-five, he had risen in ten years from second lieutenant to brigadier general. He had been put temporarily on the retired list because he would not accept a command in the Army of the West, which was engaged in fighting French royalists in Brittany. He even considered leaving for a time in order to serve as adviser on artillery to the Turkish government. He could, nevertheless, expect other more congenial army appointments in France. Though hardly popular, he was coming to be well-known, and he was liked and respected by Barras, the most powerful politician of the capital.

Now that Bonaparte was in Paris his understanding with Désirée was becoming clouded, for despite her avowals no more letters came. He was ready to send her his portrait, so he told Joseph in August, 'if she still wants it'.⁶ In September he suggested that Joseph find out from her brother what Désirée's intentions really were. 'Either we settle this affair,' he wrote unhappily, 'or we break it off.'⁷

Bonaparte's letters to his brother show him to have been moody to the point of despair. There were hints of suicide. 'Life is but a light dream that soon vanishes,' he wrote.⁸ Paris society, such as it was, appalled him. He intensely disliked the speculators and financiers who crowded the salons of the Directory. Ouvrard, one of these speculators, thought equally little of Bonaparte, labelling him in what is surely one of history's greatest misjudgements as 'the least notable of all those who made up the society of Madame Tallien, and the least favoured by fortune'.[9]

The continuing uncertainty about his relations with Désirée and about his career provoked Bonaparte to impetuous moves. 'If I stay here,' he confessed despondently to his brother, 'it is not impossible that a mad desire to get married (*la folie de me marier*) will take possession of me.'[10] He turned from Désirée to an old Corsican friend, Madame Permon, a woman of noble Greek origin, widow of a wealthy government contractor. According to her daughter, the future Duchess d'Abrantès, Bonaparte at this time proposed to Madame Permon, fourteen years his senior, only to be promptly refused. He likewise made unavailing overtures, with what degree of seriousness we cannot tell, to a Madame de la Boucharderie. In such an atmosphere and in such a mood he was to make the acquaintance of Josephine – associate of Thérèse Cabarrus, good friend of Tallien and Barras, and, in this hectic autumn of 1795, shining ornament of Parisian society.

In turning to women considerably older than himself Bonaparte may well have been demonstrating the powerful subconscious influence exercised on him by his mother. All through his life he kept a deep affection for the handsome, dominating Letizia Ramolino, who had married at the age of fourteen and had borne Napoleon – her fourth child – when she was still only nineteen. 'She was a woman of great courage and great talent,' Napoleon told Dr O'Meara at St Helena, 'proud and high-minded.'[11] Was it this lurking image of his mother that aroused his uncertainties with respect to the youthful Désirée? When, soon after, he proposed to Madame Permon he sought the hand of someone who lacked only a few years being his mother's age. Josephine could make no such claim, to be sure, but she was cast in an entirely different mould than was Désirée. She was six years older than Bonaparte, she was a widow, she was the mother of two children, and life had brought her extraordinary trials.

The fateful meeting of Bonaparte and Josephine arose out

of political events in the capital. Appointed in August to the topographical bureau of the Committee of Public Safety, Bonaparte plunged with expert enthusiasm into plans for a French invasion of northern Italy. Quite unexpectedly he was projected to the very centre of the public stage. When, in October, the three years of rule by the Convention came to an end and the new Constitution of 1795 was to be submitted to popular ratification, resentment at some of its provisions led to mob demonstrations in the street and threats of an imminent attack on the government offices in the Tuileries. Barras, responsible for the defence of the capital, placed Bonaparte in charge of the artillery, and his cannonades from outside the Church of Saint-Roch on the rue Saint-Honoré – Carlyle's famous 'whiff of grapeshot' – helped to disperse at a cost of two or three hundred casualties the mobs threatening the Tuileries. This was the celebrated day of Vendémiaire (5 October) that saved the government and confirmed Bonaparte's reputation. 'We have disarmed the Sections,' Napoleon wrote to his brother, 'and all is quiet. As usual, I was unharmed.'[12] Removed some time before from the active list, he was now restored as general of division, second in command of the Army of the Interior.

The meeting with Josephine soon followed. If Bonaparte had earlier been briefly presented to Josephine in the salons of the Directory it could have been little more than a passing encounter. At St Helena Bonaparte admitted that as a young officer he had been awkward and extremely timid in the company of women. Chance now brought him into the presence of one who by nature and experience was well qualified to conjure away any such inadequacies.

The *Moniteur* for 14 October carried a notice stating that Barras had announced in the Convention a few days before that all unauthorized weapons in the sections *Lepelletier* and *Théâtre français* were to be surrendered to the authorities. When a commissioner visited the Beauharnais household to enforce the rule, the boy Eugène, not yet away at school, protested in truly Roman fashion at having to surrender the sword of his father – once a general in the armies of the Republic. He was told, not unkindly, to seek permission from

the commanding general in Paris. In this way General Bonaparte at his headquarters in the rue des Capucines received a
visit from a solemn, fourteen-year-old boy, asking as a matter
of honour to retain his father's sword. Moved by the request,
Bonaparte agreed. Soon after, an elegant lady called to thank
Bonaparte for his sympathy to her son and for his respect to
the memory of her husband. Struck by her charm, Bonaparte
requested and was granted permission to visit her in her apartment in the Chaussée d'Antin.

It is not hard to imagine this meeting between the revolutionary soldier and the former viscountess. Josephine, radiant
in her new social position, was mistress of the art of charm.
Bonaparte was pale, thin, awkward, careless of his appearance,
with lank hair reaching to his shoulders, wearing ill-fitting boots
and wretched clothes – presenting anything but the image of a
victorious general of the new Republic. His appearance, however, did not prevent him from being invited to call again. 'One
day,' he long afterwards recalled, 'when I was sitting next to
her at table, she began to pay me all manner of compliments on
my military qualities. Her praise intoxicated me. From that
moment I confined my conversation to her and never left her
side. I was passionately in love with her, and our friends were
aware of this long before I ever dared to say a word about it.'[13]

Napoleon much later told General Bertrand that he had been
led to believe by Josephine that she possessed a considerable
fortune. As an ambitious young man, he had naturally wished
to advance himself, and so he managed to rout out her banker,
Emmery, and make inquiries. He learned the Josephine's
fortune was not considerable at all. Her mother, so Emmery
said, had a plantation worth about fifty thousand francs a
year from which he was authorized to draw from twenty to
twenty-five thousand francs yearly at Josephine's request.
Only ten days before this conversation Josephine had cashed
a bill of exchange for ten thousand francs. She had money,
then, but hardly a large fortune, especially in view of the
current inflation of prices. Yet there were reasons for this
marriage which the older man, looking backward, would be
more likely than his younger self to set high in importance. 'On

the whole,' Napoleon observed philosophically to Bertrand, 'the marriage was an excellent thing for me. A good French family suited me very well, as I was a Corsican by birth.'[14]

Within two weeks of their first meeting Bonaparte was made commander-in-chief of the Army of the Interior, assuming new burdens of work and responsibility. 'My health is good,' he informed his brother, 'but I lead a terribly busy life.'[15] Social visits were not easily managed, and his connexion with the widow Beauharnais was almost in danger of lapsing. It was Josephine who saved the day. On 28 October she wrote him her first letter:

Josephine's first note to Bonaparte

You no longer come to see a friend who is fond of you. You have completely deserted her. You are wrong, for she is affectionately attached to you. Come tomorrow to lunch with me. I need to see you, and to talk with you about your affairs. Good night, my friend. *Je vous embrasse.*[16]

Probably on the same day Bonaparte wrote her a note:

I cannot imagine what has been the cause of your letter. I beg you to allow me the pleasure of believing that no one desires your friendship as much as I do, or is as ready as I am to give proof. If my affairs had permitted I would myself have been the bearer of this letter.[17]

This was the simple beginning to what, soon enough, exploded into an ardent affair. An undated letter, usually listed first in the collection of letters from Bonaparte to Josephine, and probably of December, tells the story:

The first love letter from Bonaparte

At seven in the morning
I awake, full of you. Your portrait, and the memory of the
intoxicating evening of yesterday leave my senses no rest. Sweet
and incomparable Josephine, what strange power do you have
over my heart? Are you angry? Do I behold you sad? Are you ill
at ease? My heart is broken with grief and my love permits me no
rest . . . But how can I rest any more when, yielding to the feeling
that masters my innermost self, I drink from your lips and from
your heart a flame which burns me. Ah, this night has shown me
how far your portrait falls short of your true self! You leave at
noon: in three hours I shall see you again. Till then, *mio dolce amor*,
a thousand kisses; but give me none, for they set my heart on fire![18]

The frustrations, the pent-up emotions, and the ardours of
the young Corsican pour forth in this and subsequent letters –
historic documents in the language of passion. We do not need
letters from Josephine to realize how entirely she was able to
captivate this officer who now moved awkwardly into a world
of which she seemed to be so completely the bewitching genius.
Did she love him? In 1804 she told Count Ségur that she had
'inner struggles and long reluctance' before she could agree
to marry Napoleon.[19] We cannot read her heart. It is evident
that she gave herself to him as she had to others before him.
Yet, if we are disposed to think that little but the calculation
of material advantage entered into Josephine's surrender to
Bonaparte's ardent courtship, we must remind ourselves how
strangely this dark, unfathomable soldier differed from the
Talliens, the Barras, and the Ouvrards whom she had come to
know.

The young general was daily growing in authority. One of
his aides, Marmont, later to become a marshal of France,
described him as having at this time an extraordinary self-
possession, an air of grandeur that was quite new, and an ever-
increasing sense of his own importance:

Bonaparte was in love in the full sense of the phrase, in all its
force and in its widest meaning. It was, by every appearance, his
first passion, and he experienced it with the full energy of his nature.
. . . Although she no longer had the freshness of youth she knew
how to please him, and we know that to lovers the question, 'why',

is superfluous. One loves because one loves, and nothing is less susceptible to explanation and analysis than this emotion.[20]

In January 1796 Hortense Beauharnais, though only thirteen, was invited by Barras to come with her mother to dinner at the Luxembourg Palace. She was seated between Bonaparte and her mother. 'In order to speak to Josephine,' she recalled, 'he constantly thrust himself forward with such vigour that he tired me out and forced me to draw back. He spoke with fire in his voice and was solely preoccupied with my mother.'[21] It was long, indeed, before either Hortense or her brother Eugène could come truly to like Bonaparte and approve of his suit. Nor could they be at first sure of the new state of affairs. There was the inevitable lovers' quarrel, with its 'dreadful scene', as Bonaparte later recalled it in a letter to Josephine. Moreover, in January and February Josephine still invited other friends – Barras among them – to dinner at the rue Chantereine. Phrases such as '*Je vous embrasse*' and '*Je vous aime tendrement*' are the common termination of her letters to Barras. These may well have been only rhetorical flourishes. As for Bonaparte, beyond any doubt he had succumbed utterly to Josephine's spell.

In February 1796 the banns for the wedding of Josephine and Bonaparte were issued. A marriage of the conventional type was not to be expected or even possible in revolutionary Paris. As early as September 1792 the legislature had entrusted the registration of marriages to the civil authorities, and in the following year, as the anti-religious tides rose, a decree of the Commune of Paris had closed all churches in the capital. Whatever the feelings of individuals – and there were many who now looked to a revival of Christianity – the new era following the downfall of the Jacobins had not as yet seen any restoration of religion to a position of importance. Given these circumstances, therefore, the wedding of Josephine and Bonaparte would inevitably be 'revolutionary' and 'republican'.

At this very time the career of the young general was about to attain new dimensions, giving him a leading role not merely on the French stage but also on that of Europe. Barras was later pleased to insist in his *Memoirs* that it was he who arranged that Josephine should leave the 'seraglio' at the Luxembourg for the arms of Bonaparte, and that it was he who likewise arranged for the command of the Army of Italy to accompany this marriage as a kind of splendid wedding gift. Actually Bonaparte was so clearly in the ascendant in these months that Barras can have little claim to be the architect of his career. Moreover, within the board of the five directors the voice that spoke with principal authority on military matters was not the voice of Barras but that of the great republican general and 'Organizer of Victory', Lazare Carnot. Carnot had become aware of Bonaparte's brilliant work in the topographical bureau and had concerted with him the plans for the Italian campaign. When the decision about a commander had to be made, Carnot staked his reputation on giving Bonaparte the post. For those who wish to pinpoint such details the facts are that the wedding banns were published on 19 February; on 25 February the nomination for the command of the Army of Italy was decided upon; on 2 March the appointment was signed; on the same day Bonaparte asked the director of the *Dépôt de la Guerre* to provide him with all available books, atlases, and charts dealing with Italy; and on 7 March he received his official letter of service. Amid this military hurly-burly Josephine, as best she could, undertook the preparations for her second marriage.

A hastily composed contract of marriage was signed on the afternoon of 8 March in the office of the notary, Raguideau, in the rue Saint-Honoré. Strikingly different from the elaborate contract that had accompanied Josephine's wedding in 1779, it suggested a curious independence on the part of the two signatories. The first article now stipulated that there should be no community of goods of any kind and that neither would be responsible for the debts of the other. The ensuing articles provided that Josephine was to have control and custody of her two children, that each spouse would pay half the marriage costs, and that if the marriage should be dissolved Josephine, as well as her heirs, would be entitled to all clothes, silver, and jewels for her personal use, as well as all the furniture and other things that otherwise belonged to her. Bonaparte agreed to settle upon his wife the relatively modest annual sum of fifteen hundred francs, in metallic currency. It remains true, therefore, that the impoverished Bonaparte, without home or belongings, contributed little more to the marriage than the shabby uniforms he wore. This situation is reflected in the story about Josephine's adviser, Raguideau, 'one of the shortest men', says Bourrienne, 'I think I ever saw in my life'.[22] On looking over the contract, Raguideau urged her not to sign it, saying in effect, 'this man is bringing you nothing but his cloak and sword'. Bonaparte, according to the story, overheard him, but made no comment save to tell Josephine that Raguideau was a shrewd lawyer and that she should entrust her affairs to him. Eight years later, however, amid the jewels, silks, and splendours of the imperial coronation, the long-memoried Napoleon is reported to have turned to Raguideau, whom he had taken pains to invite, and to have said to him, 'Well, Raguideau, what do you think of my cloak and sword now?'[23] If the story is not true, it ought to be.

A curiously melodramatic quality characterizes this second marriage of Josephine. The incident – for it was hardly more – takes us to a once elegant but now dingy room, the mayor's office of the second *arrondissement* of Paris. If the visitor today wishes to find this spot he must walk away from the Opera, along the Avenue de l'Opéra, until he comes to the narrow rue d'Antin on his right. At No. 3, he will find what was once the *hôtel* Mondragon, a fine eighteenth-century residence that formerly was in the Mondragon family, which under the Revolution had become the property of the municipality. Here a second-storey room, still having the marble fireplace, the large gilt mirrors, and the delicate Louis XV panelling of its former owners, had been rudely furnished as headquarters of the *arrondissement*. And here, on the night of 9 March 1796 Josephine came with a little group of witnesses to be married. Paul Barras, one of the five directors, Jean Tallien, member of the legislature, and Jérôme Calmelet, friend and financial adviser to Josephine and once tutor to Hortense and Eugène, were her three companions. The room, as Josephine recalled years afterwards, was miserably lighted by a single candle, which no one thought to trim, flickering in a tin sconce. The mayor, tiring of the long wait, had finally departed, leaving all authority to one Antoine Lecombe, a minor official hobbling about on a wooden leg. In these utterly drab surroundings the little wedding party waited restlessly for over two hours until at long last the clatter of footsteps was heard on the stairs and the newly appointed commander of the Army of Italy, accompanied by his aide, rushed in, having abandoned for the moment his books, his maps, and his statistical tables.

The ensuing civil ceremony by which Josephine became Bonaparte's bride was over in a few minutes. It has been pointed out that the proceedings were strewn with legal uncertainties. Such a ceremony was not recognized by the Church; it was performed by a subordinate lacking the proper legal authority; and it involved one witness – Bonaparte's aide – who had not reached the required legal age. Owing to the difficulty of obtaining the necessary documents from overseas, the officials had accepted sworn statements in lieu of the conventional baptismal certificates. Consequently the bridegroom was able gallantly to overstate his years by two and the bride coyly to understate hers by four, thus reaching a common ground of inaccuracy and historical confusion with the age of twenty-eight. The ages to which they swore would have made Josephine twelve at the time of her first marriage and Napoleon one month younger than his brother Joseph. Despite this catalogue of errors, to say nothing of deceptions, legal authorities have held that the marriage, given the conditions of the time and the intentions of the participants, must be accepted as valid.

No members of either family were present. None, apparently, had been invited. None, indeed, seem even to have known in advance of the marriage. Madame Renaudin and the former Marquis de Beauharnais quickly gave their approval. They might well do so, for they, too, were contemplating matrimony. The remarkably durable Monsieur Renaudin, for over thirty-four years an insuperable obstacle to their hopes, died in December 1795. After all these years of 'acquaintance' the elderly couple could be, and indeed soon were, wed.

Napoleon saw fit to inform only the Executive Directory of his wedding. On 11 March, the busy day of his departure for Italy, he wrote briefly to Letourneur, president of the Directory, as follows:

I have asked Citizen Barras to inform the Executive Directory of my marriage to Citizeness Tascher Beauharnais. The confidence which the Directory has on all occasions shown me makes it my duty to keep it informed of all my actions. This is a new tie binding me to my country; it is a token of my firm resolution to entrust all my fortunes to the Republic.

The General in Chief of the Army of Italy,
Buonaparte[24]

At this time, too, Napoleon seems to have established the use of the name 'Josephine' for his bride, a name that became official only with the proclamation of the Empire in 1804.

One letter soon reached Bonaparte from Marseilles. On hearing at last of the marriage, the young Désirée Clary wrote her farewell:

My life is a dreadful torment for me since I can no longer devote it to you . . . So you are married! I shall never accustom myself to this thought. It is destroying me, and I cannot survive. I will let you see that I am more faithful than you to our pledges, and even though you have broken the ties that once bound us I shall never become engaged – I shall never marry another . . . I wish you every kind of happiness and prosperity in your marriage; I wish that the wife you have chosen will make you as happy as I had intended to do, and as you deserve. But, in the midst of your happiness, do not forget Désirée; sympathize with her lot.[25]

Two years later Désirée married Bernadotte, one of Bonaparte's most distinguished generals, soon to become marshal of France, and ultimately crown prince and then king of Sweden. When in due course a son was born to Désirée, she asked Bonaparte to serve as godfather. He did so, naming the child Oscar in tribute, we are told, to the poet Ossian. This Oscar married another Josephine, the daughter of Eugène de Beauharnais, and in time the pair reigned, too, on the Swedish throne.

At the end of the brief wedding ceremony the house on the rue Chantereine awaited Josephine and Napoleon. So likewise did the dog, Fortuné. 'See this fellow,' Bonaparte said later to some of his visitors, referring to the mongrel, 'he took possession of Madame's bed on the night I married her. I was told frankly that I must either sleep elsewhere or share the bed with him. Not a very pleasing alternative! Take it or leave it, I was told. The darling creature was less accommodating than I was.'[16] Thereupon Bonaparte displayed to his listeners the scars that Fortuné's teeth had left that night on his leg. This was the Bonaparte who had boasted of coming through the revolutionary day of Vendémiaire unscathed.

On the next day, 10 March, Napoleon and Josephine paid a surprise visit to Hortense de Beauharnais at Madame Campan's school in the pleasantly rural surroundings of Saint Germain-en-Laye. Bonaparte, in a genial mood, announced his intention of placing his sister Caroline, now fourteen years old, in this same establishment. Caroline, he cheerfully assured Madame Campan, knew absolutely nothing, and it does seem to be true that at this time she could neither read nor write.

Eleven March was the day of preparation for the soldier's departure. In the evening a carriage drew up at the *porte cochère* on the rue Chantereine. Bonaparte, accompanied by General Junot, climbed in, leaving his bride of two days in order to take command of the Army of Italy. The Directory in its wisdom had withheld a passport from Josephine, feeling that her husband should devote himself without distraction to his command. He was about to launch a campaign so spectacular in its successes that almost overnight the names of obscure Italian villages – Arcola, Rivoli, Castiglione – would become an imperishable part of the history of France. The honeymoon had been all too short, but indubitably, there had been advance credits.

❖ 10 ❖

'Parting is such Sweet Sorrow'

WHATEVER that strange marriage in the mayor's office of
the rue d'Antin may have meant to Bonaparte, to Josephine it
could well have seemed little more than an anchor to windward
in time of storm, an arrangement of convenience and respectability into which she had been swept by the ardours of the
young revolutionary general. The sequel could hardly have
been unexpected. Throughout the first twelve months of their
wedded life Mars, not Venus, prevailed, so that Josephine and
Napoleon spent little more than two months together, usually
just a few days at a time, and always in the dazzling glare of
public responsibilities.

Separation brought profound unhappiness to Bonaparte.
While conducting the great Italian campaign that pressed so
hard on the heels of his marriage, he sent to his wife in Paris a
series of letters that tell the story of a passionate attachment
flaming amid momentous events. Josephine was soon to
realize that in marrying the young general who had fallen so
ardently in love with her she had also attached herself to a
segment of history. The letters she wrote to her husband – and
it is clear that there were more than a few – have not survived.
Those of Bonaparte, thanks to chance, we can still read. Josephine kept them with her, we now know, all her life, and soon
after her death a valet found some of them in the dust of a
closet at Malmaison. He sold them, and after curious adventures they, along with others, were published.

The letters began almost with Bonaparte's departure:

Every moment takes me farther from you [he wrote], and at every
moment I find it harder to bear the separation. You are the ceaseless
object of my thoughts – my imagination exhausts itself in won-
dering what you are doing. If I think of you as sad, my heart is

torn and my misery increases. If you seem gay and frolicsome with your friends, then I reproach you for having forgotten so soon our unhappy separation of three days. You would seem to be inconsiderate and therefore not to be stirred by deep emotions . . . Write to me, gentle friend, and write at length! Accept a thousand kisses of love – as tender as they are true.[1]

The journey to the Italian border brought Napoleon to his mother and sisters, now living near Marseilles in a condition not far from penury. Here he could break the news of his marriage. Bonaparte had doubtless anticipated what the shrewd Letizia Bonaparte would think of this marriage of her son to a widow with two children. He had tried to prepare the way by having Josephine compose a dutiful letter to her mother-in-law, and when this plan failed he had no alternative but to draft a letter himself for Josephine to copy. This he now brought with him. The scheme was hardly effective, for Letizia, full of misgivings, expostulated with her son. Yet the deed was done. Since she was clearly unwilling, and doubtless unable, to compose the necessary maternal acknowledgement of the letter that Napoleon had brought, he was now under the odd necessity of dictating a second letter – this to serve as Letizia's answer to the one he had earlier composed for Josephine!

I have received your letter, Madame, and it has enabled me to enlarge the picture I already had formed of you. My son has told me of his happy marriage, and henceforth you have my esteem and my approval. All that is now lacking is for me to see you. Be assured that I have all the tenderness of a mother for you, and that I cherish you as I do my own children.[2]

One or two letters to Barras, written during the journey, give evidence of Napoleon's amicable relations with the most prominent figure in the Directory, and even more of his almost pathetic eagerness to have news of Paris. Josephine dominated his thoughts. Arriving at army headquarters in Nice, Bonaparte wrote thus to his wife:

I cannot pass a day without loving you. I cannot even drink a cup of tea without cursing the glory and the ambition which keep me apart from the soul of my existence . . . If I leave you with the speed of the torrential waters of the Rhône, it is only that I may return to you the sooner. If, in the midst of the night, I arise in order to work, it is only to speed the days before the arrival of my beloved. Josephine! Josephine! Do you remember? . . .[3]

It is easy and tempting to make the assumption that Josephine, so lamentable a correspondent in the eyes of her first husband, was no less so to her second. This seems hardly the case – at least, not yet. 'I have received *all your letters*,' Bonaparte writes on 3 April, 'but none has made such an impression on me as your last.' He then goes on to express concern at the tone of this letter, saying that it has gravely disturbed him, implying that either she may be ill or that she may be developing a dissatisfaction that is causing her to love him the less:

There was a time when I took pride in my courage. Then, in fixing my gaze on the harm which men could do me, or in the fate which destiny reserved for me, I could face the most extraordinary misfortunes without even wrinkling my brows, without even being surprised. But now, the idea that my Josephine could be unhappy, or could be ill, and above all the cruel, distressing thought that she could love me less, withers my soul, chokes my blood, renders me sad and downcast, and does not even give me the courage of fury and despair. . . . Sweet one, forgive me, for I am raving! Nature loses control over the one who feels so keenly, over the one who loves you so.[4]

Strange, reminiscent overtones arise from this letter. Is it actually written by the commanding general of the Army of Italy to his bride? Or are we tempted to believe that in some mysterious way we have gone back fourteen years, and that this is a letter to Josephine from a young captain in the Sarre infantry regiment, miserable at the lack of news from his wife – a letter penned by him as he waits at Brest in December 1782 for the ship that is to take him to America?

Arriving at Nice, Bonaparte at once plunged into the business of war, reviewing his troops, drafting order after order, and making all preparations for the imminent moves against the Piedmontese and Austrian armies. He was quickly finding himself. General Marmont observed that although at this time Bonaparte was awkward in gestures and lacking in natural dignity, he was soon able by his manner of speech and by vigorous professional attention to every detail of his task to impose his will upon the Army of Italy. Masséna said that when Bonaparte put on his general's hat he seemed two feet taller. Striking first at the Piedmontese forces and dividing them from their Austrian ally, he quickly won victories that by 28 April resulted in the Armistice of Cherasco. In two weeks he had obtained control of the Piedmontese fortresses and thus could send the following curt, triumphant report to the Directory at Paris:

Concerning the conditions of peace with Sardinia, you may dictate what you please: all the fortresses are in my hands. . . . If you continue to give me your confidence and approve my plans, I am sure of success. Italy is yours.[5]

Despite the intoxication of his first victory, Bonaparte's domestic anxieties gnawed at him. He spoke often of his wife to Marmont. 'He referred to his love,' so the latter recalled, 'with the open-heartedness, the impetuosity, and the delusions of a very young man. The continued delays she put in the way of her departure tormented him painfully, so that he gave himself up to the pangs of jealousy and to a kind of superstition which seemed inherent in his nature.'[6] In a private letter to Barras, Bonaparte disguised his emotions in a very simple statement: 'I wish very much for my wife to join me.'[7] He wished in vain, for the soldierly Carnot, powerful voice in the Directory, still thought it best for his most promising general to fight without domestic entanglements.

Bonaparte tried desperately to maintain his ties with Josephine. On 24 April he sent her a letter by his brother Joseph, warmly acknowledging two letters received from her. Five days later he sent still another letter, this time by means of Murat, urging her to accompany Murat when he returned to Italy. Still Josephine did not act. In May the correspondence was briefly interrupted by the second phase of his campaign, for with Piedmont out of the way the major problem now was to tackle Austria. Moving fast, Bonaparte crossed the River Po at Piacenza; on the tenth came the dramatic crossing of the Adda by the bridge of Lodi; on 15 May Bonaparte received a hero's welcome as he entered Milan. From here the victorious young general wrote to the Directory a triumphal announcement of a sort that would often be heard in the future:

> Tomorrow there will go to Paris, Citizen Directors, twenty superb paintings, chief among them the celebrated *Saint Jérôme* of Correggio which had been sold, I am assured, for 200,000 livres. I shall have others sent soon from Milan, among them paintings by Michelangelo.[8]

An attached paper listed works by Leonardo, Titian, Raphael, and Veronese, as well as scores of other treasures.

Amidst these triumphs the spell of Josephine continued to exercise its power. In answer to a letter from Murat, passing on what, if true, would have been exciting domestic news, Napoleon wrote to Josephine from his headquarters at Lodi on 13 May as follows:

> So it is true that you are pregnant! Murat has written to me; but he says that you are ill and that he does not think it wise for you to undertake so long a voyage. . . . You write that you have changed much. Your letter is short, sad, and in a trembling hand. What is it, my adorable one? Oh, do not dwell in the country; remain in the city; try to amuse yourself, and realize that there is no torment more real for my soul than to think that you are suffering and unhappy. I would have thought I would be jealous, but I swear to you that I am not. Rather than know you to be melancholy I almost think that I would myself find a lover for you. Be gay and happy, then, and know that my happiness is linked with yours![9]

On the following day he wrote to his good friend Barras: 'Murat tells me that my wife is ill; this causes me a sorrow of which you can have no idea.'[10]

What, meanwhile, was Josephine doing in Paris? Murat was a better soldier than diagnostician, for Josephine was not pregnant, nor, in spite of some minor indispositions, was she in any serious sense ill. She was engaged in the busy round – appearing in the salons, receiving and writing letters, seeing her friends, keeping in touch with her children, and planning the redecoration of her home. Through the hostile pen of the lady who was later to be the Duchess d'Abrantès we have as

sly a thumbnail sketch of Josephine as perhaps any woman
has ever written of another: 'She was still charming at this
period . . . Her teeth were frightfully bad, but when her mouth
was shut she had the appearance, especially at a few paces
distant, of a young and pretty woman.'[11] We catch another
glimpse of Josephine in an item of gossip in one of the Paris
newspapers, the *Ami des Lois*:

> The story is being told in the Paris salons, as if it were a re-
> markable event, of the change in coiffure of mesdames Tallien
> and Buonaparte. Both had long been distinguished for their
> superb black tresses; but at last they have been compelled to yield
> to the craze for blond wigs. A woman with black hair would be
> painfully conspicuous in good society, though men with dark hair
> are still à la mode.[12]

Murat had arrived early in May with Bonaparte's letter
telling of the armistice with the King of Sardinia and begging
Josephine to return with Murat via the short route through
Turin.

> It is possible [wrote Bonaparte] that I may see you in two weeks.
> My happiness is that you should be happy; my joy that you should
> be gay; my pleasure is that you should have pleasure too. Never
> has a woman been loved with more devotion, more warmth, and
> more tenderness. . . . If I were to lose your love, your heart, your
> adorable self, I would have lost all that makes life happy and dear
> to me.[13]

Bonaparte's scolding words that followed this tender passage
were playful, reproachful, and, to some degree, barbed:

> Why do you expect me not to be sad? No letters from you! I
> receive one only every four days, whereas, if you loved me, you
> would write to me twice a day. But you must chatter every morning
> with these young sprigs of visitors, and then you must listen to the
> nonsense and the follies of a hundred coxcombs until the small
> hours. In well mannered countries everyone is at home by ten,
> and a wife writes to her husband, she thinks of him, she lives for
> him.
>
> Farewell, Josephine! You are a monster whom I cannot explain.
> I love you more every day. Absence heals small passions, but those
> which are great it only increases. . . .

It will be a happy day when you cross the Alps. This will be the finest reward for my efforts and for the victories I have won.[14]

The poet Arnault was with Josephine on one occasion when she read him passages such as these from Bonaparte's letters. She seemed amused at her husband's ardour, the poet thought, and was likewise puzzled by his signs of jealousy. 'I can still hear her,' commented Arnault, 'saying in her creole accent "What an odd fellow, this Bonaparte! [Il est *drolle*, Bonaparte!]"'[15]

Josephine busied herself, too, with an activity that was deeply rooted in her warm, creole nature and was to grow with the years – the tireless use of her position to do favours for her friends, and even for her casual acquaintances. At this time there appeared a Belgian nobleman, Count Mérode, who had fled to Prussia during the Terror and now, seeking to regain his property, wished to have his name stricken from the list of *émigrés*. His agents in Paris approached both Josephine and one of her new companions, the somewhat disreputable Madame Campi. This wife of an Italian banker now lived with a Belgian count who occupied himself profitably by speculating in military supplies. Josephine obligingly helped Mérode's cause by taking some of the necessary documents to her important friends at the Luxembourg Palace, with the result that the count's name was quickly stricken from the *émigré* list. Madame Campi asked for, and received, cash outright for her share in the questionable transaction. Josephine's reward we can only conjecture. She had been 'helpful' to Count Mérode as she likewise was to others. She encouraged her friend Antoine Hamelin, for example, to go to Italy, saying that she was sure that she could persuade her husband to do something for him. She had definite reason to say this, for Bonaparte, pathetically eager to please, had recently written to her with what he surely must soon have realized to be dangerous generosity saying, 'If you want a place for anybody, you can send him. I will give him one.'[16]

At this point an odd figure enters the life of Josephine – a figure who in contrast to the heroic proportions of Bonaparte emerges as a sheer embodiment of the spirit of comedy – or, better still, of farce. Between General Napoleon Bonaparte and Captain Hippolyte Charles, officer of hussars, one can find little in common save that both wore uniforms (one can hardly call Charles a soldier) and that both were under the average in height.*

Hippolyte Charles was nine years younger than Josephine. During the early years of the Revolution he had volunteered in the national guard and, after some harmless, nondescript duty, had found a comfortable berth as adjutant to General Leclerc in Marseilles. Accompanying Leclerc to Paris in the spring of 1796, he there met Josephine. Captain Charles occupies his minuscule niche in history as a perfect embodiment of an ageless type – the society wit, the drawing-room comic, the buffoon, the 'character', the 'card'. He emerges as the utterly consistent, the invariably dependable, funny man. He was capable of the type of humour that led him to glue General Junot's sabre, with what consequences one hesitates to imagine, in its scabbard, or to turn up at Josephine's salon dressed as a creole. Again and again he would put the room in a roar with his sallies, and would so convulse Josephine, we are told by one of her friends, that on these occasions she would be compelled to hide her teeth (*'qui étaient affreuses'*) behind her handkerchief.

Captain Charles was, to be sure, more than a drawing-room comedian. He was young, dapper, with olive skin, jet-black hair, blue eyes, chiselled features, and tiny hands and feet. He presented an altogether dashing figure in his fine hussar's uniform of sky-blue, his red morocco boots, his tight Hungarian breeches, his heavily braided dolman, or jacket, worn as a cape, his scarlet sash, his clanking sabre in a sheath of silver and copper, and his black shako ornamented with a scarlet band, silver braid, and red-white-and-blue cockade. If not the lion, he might well be called the lap dog of Directory

---

*The measurement of five feet two inches, often given for Napoleon, is in reality based on the French inch, or *pouce*, which, when converted by applying the proportion of fifteen to sixteen, comes out at the English five feet six – a dimension confirmed by the autopsy at St Helena. Captain Charles, without benefit of autopsy, is credited with a similar height.

society. Josephine, delighting in his trivial gallantries, paid him an attention she did not bother to disguise.

In the light of the obviously warm friendship of the two, one is tempted to explain Josephine's delay in leaving Paris – and the consequent exasperation, not to say agony, of her husband – as caused by this fantastic little captain of hussars. Yet that clearly is not the whole story, and in justice to Josephine one must quote the letter that more than two months after Bonaparte's departure General Carnot, member of the Executive Directory, sent to him on 21 May. The phraseology deserves careful notice.

It is with great reluctance that we yield to the desire of Citizeness Bonaparte to join you. We were afraid that the attention you would give to her would turn you from the attention due to the glory and safety of your country. Hence we had long resisted her wishes, and we had agreed with her that she could set out only when Milan was yours. You are there, and we have no more objections to make. We hope [Carnot added neatly] that the myrtle with which she will crown you will not detract from the laurels with which you have already been crowned by victory.[17]

This letter goes far to explain and perhaps to justify Josephine's delays up to this point. It raises serious questions about her subsequent conduct, however, for more than a month was to elapse between the date when this news was issued and the date when Josephine actually left Paris for Milan. During these weeks Josephine's letters to her husband were brief to the point of being meaningless. Even worse, she ceased to write. The effect upon Bonaparte was shattering.

Within ten days of his entry into Milan Bonaparte began the drive eastward against the Austrians. 'No letter since the 17th,' he wrote late in May to his wife:

No news of my *bonne amie*. Could she have forgotten me, or have forgotten that there is no greater torment than not to have a letter from *mio dolce amor*? They gave me a great fête here; five or six hundred elegant and beautiful figures sought to please me; none had that sweet and music-like countenance which I have engraved on my heart. I saw only you, I thought only of you! . . . And how goes your pregnancy? I imagine constantly that I see you, *avec ton petit ventre* – it must be charming![18]

In June his frenzy reached almost the point of incoherence:

Josephine! Where will this letter be delivered? If at Paris, my misfortune is sure; you no longer love me. I would have nothing to do but die. . . . Could it be possible! All the serpents of the Furies are in my breast, and I am already only half alive. . . . I detest Paris, women, and love. . . . My condition is terrible . . . and your conduct? . . . but must I accuse you? No. Your conduct is that of your destiny . . .[19]

Other letters, written while the campaign against Austria moved to a new climax, are similar. They were composed at a time when Genoa, Tuscany, Rome, and Naples were falling subject to the will of the French conqueror. While Bonaparte undertook the siege of Mantua, while he entered Modena and Bologna in triumph, and while he concluded the armistice of Foligno with the papacy (stipulating the usual haul of art treasures for France), letter after tormented letter went from him to Josephine.

Since the 6th [he wrote in June] I hoped and believed that you had arrived at Milan. Scarcely had I left the battle of Borghetto when I rushed here to seek you. You were not to be found! Some days later a courier told me that you had not left, and he brought me no letters from you. My heart was shattered with sorrow.[20]

He wrote austerely to Carnot, thanking him for his attentions to Josephine; but, now, knowing that Josephine could come if she would, he also wrote in deepest gloom to Barras: 'I am desperate. My wife does not come. Some lover keeps her in Paris. I curse all women, but I embrace heartily my good friends.'[21]

Whether because of lovers or friends, Josephine was clearly too preoccupied to write. Hence the refrain from Bonaparte continued. 'My life is a perpetual nightmare,' he began a letter of mid-June, 'I no longer live; I have lost more than life, more than happiness, more than repose.'[22] Towards the end of the month he wrote again to Josephine:

In a month I have received from *ma bonne amie* only two letters of three lines each. Is she having affairs? Does she feel no need to write to her good friend?... A day will no doubt come when I shall see you, for I cannot believe that you are still in Paris. Then I shall show you pockets full of letters which I have not sent to you because they were too foolish![23]

Torturing memories of the gay life that Bonaparte had seen Josephine share with the leaders of the Directory haunted his memory:

You should have started on 24 May; stupid that I was, I expected you by June. As if a pretty woman could abandon her habits, her friends, her Madame Tallien, a dinner with Barras, a performance of a new play, the dog Fortuné – yes, Fortuné! You love everything more than you do your husband; for him you have only a little respect – merely a part of the general kindliness in which your heart abounds![24]

Napoleon's closest friend and confidant had long been his brother Joseph. Made miserable by the conflicting reports that Josephine was ill, and that she was enjoying herself all too well, the unhappy husband wrote thus to his brother:

Mon ami, I am in despair. My wife, all that I love in this world, is ill . . . I beseech you to tell me what ails her and how she is doing. . . . You are the only man on earth for whom I have a true and constant affection. After her, after my Josephine, you are the only one who arouses in me a feeling of concern. Reassure me! Tell me the truth! You know I have never been a lover, that Josephine is the first woman I have adored. Her illness causes me to despair.

Everyone abandons me. I am alone, a prey to my fears and to my misfortune. You, likewise, do not write.

If she is well, let her make the trip; I ardently desire her to come. I need to see her, to press her to my heart. I love her madly, and I cannot continue, far from her. If she no longer loved me, I would have nothing left to do on earth.[25]

Against these genuine emotions – the feelings of a man deeply unhappy – must be set the actions of Josephine and her acquaintances in these last weeks at Paris. For over two months she had been denied permission to leave the capital, and she had made some play of her slight indispositions. By 21 May Carnot had told Bonaparte that the obstacles to her departure no longer existed. Nevertheless, a full month elapsed before

Carnot wrote on 22 June as follows: 'Your dear wife is at last to rejoin you, though still not fully recovered [*encore assez mal rétablie*]; she takes with her the particular regrets of my entire family.'[26] Ill health may have contributed to the delay, yet a more obvious contribution, surely, came from the gay circle of which Hippolyte Charles was the presiding genius. Seeing, however, that General Junot was also being summoned to Italy, and that Captain Charles would go along as his adjutant, the prospective journey now took on a piquancy it formerly had lacked.

Passports were issued on 24 June for Josephine, Joseph Bonaparte, Nicholas Clary (Joseph's brother-in-law), General Junot, Captain Charles, Louise Compoint (Josephine's maid-companion), and four servants. The Duke of Serbelloni, who had brought letters from Italy for Josephine and in whose palace at Milan Bonaparte made his headquarters, was also of the company, as was Antoine Hamelin, the Paris acquaintance whom Josephine had enthusiastically promised to introduce to Bonaparte in the expectation of her husband finding him a job. The dog Fortuné also went along, at what peril to the rest of the group we do not know. The several carriages needed for the party were provided with a cavalry escort, so that now for the first time Josephine had a taste of the military honours that in a few years would be customary.

It is altogether characteristic that Josephine found herself at the last minute short of money, explaining as best she could that the sums promised by her husband had not arrived. Poor Antoine Hamelin lent her four thousand francs (nearly all he had); and when further he was obliging enough to offer to call for a veil that Josephine had ordered from the *modiste*, he discovered that he must provide the six hundred francs to pay for that also. In one way or another the preparations for departure were completed. Paris still had its charms, so potent that when on 26 June Josephine made her farewells and set off from the Luxembourg Palace, she burst into tears. She might well do so, for she would never again see the city as it had been during the two heedless, hectic years she had experienced following her liberation from the prison of the Carmelites.

❦ II ❦

Wife of a Hero

JOSEPHINE now began to move against a background of heroic proportions. Bonaparte found it easier to consolidate the conquest of Italy than to consolidate the conquest of his wife. The events of this momentous year of 1796 were drawing her into an extraordinary position of public prominence for which nothing in her marriage to Alexander de Beauharnais and nothing, surely, in the dissolute circles of the Directory had prepared her. She left Paris not simply for a rendezvous with her husband, but for a rendezvous with destiny.

Wars and the threat of wars had coloured every stage of her existence. She had been born on Martinique at a time when it had just resumed its French status after British conquest during the Seven Years' War. She had reached the crisis of separation from her first husband on the occasion when he left her to serve in Martinique with the French forces fighting in support of the American colonies. She and this first husband had shared imprisonment during the French Revolution, and he had met death, in part at least because of his failures as a general during the revolutionary wars.

Now she was married again, and to a man whose only training had been for battle and whose career was soon to place him on that lofty pinnacle shared only by the world's greatest soldiers. When Josephine left for Italy she undertook a life that, month after month and year after year, would be overshadowed by war's alarms. The sounds of cannon and of marching men, now echoing through Italy, would, during nearly two decades, resound in Egypt and Syria, then again in Italy, in Switzerland, in Holland, and in Germany, then in Spain, Portugal, and in far distant Russia. They would be heard in the great German

War of Liberation and in the desperate, brilliant, unavailing battles of 1814, fought by Napoleon as he retreated towards Paris across the rolling plains of Champagne.

Josephine was launched upon her career as wife of a hero. Late in June the carriages with their cavalry escort left the narrow streets of Paris and made their way along the fine French highways to Lyons. From there, in the pleasant weather of early summer, they climbed the Mont Cenis Pass and then descended into the history-strewn plain of Lombardy. General Junot, always the dashing soldier, found it agreeable to share his carriage with Josephine's maid-companion, Louise Compoint. In the course of the journey they evidently shared more than the carriage, for at the end of the trip Josephine, assuming a virtue which to some might have seemed excessive, insisted that Bonaparte dismiss poor Louise for unseemly behaviour. The truth may be, as the Duchess d'Abrantès thought, that Josephine was more angry with Junot for taking liberties with her *demoiselle de compagnie* than she was with Louise for granting them. Whatever the explanation, it was the woman who paid. Junot may have nursed a grudge against Josephine for this outcome; while this is only a conjecture, it is a matter of record that hardly more than two years later he was the one who during the Egyptian campaign was bold enough to convey to an outraged Bonaparte the rumours of Josephine's scandalous goings-on in Paris. During these pleasant days of 1796 so painful a future could not be foreseen. Hippolyte Charles, as we may guess, proved an entertaining carriage-companion for Josephine. Entertainment of another sort greeted her at Turin, for here the ruling family, conscious of Josephine's important new status, received her with Junot and Joseph, offering them a state dinner.

After a journey lasting two weeks the weary cortège clattered into Milan on the evening of 10 July. As the foam-flecked horses drew up before the monumental granite façade of the Serbelloni Palace with its Ionic columns and great triangular pediment, Josephine learned amid the bustle of lackeys and torch-boys that General Bonaparte, who had so ardently desired her presence, was away from his headquarters. Deeply involved in the military campaign and the civil affairs of Italy, he had left urgent instructions with the commanding officer at Milan that a courier was to be sent at once, bringing him the news of his wife's arrival. Within three days Napoleon was back at Milan.

The many delays and the long journey at last ended in a lovers' meeting. Amid the grandeurs of the Serbelloni Palace, where Bonaparte had filled the marble halls with Italian works of art and French furniture, Josephine rediscovered the ardours of her husband. One of the companions of the trip was struck by Bonaparte's constant attentions to his wife. 'He loved his wife passionately,' Antoine Hamelin wrote. 'From time to time he would leave his study in order to play with her as if she were a child. He would tease her, cause her to cry out, and overwhelm her with such rough caresses that I would be obliged to go to the window and observe the weather outside.'[1] Unhappily, the reunion, like the two-day honeymoon of March, was cruelly short.

Bonaparte was now entering the climactic stage of the campaign with Austria for the control of the entire peninsula. Arriving in Milan on 13 July, he was away again by the 15th. He had already besieged the powerful fortress of Mantua without which his other north Italian victories would become meaningless. Three successive efforts by the Austrian commanders to break this siege in the latter half of 1796 were to absorb all Bonaparte's military efforts and were to result in some of his greatest victories. In the end, the French tricolor flew over Mantua and then Bonaparte could proceed with the complex problem of reorganizing all northern Italy. Simultaneously he drove the Austrian armies across the Venetian territories, up through the Carnic Alps and actually on to Austrian soil, so that by March of 1797 this incredible young general was within a hundred miles of Vienna. An armistice was followed by summer negotiations in which the directors at Paris took only the slightest part and that in October resulted in the Treaty of Campo Formio with Austria. This treaty, one of the most spectacular in her history, gave France Belgium, the Rhineland, the effective control of a reorganized northern

Italy, and in the Mediterranean the strategically invaluable base of the Ionian Islands.

Josephine's interests were neither political nor military, nor were they ever significantly to become so. Six letters from Bonaparte written during the first six days of his departure from Milan attest the warmth of the hero's devotion to Josephine. He was happy, too, to have letters from her. Yet within a week the harsh note of suspicion and anger flashes out in a letter written to Josephine at eight o'clock in the morning from his headquarters at Castiglione. Clearly, Napoleon had not been oblivious to the presence at Milan of Hippolyte Charles, whom he remembered well enough to describe years later as having 'the face of a womanizer'. The conventional and kindly remarks with which his letter to Josephine had begun suddenly changed to a savage outburst and a cry of anguish, all in a strange jumble of bad spelling and bad grammar that defies accurate translation:

By this time you must know Milan well. Perhaps you have found this lover you came here to seek. Only, you will have found him without my offering him to you. That's the idea, isn't it? Surely, no! Let us have a better idea of our merits. In this connexion, I am told that you have known for a long time and know *well* [heavily underlined] this gentleman whom you recommend to me for a business contract. If this were true you would be a monster! What are you doing at this hour! Are you asleep? And I am not there to feel your breath, to contemplate your grace, and to overwhelm you with my caresses! Far from you the nights are long, stale, and melancholy. With you, one regrets that it is not always night!

Adieu, my fair beloved, my incomparable, my divine one! *Mille baisers amoureux, partout! partout!*[2]

Bonaparte had written such letters before and he would write them again. Tormented with jealousy, he would cry out his complaints, and yet in the end he would assure his wife of his love and his ardent longing to see her again. Within a few days, having heard from Josephine that her indispositions were over and that her health was good, he wrote requesting her to come to his new headquarters at Brescia. And come she did.

Josephine's only connexion with politics arose from the polite eagerness of local rulers to welcome and entertain the wife of the ever-victorious French commander. Travelling from Brescia to Verona she had the startling experience of being held up by the military moves of the enemy, seeing the misery of the wounded, and, near Mantua, coming under fire from the fortress. Unnerved and weeping she was comforted by her husband. 'Wurmser,' he told her, referring to the Austrian commander, 'will pay me dearly for these tears.'[3] Then Josephine left her husband in order to cross the Po and move southward into safer territory. She visited Ferrara, Bologna, and Parma. At Lucca her party was received by a guard of honour and given a public reception. In Tuscany the government provided a cavalry escort, and the grand duke offered her a fête. After visiting Leghorn Josephine returned early in September to Milan.

About this time Josephine sent off a letter to her aunt at Paris, now the wife of the eighty-one-year-old former Marquis de Beauharnais. Josephine's letter, which conveys the spirit of these Italian months, was obligingly taken to Paris by the Duke of Serbelloni:

M. Serbelloni will inform you, my dear aunt, of the way I have been received in Italy – fêted wherever I have gone, given receptions by all the princes of Italy, even by the Grand Duke of Tuscany, brother of the Emperor. Ah, well, I would prefer to be an ordinary individual in France. I don't like the honours of this country, and I am often bored. It is true that the state of my health does much to render me sad, for I have much discomfort. If happiness could ensure health, then I should be doing well. I have the best husband in the world. I never lack anything, for he always anticipates my wishes. All day long he adores me, as if I were a goddess. He couldn't possibly be a better husband. M. Serbelloni will tell you how I am loved. He often writes to my children for he loves them very much. He is sending Hortense, by the kindness of M. Serbelloni, a fine enamelled repeating watch surrounded with fine pearls; to Eugène he sends a handsome gold watch.[4]

It was pleasant now to be able to do favours when so often before she had had to beg them. 'I shall try to have a little money sent to you,' she told her aunt, 'since you have requested it as soon as possible.' Generous-hearted Josephine! By the same messenger she wrote to her old friend Barras saying that the Duke of Serbolloni was bringing presents for all: a hat of Leghorn straw for Madame Tallien, sausages and cheese for her husband, a coral necklace for their little daughter, Thermidor, and a case of liqueurs for Barras.[5]

One episode of this Italian period makes an odd reversal in the relations of Bonaparte and Josephine. His letters again and again had demonstrated his misery at her absence and his gnawing suspicion of her fidelity. Now it became the turn of Josephine to worry and to doubt. She approached Berthier, a capable officer of the old régime who had risen to be general of division and chief of staff to Bonaparte, and she persuaded him to write to her regularly from headquarters reassuring her of her husband's devotion. Twelve of these curious reports, running from October 1796, when Bonaparte was engaged in the critical campaign around Mantua, to February 1797, when the city fell, must, surely, have given Josephine every possible assurance. The refrain from Berthier is constant: Bonaparte's health is good; Bonaparte loves you; have no doubts, he adores you; Bonaparte declares there is none equal to you in the world; he longs to be back in Milan. 'You possess his heart,' Berthier wrote: 'he loves you, he adores you; he is miserable over these fancies and delusions which lead you to believe that he is dead; Bonaparte loves you truly. Do not spurn his tender feelings.'[6]

Whatever reassurances Berthier was able to give to Josephine, he failed most obviously to reassure her husband. All Bonaparte's mingled emotions appear in a letter of November to Josephine:

I no longer love you, on the contrary I detest you! You are hateful, clumsy, stupid, mean! You never write to me! You no longer love your husband. Even though you know what pleasure your letters give him, you will not send him even six hasty lines.

What do you do all day, Madame? What important business is it that gives you no time to write to your beloved husband? What attachment has stifled and cast away the love – the tender and constant love – that you once vowed to me? Who can be this wonderful new lover who claims all your time, dominates your days, and hinders you from giving any attention to your husband? Beware, Josephine! Some fine night the door will be burst open and I shall stand before you!

Seriously, my dear one, I am disturbed at not hearing from you. Write to me soon – four pages of those loving words which will fill my heart with emotion and happiness.

In a few days I hope to clasp you in my arms and to cover you with a million kisses, as burning as the equator.[7]

By an unhappy turn of events, when the soldier did return from the wars to Milan late in November, Josephine was not there – she was on a flying visit to Genoa. According to Berthier, Napoleon was so upset at not finding Josephine that he fell ill with swellings of the head and signs of erysipelas. 'Come,' Berthier wrote anxiously to her, 'he is afflicted and gravely upset.'[8] Josephine came, and, as usual, reconciliation followed. Later in December she gave a great ball at the Serbelloni Palace, and in the brilliance of this occasion and amid the pressure of his work, Bonaparte drowned the memories of the unhappiness brought upon him by this baffling, elusive creature who had become his wife.

After the domestic troubles of the preceding months the triumphant conclusion of the Italian campaign brought about a new accommodation between Bonaparte and his wife. Josephine was swept along by the tide of vast events. In May 1797 her husband transferred his residence for the hot, summer months from the Serbelloni Palace in Milan to the Castle of Mombello, some ten miles away. Here, in pleasant rural surroundings, he now maintained a state that was almost regal. A visitor has given a striking picture of this new conqueror:

I was received by Bonaparte . . . in the midst of a brilliant court rather than the headquarters of an army. Strict etiquette already reigned around him; his aides-de-camp and his officers were no longer received at his table, and he had become fastidious in the choice of his guests whom he admitted to it. An invitation was an honour eagerly sought, and obtained with great difficulty. He dined, so to speak, in public; the inhabitants of the country were admitted to the room in which he was eating, and allowed to gaze at him with a keen curiosity . . . His reception-rooms and an immense tent pitched in front of the palace were constantly full of a crowd of generals, administrators and big contractors; besides members of the highest nobility, and the most distinguished men in Italy who came to solicit the favour of a momentary glance or the briefest interview.[9]

Josephine played the part of hostess – wearing a cameo necklace presented to her by the Pope – and by common report played it well. With the assistance of the Austrian envoy, the Marquis di Gallo, she was able to introduce an elegance of manners previously unknown among the rough warriors of the French Republic. Numbers of the Bonaparte family arrived: Madame Letizia; the three sisters Elisa, Pauline, and Caroline; two brothers, Joseph and Louis; and also the fifteen-year-old Eugène Beauharnais. Even Bonaparte's Uncle Fesch turned up from Corsica, having conveniently put aside his priestly vestments to pursue the more lucrative occupation of army contracting (from which he would return in time to become archbishop of Lyons and cardinal). The celebrated Grassini, *prima donna* of La Scala at Milan, was invited to attend. What with elegant soirées and musicales, dances, games of *vingt-et-un*, boar hunts, and excursions to Como and Maggiore, life was a constant round of excitement and pleasure.

The French diplomat, Miot de Melito, has left a pleasant record of life in the warm days of that Italian summer. On one occasion he and General Berthier accompanied Napoleon and Josephine on a trip to Lake Maggiore. His account gives a vivid picture of the carriage and its four occupants moving through the enchanting countryside that borders the lake; and one has the picture, too, of the diplomat and the soldier, seated side by side, officially correct yet frozen with embarrassment while, facing them, their commander takes what Miot de Melito describes as 'conjugal liberties' with his wife. A young French playwright and poet, Carrion de Nisas, also has recorded in his diary his impressions of Josephine during these days:

Madame Bonaparte is neither young nor pretty, but she is

extremely modest and engaging. She frequently caresses her husband who seems devoted to her. Often she weeps, several times daily, for very trivial reasons . . .[10]

One small tragedy marks this summer. The dog Fortuné, spoiled hero of so many adventures, accompanied his mistress to Mombello. Here Napoleon's cook also had a dog, large and fierce; and this animal, tiring at long last of being bitten every day by Fortuné, turned upon him and brought his mongrel, combative life to a close.

Another problem received attention, though with no such finality as had overtaken Fortuné. For a time, at least, Captain Hippolyte Charles no longer danced attendance on Josephine. He was first ordered to Rome on a minor assignment. Returning to Milan, he once again met the baleful eye of Napoleon, who in November instructed Berthier to order the young hussar back to Paris. Some stories would have it that only the friendship of Junot and Duroc kept him from being shot, for in addition to his boudoir activities Captain Charles had been speculating flagrantly and corruptly in army supplies. In point of fact he managed, somehow, to postpone his departure until December.

In September, meanwhile, as rumours began to develop that Bonaparte's plans for Italy necessitated the destruction of the ancient Venetian Republic, a new, so-called democratic régime (actually dominated by the French) overthrew the old oligarchy of the Adriatic city. A Tree of Liberty was planted in front of St Mark's. Bonaparte was invited to visit Venice, but for political reasons was reluctant to do so. Josephine went instead with a retinue that included General Marmont and stayed for four days. Politics apart, it must have been an enchanting visit. The Venetians did their best for the wife of the man who was now master of their fate: on the first day they provided a regatta and a parade of boats; on the second, water excursions and a picnic at the Lido; on the third, an illuminated procession with fireworks on the Grand Canal followed by a ball in the Doge's palace. '*Vénise élégante et voluptueuse*,' Marmont called it, though another French observer, Carrion de Nisas, was principally struck by the extravagance of it all and by what he called the wicked prodigality of Josephine, whose jewels and bracelets, he thought, would have paid the costs of two or three months of the military campaign.

A curious sequel resulted. Soon after Josephine returned to French headquarters at Passariano a Venetian delegation headed by the great patriot, Dandolo, arrived, hoping desperately to preserve the independence of the city. The delegation was well equipped with money, with which it was ready to bribe anyone on Bonaparte's staff who could help the cause of Venice. Dandolo ventured to offer Josephine a hundred thousand ducats for her assistance, the money to be paid when her husband had acted favourably. In response Josephine delighted Dandolo by speaking up warmly on behalf of Venice at a dinner. After the meal Josephine invited another of the Venetian delegation to walk in the garden with her, and as they strolled in the night she made no objection when he slipped on her finger a magnificent diamond ring. Since the fate of Venice was already settled, these romantic manoeuvres were unavailing: Josephine did not receive the promised ducats; Venetian independence was destroyed; but there is nothing to show that she ever returned the diamond ring.

With the official conclusion of the Treaty of Campo Formio with Austria in October, Bonaparte's great work in Italy was done. In November he left Milan for the Rhineland, to engage with Austrians in important conferences at Rastatt about the reorganizing of Germany. He therefore preceded Josephine from Milan, taking the shorter route through Switzerland. Before Josephine left Italy she was busy with various minor matters. She wrote to Barras asking him to do what he could for her cousin Françoise, daughter of the celebrated Aunt Fanny. Françoise had earlier married Alexander de Beauharnais' brother François, had divorced him when he emigrated, and, like Josephine, had spent some time in prison. Emerging, she had married Charles Castaing, a mulatto from Santo Domingo who had rented rooms in her house – all to the considerable embarrassment and concern of her relatives.

In this period, too, Josephine had decided that the house on the rue Chantereine was not elegant enough for the new conqueror of Italy. While still at Passariano she had written to an old friend, the architect Vautier, saying that there were funds in Paris under the control of her agent, Calmelet, adequate for the business of remodelling. He should, therefore, spare no expense in redecorating and refurnishing her house, which she desired to have done over, both upstairs and down, 'in the latest elegance'.[11] Whether Josephine sent more detailed instructions, or whether all was left to the taste and discretion of the architect and the Paris cabinet-makers is not clear. What is crystal clear is that Vautier did spare no expense; he got the artist, David, for example, to design the frieze for one of the salons, and he commissioned the celebrated *ébénistes*, the Jacob brothers, to make the furniture. The spectacular results were such that a shaken Bonaparte still remembered every costly detail when he talked about the matter to Las Cases at St Helena nearly twenty-five years later. On leaving Italy he had been told by Josephine that she had ordered the redecorating of their home. Returning to Paris before her he was stupefied at the transformation. The place itself, he told Las Cases, was not worth more than 40,000 francs; consequently he was astonished to receive bills from the decorators amounting to 130,000 francs. It was useless, he realized, to complain, since the agent showed him a letter from Josephine asking for everything to be handmade and in the latest mode. In a court of law, clearly, he would not have had a leg to stand on. And this was not all, for further bills came in that ultimately raised the costs to a fantastic total of 300,000 francs. Bonaparte got what little comfort he could from reminding himself that these sums were in inflated currency.

Meanwhile Josephine was on her way to Paris, leaving Milan in late November and taking the route which passed through Turin and Lyons. At Lyons, where the town was illuminated in her honour, there were balls and fêtes; a crown of roses was offered to Josephine and a laurel wreath was given her for her husband. At Moulins further illuminations appeared, among them being a large display which in limping verse paid particular honour to Josephine:

Companion of the hero admired by every nation,
In thee our hearts acclaim his source of inspiration.

Josephine, moved to unexpected eloquence, made a little speech in which she assured the people that Bonaparte loved all republicans and that for them he stood ready to shed the very last drop of his blood. In the morning as she left for Paris huge crowds gathered to bid her farewell. Josephine was not, however, to travel in solitude, cogitating these flattering tributes to Bonaparte and herself. Hippolyte Charles, who had managed to delay at Milan even longer than she, caught up with her en route, so that despite all risks and all threats they could make part of the journey together. Josephine urged him to resign his commission as a soldier and to become an army contractor; it was soon to appear that she, too, was closely involved in some of this business. Three stages before reaching Paris the pair separated.

When she reached the capital on 2 January 1798 Josephine found that her husband, having left the negotiations at Rastatt, had preceded her by several weeks. He had time, therefore, to adjust himself as best he could to the costly new splendours of the rue Chantereine, and amid his plans for further campaigns to prepare a welcome within its walls for his still unpredictable wife.

❧ 12 ❧

Joséphine Infidèle

THE victorious Bonaparte arrived in Paris at the beginning of
December 1797. Four weeks were to elapse before Josephine
rejoined him, yet, seeing that her delays were by now routine
and notorious, he could hardly have been greatly surprised.
He did not know that Captain Charles, ordered in November
to return to Paris, had failed to do so. Bonaparte, in truth, had
little time to brood, for he was enjoying the sweet taste of
power. With Italy at his feet he had gone post-haste to the
Rhineland, where his triumphs continued. Here, during his
brief stay at Rastatt, he dominated the discussions of the
German princes on the reorganization of western Germany.
He had also negotiated for the transfer of Venice to the
Austrians, and he had further arranged for the transfer of
Mainz, a key military post and one of the chief cities of the
Rhineland, to France. These were impressive achievements
demonstrating that the man who awaited Josephine was now
beginning his great role as the arbiter of Europe.

Bonaparte's winning of Mainz, whose loss to the Prussians
had led to Alexander de Beauharnais' death in 1794, crowned
the triumph of Josephine's second husband. Mainz was now
the glittering symbol of a victory that had confirmed France
in possession of Belgium and the entire Rhineland, giving her
the 'natural frontiers' neither Richelieu nor Louis XIV had
been able to win. When the directors, therefore, honoured
Bonaparte with a magnificent public reception in the gardens
of the Luxembourg Palace he was at the height of his popu-
larity. He skilfully and generously shared his fame with the
directors. 'You have succeeded,' he told them, 'in fashioning
a mighty nation, whose wide territories are bounded only by
the limits that Nature herself has appointed.'[1] The huge crowd

listened in intent silence to every word which he spoke and wildly cheered him when he was through. They had no ears, on the other hand, for Barras, who followed. This wily director was unable to command even the semblance of attention for the unctuous phrases of congratulation he poured upon Bonaparte.

There could be no question of Bonaparte's enormous prestige. He was applauded when he appeared at the theatre. He was welcomed by the *savants* of the Institute of France. The central administration ordered the name of the rue Chantereine to be changed to the rue de la Victoire in order to pay tribute to the conqueror of Italy. The public jealously guarded his fame. When a Paris newspaper printed a report that a royalist citizen of Brittany had contemptuously named his dog Bonaparte, the news aroused a storm of indignation. The possibility of public demonstrations of protest in Paris was averted only when a correspondent at Avranches was able to report that there had been complete misunderstanding. The dog, he explained, an animal of great beauty and docility, actually was named Peace.

Ironically enough, the victorious Napoleon had no immediate public role to play in Paris. A general back from the wars, Bonaparte had put down his Italian command; he had every reason to be dubious about the prospects of the cross-Channel invasion of England that the Directory now had in mind as a next move; and he was too young to be eligible for election as one of the five directors.

In this situation Bonaparte played his cards carefully. He avoided public debate on matters of politics and chose instead to discuss science with the scientists, mathematics with the mathematicians, and philosophy with the philosophers, with the result that he was elected before the year was out to the Institute of France, taking his place in the class of sciences and arts. The letter of acceptance which he wrote to the president of the Institute neatly veiled his political ambitions. 'The true conquests,' the soldier declared, 'the only ones that cause no regret, are those which are made over ignorance.'[2]

A breathless Josephine arrived on the second day of the

new year with the plaudits that had accompanied her triumphal progress from Lyons to Paris still ringing in her ears. Her delays had caused great confusion in the plans for the state reception that Talleyrand, now minister of foreign affairs, had arranged at his official residence, the *hôtel* Galliffet in the rue du Bac. Josephine's failure to arrive in Paris when expected had put Talleyrand to great cost and inconvenience. On three successive days notices of postponement had to be sent out and huge quantities of flowers were wasted and had to be re-ordered. In the end, nevertheless, the fête was magnificently managed, with a general attendance of several thousand guests, a supper for three hundred, music by the best singers from the opera, and toasts proposed by Talleyrand. The women, it was noted, were simply and elegantly dressed in 'antique style' – a mode which reflected the turn of fashion from the reckless styles of the preceding years. Despite all the honours, Josephine seemed very distrait, in part because of her late arrival in Paris, in part because of the painful words she had had with Bonaparte over her extravagance in re-furnishing their house, in part, no doubt, because her affair with Captain Charles gave her an uneasy conscience. Count Girardin, good friend of Joseph Bonaparte (whom Josephine detested), noted that Napoleon, who kept very close to his wife during the reception, seemed devoted to her – 'very amorous and excessively jealous', he wrote. Girardin was hardly an unprejudiced witness. He estimated Josephine's age at 'nearly forty' (a hostile error of more than four years), he declared most ungallantly that she was no longer beautiful, and he insisted that she fully looked her years. Girardin added with what charity he could muster that Josephine had an elegant bearing and that he was sure her kind heart would never grow old.[3]

In these triumphant days a meteoric challenger for Josephine's place in Bonaparte's affections shot briefly across the horizon. Germaine de Staël was the daughter of Necker, once the financial genius of the French monarchy. Wife of the Swedish ambassador to France, ex-mistress of Talleyrand, of Narbonne, and of many others, she was as devoted to the literary and intellectual life of the capital as Josephine was indifferent to it. Madame de Staël had developed a vast admiration for Bonaparte, sending to him in Italy letters now lost in which she compared him to the Roman Scipio and to the medieval hero, Tancred. These ardent letters from the one whom he chose to describe as 'that hussy, Staël²', Bonaparte never answered.

Germaine now flung herself at Bonaparte with an intensity that on occasion brought him close to panic. He characterized her variously as 'a veritable pest', as 'an old crow', and as 'a madwoman who should be taken into custody by the police'. Her campaign was conducted on several fronts. Germaine wrote to Bonaparte saying that it was an error in human institutions for him to have married the 'sweet and gentle' Josephine. Nature, rather, destined a soul of fire (Germaine) to receive the adoration of a man such as he. On another occasion she called at the rue Chantereine, and when told that the general was naked in his bathtub sought to rush past the astonished footman, crying, 'No matter! Genius has no sex!'⁴

On the evening of Talleyrand's reception at the *hôtel* Galliffet Germaine tried again. Finding herself beside the general, she bombarded him with questions, and in the ensuing exchange met her match. 'Who is the woman you love the most?' she asked. 'My wife,' Bonaparte replied curtly. 'Who is the one you esteem most highly?' – 'The one who manages her household the best.' 'Who would be for you the first among all women?' – 'The one, madame, who bears the most children.' The victory in this exchange clearly went to Bonaparte and left Germaine capable of no more than the final, flustered comment to her neighbours: 'Your great man is a very singular fellow!'⁵

The Directory was now concerned with bringing the war with England to a successful close. To this end it sent Bonaparte early in February on an inspection tour of the Channel ports, seeking his opinion on the feasibility of a cross-Channel invasion that would lead, as Hitler more than a century later hoped it would, to the destruction of the stubborn island power. The unfavourable report that Bonaparte quickly submitted to the directors brought into prominence the alternate plan, already seething in his mind, for the expedition to Egypt.

While matters of high policy were thus under consideration in Paris, Josephine picked up the threads of her old life and began some new ventures. She was still a good friend of Barras. It is clear also that she now took an active, personal interest in firms concerned with army contracts – an interest that went beyond a simple willingness to do favours for her friends. It is also clear that the fantastic Captain Charles (having resigned his hussar commission) still had his place in her life.

Josephine wrote several letters to Barras during this period, one of them in mid-January being couched in warm phrases and asking him to dine with Bonaparte and herself in the company of several members of the Institute. After Bonaparte left on 10 February for his inspection tour of the Channel coast, Josephine had quite cosy relations with Barras. This is the clear implication of a letter to Barras' secretary, written on the evening of Bonaparte's return to Paris on 21 February:

> Bonaparte has come back tonight. Will you, my dear Bottot, express to Barras my regrets that I cannot dine with him tonight. Tell him not to forget me. You know better than anyone how I am placed. Farewell, I send you my sincere friendship.[6]

However close Josephine's connexion with the principal director may have been, it could hardly equal the closeness of her continuing connexion with Hippolyte Charles. The most charitable explanation – if charity is called for at this point – is that Josephine, along with Charles and possibly Barras, had become deeply involved in the financial affairs of the Bodin Company. This was one of the many concerns mushrooming in this period that held, or sought, contracts for government supplies. Charles had surrendered his army commission to work more closely with the company, if not actually to be a partner in it. Josephine, too, was much more than an innocent bystander. For what could only be selfish financial reasons this wife of a victorious general sought to make secret profit out of the economic necessities of a country at war.

Under the heavy pressure of a steadily enlarging war, the

government had been faced with a baffling supply problem. It had very little cash. Hence it had to make contracts with suppliers who operated on a very large scale and were willing to accept financial payments on a deferred, long-term basis. The *Compagnie Flachat* and the *Compagnie Dijon* were outstanding examples of companies which played a major part in such operations. Simultaneously, bankers such as Ouvrard and public figures such as Barras and Talleyrand were able to make huge fortunes through loans, currency speculation, and similar devices. Other lesser groups, among which the *Compagnie Bodin* was one, tried to move into these lush financial pastures. This company followed the common practice of shortchanging the government, both in the quantities and the quality of supplies it furnished. It was not averse to altering figures in its invoices after they had been officially approved, and it had a reputation for providing the government with poor horses and cattle it had taken by requisition from French farmers and peasants, often without troubling to pay for them.

Information about this unsavoury Bodin Company reached Joseph Bonaparte, inveterate enemy of Josephine. He then hastened to inform Napoleon. Following this, the brothers confronted Josephine in what must have been an extremely painful interview. Among the papers of Hippolyte Charles have survived a few letters from Josephine that were unknown to her earlier biographers and that put her in as unfavourable a light as any known documents in her entire life. She wrote to Charles in great agitation to say that on the day before Joseph had had a long conversation with Napoleon, after which the two had put her through a most savage interrogation. Did she, they asked, know this Citizen Bodin? Had she been responsible for getting him supply contracts with the Army of Italy? Did Captain Charles lodge with Bodin at No. 100, Faubourg Saint-Honoré, and did Josephine go there daily?

The answers Josephine told Hippolyte she had given to Napoleon suggest that the ruthless interrogation had brought her close to hysteria:

I replied that I knew nothing about what he was saying to me; if he wished a divorce he had only to speak; he had no need to use such means; and I was the most unfortunate of women and the most unhappy. Yes, my Hippolyte, they have my complete hatred; you alone have my tenderness and my love; they must see now, as a result of the terrible state I have been in for several days, how much I abhor them; they can see my disappointment – my despair at not being able to see you as often as I wish. Hippolyte, I shall kill myself – yes, I wish to end a life that henceforth would be only a burden if it could not be devoted to you. Alas! What have I done to these monsters? But they are acting in vain, I will never be a victim of their atrocious conduct!

Following this outburst came specific instructions:

Tell Bodin, I beg you, to say that he doesn't know me; that it has not been through me that he got the contracts for the Army of Italy; let him tell the door-keeper at No. 100 that when people ask him if Bodin lives there he is to say that he doesn't know him. Tell Bodin not to use the letters which I have given him for Italy until some time after his arrival there when he needs them . . . Ah, they torment me in vain! They will never separate me from my Hippolyte; my last look will be for him!

I will do everything to see you today. If I cannot, I will spend the evening at Bodin's and tomorrow I will send Blondin [a servant] to let you know the time when I could see you in the garden of Mousseaux. Adieu, my Hippolyte, a thousand kisses, as burning as is my heart, and as amorous . . .[7]

In a subsequent letter to Captain Charles, Josephine told him that she had just written to the minister of war arranging to submit some papers. Papers about what? Could her action have concerned army contracts, or had it something to do with Hippolyte's retirement from military service? She added further that she had written to Barras asking him 'to return the letters which he had promised'. We can only conjecture what these were. The letter to Captain Charles ends as follows:

I am going, my dear Hippolyte, to the country. I shall be back between half past five and six, looking for you at Bodin's. Yes, my Hippolyte, life is a continual torture. You alone can make me happy. Tell me that you love me, and only me. I shall be the happiest of women.

Send me, by means of Blondin, 50,000 livres from the notes in your possession. Callot is demanding them. Farewell, I send you a thousand tender kisses. *Tout à toi*.[8]

When a wife writes such letters to a lover, the reasonable inference is that relations with her husband have reached the breaking point. Actually, no such decisive development was to occur. When Bonaparte returned from his inspection tour, his mind was much more on grand strategy than on the problems of his private life. He drafted a report to the Directory saying that a cross-Channel invasion was out of the question. He then turned his powerful energies to the plan that had always fascinated him, which the Directory now was prepared to authorize – that of an expedition to Egypt. Nearly two hundred detailed letters and orders from him found in his published *Correspondence* show how deeply absorbed he was during the next two months in every aspect of the complicated preparations. He had little time for Josephine, and whatever anger he did show seems to have arisen as much from her evident connexion with the Bodin Company as from what he knew of her relations with Captain Charles. Josephine suspected that it was her new brother-in-law, Joseph Bonaparte, who was trying to make trouble. Three months later she told Barras that Joseph's attitude to her was 'abominable', and that she knew he had vowed not to rest until he had separated Josephine from her new husband. 'He is a vile, abominable person,' she wrote heatedly, 'some day you will know what he is like.'[9]

If there had been serious prospect of a rupture, it is hardly likely that Bonaparte would then have bought the house they had been renting for the past two years. On 26 March 1798 he purchased the establishment on the newly named rue de la Victoire – Pompeian frescoes, mirrors, cupids, pink roses, white swans, and all – for 52,400 francs. The price was substantial, yet far less than the 300,000 francs that Josephine had incurred for its refurnishing and redecoration. The fantastic purchase was doubtless the only way for the soldier to safeguard his interest in the huge sums he had already been obliged to pay.

Some of Josephine's family complications briefly touched the activities of Bonaparte. Her sister-in-law, Françoise de Beauharnais, had a daughter by her first marriage, Emilie, whom Louis Bonaparte wished to marry. Emilie would have none of him, and so the family, with Bonaparte's help, rounded up one of his aides-de-camp, Antoine Lavalette. The marriage took place in the spring of 1798 at the home of Josephine's elderly father-in-law. One wonders whether he obligingly offered his home so that the family would not have to accept the mulatto who was Françoise's husband as host on this occasion. Perhaps also because of the social questions raised, Josephine and Bonaparte stayed away, sending Hortense de Beauharnais and Caroline Bonaparte as their representatives.

The ever-thoughtful Josephine set to work at once to do something for the young Lavalette who had just married her niece. On the very eve of Bonaparte's departure for Egypt she wrote from Toulon to Barras requesting a recommendation from the director for Lavalette. She also wrote to Barras's secretary in the same vein. 'My niece has charged me,' she explained, 'to fulfil a solemn engagement . . . A letter from the director saying that he takes an interest in us is all we need.'[10]

By May the secret plans for a French attack on Egypt had been completed. This campaign, it was hoped, would undercut British sea power in the eastern Mediterranean, end the menace from France's only great rival, and permit Bonaparte to realize his great dreams of conquest in the Orient. Josephine was to accompany her husband at least as far as Toulon and to join him later in Egypt. The pair therefore left Paris on 4 May and arrived at Toulon on the 9th. There a considerable delay ensued. The correspondence makes it clear that Bonaparte did seriously intend his wife to follow him to Egypt when circumstances made it safe for her to do so. Meanwhile she would go to Plombières, a most pleasant resort in the Vosges Mountains, where the waters were widely believed to be effective in overcoming sterility. Some of this news about herself Josephine conveyed in a letter to Barras from Toulon, ending with the hope that he would not forget 'a friend who is devoted to you and whose friendship is as tender as it is sincere'.[11]

Bonaparte's huge fleet of more than three hundred transports and fifty escorting ships of war, which left Toulon on 19 May, has been described as the most spectacular expedition since the Crusades. Luck was with him, for Nelson, who with his British squadrons had maintained a long vigil in the Mediterranean, might easily have inflicted heavy damage. Fortunately for the French, however, Nelson's warships did not find the transports. En route to Egypt Bonaparte stopped briefly to seize Malta, a key point in the strategic control of the Mediterranean. From here he made sail for Alexandria where, once again escaping Nelson by a hair's breadth, he put his army of forty thousand ashore at the end of June.

What followed was a magnificent piece of military bravura undertaken in company with a scientific programme of genuine importance. The demonstration of brilliant personal showmanship was nevertheless marred by a sorry catalogue of military miscalculations and blunders, the outcome of which was to be a humiliating French surrender. The Egyptian campaign is, to be sure, a distant episode which touches the life of Josephine only indirectly. Because events did not permit her to join her husband in Egypt, she indulged in reckless behaviour in France that further injured her reputation and caused her husband the most poignant anxiety and the wildest indignation.

Josephine might well have found in Egypt a land of romance far surpassing what she had known in Italy. The British, however, were on the alert, and Bonaparte did not wish his wife to run risks. The agreement, therefore, was that she should stay in Toulon until news came that the French ships had safely passed Sicily. Then, unless explicit word came for her to sail, she would proceed to take the waters at Plombières and wait upon events. Nothing, so Bourrienne wrote, could have been more affecting than their parting. After Bonaparte had sailed, he found that his elaborately worked out plans led only to confusion, for although he wrote to his brother Joseph while passing the island of Corsica, saying that he was now instructing his wife to join him, his letter arrived too late for her to obey.

Before the end of May Josephine had begun the long trip northward to Plombières, sending a warm note to her old friend Barras before leaving. She likewise kept in touch with him en route. True to her nature she wrote from Valence passing on a letter of recommendation concerning an 'unfortunate citizen' whom she had just met. It was awkward that she could not quite remember his name. She wrote again from Lyons to warn Barras that General Brune, the French commander in Switzerland, was trying to break the government contracts held by the Bodin Company. 'Write on their behalf, I beg you, to General Brune,' she urged. 'Both you and I owe everything to them . . . You will do them a great favour by writing on their behalf to General Brune, and I beg you to waste no time.'[12]

By mid-June Josephine was agreeably installed high amid the pine forests of the Vosges. Under the direction of Citizen Martinet, the local doctor at Plombières, she could rest, relax, and take the sulphur waters that had been famous ever since the days of the Romans. She was staying, so she wrote to Barras, in the simple home of an elderly couple whose charming devotion to each other reminded her of Ovid's Philemon and Baucis. Having given this news, she sought word of Barras and of her husband. 'I am so unhappy to be separated from him,' she wrote, 'that I have a sadness I cannot overcome. On the other hand, his brother, with whom he corresponds so closely, acts so abominably towards me that I am always uneasy when I am far from Bonaparte.'[13] There is truth in what Josephine wrote: in the presence of her husband she quickly realized how much of a spell she exercised over him, while in his absence she brooded upon the hostility of her Bonaparte relatives, never sure what influence their unkind tongues might have.

Her letter to Barras is revealing in other ways. 'I wish that the waters of Plombières could be prescribed for you,' she told Barras coyly, 'so that you could decide to come here and take them. It would be most obliging of you to have an ailment in order to be able to cause me pleasure. I am very devoted to you – I like you for what you are, my dear Barras; this is a feeling due to you when one has the pleasure of knowing you, and no one experiences it more than I do.'[14] Amid these cloying words the true picture of Barras – the vicious, dissipated roué of the Directory who ultimately was to include in his *Memoirs* as savagely hostile a picture of Josephine as any that ever was written about her – dissolves like a dream. But Barras as yet had not been driven from office by Bonaparte.

Josephine also enclosed a letter to be forwarded to Bonaparte. 'You know him,' she explained to Barras, 'and you know how he would hold it against me if he had no news of me. His last letter is very tender and sentimental. He asks me to rejoin him soon, for he cannot live without me. And so I am taking the prescribed cure in order to be able to rejoin him quickly. I love him well, despite his little faults.'[15]

What these words really meant, and what Josephine would have done, we cannot say, for two days later a sudden accident broke into the pleasant pattern of her life. It was occasioned by a dog. Josephine was sitting sewing in an upstairs room with a few friends when her companion, Madame Cambis, called her to a wooden balcony some fifteen feet high to observe a small, handsome dog that happened to be passing by in the street. The entire company rushed out, the balcony collapsed, and Josephine fell so hard as to receive extremely painful, yet fortunately superficial, pelvic injuries. No one was gravely hurt, though in her fall Josephine broke the leg of a colonel of cuirassiers who happened to be below. Immediately she came under the care of Dr Martinet who, calling in other doctors from the neighbourhood to assist in the care of a celebrated patient, first wrapped her in the skin of a newly slaughtered sheep and then, in the fashion of the day, embarked on so madly elaborate a régime of infusions, baths, douches, lavings, bleedings, poulticings, plasterings, and applications of leeches that Josephine's survival seems little short of miraculous. She was required to stay at Plombières for more than two months during which every detail of her treatment was immediately proclaimed to the world in the learned pages of Dr Martinet's own *Physico-Medical Journal of the Waters of Plombières for the Year VI of the Republic*.

We can follow the course of Josephine's recovery with much

less clinical detail in some letters to Barras. It was a painful business, so she told him early in July, and she still could not walk. But his charming letter, she added, 'has put balm on my bruises'.[16] By mid-July Dr Martinet was able to report officially to Barras that Citizeness Bonaparte continued to enjoy perfect convalescence, that she walked for more than an hour daily, and that the pains in the lower regions were subsiding. Josephine would hardly have agreed.

I have received a charming letter from Bonaparte [she told Barras]. He says that he can't live without me. I am to rejoin him and to embark at Naples. I wish my health would permit me to start at once; but I don't see the end of my cure. I cannot stand upright for more than ten minutes without terrible pains in the loins and lower abdomen. I do nothing but cry. The doctors say that in a month I shall be cured. If I find no relief in two weeks I shall go to Paris.[17]

This picture, clearly, was exaggerated. Josephine told her friend, Madame Marmont, wife of the general, a different story. She planned first to go to Paris, she said, making no reference to her trouble, then the two of them would travel the length of Italy and join their husbands in Egypt. When the near-by municipality of Épinal invited her to a public reception to be held shortly, she replied that she would have to wait ten days before deciding to accept. But, in the end, accept she did. Accompanied by Hortense and Madame Beurnonville, she was met and escorted by the National Guard and a band. The party proceeded through a triumphal arch, along streets decorated with greenery, and to sound of cannon shots. At the town hall she saw a statue of liberty with inscriptions honouring Bonaparte. She received a bouquet and heard an address by the president of the municipal council. At night there was a banquet, followed by illuminations, fireworks, and supper while crowds thronged the streets. In this way Épinal indirectly honoured the soldier who at this moment had won the Battle of the Pyramids and was preparing to enter Cairo and declare Egypt a French protectorate. Returning to Plombières, Josephine found a ceremonial sword that had been sent her by the Directory as a gift for her victorious husband. The details of Bonaparte's triumphs were not known at this time either to the Directory or to Josephine, yet in view of his growing fame and the obvious share that would be hers, it is almost incredible that she should have valued her marriage so little, and should have risked it again and again, as she did now, by her irresponsible conduct.

Since Josephine was clearly recovering from her accident, the prospect of joining her husband now still lay before her. The plan was to go first to Paris before proceeding to Italy and Egypt, and with this in mind, early in August, she sent her daughter Hortense ahead. Josephine must have left about 10 September, since two days later she was in Nancy where, as at Épinal, she was royally welcomed. By 15 September, when she reached Paris, alarming news from Egypt awaited her. This told of Nelson's spectacular victory of 1 August, when his ships had come upon the French fleet anchored at the mouth of the Nile, in Abukir Bay, and in a fierce night engagement had totally destroyed it. Josephine's first impulse was to write to Barras informing him how disturbed she was at these reports just arrived from Malta. 'As I am much disturbed at the news from Malta, my dear Barras,' she wrote, 'permit me to visit you this evening at nine. Give orders for no one to enter.'[18] The report of the loss of the French fleet now made any plans to visit Egypt totally out of the question, so that Josephine was flung once again into a circle of acquaintances who did her reputation no good. Since communications with Egypt were broken, she had no way of knowing, and certainly no way of counteracting, the tormented emotions of her far-distant husband.

The months in which Bonaparte once more became acutely distressed at the thought of Josephine's infidelities were the months in which he was deeply embroiled in the dramatic conquest of Egypt. Landing at Alexandria, he won the Battle of the Pyramids on 21 July and occupied Cairo three days later. Following these victories came the naval disaster at Abukir Bay. Before this had happened Napoleon wrote to his brother Joseph exulting in his victories and yet in personal matters showing himself to be deeply unhappy. Although he did not mention Josephine by name, the inference was unmistakable.

I have much, much domestic trouble, for the veil is completely torn away. You are the only person left to me in this world; your friendship is very dear to me; if I were to lose this, or if you were to betray me, nothing could keep me from becoming a complete misanthrope. It is a sad state of affairs when all one's affections are concentrated upon a single person. You will know what I mean.

See to it that I shall have a country place upon my arrival, either near Paris or in Burgundy. I count on passing the winter there and seeing no one. I am sick of people! I need solitude and isolation. Greatness wearies me, my feelings are dried up, glory is empty. At twenty-nine I have exhausted everything . . .[19]

This letter, addressed to 'Citizen Joseph Bonaparte' in Paris, never reached him, for the ship carrying the bearer was seized by the British and the documents were sent to London. The first part of the letter, giving political news, was quickly printed by the British in a volume entitled *Political Correspondence*. The second part, 'by reason of its being a private letter', was veiled by the Foreign Office in decent obscurity. It lies to this day among the Additional Manuscripts of the British Museum with a simple endorsement in the handwriting of Nelson, 'found on the person of the courier'.[20]

What Bonaparte hinted at was discussed more frankly in another letter, written on the day before and, like his, captured by the British. Its author was Josephine's sixteen-year-old son, Eugène de Beauharnais, now serving as an aide to Bonaparte. This solemn, sterling youth painfully put together some frank words for his mother on the reports of her scandalous goings-on in Paris:

My dear mama, I have so many things to say to you that I don't know where to begin. Bonaparte has been extremely sad for five days, as a result of an interview with Julien, Junot and Berthier. This conversation has affected him more than I would have believed. All I have heard amounts to this: that [Captain] Charles travelled in your carriage until you were within three posting stations of Paris; that you saw him in Paris; that you were with him at the Theatre of the Italians in the private boxes; that he gave you your little dog; that even now you are with him. Such, in scattered phrases, is everything that I have heard. You know, mama, that I don't believe this; but what is certain is that the general is very upset. However, he redoubles his kindnesses to me. He seems to say, by his actions, that children are not responsible for the faults of their mother. Your son, however, chooses to believe that all gossip is manufactured by your enemies. Your son loves you as much as ever and is as eager as ever to greet you. I hope that when you do come all will be forgotten.[21]

Since Eugène's letter likewise was captured by the British it had no influence on his mother's behaviour. It is, nevertheless, an extraordinarily revealing document. Written within a month of Bonaparte's landing in Egypt, it could not have been based on any new reports of Josephine coming from France and was probably an outcome of the raking-over of old scandals by the officers on Bonaparte's staff. Something of this earlier behaviour of Josephine and Hippolyte Charles was, of course, known to Bonaparte. He had written bitterly about it while in Italy, and subsequently there had been the painful scene of mid-March at Paris when Joseph and Napoleon had put Josephine through the interrogation as a result of which she had written to Charles talking feverishly about divorce. Eugène's letter suggests that in some conversation with his officers Bonaparte had let all his pent-up doubts and anxieties burst forth – as they did in the letter to Joseph.

Napoleon's secretary, Bourrienne, has in his *Memoirs* a most circumstantial narrative of a smilar explosion, which according to Bourrienne's dating would have occurred seven months later, during the advance from Egypt into Syria. Bourrienne says that he saw Bonaparte walking with General Junot 'near the wells of Messoudiah' and that the commander seemed pale and distraught, striking his head with his hand several times as Junot spoke to him. When Bourrienne approached, Bonaparte launched into a wild attack on him:

So! I find I cannot depend upon you. – These women! – Josephine! – If you had loved me you would before now have told me all I have heard from Junot – he is a real friend – Josephine! –

and I six hundred leagues from her – you ought to have told me. That she should have thus deceived me! – Woe to them! – I will exterminate the whole race of fops and puppies! As to her – divorce! Yes, divorce! A public and open divorce! – I must write! – I know all! – It is your fault – you ought to have told me!

Bourrienne attempted to quiet Bonaparte, urging that it would be unreasonable to rely on hearsay evidence while so far away in Egypt. It would be unwise, he urged, to write letters that could be intercepted. As for divorce, 'it would be time to think of that hereafter'.[22]

One soon learns to suspect memoirs of the Napoleonic period written long after the event, especially when they report conversations with such confident stenographic accuracy. Indeed, it has been asserted that Bourrienne could not have been at Messoudiah at the time when Bonaparte was there. Yet the general picture of an unhappy Bonaparte, alternately brooding and storming over his married fate, seems difficult to challenge.

Another episode, important enough to mark a new stage in Napoleon's relations with Josephine, can be discerned in the complex happenings of the Egyptian campaign. Until this point, despite his anger and his unhappiness, Bonaparte seems to have been faithful to his wife. He now embarked upon the first of those fleeting extramarital adventures that were to run consistently for the rest of his life and to accumulate so rapidly that the scholarly Frédéric Masson has been able to write a learned book of 325 pages cataloguing and describing the lot.

Marguerite-Pauline Bellisle, a nineteen-year-old dressmaker of Carcassonne, had become the wife of a young Lieutenant Fourès of the Chasseurs. When he was ordered to Egypt, she put on an officer's uniform and stowed away aboard ship. Blessed with 'a rose-petal complexion, beautiful teeth, and a good geometrical figure', she soon became one of the striking personalities of the Egyptian Tivoli – a pleasure garden at Cairo modelled on the similar gardens in Paris. Bonaparte saw her, was attracted, and showered her with presents. Consequently, in December 1798 Lieutenant Fourès was given an urgent commission to carry dispatches to Paris. He had no choice but to leave, and his wife with her rose-petal complexion and geometrical figure was installed in a pleasant villa adjoining the Elfi-Bey Palace where Bonaparte had his headquarters.

The gods frequently take pleasure in outwitting clever mortals. Lieutenant Fourès' ship was captured by the British when only one day out from port. This might well have meant his permanent removal from the scene had not the British intelligence service been functioning well. With unexpectedly sly humour they immediately returned the young French officer under parole to Cairo. Outraged at what he found and unwilling to be quiet, Lieutenant Fourès demanded and obtained a civil divorce. On Bonaparte's eventual return in June 1799 from his unsuccessful six months' campaign in Syria, Madame Fourès paraded publicly as Bonaparte's mistress. When 'Bellilotte', as she was called, rode with the general in his open carriage through the streets of Cairo, Eugène, as aide-de-camp, was required to serve as escort. The boy found his duty so embarrassing that he requested General Berthier to transfer him to a regiment of infantry. He then had a painful scene with Bonaparte, after which, as Eugène relates in his memoirs, the public carriage rides stopped.

Kircheisen, the most learned of Napoleon's biographers, says that Napoleon took the *affaire Bellilotte* seriously. He wrote her letters during the Syrian campaign and later instructed her to follow him when he returned to France. This she did, but she was too late, for by the time of her arrival Napoleon and Josephine had become reconciled. Bonaparte never again saw the dressmaker of Carcassonne, though she received a house and a liberal allowance from him under the Empire, lived to paint pictures, to be a friend of Rosa Bonheur, to write a novel, *Lord Wentworth*, to spend some time in Brazil, and to flourish happily until her ninetieth year, recalling those long-distant days in Egypt. This transient shadow in the life of Josephine died in 1869 in her Paris apartment, surrounded by a strange assortment of monkeys and uncaged birds.

The Josephine who returned to Paris from Plombières in September 1798 quickly resumed her familiar heedless ways.

Joséphine Infidèle

After two and a half years of marriage, only a small part of which had been spent with her husband, it seems that she still did not know what kind of man he was. To her only the present mattered, and so she lost no time in renewing the connexion with her good correspondent, Barras. He was, after all, on the scene, while her husband was a thousand miles away, with the date of his return, to say the least, uncertain. Bonaparte might never come back; Barras was the most powerful of the directors; he could help in the Bodin Company's affairs, which seemed daily to go from bad to worse; he could do favours for her needy friends; and, as she more than once reminded him point-blank, he could entertain her at dinner, discreetly and alone.

No characteristic in Josephine is more persistent than her willingness to ask favours for her friends. One of the oddest of her requests concerns Caroline Wuiet, an infant prodigy who at the age of five had played the piano before Marie Antoinette and had composed a three-act play at the age of twelve. An emigrant during the Revolution, Caroline had later returned to France and had become something of a social figure in the circles of Madame Tallien and Madame Bonaparte. She became the editor of a literary journal, the *Phoenix*, which was a *mélange* of gossip, poetry, financial news, anagrams, and charades. Finding one of her major expenses to be clothing, the emancipated Caroline hit upon a happy solution: she would simplify matters by dressing as a man. Convenient as this solution seemed, it caused immediate difficulties with the police – far less tolerant then than now – who ordered Caroline to desist. Quick to support her friend, Josephine wrote to the office of the minister of police as follows:

You will see from the attached note, estimable citizen, that Citizeness Caroline Wuiet (a distinguished artist whom I take the greatest pleasure in helping) wishes to obtain permission to wear men's clothes occasionally. I ask for her your accustomed courtesy, since the citizen minister has kindly promised to act favourably in her case. Greetings and friendship,

Lapagerie Bonaparte[23]

Josephine made some effort, in this period of her husband's

absence in Egypt, to revive the salon life of a former age. The task was not easy. Miot de Mélito recalls in his *Memoirs* that the times were too confused for any true elegance to develop. The drawing rooms, he said, were full of contractors, generals, savants, ladies of the old aristocracy, and ladies of gay adventure. 'One idea alone, common to all, dominated and absorbed people of totally different origins and education – the desire to make money. Every means was justifiable to acquire it.'[24] Other writers give a somewhat less critical picture, telling how the crowd of guests that Josephine was able to attract pushed into the house on the rue de la Victoire, where she presided with what one of them calls 'a touching simplicity, endless assurance, and an engaging frankness which won all hearts'.[25]

The long roster of Josephine's guests included reigning beauties such as Thérèse Tallien and Madame Récamier. With them came Bonaparte's sisters – Pauline, Caroline, and Elisa – and the wives of many of the newly famous generals of France. Aunt Fanny de Beauharnais, still tireless as a writer, was there. So likewise was the aged Madame de Houdetot, long ago the inspirer of an unrequited passion on the part of the young Rousseau. Among the men were the painters David, Gérard, and Girodet-Trioson, the musicians Méhul and Cherubini, and the playwrights and poets Ducis, Arnault, Joseph Chénier, and Legouvé. The list is impressive. By common agreement Josephine shone as a gracious hostess at such affairs, and while she made no claim to equal the conversational brilliance of the formidable Madame de Staël, bit by bit a new society with some pretence to civility and grace began to supersede the crude extravagances of the Directory era.

Did Josephine renew her relations with Hippolyte Charles when she returned to Paris in this autumn of 1798? In the previous March she had written to him in wildly extravagant terms, speaking of a possible divorce from her husband and protesting her undying affection. We have three letters of 1799, the first of which, written in February, would seem to indicate the approaching end of a chapter. A continuing link between the two was the Bodin Company, for in this February letter it is clear that Josephine had still been using her influence to establish new contacts for the company with the Army of Italy. Josephine told Charles that she wished to see him for a few moments on the following day in order to speak about a matter that concerned her. Then she added, with what sounds like bitterness or disillusionment: 'You can be assured, after this interview, which will be the last, that you will no longer be tormented by my letters or by my presence. The respectable woman who has been deceived [*l'honnête femme trompée*] retires and says nothing.'[26]

Was this the end? Not if we are to believe the rumours of 1799. Gossip had it that Captain Charles haunted the country-side near Paris where Josephine was in process of acquiring the estate of Malmaison, and that amid the shades of evening the slight figure of this young man could be seen there es-corting Josephine as she walked abroad. Louis Gohier, who was elected to the Directory in June 1799 and whose wife was a close friend of Josephine, urged her to give up Captain Charles and, when she seemed unwilling, told her that if she proposed to continue her affair she should divorce Bonaparte and marry Charles. Fortunately for Josephine's place in history she chose not to take Gohier's last advice. Sometime during the autumn the parting came with Hippolyte. A brief, austere letter that she wrote to Captain Charles in October 1799 concerned itself simply with the seemingly interminable affairs of the Bodin Company. Another letter, written after Bona-parte had seized political power in France, informed Charles of her unfortunate failure to obtain a political appointment for one of her friends. Josephine assured Charles, who was drifting out of her life, that her feelings towards him had not changed. Her friendship, she said, was most tender and most lasting. Whatever this may have meant, the little captain of hussars was through; there is no evidence of further contacts, and on his deathbed in 1837 he asked that Josephine's letters to him be burned. His executors tried to do what he asked, and only the chance survival of five letters makes it possible to elaborate and confirm the many contemporary stories of this reckless and unfortunate episode.

In these same months before the return of Bonaparte, Josephine plunged into a venture that was to give colour and character to all her subsequent doings – the purchase of Malmaison. For the increasing importance of her station the small town house on the rue de la Victoire clearly was not enough. Never well supplied with funds – on the contrary, plunging ever more deeply into debt – Josephine now regarded herself as the wife of a conqueror from whom the spoils of war could be counted upon in ever-increasing amounts to solve her financial problems. Jewels, rare objects, paintings, and sculptures already were pouring in upon her, so it is hardly surprising that she should have approached the purchase of a country estate with airy disregard for the costs. Bonaparte, too, was now thinking of some country retreat where he could rid himself of the cares of the world. For Josephine the country had always had an attraction, and she had pleasant memories of her early years in Martinique, of the rural seclusion of Noisy-le-Grand and Fontainebleau, during her first marriage, and of the green, wooded retreat at Croissy where she had gone with Madame Hosten to escape the dangers of Paris under the Reign of Terror.

The estate of Malmaison, some eight miles west of the heart of Paris, lay just across the Seine from Croissy, in the parish of Rueil. The name Malmaison – 'Evil House' – has been associated by some with a medieval leper hospital. If so, the association was now lost in the mists of the past. Malmaison was a venerable, former seigneurial domain of substantial proportions with pleasant vistas, farms that could be leased out for income, ample outbuildings for livestock, and vineyards that had gained some local reputation. The estate was in the hands of the Lecoulteux family – members of the former administrative nobility who had lost their money during the Revolution and who had permitted the property, both inside and outside, to become badly run-down. It was not unknown to Bonaparte, who on his return from Italy was reported to have offered 300,000 francs for it. In the spring of 1799 Josephine undertook negotiations again, using the mayor of Croissy, M. Chanorier, as her agent, and relying also on the expert help of her old Parisian adviser, M. Raguideau. After much haggling the price was brought down from 300,000 francs to 225,000 francs, with extra sums to be paid for the furnishings and for other rights raising the total to more than 271,000 francs. When the contract was signed on 21 April 1799 Josephine did not have the funds to make even a token down-payment. She was forced, consequently, to borrow 15,000 francs from the estate steward for this purpose, so that with his obliging assistance the transaction was sealed. However dilapidated and unfashionable the furnishings of Malmaison then seemed, Josephine was sure that the near future would make possible an almost magical transformation. And Bonaparte could foot the bills.

Josephine entered into possession with mixed feelings. 'Since I have become a country-dweller,' she wrote to Barras in September with mock concern, 'I have become so uncivilized that the fashionable world frightens me.'[27] Her concern turned out to be short-lived. Soon remodelled at heavy expense, Malmaison grew in beauty and comfort until its quiet elegance furnished the setting for some of Josephine's most precious hours.

❧ 13 ❧

Mistress of the Tuileries

ONE evening in October 1799, Josephine dined with Gohier, president of the Directory, and his wife in their apartment in the Luxembourg Palace. Gohier had been a moderate in the early years of the Revolution; he had also been astute, with the consequence that he had finally reached his present exalted station. Josephine and his wife (who once had been his cook) had become close friends. During the dinner dramatic news, not altogether unexpected, was brought to them. The 'military telegraph' – a recently developed device that sent visible signals in simple semaphore code from one hilltop to another and could span France in two days – reported that General Bonaparte had landed on the south coast of France. Aware of the troubled situation at home and eager to profit from it, he had left his army under General Kléber to languish on the sands of Egypt, where two years later it surrendered to the English. Accompanied only by a few intimates, Bonaparte had risked the dangerous Mediterranean crossing and after a sixteen-day voyage, which more than once brought glimpses of British sails on the horizon, had arrived safely at Fréjus.

He was returning to an explosive world. The unsavoury intrigues in the life of Josephine were but a pale reflection of other intrigues carried out on a national scale by politicians, soldiers, and businessmen. The Constitution of 1795 – that work of caution intended to give the country stability after six years of revolution – had proved vastly disappointing. The two elected chambers were crowded with nonentities; the ministries were corrupt; and the board of five directors wielding executive power lurched from crisis to crisis, never knowing when a sudden coup would remove one or other of its members. In Paris, Jacobin groups had begun to reappear. This dark picture had some mitigating features, for the country had weathered the worst economic storms and some important technical reforms were under way. Even so, the actual régime smelled of decay. One ambitious politician manoeuvred to outwit another, and for many it seemed that the strong hand of the soldier would give the only solution to the political problem.

The general foreign situation was alarming. War had been resumed in the preceding March, so that France was now threatened by a Second Coalition. One Austrian army was advancing in Germany through the Black Forest. Another, supported by Russian divisions and commanded by the brilliant general Suvorov, overran northern Italy, drove out the French, and entered Milan, where Cossack cavalry appeared on the recent scene of some of Bonaparte's greatest triumphs. Another Russian army had invaded eastern Switzerland and in August had seized Zurich. These were dangers that now called for drastic action.

Josephine quickly declared to Gohier that her husband's return would be no threat to liberty – an involuntary recognition, surely, of the widely felt concern over what a victorious general might do. Equally revealing were her further admissions: she had nothing to fear, she said, from calumny, but she must at all costs reach Bonaparte before his brothers did, since these men – 'who have always detested me' – could do her great harm. She told Gohier, moreover, that Bonaparte would be grateful to know she had always been welcome in this director's house.[1]

Thereupon Josephine and Hortense set out for a rendezvous with Napoleon, driving southward at top speed to the meeting that would enable Josephine to counteract the wagging tongues of Paris and make amends for the long silence that the breach in communications with Egypt had imposed. The wife of Napoleon's secretary, Bourrienne, had likewise been notified of her husband's return to France and drove northward towards Paris to await him there. In so doing she met the carriage of Josephine and Hortense, driving south. As mother and daughter were both asleep, Madame Bourrienne did not awaken them. One is left simply with a tiny vignette of urgent feminine traffic on the highroad to Paris.

Josephine's luck was against her. She took the easterly route through Burgundy, while Bonaparte, heading northward, branched off at Lyons and took the other highroad to Paris, one that lay somewhat farther to the west. It was impossible, therefore, for the pair to meet. At Lyons Josephine received definite information that her husband had already passed this point and would actually by then be in Paris. So she could do nothing but turn back, with the gnawing realization that in addition to her long silence and to whatever rumours may have arisen about her behaviour, Bonaparte now could reproach her with the crushing fact that she was absent from Paris at the climactic moment of his homecoming.

Bonaparte's journey through France had been a triumphant progress. Crowds hailed him in the towns through which he passed; in some places torches illuminated the highways. Eugène, who was with him, described the reception at Lyons as delirious. Yet these were hollow triumphs. On 16 October Bonaparte reached his home on the rue de la Victoire, only to be devastated by anticlimax and disappointment. Josephine had gone, and two days were to elapse before his unlucky, unhappy, and exhausted wife could rejoin him.

Back in Paris, Josephine found no quick way to melt her husband's heart. The door of Bonaparte's bedroom remained locked, and no amount of appeals or protestations, no floods of tears, could open it. Madame Junot gives us a picture of a grief-stricken Josephine extended full length on a small back stairs, after hours of entreaty, 'suffering the acutest pangs of mental torture'. A maid, the faithful Agatha Rible, suggested that Josephine strengthen the assault by mobilizing the efforts of the two children. Hortense's tears we can easily imagine; yet it strains credulity, surely, to believe that Eugène, newly returned from Egypt and by now a veteran of desert battle who had been wounded in the head as he fought in Syria, could have joined in such an onslaught. In the end, predictably, Josephine was the victor. Napoleon received his wife in the bedroom, where his brother Lucien, making his visit late on the following day, still found them.

Josephine had won a victory over her husband and also over the entire Bonaparte clan.

Whatever might be his wife's errors [Madame Junot wrote], Bonaparte appeared entirely to forget them, and the reconciliation was complete. Of all the members of the family, Madame Leclerc [Pauline] was most vexed at the pardon which Napoleon had granted to his wife. Bonaparte's mother was also very ill-pleased; but she said nothing. Madame Joseph Bonaparte [Julie Clary], who was always very amiable, took no part in these family quarrels; therefore she could easily determine what part to take when fortune smiled on Josephine. As to Madame Bacciocchi [Elisa] she gave free vent to her ill-humour and disdain; the consequence was that her sister-in-law could never endure her . . . Caroline was so young that her opinion could have no weight in such an affair. As to Bonaparte's brothers, they were at open war with Josephine.[2]

Now reconciled with Napoleon, Josephine soon found herself involved in one of the great coups of history. In this late autumn of 1799 an elaborate plot was devised that was to make her husband master of France; one consequence of this was that Josephine would sit beside him in semi-regal state as mistress of the Tuileries. This Coup of Brumaire, carried out by a small group of ruthless men in the foggy November month of the Republican calendar, is a classic example of how a determined minority, backed by the bayonets of obedient soldiers, can overthrow a spineless régime.

Many politicians had thought of organizing such a coup, and Bonaparte was only one of several generals whom they had in mind to help them overthrow the outworn Directory. Among the five directors Barras had quite clearly outlived his usefulness. Three others were nonentities. The fifth, Sieyès, had considerable hopes that he could manoeuvre power into his own hands. Sieyès was an extraordinary character – a former priest and ex-Jacobin, author of one of the most famous revolutionary pamphlets of 1789, and an inveterate phrase-maker. He had survived the storm of revolution for ten years, had recently been elected director, and now saw in General Bonaparte the man of the hour. To be certain of his own

prominent role when the crisis came Sieyès quietly began to
take riding lessons, for the day would arrive, he assumed, when
he would be called on to ride triumphantly with Bonaparte's
cavalcade through the streets of Paris.

Although Bonaparte had deliberately worn civilian clothes
on his return from Egypt, he neglected few dramatic effects.
On occasions he wore a Turkish fez and carried a scimitar
underneath his green civilian overcoat. He attended the
meetings of the Institute where he spoke learnedly of the
antiquities of Egypt. He subscribed to every newspaper in
Paris, and constantly widened his circle of friends. The salon
of the house in the rue de la Victoire saw a steady stream of
soldiers and politicians – men interested, like him, in a change
of régime. On these occasions, Josephine's role was that of
the gracious hostess; she engaged one group after another
with pleasant nothings while her husband's political discussions proceeded.

Gradually the plot crystallized. In addition to Sieyès, only
one other director, Roger-Ducos, could be considered safe.
If the remaining three, Barras, Gohier, and Moulin, could be
compelled to resign, then an appeal (backed by bayonets) could
be made to the legislative branch and a provisional new régime
be appointed. This new régime, if Bonaparte were the head of
it, would have an unrivalled opportunity to give France the
leadership and discipline it so sorely needed. In addition to
Bonaparte's loyal brother-officers a few prominent civilian
figures were to be drawn in. Notable among these were Cambacérès, the distinguished minister of justice; Talleyrand, at
the Ministry of Foreign Affairs; Joseph Fouché, an ex-terrorist
who had become minister of police; and Napoleon's own
brother, Lucien, now most fortunately serving as president of
the Council of Five Hundred. The date of the coup was fixed
for the 18th of Brumaire (9 November 1799).

On the day preceding the coup Josephine wrote to her good
friend Gohier, one of the uncertain members of the Directory,
in the following cordial terms:

Will you, my dear Gohier, and your wife have breakfast with me
tomorrow at eight o'clock in the morning? Do not fail; I must

speak to you about very interesting matters. Farewell, my dear Gohier, count always on my sincere friendship.[3]

What Gohier could have counted on in addition to 'sincere friendship', had he accepted the invitation, would have been detention at the point of a bayonet followed by the loss of his job. He did not rise to the bait. Guarding his own immediate freedom of action, he sent his wife instead, who on arriving found, not breakfast, but a house crowded with soldiers. Gohier soon learned from her of this ominous gathering of military men and at once informed the other directors. For them, however, it was now too late. Sieyès, who was in the plot, had been up since dawn, taking his last riding lesson, for which, as it turned out, he would have absolutely no use.

Josephine the Conspirator

Since seven o'clock on that fateful morning Josephine's salon had been so crowded with Napoleon's brother-officers that late arrivals were obliged to stand in the courtyard outside. By a very ingenious trick the members of the Council of Ancients had been summoned to meet at the Tuileries, but the instructions were so issued that unsympathetic members received their notices only after the others had met and the voting was over. Those who did assemble were informed by Bonaparte of an entirely fictitious Jacobin conspiracy and at once obligingly voted two decrees. One of them appointed Bonaparte commander of all the armed forces of the capital; the other required the two assemblies to adjourn and transfer their meetings next day from Paris to the suburban château of Saint-Cloud, ostensibly to be away from the dangers of the Paris mob.

The directors were quickly brought under control. Talleyrand, who turned up among the earliest at the rue de la Victoire, was sent by Bonaparte to obtain the resignation of Josephine's old friend, Barras. He was provided with ample funds which he was to use, if necessary, to speed Barras' resignation. The bribe was not needed, so that Talleyrand, true to form, ended the morning that much the richer. Realizing the situation, Barras had at once signed the letter Bonaparte prepared for him and retired to his country estate. Here this figure – 'unrestrained in his pleasures', 'rotten with vice', 'corrupt to the marrow' (some of the phrases that have been used to describe him) – built up his hostility to Napoleon and in good time produced those memoirs in which he spewed his venom against Josephine, adding to the little tale of scandal which he knew only too well many repulsive fabrications of his own. Josephine had lost a lover and patron and acquired her most vicious enemy. Of the other directors, Gohier and Moulin were simply bullied into submission, while Sieyès and Ducos, actually with little to do, were counted as supporters of the plot. Thus, when Bonaparte returned home to Josephine he was able to tell her, like a businessman at the end of a strenuous day, that things were going well.

The truly critical events remained for the morrow, since it was then necessary for Bonaparte to appear at Saint-Cloud, in his new capacity as military commander of Paris, to warn the Council of Ancients and the Council of Five Hundred of the 'Jacobin dangers' in the city, by this means obtaining their authorization to create a new provisional government. When the moment came, his appearance before the Ancients proved to be a near fiasco. The young soldier's oratory did not rise to the occasion; what should have been an eloquent harangue turned into an embarrassing business of question and answer in which he tried awkwardly to counter the charges and accusations the suspicious members flung at him. Bourrienne, who sat beside Bonaparte, truly described the episode as a confused conversation devoid both of dignity and sense. Tugging at the general's coat, he at last quietly persuaded his master to withdraw.

At this critical moment of tension Bonaparte found time to have Bourrienne send off an express messenger to Josephine assuring her once again that all was going well. The immediate sequel disproved him. The encounter with the Council of Five Hundred at the *orangerie* of Saint-Cloud, despite the help of brother Lucien, proved even worse than in the Council of the Ancients. In the remodelled *orangerie* the legislators received him with a wild tumult of reproaches. Resplendent in their red togas – those classic garments by means of which they vainly sought to reproduce the ancient dignity of the Roman republic – the members flung charges of dictator and tyrant at Bonaparte. Unable to speak above the din, he was in actual danger of being mobbed, when his brother and a few guards at last managed to get him out of the hall.

Lucien, as much as Bonaparte, won the day, for he harangued the grenadiers stationed outside and urged them to go in and expel the deputies by force. General Murat and General Leclerc – the two brothers-in-law of Napoleon – then led in their troops. The naked bayonets did the trick, and the deputies stayed no longer. They fled through the long casement windows of the *orangerie*, rushing across the lawns and scattering their red togas on the rose bushes of the park as they dispersed in the gathering gloom. Enough of the members were later brought back to join with the Ancients in a feeble pretence at legality. They declared an end to the Directory and appointed Bonaparte, Sieyès, and Ducos as provisory consuls. These three were to govern during the crisis and to set to work upon a new constitution.

Towards midnight Eugène was instructed to carry the good

news to Josephine. By the narrowest of margins and by the ruthless threat of force one of the great coups of history had succeeded. Bonaparte had become master of France.

Five days after the Coup of Brumaire Bonaparte and Josephine took their leave of the house that had been their home for nearly four years. The pink roses, the mirrors, and the cupids of the rue de la Victoire made up a décor singularly inappropriate for the new master of France. His official residence was now to be the Luxembourg, that splendid palace built nearly two centuries earlier by the order of Marie de Medicis, the Italian wife of Henry IV.

The Revolution, to be sure, had sadly dimmed the splendours of this royal residence. Louis XVI and Marie Antoinette had been confined there in 1792 when monarchy fell. Under the Terror it had become a prison, counting among its inmates Camille Desmoulins, Danton, and the Englishman, Tom Paine. When it was turned over to the directors in 1795 it gave the impression of a vast, dilapidated barracks – chill, neglected, and almost empty of furniture. The directors were each allotted an apartment where they lived at first in Spartan simplicity. Barras, however, soon set the tone of ostentatious luxury, and so Josephine in the course of her visits to him and to Gohier had already found opportunity to familiarize herself with these new surroundings. She and her husband were now housed in the wing to the right of the main entrance known as the Petit Luxembourg, overlooking the rue Vaugirard. In taking up residence here, Josephine was not far from a building which held grim memories. Less than half a mile away, on the same rue Vaugirard, stood the former convent of the Carmelites, where only six years earlier Josephine and Alexander de Beauharnais had been imprisoned. From here her husband had gone forth to the guillotine and here she had sat in a reeking cell expecting death at any moment.

All this was now a distant nightmare, almost lost in the past. Little question remained of Bonaparte's overwhelming powers. A new constitution, quickly completed under his direction, specifically named Bonaparte, Cambacérès, and Lebrun as consuls and placed all decisive authority in their hands. More precisely, it gave ultimate power to Bonaparte. The other two consuls had at best a consultative voice. They were to sign a register to indicate their presence, and could record in it, if they desired, their opinions on any issue; 'after which,' so ran Article 24, 'the decision of the first Consul shall suffice.'

In the Petit Luxembourg Bonaparte had his suite of rooms on the ground floor, where he immersed himself in a flood of public activities. Josephine's apartments were directly above his. Their stay in these once royal quarters proved short – a mere three months – for Bonaparte had much more splendid plans in mind. Even in these transient days, however, there was work for Josephine to do. Although he had no intention that his wife should play a political role, the first consul wished her to serve as his graceful hostess, one who could restore to France something of the dignity and polish the Revolution had so savagely destroyed. She did what she could in the face of difficulties, some of which Bonaparte himself created. When guests were invited to luncheon, they soon found that the first consul would not tolerate a long stay at the table. He was always served first, so that he would often finish a course before the last guest had unfolded his napkin. Guests had no chance to catch up, for the main dish would quickly be followed by a simple dessert. In fifteen or twenty minutes the first consul would be through with his mushrooms, pastry, and wine, and the guests, finished or not, would then have to leave the table with him.

Quite generally a new tone came over public life. The titles, *monsieur* and *madame*, replaced the Revolutionary terms, *citoyen* and *citoyenne*; the use of *vous* came back in place of the more familiar *tu*; and at the Luxembourg it became increasingly common to address the first consul as 'Your Highness'. Something was done, too, about women's dress. Bonaparte made it clear that domestic silks and satins were more desirable than the diaphanous imported fabrics of the scandalous Directory years. On one occasion when he disapproved of the extreme décolletage of some of his guests at a reception, he ostentatiously ordered the servants to throw more wood on the fires, loudly expressing his fears lest the 'half-naked' guests should freeze. In view of the rough, barrack-room manners of Bonaparte's brother-generals, such changes in dress and manners did not come easily – yet changes there were, and the effects were noticeable. 'It was not exactly a court,' the Princess Dolgoruki said of this society, 'but it was no longer a camp.'[4]

Josephine was breaking with her past and trying to heal recent wounds. Within a few weeks of moving into the Luxembourg she wrote to a certain Lagrange in Paris, a man who had been one of her financial agents. She told him that she was now terminating her interest in companies supplying equipment to the army, and asked him to wind up her affairs. He was, she warned him, to use 'all the discretion and delicacy' of which he was capable.[5] As wife of the first consul it was now her business to contribute in what small ways she could to a general relaxation of tensions. She coaxed Gohier, the ex-director, into accepting a position in the new régime, after his having been unceremoniously retired with the old. The *Moniteur* recounted that during his scuffle with the deputies in the *orangerie* at Saint-Cloud on the day of 19 Brumaire Napoleon had been shielded by a grenadier from the blow of a dagger, and that this grenadier, Thomas Thomé, had had the sleeve of his tunic torn. Thomas was therefore invited to breakfast and dinner at the Luxembourg, where the ever-sympathetic Josephine embraced him and generously put on his finger a diamond ring worth two thousand crowns.

The haphazard, disreputable society that had flourished under the Directory no longer was tolerated. A letter of invitation was necessary before guests could be received at the Luxembourg. Josephine, once so self-indulgent, learned to accommodate herself rigorously to the wishes of her husband. She dressed to please him, and she managed somehow to be punctual, so that if on the spur of the moment Bonaparte decided to go to Malmaison, then Josephine, radiating charm, was invariably ready to accompany him. She was aware of the hostility of Napoleon's mother. Letizia Bonaparte was stubbornly determined to maintain her position as head of the family and consequently she resented Josephine's new prestige. Josephine managed at least to save the appearances. Especially in the presence of Napoleon she gave way to 'Madame Mère' as gracefully as she could.

Life at the Luxembourg Palace gave Josephine her first taste of what it meant to be married to the ruler of France. To dwell thus in royal surroundings was a novel experience for her. Yet the ceremonial routines Bonaparte introduced here had no more than a temporary importance in his plans, for the soldier who had now become master of nearly thirty million people would be satisfied with nothing less than to make the Tuileries his home and to sleep in the bedchamber of the former kings of France.

Today the Tuileries are only a name, perpetuated in the splendid gardens and walks lying between the Place de la Concorde and the vast buildings of the Louvre. Reaching out to the westward from either side of the central mass of the Louvre, like huge arms, are the long buildings which terminate in two elegant Renaissance pavilions – the Pavillon de Flore overlooking the Seine, and the Pavillon de Marsan overlooking the Rue de Rivoli. Such is the picture today. In the long empty space between these pavilions once stood the historic Palace of the Tuileries, begun by the architect Delorme for Catherine de Medicis in 1563, enlarged by Henri IV and Louis XIV, and, along with the Louvre with which it was connected, a principal residence of every ruler of France until the fall of the Second Empire in 1870. Gutted by fire in the savage uprising of the Paris Commune in 1871, the melancholy ruins stood gauntly until the following decade when every blackened stone was removed and the Tuileries became a ghostly memory.

From the Tuileries Louis XVI and his family had tried to flee France in 1791. Failing in their attempt, they were returned virtually as captives. Here, on 10 August 1792 monarchy fell, as the Paris mobs butchered the devoted Swiss guards in the courtyard and then surged inside to loot and sack the royal quarters. Under the Terror the Committee of Public Safety met for a time on the ground floor in what had been Marie

Antoinette's apartments. The old royal theatre within the palace was converted into a meeting-place where the Convention sat until 1795, then making way for the Council of Ancients. Amid the hectic disorder of the republican years the whole palace had become a veritable maze of offices and whitewashed corridors. Bonaparte knew the building well, for on the fifth storey of the Pavillon de Flore was the topographical bureau of the Committee of Public Safety – the busy workshop to which he had climbed day after day in order to ready his plans for the Italian campaign of 1796. Amid the press of republican business all semblance of royal splendour had long since disappeared. To serve the crowds of hangers-on within the palace there were stalls for lemonade alongside shops selling tobacco, pastries, and patriotic prints. The public could also patronize a barber's and a draper's shop. Jostling among the endless succession of men coming and going, professional beggars plied their trade. Clearly, to reconvert such a shambles to the dignified purposes that Bonaparte intended was a major undertaking. His plan was to employ the southern half of the Tuileries lying between the central entrance and the Seine as his official residence. The northern half, away from the river, could still harbour its army of officials.

Bonaparte first summoned his architect, Lecomte, to arrange for a thorough cleaning of the apartments. Everywhere the famous republican symbol, the red cap of liberty, was painted or stencilled on the whitewashed walls. 'Get rid of all these things,' Bonaparte told Lecomte, 'I don't like to see such rubbish.'[6] In the long, upper gallery of the Tuileries he had the painter David place a fine antique bust of Brutus that had been brought from Italy. Then it occurred to him to select other busts so that he would have as a background a gallery of heroes. The choices were interesting: they included Demosthenes, Alexander, Scipio, Cicero, Cato, and Caesar. The representatives of modern times were largely soldiers: Gustavus Adolphus, Condé, Turenne, Marlborough, Prince Eugène, Marshal de Saxe, Frederick the Great, and Washington, as well as three of Bonaparte's own dead comrades, Dugommier, Dampierre, and Joubert.

Moving day which came on 19 February 1800 was blessed by a singular tribute from the French people. On the preceding day the spectacular results of the plebiscite on Bonaparte's new constitution had been announced: 3,011,007 votes were in favour of it and only 1,526 against. Under the circumstances, Bonaparte had good reason for making his departure from the Luxembourg to the Tuileries the occasion for a splendid public parade. This was largely military in nature, with a fine display of brilliantly uniformed officers, well-disciplined troops, and martial music. The civilian contribution was distinctly less impressive. Since the fine carriages and coaches of the old régime had long since disappeared, the ministers, councillors of state, and other officials rode in nondescript hackney-carriages on which the licence numbers had economically been concealed by pasting pieces of brown paper over them. Bonaparte's private carriage, in contrast, was drawn by the six splendid white horses presented to him by the Austrian emperor after the Treaty of Campo Formio, and he wore the magnificent sabre given to him at the same time. No ladies, not even Josephine, rode in the procession. The new mistress of the Tuileries had preceded her husband to the palace where, elegantly dressed and surrounded by her attendants, she watched the spectacle from the upper windows of the Pavillon de Flore. When the troops and the carriages entered the great courtyard, Bonaparte changed from his carriage to horseback for a military inspection. Standing at the main entrance to the Tuileries and surrounded by his generals, he saluted the various regimental colours, some of them already faded by the sun of Italy and Egypt, some blackened by gunpowder and torn by bullets. Then he greeted his wife within the palace where she was to make her official home for the next ten years.

Josephine's private apartments in the Tuileries were on the ground floor, lying to the left, or southern side, of the central entrance as one approached from the courtyard of the Carrousel and extending all the way to the Pavillon de Flore. Her windows did not overlook this courtyard, but faced westward in the other direction across the Tuileries gardens towards the Champs-Élysées. These gardens had become public areas and as Josephine's rooms were practically at ground level and there were no railings or protective balustrades, inquisitive Parisians could approach close enough to see and hear what was going on inside. Hence it was necessary for privacy to keep the windows closed or the curtains drawn.

Josephine occupied the ancient apartments of Marie Antoinette, rooms that were heavy with grim memories. 'I shall not be happy here,' this daughter of a Martinique planter told Hortense, 'I have dark misgivings . . . I feel as if the shadow of the queen is asking me what I am doing in her bed. There is an air of monarchy about this palace that one cannot breathe with impunity, and I am still disturbed by it.'[7]

There were even grimmer associations. Josephine's very bedroom had once served as the seat of the Committee of Public Safety – that all-powerful committee of twelve, dominated by Robespierre, which had ruled France so ruthlessly under the Terror. The two adjoining salons had been crowded with secretaries of the Committee, and the large vaulted entrance hall adjoining the Pavillon de Flore had served as a vestibule for those coming on public business. This entrance hall had witnessed the end of the greatest of the Terrorists. Here, stretched out on a table throughout the night of 27–8 July 1794 the half-conscious Robespierre had lain in ghastly agony, his roughly-bandaged jaw shattered by a pistol bullet, while the Committee within deliberated on his fate. From here he was carried to the guillotine. With such associations, the dark misgivings of Josephine are easy to understand.

Putting aside her uneasiness, Josephine undertook the congenial task of refurnishing her surroundings in a manner that soon would be known as *le style Empire*. She was not permitted to expend great sums on new creations from the cabinet-makers. Yet much could be done with upholstering and decorative details. The furniture in the first salon was covered with silk taffeta of a violet-blue colour, having honeysuckles of a chestnut colour embroidered upon it. On the wall hung a seventeenth-century painting of St Cecilia, by Domenichino. The larger, second salon was decorated with yellow and brown satin fringed with red, with which the mirrors were draped but not framed. Around the walls were console tables of porphyry and marble with vases, either of Sèvres porcelain or of rose-coloured granite with bronze decorations. The room was lighted by candles massed in crystal chandeliers. The bedroom next to it had blue-and-white striped coverings, fringed with gold, on the furniture. The mahogany bed, standing in an alcove, was very heavy, with elaborate bronze-gilt ornaments. From an adjoining *salle de bain* a small staircase led to Bonaparte's study on the floor above. Also adjoining was a small library having grilled book-cases of inlaid rose-wood. In this room hung a copy of Raphael's 'Madonna of the Chair'. The suite also included a low-ceilinged, mirrored dressing-room with embroidered muslin curtains fringed with blue and white. Near by was a room for Hortense.

On the floor above Josephine's were the rooms of the first consul – a historic suite, much grander in scale, that included the famous *cabinet de travail* so minutely described for posterity by his secretaries. Here was the imposing Gallery of Diana, employed for ceremonial receptions, as well as other salons appropriate to the dignity of the new master of France. In such a setting Bonaparte was already assuming a semi-imperial air. Josephine, on the other hand, hesitated to accept the full burden of so much grandeur, and for this reason the Tuileries could never hold the place in her heart that the rustic beauty of Malmaison so easily commanded.

❖ 14 ❖

The Consulate

JOSEPHINE became mistress of the Tuileries in her thirty-seventh year. Elegant, affable, and worldly-wise, she had now reached the very centre of a world that was separated from the island life of her childhood by far more than mere time or distance. The inexperienced girl who just twenty years before had come almost penniless from Martinique had grown into a woman who commanded an obeisance from every lady in France. Yet there is no tedium like the tedium of greatness, and as life became more splendid it also became less dramatic. The intense personal excitement Josephine had known in the revolutionary years was now followed by a new career dominated by set patterns of ceremony and decorum, and acted out in the full glare of publicity in the salons of the Consulate and on the throne of imperial France.

Josephine and Napoleon began to settle down to a life of mutual accommodation, in which each understood the other far better than ever before. The fires that had burned so fiercely in the young soldier's letters had subsided, even as the once raffish behaviour of Josephine was put aside in face of the conventional demands of her new position. The relations of the two came to be marked by a genuine, comfortable affection, and by a recognition on the part of Napoleon that Josephine had a role to play in the new France that was taking shape. Thus, the interest and meaning of these years of the Consulate arise not so much from what Josephine did as from what she was. In an official society where for nearly a decade women had had no place she now brought her own unforgettable charm.

The ceremonial of the Tuileries was at first relatively simple. Dressed in the new consular uniform he devised – a scarlet tunic with gold embroidery – Bonaparte would receive members of the diplomatic corps twice monthly. At regular intervals other receptions were held for the senators, the members of the legislature, the generals, and high public officials. The guests would be formally presented to him, then conducted downstairs from the audience-chamber to Josephine's apartments for a less formal greeting. Every ten days, precisely at noon, there would be a sparkling review of troops in the great courtyard of the Tuileries – the Carrousel. Every ten days, too, there was a formal dinner in the Gallery of Diana, sometimes with as many as two hundred attending. Napoleon drew his guests from the official world, for quite sensibly he chose to recognize and honour those who served him. He could hardly as yet turn to the nobility of the old régime, who in large numbers were now coming back to France, and he quite definitely wished to get away from the unattractive adventurers who had elbowed their way to the forefront under the Directory.

A typical evening reception held by Josephine in the salons of the Tuileries at this period can be reconstructed from the vivid *Memoirs* of Bonaparte's valet, Constant. On these occasions, beginning at eight in the evening the apartments of Madame Bonaparte, which were situated on the ground floor overlooking the gardens, would be crowded with company. A dazzling display of splendid dresses, feathers, and diamonds was provided by the throng who so packed the salons that it was found necessary to throw open Josephine's bedroom to relieve the crush. When, after considerable embarrassment and trouble, the company had been arranged as well as possible, Madame Bonaparte was announced and would enter, conducted by Talleyrand. She usually chose to wear a dress of white muslin with short sleeves, and a pearl necklace, and she had her hair simply braided and confined by a tortoiseshell comb. The buzz of admiration that greeted her entrance must have been extremely gratifying, so Constant thought, noting further that at these times she was invariably at her most graceful and most elegant.

Still holding Madame Bonaparte by the hand, Talleyrand

would present the members of the *corps diplomatique* to her, one after another, not mentioning them by name but designating the courts they represented. He then conducted her through the two drawing-rooms. As he was doing this, the first consul would enter unannounced. His dress for such occasions consisted of a very plain uniform coat, white woollen breeches, and top boots. Round his waist he wore a tricoloured silk scarf with a matching fringe, and in his hand he carried his soldier's black hat. He would move quickly through the company, his simple costume making a striking contrast to the embroidered coats, the cordons, and the jewels of the ambassadors and foreign dignitaries, even as the simple charm of Josephine's dress gave her distinction amid the splendour of the ladies surrounding her.

Josephine moved easily and smoothly in this new life of formality, where her natural flair helped to make the transition less difficult. Just as the first consul now equipped himself with an intendant and four prefects of the palace, so also Josephine had her ladies-in-waiting to give dignity and substance to her position. Her preferences were for those who had already known the society of the *ancien régime*. Madame Campan, for example, once the companion of Marie Antoinette and later the founder of the school at Saint-Germain that Hortense had attended, came frequently to the Tuileries. From her Josephine obtained much advice on fine points of ceremony. Other familiars were Madame de la Tour du Pin, Madame de Valence, and Madame de Montesson, all of them substantial representatives of the old order. The most prominent of this group was the former Marquise de Montesson, who thirty years before had become the morganatic wife of the Duke d'Orléans, great-grandnephew of Louis XIV. Josephine had come to know her at the summer resort of Plombières. Now elderly, Madame de Montesson opened a salon in Paris that recaptured much of the elegance of the old régime, and in her person something of the very flavour of royalty returned to the Tuileries. Gentlemen first reappeared in silk stockings and buckled shoes in her salon, and her servants were the first to resume the liveries that had been forbidden during the Revolution. Josephine warmed to such society, and in this elegant atmosphere of aristocratic good feeling declared to Madame de la Tour du Pin that it was her wish, and also her husband's, to end the sufferings of bygone years and bring reassurance to all.

Informal occasions, perhaps even more than formal, saw Josephine at her best. Devoted to the theatre, she went whenever she could. Pleasant little gatherings would often follow these excursions, at which the guests who were invited to the yellow salon of the Tuileries would find Josephine happily chattering, embroidering, playing whist or backgammon, and occasionally joining her husband and his friends at billiards. Bonaparte, who always worked at a furious pace throughout the day, found these late affairs very tiring and would sometimes leave in order to go to bed. Josephine would then excuse herself, ascend to her husband's apartments, and sitting at the foot of his bed would read to him in her melodious voice until, like a child, he was nearly asleep. Then she would return to her company. There seems no reason to quarrel with the verdict of the valet, Constant. Servants passing in a corridor, he said, would stop to admire the very tones of her voice. The sceptic, to be sure, might well think of a less flattering and more calculating reason for their eavesdropping. Even so, Constant's words deserve to be recorded. 'People spoke as one,' he recalled, 'of the perfect grace, the skill both natural and cultivated, which was displayed by Josephine in the salons of the Consulate.'[1]

Reconciliation with members of the old aristocracy, however well-intentioned, had its dangers. Not all these men were prepared to accept the consular régime. Innocent of any desire for political intrigue, Josephine nevertheless became associated with certain pressures from abroad to bring back the monarchy. The two brothers of the guillotined Louis XVI had emigrated, and the elder, then known as the Count de Lille and later to become Louis XVIII, nursed the vain hope that General Bonaparte would do what General Monk had done in England at the end of the Cromwellian period – help in the restoration of an exiled monarchy. In February 1800, and again in June, he wrote to Bonaparte from Warsaw appealing for assistance. The first consul sent a famous and shattering reply for which the future Louis XVIII never forgave him:

You must no longer look forward to your return to France [Bonaparte wrote harshly]. Your path would assuredly lie over one hundred thousand corpses. Sacrifice your personal interests to the peace and happiness of France. History will record its gratitude to you for doing so . . . I am not insensible to the misfortunes of your family and I will gladly do what I can for your peace and repose in your retirement.[2]

Thoroughly rebuffed by Bonaparte, the Bourbons still thought of Josephine. The Count de Lille had many sympathizers in France, among them the former Marquis de Clermont-Gallerande, member of a royalist committee in Paris that secretly hoped to bring back the monarchy. Josephine had long been regarded by Clermont-Gallerande as a royalist – and some of her friendships during the revolutionary years would certainly give colour to his belief. Such information was passed on to the brother of Louis XVI. 'The support which she gives to those of my faithful subjects who have recourse to her,' the Count de Lille declared, 'entitles her to the name, *Angel of Goodness*, which you have given her. Convey my regards, therefore, to Madame Bonaparte. They will not surprise her; on the contrary, unless I am much mistaken she will be happy to receive them.'[3]

Josephine may well have had strong personal sympathies with the royalists, for much in her background would lead her in their direction, and certainly from her own experiences she had little reason to love the Revolution. She might even argue selfishly that there would be, theoretically, a safer future if her husband were 'mayor of the palace' on the steps of a legitimate throne. The man who seizes power by the sword is always in danger of losing it by the sword. Yet to argue in this way is to misunderstand Bonaparte completely, and Josephine was by now close enough to the centre of great events to have some sense of his unique qualities. What she could do, and what she did do in full measure, was to give her help and sympathy to the growing number of *émigrés* who, having left

France during the Revolution, now wished to return. Most of them were in difficulties because they were still included among the hundred thousand names of those who had been declared enemies of the Republic. Such people had forfeited their property and their civil rights. Bonaparte had seen to it that these lists were now closed, yet official action was necessary to have anyone struck off. Josephine had a long history of willingness to do favours, and now letter after letter indicated how eagerly such *émigrés*, or their good republican friends, petitioned her, and how generously she responded. 'Madame Bonaparte has the honour to convey her compliments to Messieurs de Villeneuve,' so reads a typical letter of June 1800, 'and to inform them that they have been stricken from the lists.'[4] Another letter revives the name of Jérôme Calmelet, old friend, financial adviser, and witness at Josephine's wedding to Napoleon:

> Calmelet has the honour to present his compliments to Citizen Fontenay. On the day before yesterday he managed to give the letter to Madame Bonaparte who has promised to say a word about it to her husband. Citizen Fontenay will know the outcome very promptly.[5]

There were, to be sure, royalists and royalists. Many, accepting the new régime with whatever grace they could muster, were grateful to Josephine for her help and friendship. Others were of a different sort, and nothing that Josephine did could prevent the extremists from attempting to solve their problems by violence. In October 1800 a plot to assassinate Bonaparte while he attended the opera was uncovered. Four conspirators were executed. On the following Christmas Eve, Bonaparte and Josephine had an even narrower escape from assassination. Their party had set out in several carriages from the Tuileries to attend a performance of Haydn's *Creation* at the Opéra. En route they found the street blocked by a wagon with a large barrel lashed to it. This was the famous 'infernal machine' – an innocent-looking barrel packed with gunpowder and grapeshot and having a lighted fuse. The escort did not notice the fuse and simply pushed the wagon aside. Napoleon, riding in the first carriage with three of his generals, passed safely by. Josephine was some distance behind him with her daughter and her sister-in-law, Caroline, and thus she and her party were nearer the explosion that seconds afterwards killed twenty spectators and injured sixty. The ladies were prostrate with fright and Hortense was cut by flying glass. Despite all terror the party proceeded to the Opéra, where Bonaparte received an ovation and Josephine controlled herself as best she could in the face of this alarming evidence of opposition to the new order.

Although the consular régime had been welcomed in France with the hope that it would bring peace to a war-weary country, in the year 1800 new crises began to blow up. The Second Coalition was growing in strength, the military situation in Italy was becoming catastrophic, and other dangers threatened in Switzerland and Germany. Within a few months of his seizure of power, Bonaparte determined to assume the Italian command in person and, as in 1797, to shatter an enemy coalition by the speed and unexpectedness of his manoeuvres. For the third time in four years he was obliged to leave his wife and meet the challenge of war.

Setting out from Paris on 6 May, he reached Geneva in three days and from there sent to Josephine the first of a series of letters, warm and cordial enough, yet lacking the fire he had shown in 1796 and 1797:

I am at Geneva, my dear [he wrote in the first]. I shall leave to-night. I have received your letter of 16 April. I love you very much. I wish you to write to me often and to remain convinced that my Josephine is very dear to me.[6]

From Lausanne he wrote simply that his health was good, that the country was beautiful, and that perhaps in two or three weeks Josephine could set out to join him. If she did so, she would have to travel incognito and be certain to reveal none of his plans.

Bonaparte had reason for secrecy, for he was about to confront the Austrians with one of his most dramatic surprises. Making the circuit of Lake Geneva, he pushed south into the Valais and in this way approached the Great St Bernard Pass. Here, in an exploit immortalized in David's painting, he led over the Alps an army of thirty thousand men, practically in single file, scrambling upwards until the mountain paths became so steep and narrow that wheeled traffic was impossible and cannons had to be dragged through the snow and ice on sleds or hollowed-out logs. The sequel was to be another triumphant campaign in the familiar plains of Lombardy. With the crossing of the Alps so masterfully achieved, an understandable elation took possession of Bonaparte. En route to Milan he wrote Josephine a letter in which, despite his staccato, string-of-sausage style of prose, something of his old ardour reappeared:

I am in bed. I leave in an hour for Verseille. Murat should be at Novara by tonight. The enemy is greatly demoralized. He still doesn't know where we are.

I hope within ten days to be in the arms of my Josephine, who is always very good when she doesn't weep or act the coquette. Your son arrived tonight. I have visited him; he is well. A thousand tendernesses. I have received the letter from Hortense. By the next courier I shall send her a box of very good cherries.[7]

Since the military plans were moving so smoothly, Bonaparte had every reason for confidence. From Milan he wrote to say that because he would be in Paris within a month there was no need for Josephine to come to headquarters. Events soon proved him an expert prophet, for on the fourteenth of June he won the spectacular victory of Marengo, a single engagement that effectively destroyed Austrian power in northern Italy. 'My first laurel must be for my country, my second will be for you,' he wrote exultantly to his wife. Despite the behaviour that had caused him so many sorrows she still had the power to move him. 'In attacking Alvinzi [the Austrian commander] I thought of France; when he was beaten I thought of you.'[8]

More than purely military calculations were involved in Bonaparte's decision that Josephine should not come to Italy. Even before the victory of Marengo, Madame Grassini, the twenty-seven-year-old prima donna of La Scala had sung for him in Milan. That superb voice, the finest in Italy, now stirred Bonaparte more deeply than it had three years before when he first heard it at Mombello. When La Grassini was invited to visit his headquarters she eagerly responded, and in a manner far more discreet than had been the case with Madame Fourès in Egypt, Bonaparte made his conquest. It was arranged that Madame Grassini should precede Bonaparte to Paris for an appearance at the Theatre of the Republic. Lucien Bonaparte, Napoleon's minister of the interior, was formally instructed to have prepared the words and music for an Italian duet that Grassini and the tenor Bianchi would sing on the national festival of 14 July – a duet celebrating 'the deliverance of the Cisalpine Republic and the glory of our arms'.[9]

All this was done and even more, for in August Grassini sang again in the church of the Invalides, now the Temple of Mars, in honour of the great victory of Marengo. Yet the prima donna was but a minor disturbance in the main currents of Bonaparte's life. She seems to have resented how little attention Bonaparte found time to pay her on his return to Paris, and soon turned from him to Rode, a well-known violinist. Some transient attachment between the pair remained, however, enough so that two years later Josephine wrote to a friend on the occasion of one of Grassini's visits to Paris as follows:

I am very unhappy, my dear. Every day Bonaparte makes scenes without giving any explanation. This is no way to live. I have tried to find out what could be the reason and I have learned that for the past eight days La Grassini has been in Paris. It seems that she is the cause of all the unhappiness I experience. I assure you, my dear, that if I had been at fault in any way I would tell you. You would be doing me a favour if you would send Julie [a maid] to see if he is visiting anyone. Try also to learn where this woman is staying.[10]

This, to be sure, is looking ahead, and during the first year of the consulate after Bonaparte's return from Italy life at the Tuileries proceeded on an amicable and affectionate basis.

Josephine found considerable pleasure in renewing her summer visits to the pine woods and the mineral waters of

Plombières. She went without her husband, as well she might, for the imagination boggles at the thought of Bonaparte in that atmosphere of sulphur water, embroidering, and trivial gossip. In Josephine's case, however, there were what she might well consider legitimate and substantial reasons for her going. Joseph Bonaparte's wife, Julie Clary, who had been childless for six years, took the waters of Plombières and in the following year triumphantly bore her husband a daughter. Josephine could have some reason to hope that her failure to bear Napoleon a child could meet the same happy solution as had been the case with Julie. To Plombières, therefore, she made her pilgrimage in the summer of 1801 with a company that included Hortense, Madame Lavalette, and Napoleon's mother (surely an incompatible member of this holiday group).

During her absence Bonaparte regaled his wife with the timeless trivialities penned by the husband who remains behind:

The weather is so bad here that I am staying in Paris. Malmaison without you is too melancholy. The festival [14 July] was fine though it tired me somewhat. The plaster which has been put on my arm is causing me to suffer greatly. I have received some plants for you from London and have sent them to your gardener. If the weather is as bad at Plombières as it is here you must be very uncomfortable. A thousand amiable greetings to *maman* and to Hortense.[11]

The weather was good enough at Plombières for Josephine to enjoy her stay thoroughly. On her return journey, too, she and her party were royally treated when they passed through Nancy. The town offered her a civic reception and a dinner, following which the company attended a play and a ball. Travel, for Josephine, had now become in almost all respects a kind of royal progress, and there is every reason to think she liked it.

Josephine's domestic affairs were soon affected by matters of public policy. When she moved into the Tuileries her daughter was seventeen. Though seldom described as actually beautiful, Hortense was intelligent and amiable, with a considerable talent for theatricals. At her age marriage was the obvious next step. In the last year of the Directory Josephine had enlisted the aid of Barras in seeking a wedding with the son of Reubell, an old Jacobin and one of the original directors. This plan had not materialized. Hortense then had a passing infatuation for one of Bonaparte's aides, Duroc, yet it was clear that the choice of her partner would have to be based on other reasons than infatuation and made by other persons than herself. Josephine's intention now was that Hortense should marry Napoleon's younger brother, Louis, and her reasons for this unlikely choice take us directly into Bonaparte family politics.

As we know, the Bonaparte clan had never looked favourably upon Josephine. While Napoleon's prestige and power steadily rose, it was natural for his brothers and sisters to think of the future in terms of their own family interests. Bonaparte was a soldier, to whom the hand of Death could beckon at any moment. Joseph, who was older than Napoleon, and Lucien, who was the next younger, had both engaged in an intrigue for the control of the succession. This Conspiracy of Marengo took shape in the year 1800. The brothers were prepared to accept Napoleon's lifetime rule on the assumption that Joseph, and then Lucien, would be next in line. A small brochure, urging the need for a 'succession' and entitled, *Parallel Between Caesar, Cromwell, and Bonaparte*, appeared in October; its anonymous author was Lucien Bonaparte.

Josephine was aware of this family hostility, and also that her childlessness might possibly lead her husband to divorce her and remarry. If she could not give Napoleon an heir, she might boldly destroy the plans of the brotherly opposition by having Hortense marry into their number. Therefore she undertook to encourage a marriage between Hortense and Louis. There were complications, however, because for a time in 1798 Louis had shown an interest in Josephine's niece, Emilie de Beauharnais. Emilie, as we have seen, was removed from the picture by being married to Antoine de Lavalette. Louis once more became available, and Josephine's plans fitted in well with the fact that Louis, nine years younger than

Napoleon, was a great favourite of the first consul, and owed to him his education and his military advancement. 'We have no need to torture our brains in looking for a successor,' Bonaparte told his secretary, Stanislas de Girardin. 'I have found one in Louis. He has none of the defects of his brothers and all their virtues,'[12] So generous an evaluation of Louis unmistakably demonstrated a blind spot on the part of Napoleon, however much we may credit him with a warmth of affection for a younger brother who, unhappily for himself and for others, suffered some tragic disabilities.

In the early autumn of 1801 the marriage plan gradually crystallized, for during his visits to Malmaison Louis showed signs of becoming seriously interested in Hortense. He sent her a twenty-page letter presenting in elaborate detail the history of his emotional life. Hortense's *Memoirs* permit us to learn very little of her personal feelings in this matter – she refused to complain publicly – yet the facts about Louis are clear enough. He was a devotee of romantic melancholy, a man touched by those currents of 'sensibility' that had produced Goethe's *Werther*, Rousseau's *La Nouvelle Héloise*, and Bernardin de Saint-Pierre's *Paul et Virginie*. Unattractive in appearance, he had a mild paralysis of one side and he suffered repeatedly from vertigo, constrictions of the throat, and head-aches. This moody and introspective youth went unhappily about with inexpressive face and dull eyes that rarely showed any feeling save suspicion. The suggestion, clearly, is of emotional unbalance. It is difficult to believe that Josephine, warm-hearted and devoted to her daughter, could have agreed to such a marriage if she had suspected the misery that would result. The explanation must be that she could not have known all the unhappy circumstances, and that she acted simply and protectively from an ill-considered calculation of family advantage, that of Hortense included.

The betrothal plan succeeded. Hortense and Louis were married in January 1802 in a civil ceremony followed late in the same evening by a religious marriage performed by the papal legate, Cardinal Caprara, who to his intense surprise had been summoned at the last moment to officiate. The pair took up their residence at Josephine's old home in the rue de la Victoire; yet after two months Louis left his wife for the south of France. He did not return until October, when a son, Napoléon-Charles, was born to them. This marriage, as could have been predicted, proved disastrous; it was embittered by complete incompatibility, by constant strife, and by scandalous gossip of the cruellest sort, spread about by Madame de Rémusat and others. This gossip descended to the depths of asserting that Napoleon himself was the father of Hortense's child. After some years of total unhappiness during which two more sons were born and the ill-matched couple were promoted by Napoleon to the throne of Holland, they separated. Hortense lived until 1837 and Louis until 1846. Josephine's plan had not worked; it did not in the end save her from divorce, and it did not produce a child whom Napoleon was willing to accept as his direct heir in default of a child of his own by Josephine. Yet strangely enough, Josephine in the end had her triumph. The third son of Hortense, born in 1808 and baptized Charles-Louis-Napoléon, was one day to be known to history as the Emperor Napoleon III.

Early in 1802 the press of great affairs took Josephine with her husband to Lyons for the inauguration of the new Italian Republic. Following his Italian victories, Bonaparte had in 1801 made the Peace of Lunéville with Austria. Negotiations for peace were also under way with England. He therefore found it tempting to meddle in the affairs of Italy, drafting a new constitution for the Cisalpine Republic he earlier had put together out of some of the northern Italian states. To complete his work he had summoned several hundred Italian delegates from the Cisalpine to meet him at Lyons. At a dinner in the Tuileries shortly before leaving, Bonaparte spoke to Josephine about the trip and asked her if she knew what people were saying. Josephine replied that it was being asserted that he was about to have himself elected king of Italy. At this Bonaparte laughed, yet the forecast was to become true.

Early in January 1802, they made a midnight departure from Paris, completing the long journey southward over snow-covered roads in less than three days. At Lyons the weather continued to be bitterly cold. Although Bonaparte was busy enough with his Italian problems, he also engaged in a round of social activities, and here for the first time Josephine was vested with official dignity and appeared beside her husband at concerts, balls, illuminations, and civic receptions. In addition there were visits to various industrial establishments in the city.

The Italian delegates at Lyons made the unfortunate mistake of nominating one of their own number, Melzi, to be president of what was now to be called the Italian Republic. They were rescued from their blunder when Talleyrand hinted tactfully that the honour should go to Bonaparte – an honour that they then quickly proposed and he gracefully accepted. As usual, a number of Italians, eager for posts in the new government, calculated that the best line of approach was through Josephine. This was the case with the candidate for the vice-presidency and also with the aspirant for the ministry of finances. This latter intriguer gave Josephine a sapphire *parure* said to be worth a hundred thousand francs. Bonaparte discovered this and, outraged, demanded that she return the jewels, but according to the recollections of her old friend, Antoine Hamelin, she managed not to do so.

From Lyons Josephine wrote an unhappy letter to Hortense:

At last I see the time approaching when I shall be able to hold my dear daughter in my arms; I shall forget, when I see you, all the sadness I have felt in this country . . . I will tell you everything that has happened during my stay at Lyons, and will describe the fêtes and performances offered to us. But when you are not here to share it there is no pleasure for your mother. Kiss your husband for me. Tell him that I am beginning to love him deeply and that I thank him for his little notes which are very kind.[13]

By the end of the month they were back in Paris.

At a diplomatic reception in March 1802, Bonaparte announced the signature of the Peace of Amiens with England. His visitors noticed that the first consul had abandoned the military costume that had been usual ever since Marengo and now wore a silk habit, white stockings, and buckled shoes. In April the papal legate, Cardinal Caprara, who had married Hortense and Louis in January, celebrated a pontifical Mass at Notre Dame assisted by the combined choirs of the Conservatory. This was to commemorate the signing of the Concordat between France and the papacy by which, after more than a decade of turmoil, the Roman Catholic Church was restored to an official position in the state. It was a Mass preceded by a splendid procession from the Tuileries to the cathedral, the like of which had not been seen since the days of the Bourbons. The carriages of the ministers and ambassadors were each drawn by four horses, those of the second and third consuls by six, and Bonaparte's carriage by eight. For the first time all the attendants were in full livery: yellow for the ministers, red and blue for the second and third consuls, and green for Bonaparte. Josephine did not share in these proceedings. The first consul rode alone, dressed in scarlet velvet embroidered with golden palm leaves and wearing a hat with tricolour plumes. Amid such splendours monarchy could not have seemed far distant. The Mass was celebrated in the presence of four battalions of infantry, and it was saluted by sixty salvos of cannon. At the end of the ceremony the archbishops and bishops, as provided in the Concordat, tendered their allegiance to the first consul.

A week later the Prussian minister at Paris wrote to his government summarizing his impressions of the new régime as follows:

Everything around the first consul and his wife is resuming the general character and etiquette of Versailles. Ostentatious luxury, fine carriages, liveries, crowds of servants are seen on every side. Much care is taken in the reception of foreign gentlemen; and the foreign ladies who are presented to the first consul and his wife are announced by one of the prefects of the palace. He is developing some liking for the chase, and the forests where the kings of France and the princes of the blood once hunted are now being reserved for him and the officers of his suite.[14]

An almost immediate sequel to the signing of the Peace of Amiens was a flood of visitors from across the Channel. Before the year's end an estimated ten thousand Englishmen had arrived in France. All wished to have a glimpse of the Tuileries and its celebrated inhabitants, and a few, such as Lord Erskine, Lord Holland, and Charles James Fox, were honoured with invitations to dine. From such visitors come accounts of the new era. John Dean Paul, the author of *A Journal of a Party of Pleasure to Paris in the Month of August 1802*, tells of going to the Théâtre Français and seeing Bonaparte with Josephine and their entourage in a box. 'He is a little man,' Paul observed, 'but with an intelligent spirited countenance, and an eye that speaks an uncommon mind; he wears his lank hair out of powder, very short, and was dressed in a blue coat most richly embroidered.'[15] Paul briefly noted the presence of Madame Bonaparte and her ladies, but had eyes, evidently, only for the first consul.

In Edmund Eyre's *Observations Made at Paris During the Peace* we have other notes on Paris in this new age. Eyre was shocked in good, substantial, English fashion at the statues that adorned the gardens of the Tuileries. He was shocked even more at the beauties who 'sweep the muddy streets of the capital with flowing and Athenian muslin robes, or draw the pendant fold on their right arms to imitate the drapery of some sculptured Venus.' To judge from Eyre's account, some of the naughty extravagances of the Directory period still survived in this new and disciplined age of the Consulate:

The women of Paris have made one change for the better, amongst many for the worse, namely, having discarded the use of rouge for the toilet. Their dresses are certainly elegant, but indelicate, and give to every woman a *meretricious* appearance. They appear in public places in a state of undress really immodest . . . in truth, the gross display of bosom and shoulders seems to inspire sensations of disgust and disrespect, rather than of admiration. I do not wish to see the ladies swaddled up like mummies, nor that the sweet symmetry of their forms should be lost in an unnecessary mass of clothing; but I could desire fashion only to reveal so much as should mingle admiration with respect.[16]

The respectful Edmund Eyre then went to Malmaison, hoping to view the château and catch a glimpse of Josephine, 'but the guards, who are stationed at the gates and neighbouring barracks, peremptorily resist the solicitations of all strangers, who are denied all admission.'

In this mellow and promising period Josephine wrote to her mother at Martinique. 'The frigate which is leaving for Guadeloupe,' she explained, 'to bring General Lacrosse the news of peace with England is the carrier of my letter.' Josephine begged her mother to come to France, assuring her that her husband joined in the request. 'You will like Bonaparte very much,' she told her mother, 'he is making your daughter very happy; he is kind, pleasant, in every way a charming man, and he truly loves your Yeyette.'[17] In a subsequent letter Josephine renewed her invitation and announced that splendid presents were on the way for Madame Tascher: a box set with diamonds and having portraits of Josephine, Napoleon, Hortense, and Eugène (the gift of Napoleon); and a chaplet that the Pope had blessed and sent to Josephine on the conclusion of the Concordat. Neither presents nor appeals, however, could persuade the ageing mother to leave the island where she had been born.

During the summer of 1802 Josephine again renewed her visits to Plombières. Bonaparte's letters to her showed warm affection:

I have not yet heard from you; I believe that by now you have begun to take the waters. Here we are a little sad, even though your charming daughter does the honours of the household admirably. For two days I have been suffering mildly from my complaint. Sturdy Eugène arrived last night; he looks wonderful.

I love you as on the first day, because you are above all else kind and good. Hortense says that she has written to you often. A thousand warm greetings and a loving kiss, *tout à toi.*[18]

In another he sent conventional gossip:

I have received your letter, dear little Josephine. I am sorry to learn that you suffered from the trip; but several days of rest will do you much good. I keep well. Yesterday I hunted at Marly and wounded myself in the finger while shooting a boar.

Hortense is well. Your son has been indisposed, but he is improving. I believe that this evening the ladies are to play *The Barber of Seville*. The weather is fine. I beg you to believe that nothing is more genuine than the love I have for my little Josephine.[19]

Still later he wrote again:

I have received your letter of 28 June. You don't tell me about your health or about the effect of the baths. I see that you plan to be back in a week. This will give great pleasure to your dear one who suffers the ennui of being alone. . . .

Hortense played Rosine in *The Barber of Seville* yesterday with her usual intelligence. I beg you to believe that I love you, and that I am most impatient to see you again. Without you here, everything is gloom.[20]

In this same year, 1802, Josephine played some part in the very odd business of Talleyrand's marriage. This 'king of the weather-cocks', this nobleman of the old régime who had once been bishop of Autun, who had accepted the Revolution and abandoned his holy orders, now served as Bonaparte's foreign minister. His private life had been disorderly in the extreme. To the considerable indignation of some ambassadors' wives, there now presided as hostess over the Ministry of Foreign Affairs Talleyrand's mistress, the frail, lovely, empty-headed Madame Grand. The liaison of this figure from the *demi-monde* with the ex-bishop had become so much a matter of scandal that Bonaparte, who was determined to bring about a new standard of public morality in France, told Talleyrand to get rid of her. Talleyrand demurred, proposing marriage instead. He had used the occasion of the Concordat to request from the papacy an official recognition of his Laicization. This new legal status Pius VII was now willing to grant, although nothing would induce him to give authorization for this marriage of one who had once been a bishop. No precedent existed, so the Vatican scholars declared after learned search, in the entire eighteen centuries of Church history.

Madame Grand appealed to her friend Josephine to do what she could to soften Napoleon's hostile attitude. Josephine immediately obliged, Madame Grand had a tearful interview with the first consul, and the path to a civil marriage became clear. As evidence of their interest, the names of both Josephine and Napoleon appeared on the marriage contract, and in September 1802, without any blessing from the Church, the oddly matched pair were united in a civil ceremony. How much Josephine had contributed to the restoration of morality by her assistance we may question. Years later, when Talleyrand was asked by his niece how he ever came to make so strange a marriage, he gave her a simple, and what we may take as an adequate, explanation: 'It happened,' he said wryly, 'in a period of general disorder.'[21]

For Josephine these were splendid, intoxicating days. The proclamation in August 1802 of Napoleon as consul for life with power to name his successor was overwhelmingly ratified in a national plebiscite. Josephine was in the very centre of the ensuing celebrations. A reception was held at the Tuileries for the members of the various legislative bodies and the foreign ambassadors, followed by a concert given by three hundred instrumentalists playing the music of Cherubini, Méhul, and Rameau. In the afternoon a *Te Deum* was celebrated at Notre Dame. In the evening the Tuileries were illuminated. The city of Paris erected a thirty-foot star on the towers of Notre Dame, outlined by lamps, while on the Pont Neuf rose a forty-two-foot statue of Peace. Firework displays were given at the Hôtel de Ville and along the Champs-Élysées. Josephine and Napoleon meanwhile went to Malmaison for family celebrations, where Hortense, although seven months pregnant, took the lead in amateur theatricals. A week later the Senate gave a brilliant reception at the Luxembourg, and at the end of the next week there was a dinner for two hundred at the Tuileries. Talleyrand was only one of many who encouraged Napoleon to think of a truly hereditary régime – a prospect that would mean even greater splendour for Josephine and her family.

Josephine's life in these years of the Consulate alternated between the lurid glare of public events and the mellow glow of her domestic activities. She accompanied her husband on an inspection tour of Normandy in the autumn of 1802, visiting

Evreux, Rouen, Le Havre, Honfleur, Dieppe, and Beauvais.
Everywhere there were warm welcomes from the inhabitants
and also the endless, inescapable visits to factories and commercial establishments. In May 1803 war was resumed with
England. Consequently the even longer tour through north-
eastern France, Belgium, and the Netherlands that the pair
undertook in that summer was less concerned with fostering
the arts of peace than with preparations for the cross-Channel
invasion of England that Bonaparte, after his original opposition, now definitely intended. The tour was more regal than
any of its predecessors – witness the instructions given to
Barbé-Marbois, minister of finance. Bonaparte ordered him
to select some of the finest pearls held in the treasury as well as
precious stones of varied hues, so that Josephine on formal
occasions could appear in a splendour that had not been seen
since the days of the *ancien régime*.

Before leaving on this tour Josephine had been again at
Plombières, where her short stay in these pastoral surroundings
caused her to reflect on the burdens of greatness:

I feel [she told Hortense] that I am not made for so much grandeur. I would be happier in some retreat, surrounded by the
objects of my affections. . . . I know your attachment to Bonaparte
well enough to be sure that you are being a faithful companion to
him. For many reasons you owe him your affection and gratitude.
Kiss him for me and be sure to accept for yourself all my tender
regards.[22]

She was still happiest, it would seem, amid the affections of her
family.

Malmaison continued to give Josephine some of her happiest
hours. She had arranged for its purchase, as we have seen, in
the spring of 1799 while Bonaparte was in Egypt, but had been
unable, characteristically, to find the money to meet the
purchase price of 271,000 francs. Substantial sums were soon
committed to its improvement, so that during the year 1800
Josephine's indebtedness grew at a calamitous rate, and was
made even heavier by the steady drain of her personal expenses. Talleyrand learned of this state of affairs and mentioned

it to the first consul. Bonaparte, fortunately, was then in possession of a very large sum of money paid to him by the free city of Hamburg as an indemnity for the detention there of two French citizens. Bonaparte told Bourrienne to use some of this money to pay his wife's debts, not realizing how large they were. When Bourrienne asked Josephine, she confessed that they amounted to about 1,200,000 francs, and that she did not dare risk her husband's anger by telling him. Seeing that some of the smallest charges in her bills involved expenditures for such items as thirty-eight new hats in one month and 1,800 francs worth of herons' plumes, her hesitation was understandable. She and Bourrienne finally agreed to halve the figure and put it at 600,000 francs. Bonaparte reluctantly agreed to honour this amount and Bourrienne, by vigorously beating down the creditors who no doubt had heavily overcharged Josephine in the first place, paid the bills.

No other setting has so completely associated itself with Josephine as has Malmaison. In 1799 the sadly dilapidated estate resembled a farm rather than a château. Yet its possibilities, as Josephine quickly saw, were rich, and the work of restoration and improvement became a constant excitement and challenge. Once Malmaison was acquired, Bonaparte kept watch on the purse-strings, yet he, too, developed a fondness for planning renovations and exercised to the full his natural inclination to improve whatever he saw. 'Nowhere,' wrote Bourrienne with unconscious irony, 'except on the field of battle, did I ever see Bonaparte more happy than in the gardens of Malmaison.'[23] Here Bonaparte worked, shot, chatted, and played chess. At Josephine's informal lunches he would dominate the company with talk of science, art, and literature. In the evenings he liked to tell dramatic stories or to discuss what his critical eye had observed of women's toilettes. Josephine was a pleasant rather than a brilliant hostess. Her gifts were those of sympathy and warmth. She was fond of games, embroidery, and desultory conversation. She had some little aptitude for painting and she played the harp occasionally, though, if we are to believe Méneval, always the same tune.

Quite early in her career Josephine demonstrated her

instincts as a collector. She had paintings, so she told Madame de la Tour du Pin, that were the gifts of the sculptor, Canova, of the Pope, and of the city of Milan. It would have been truer to say, so her visitor thought, that Bonaparte had 'collected' them at the sword's point in Italy. Josephine somehow managed also to find funds of her own for purchases. She wrote to her old friend, Hamelin, who was in Rome, saying that she had made available through her bankers a draft of 100,000 francs with which Hamelin could purchase art objects for her at his choice. He could even go beyond this amount if it seemed advisable. Hamelin promptly did so, to the extent of 13,000 francs, with the sad consequence that two years later he still had not been paid, even after complaining directly to Josephine about his problem. Josephine also made substantial purchases of plants, draperies, and furnishings. In 1801 she wrote to Otto, agent of the French government in London, telling him of her interest in obtaining some English trees or shrubs, and suggesting that the gardener at Kew might be willing to provide her with some unusual seeds. She wrote also to her mother in Martinique with similar requests. Other letters show her constant concern in adding to what she had originally purchased.

Talleyrand, as well as anyone, has recaptured the carefree, rustic spirit of Malmaison in these happy consular years:

I arrived at Malmaison [he wrote] and do you know what I did, and where the First Consul has established his work-room? On one of the bowling greens! They were all seated on the grass. It was nothing to him, with his camp habits, his riding boots, and his leather breeches. But I, in my silk breeches and silk stockings! Can you see me sitting on that lawn? I'm crippled with rheumatism. What a man! He always thinks he is camping out.[24]

If Malmaison represented the spirit and dreams of Josephine, life at Saint-Cloud carried much more the imprint of Bonaparte. Somewhat closer to Paris than was Malmaison, this royal residence had been bought and refurbished by Louis XIV near the beginning of his reign. Despite a petition from its inhabitants, Bonaparte was not at first disposed to take it over as a residence in addition to Malmaison. Late in 1801, however, he changed his mind, telling Berthier that Saint-Cloud would be more convenient for his purposes than Malmaison. He hoped to remodel it for a modest sum, yet when his architects, Percier and Fontaine, undertook the work they developed so lavish a programme that in the end the bills came to more than three million francs. Whatever their value, the restorations have been lost for ever, for the palace of Saint-Cloud, like the Tuileries, is totally gone – destroyed during the Franco-Prussian War of 1870.

The ambassadorial receptions at Saint-Cloud were affairs of high ceremony. The coaches drove through the tall gateways into a courtyard full of green-liveried attendants and soldiers of the guard. Ascending a fine staircase, the guests came to a circular vestibule in which was displayed David's heroic painting of Bonaparte crossing the St Bernard Pass. They then would pass through a gallery hung with paintings and having a frescoed ceiling that dated from the reign of Louis XIV. In the next salon elegantly clad ladies in silk dresses and jewels, waiting to be presented, grouped themselves gracefully beneath a large portrait of Madame Bonaparte sitting on a sofa. Josephine's four ladies-in-waiting, charming in white Indian muslin, received the guests. Talleyrand was in attendance as minister of foreign affairs and made the presentations, while numerous officials hovered in the background.

When all were assembled the guests would move into the next salon for the presentations, the ladies forming a semicircle with the men behind them. For such affairs Bonaparte would enter, escorted by two prefects of the palace. He wore usually the green tunic, trimmed with red, of the *Chasseurs* of the Guard, a dark blue waistcoat, black silk breeches, and white silk stockings. A sabre hung at his side and he invariably carried his black hat under his arm. He would move quickly from one lady to another, bowing as he heard her name and addressing one or two perfunctory questions to each. Josephine would enter shortly after her husband, likewise attended by two prefects of the palace, and make the circuit at some distance behind. She was a gracious figure in a toilette of white satin trimmed with lace, and wearing a fine diadem with three rows of stones and three fine ancient cameos. At the end of the circuit Josephine would be seated and other presentations of men and women would be made to her while Bonaparte stood chatting with a group of men in another part of the salon. The ceremonies over, the first consul and his wife would bow to the company and retire. The guests then moved quickly through a long gallery to still another grand salon where a magnificent buffet supper was served. Following this came the descent to the *rez-de-chaussée* and the tedious wait while the carriages, sometimes as many as two hundred and many of them drawn by four horses, were punctiliously summoned in order of diplomatic precedence.

Similar ceremonial marked the presentations and receptions at the Tuileries: grace and sympathy on the part of Josephine; dignity and power, interrupted by sudden flashes of brusqueness and rudeness on the part of Bonaparte. 'I have seen that dress before, madame,' he would say, or, 'Your arms, madame, are very red.' After a decade of revolution the good manners of a shattered régime are not easily restored.

Some domestic sorrows still hung over Josephine. Occasionally she was aware of the fleeting figure of Madame Grassini, tiptoeing into the private apartments of the first consul; occasionally she heard of Mademoiselle George, from the Comédie Française. On one dreadful night she was roused from her apartment by the terrified screams of Mademoiselle George, waking the household as Bonaparte experienced one of the brief, convulsive seizures that were a part of his medical history. Josephine, moreover, could not escape the persistent and growing unkindness of the Bonaparte clan. A letter to her mother in these days carries a suggestion of her troubles:

I do not write to you as often as I should like, dear mama, because I have little time to myself. . . . I imagine that you may feel some occasional concern about me, but there is no reason for this. So, I beg you, do not give way to such feelings, and believe only the news which I send you.[25]

If this represented one side of Josephine's feelings, another is found in a letter which she wrote to Bonaparte in November 1803, while he was away at Boulogne, busy with his plans for the cross-Channel invasion. This letter has a unique significance. It has been called by Masson the only certain and authentic surviving letter addressed by Josephine to Napoleon, as distinct from the few that survive as copies and the many which she addressed to others. What is it that has caused more than two hundred and fifty letters from Bonaparte to Josephine to escape time's ravages and has allowed only one from Josephine to Bonaparte to survive? What different light would the survival of more letters from Josephine to her husband shed upon the relations between the pair, and would history in this event have treated her reputation more kindly? We can only ask.

This 'one certain and authentic' letter of November 1803 tells much of the husband and wife of the Tuileries:

All my sorrows have disappeared in reading the good, sympathetic letter which contains such loving expression of your feelings for me. How grateful I am to you for giving so much time to your Josephine! If you could know, you would applaud yourself for being the means of causing so much joy to the wife whom you love.

A letter is the portrait of a soul, and I press this one to my heart. It does me so much good! I wish to keep it always! It will be my consolation during your absence, my guide when I am near you. I wish to be always in your eyes the good, the tender Josephine, concerned only with your happiness. . . .

Adieu, Bonaparte, I shall never forget the last sentence of your letter. I keep it in my heart. How deeply it is engraved there! With what emotion mine has responded!

Yes, my wish is also to please you, to love you – rather, to adore you![26]

❧ 15 ❧

Steps to a Throne

THE consulate for life meant that Napoleon was a monarch in all but name, holding in his hands control of the succession. As he rose to this new dignity, he carried Josephine up with him, with the result that an imperial crown soon marked the supreme achievement of her extraordinary career.

At the beginning of 1804 the picture in France seemed most promising, for Napoleon's great administrative reforms were well under way. Abroad, the one great flaw in his plans was that England – 'Perfidious Albion' – had re-entered the war and was busily at work whipping together a third great coalition against France. Bonaparte, nevertheless, had every confidence that he could deal with this threat, even as he had dealt with the Austrians at Rivoli and Marengo. And so it was entirely characteristic of his busy genius that he should simultaneously push forward the domestic reorganization of France, make his plans for the invasion and destruction of England, and prepare imperial titles for himself and Josephine.

As Bonaparte developed his military plans, the Channel coast rang with the preparations for war. Specially built invasion barges by the hundreds crowded the harbours, new roads were laid, ports were enlarged, and at the great camp of Boulogne an army of a hundred thousand men laboriously learned the techniques of embarkation and disembarkation. Hopeful that his plans would soon bring England to defeat, Napoleon busied himself in January with a tour of supervision and inspection:

I am very well, my dear Josephine [he wrote from Boulogne]; the rain, the wind, and the cold do me no harm. I leave in a moment to continue my inspection, and I shall soon be in Paris. I am sending you some caricatures which I have received from England. A thousand fond greetings to your little cousin and to everyone.[1]

If matters were going well on the Channel coast, troubles clearly were brewing in Paris. Some of these affected Josephine. Not all Frenchmen were satisfied with the new régime, and not all Bonaparte's generals were happy at the meteoric rise of their colleague. The secret police in Paris were soon aware of the discontent and knew that plots to assassinate the first consul, furthered by royalist groups outside France, were afoot. In August 1803 Georges Cadoudal, a fanatical leader of anti-republican forces in Brittany, was brought secretly in a British cutter across the Channel from his English exile. He turned up in Paris, where he joined with General Pichegru, another royalist who had returned by stealth after having been forced to leave France. The pair tried to win the support of General Moreau, who had been one of Bonaparte's aides at the time of the coup of Brumaire. Since then Moreau had grown very bitter at Bonaparte's steady rise and had gone into sullen retirement outside Paris. Moreau had married Mademoiselle Hulot, a creole and a friend of Josephine, as restless and ambitious as himself. When Bonaparte established the Legion of Honour, Moreau had scornfully bestowed a special collar of honour upon his dog.

The conspiracy of 1804 contemplated a domestic rising in the east of France, a simultaneous invasion of *émigrés* from across the Rhine, and the assassination of the first consul as he travelled along the road from Malmaison to Paris. The French secret police, who had their agents planted amid the conspirators, deliberately let the plot mature. Though in the end General Moreau refused to join the plot, he and his wife were so close to it as to bring embarrassment and pain to their good friend, Josephine.

On a chilly February morning Bonaparte was seated beside the fireplace in Josephine's salon at the Tuileries, holding Hortense's infant son, Napoléon-Charles, on his lap. Suddenly he addressed Josephine, 'Do you know what I have just done? I have given the order to arrest Moreau.' He rose, walked to Josephine, and held her by the chin. 'You are weeping.

Why? Are you afraid?' Her answer was short, 'No, but I don't like what people will say.'[2]

Sure enough, on this very morning Moreau was arrested as he sought to leave Paris; soon afterwards Pichegru, Cadoudal, and many others were seized. An agitated Josephine wrote to her daughter at Compiègne telling her of the arrests and declaring that many of the conspirators had been in Paris for months, contemplating the murder of her husband. 'Truly,' she wrote, 'it makes one shudder.'[3]

Spectacular consequences followed. The secret police found evidence which seemed to implicate in the plot a person of royal blood, the young Duke d'Enghien, son of the last Prince de Condé and nephew of the Duke d'Orléans. Though the evidence implicating Enghien was less than convincing, Bonaparte struck ruthlessly. The duke was living quietly across the Rhine, in Baden. On the night of 14 March a troop of French cavalry crossed the imperial border, rode to the castle of Ettenheim, and in outrageous defiance of international law seized Enghien and brought him back to France for trial by a military court.

By 20 March Enghien found himself in the ancient fortress of Vincennes, outside Paris. Josephine tried twice to save him. She had spoken to Bonaparte on Passion Sunday when they attended High Mass in the chapel of the Tuileries. 'I have done what I could,' she told Madame de Rémusat as they drove back to Malmaison, 'but I am afraid his mind is made up.'[4] A day or so later Josephine interceded again in the park at Malmaison where Bonaparte was walking with Talleyrand. 'I fear that cripple,' she told Joseph Bonaparte, who was with her, and so Joseph, obligingly for once managed to lure Talleyrand away. Her efforts were useless, for when Josephine appealed directly to her husband on behalf of Enghien, Bonaparte dismissed her with the words: 'Go away; you are a child; you do not understand public duties.'[5] Actually, Enghien's fate had been settled from the moment when he was seized, and neither Josephine nor anyone else could do anything about it. As he crossed the dry moat at Vincennes to meet his judges within, he passed an open grave, dug just two hours before. He was found guilty and shot by the light of torches before dawn broke over the castle. At St Helena Napoleon defended his actions, saying that Enghien had frankly confessed to be planning the invasion of France. In our own day Napoleon's biographer, Kircheisen, has stated that by all the rules of war Enghien deserved his punishment. Nevertheless, the conscience of conservative Europe was outraged and an irreparable breach was erected between the Bonapartes and the Bourbons.

Other punitive actions soon followed. General Pichegru, having been arrested, was found strangled in his cell, under circumstances that have defied explanation. General Moreau, loudly insisting that he had refused to join the conspirators, was given the light sentence of two years in prison, quickly commuted to exile, which he chose to spend in America. Twenty other conspirators were sentenced to death. Twelve of them, including Cadoudal, were executed; the others were pardoned. The pardoned owed much to Josephine and her kinswomen for their escape. She managed to introduce the former Duchess de Polignac, elderly mother of two of the conspirators, as well as the parents of another royalist into Bonaparte's study at Saint-Cloud. When Madame de Polignac fainted at the great man's feet he relented. Hortense lay in wait outside with the daughter of another conspirator; Bonaparte's sisters, Elisa and Caroline, confronted him with still more grieving relatives. Thanks to this mass feminine onslaught, the lives of eight of those involved in the plot against the first consul were spared.

Bonaparte's determination to convert the life consulship into an imperial régime went forward amid a loud chorus of family bickerings. The Bonaparte clan could hardly object to an empire, for the heightened prestige that would envelop the entire family was obvious. What did give concern was the perennial problem of the succession. Neither Bonaparte's marriage nor his casual affairs with several transient figures had resulted in proof that he was capable of fatherhood. It was still not clear what claims to the succession, in the event of

Bonaparte's death, could be asserted by his brothers against Josephine, whose only children were the fruits of her first marriage. Josephine had believed that some of these difficulties would be solved by Hortense's marriage to Louis Bonaparte, but this, unhappily, had not turned out well. The sickly and sullen son-in-law had shown little interest in domesticity and, despite her friendly overtures, had developed a savage hatred for Josephine. He tried to turn Hortense against her mother by raking up and retailing to her some of the scandalous gossip concerning Josephine's earlier years. Poor Hortense could do little except keep these sorry revelations, of which her mother was unaware, to herself. In the autumn of 1803 what looked like a reconciliation came about between Louis and Hortense; she became pregnant again; but concomitantly her unhappy husband began to exhibit some signs of mental disorder.

Bonaparte now talked of adopting as his heir Napoléon-Charles, the infant son of Louis and Hortense. He would do this, so he hinted, by passing over any claim that Louis might think he had to the succession, as he would also exclude his brother, Joseph, whose two children, alas, were both daughters. He had no intention of considering the other two brothers, Lucien and Jérôme, both having kicked over the traces. Lucien's first wife, the beautiful Christine Boyer, had died, and Lucien had refused Bonaparte's suggestion that he marry the widowed queen of Etruria. Instead he had secretly married a Madame Jouberthon, of whom Bonaparte strongly disapproved. Jérôme, the youngest brother, had done even worse. Cruising pleasantly with a French squadron in the West Indies, he had left his ship for a tour of the United States, where in 1803 he had impetuously married the beautiful Miss Patterson of Baltimore – an unspeakable mistake that most emphatically ruled him out.

When Bonaparte's intentions about the succession gradually became clear and the hopes of Josephine seemed about to be realized, little remained for these brothers actually to do. Lucien, once so helpful to his brother on the day of Brumaire, renounced further interest in a public career, and retired to an estate near Rome where he devoted himself, agreeably enough, to the twin pursuits of agriculture and archaeology. Although Joseph felt the keenest sense of outrage he had no desire to cut himself off from public affairs. Yet the situation rankled, and on one occasion he gave vent to his Corsican ire by firing his pistol point-blank at a full-length portrait of brother Napoleon. Having thus found relief, he continued to serve as a reasonably faithful servant of the régime.

By the year 1804 this problem of the succession was closely involved with the much larger question of proclaiming the Empire. Kingship may have been good enough for the Bourbons, but for Bonaparte, whose authority now extended over large parts of Italy, the Rhineland, and the Netherlands, nothing less than an imperial title would suffice. When Josephine and Napoleon paid a visit to Hortense in April, the first consul offered to adopt her son. Hortense begged to refuse, whereupon Bonaparte declared, 'Very well, then, I will obtain a law that will at least make me master of my family.'[6] What he had in mind was that a law regulating the succession would be included with the new legislation by means of which he was about to establish the Empire.

The plans were quickly worked out through the smoothly operating machinery of the consular régime. The tribunate adopted the principle of heredity in April, and gave approval to the title of emperor for Napoleon. The senate added its assent early in May. A legal statement was quickly drawn up, adopted by the tribunate and then formally proclaimed by the senate as a *Senatus Consultum* on 18 May. This declared that 'the government of the republic is to be entrusted to an emperor', and that his official title shall be 'Emperor of the French'. It went on to say that 'Napoleon Bonaparte, at present first consul of the Republic, is Emperor of the French', and it stipulated that 'the imperial dignity is hereditary.' The Emperor was to fix the widow's dower of the Empress, which was to be paid out of the civil list and be unalterable by his successors.

The official transition from republic to empire came with very little fanfare on this same day, when the senate proceeded in a body to Saint-Cloud. Napoleon, in military uniform, received the visitors standing with a semicircle made up of his councillors-of-state and his generals. Following the ceremony with Napoleon, the senate was admitted into the presence of the Empress, where Cambacérès offered Josephine his homage and expressed the gratitude of the French people. In extravagant words, which nevertheless had some echo of truth, Cambacérès assured her that her reputation of being always accessible to the unfortunate would be of great strength to her husband; future generations, he insisted, would learn from her that to dry the tears of the suffering is the surest way to reign over the hearts of all.

The lengthy arguments over the succession were disposed of in three articles of the *Senatus Consultum*. These dangled a gleaming prize before Joseph and Louis Bonaparte, only, alas, to snatch it away from them. Joseph Bonaparte and his male descendants, then Louis Bonaparte and his male descendants, could inherit the imperial dignity by right of primogeniture, but only *after* Napoleon had exercised his right of 'adoptive succession'. Napoleon had the right to adopt the children or grandchildren of his brothers when they reached the age of eighteen, provided that he had no male children of his own. As much as could be, therefore, the interests of Josephine's grandson had been protected, and the Beauharnais had scored a clear victory over the Bonapartes. A plebiscite held in November gave the spectacular total of 3,572,329 votes in favour of the Empire and only 2,567 against.

With the appearance of the Empire a splendid new hierarchy began to envelop the lives and activities of Napoleon and Josephine. Titles came back in a flood. Only those members of the imperial family who were in the actual line of succession were to have the title of prince or princess. Joseph, Louis, and their wives were therefore 'in', while Lucien and Jérôme were most definitely 'out', as were Napoleon's three married sisters: Elisa Bacciochi, Caroline Murat, and Pauline Borghese. The din of protest was instantaneous and deafening; and Napoleon's efforts to answer his sisters by protesting acidly, 'Truly, *mesdames*, considering your pretensions one might think that we had inherited the crown from the late king, our father,' did him no good.[7] The sense of outrage continued and would not be abated until at last the *Moniteur* soothingly announced that the sisters of the Emperor were entitled to be called 'Princess'. Even so, echoes of this family storm lasted through the entire period of the coronation.

In addition to the family of Napoleon and the existing roster of senators, councillors, and other public officials, a long list of new dignitaries soon emerged. After the hereditary princes came the six grand imperial dignitaries, the military grand officers, and the civil grand officers. Subordinate to these was the long roster including the prefects of the palace, the chamberlains, the equerries, aides, and pages. As the Empire grew in size and as Napoleon's authority enlarged, fiefs and principalities, usually with large revenues attached to them, were allotted to his most faithful and useful subordinates. Talleyrand, for example, became prince of Benevento in southern Italy; Joseph Bonaparte became king of Naples. A graded system of titles was widely applied to public offices, so that by final tally Napoleon had created 31 dukes, 452 counts, 1,500 barons, and 1,474 chevaliers.

Within the framework of this ever more dazzling imperial structure Josephine now had to organize her life. In truth, much of it was organized for her. Under the watchful and system-loving eye of the Emperor, the household of the Empress gradually attained an order, a preciseness, and a definition that the pleasure-loving, warm-hearted, extravagant Josephine never could have given it. Nothing was left to chance or improvisation. By 1808 the long lists of her officials, the exact stipulation of their duties, and even the very rooms in which they were to serve were all carefully set forth to the last detail in an imposing official quarto, *Etiquette du palais impérial*.

A lull, or at all events a change, in the feverish rush of activities connected with the proclamation of the Empire came in the summer of 1804. While the Emperor, still absorbed in the preparations for the invasion of England, spent the last two weeks of July and most of August in another of his characteristically detailed tours of inspection, Josephine was off on a new venture to try the waters of the famous Rhineland resort of Aix-la-Chapelle.

Napoleon kept in touch with his wife by means of letters couched in the easy, comfortable language that now was standard between the husband and wife. 'Madame and dear wife,' he begins on 21 July, 'during the four days that I have been away from you I have been steadily on horseback and on the move, without in any way impeding my health.'[8] Napoleon entertains her with a dramatic picture of shipwreck and rescue amid a Channel storm, and he advises her to make the trip to Aix in slow stages in order to avoid fatigue. And that is all. Nevertheless, a second letter written on this same day burns with the old ardour:

I have arrived, my dear little Josephine, in good health at Boulogne, where I shall stay for twenty days. Here I have fine troops, fine ships, and everything to make me pass the time pleasantly. All that is lacking is my good Josephine, but I mustn't tell her that. For men to be loved, they must cause the ladies to doubt and fear the extent and duration of their power. . . .[9]

On 3 August he writes again:

My dear, I hope to learn soon that the waters have done you much good, and I am sorry for the difficulties you have experienced. I wish that you would write to me often. My health is very good, though I am somewhat tired. In a few days I shall be at Dunkirk, where I shall write to you again. Eugène has gone to Blois. I cover you with kisses.[10]

From Ostend on 14 August there is a little more news:

My dear, I have had no news of you for several days. I would be relieved to learn about the effects of the waters, and about the way in which you are passing your time. I have been at Ostend for a week. Tomorrow I shall be at Boulogne for a splendid celebration. Tell me by the courier what you plan to do and when you will be through at the waters.

I am very pleased with the army and the flotillas. Eugène is still at Blois. I hear no more from Hortense than if she were in the Congo. I am writing to scold her. A thousand good wishes to everyone.[11]

Another letter from Boulogne sends the good news that Hortense – 'this dear daughter who is always good, sensible, and sympathetic' – and her infant son, Napoléon-Charles, have spent two happy days with the Emperor beside the sea.[12] One would like to have a picture of the conqueror of Marengo thus basking on the sands. Still another letter informs Josephine that in ten days he will be in Aix-la-Chapelle and that she should await him there. 'My health is good,' he writes, in answer to what seems to have been concern on her part. 'I am longing to see you, to tell you of all that you inspire in me, and to cover you with kisses. This bachelor life is wretched; and nothing can equal the worth of a wife who is good, beautiful, and tender.'[13]

A few days later, with a sort of elephantine coyness, Napoleon announces the plans for his arrival:

Tomorrow I shall be in Saint-Omer. On the 28th [of August] I shall be at Arras, on the 30th at Mons, and on 31 August or 1 September at Aix-la-Chapelle.

As it is possible that I may arrive at night, lovers beware! I would be sorry to discommode them, but one must seek his advantage wherever he can. My health is good, and I work hard. But I am too serious, and this hurts me. I long to see you and to tell you a thousand loving things.

Eugène is courting all the ladies of Boulogne, and has nothing but success.[14]

Full of his new imperial dignity, Napoleon reached Aix-la-Chapelle on 2 September. En route he had been greeted by the prefect of Arras. 'God made Bonaparte,' the prefect declared in his public oration, 'and then rested.'[15] Josephine now found herself for the first time subject to the rigorous formalities of her new position. Napoleon had arranged for her to have a house, but since it proved to be too small she had accepted the hospitality of the prefecture. Sophie Gay, an old friend who was there, noted the comical efforts of the local officials to reproduce something of the elegant ceremonial of the old monarchy – efforts that were made less embarrassing by Josephine's innate graciousness and invariable good cheer. She had reached the age, so Madame Gay candidly thought, 'when one appreciates her elegance much more than her beauty.'[16] Among other activities, the imperial couple attended a *Te Deum* in the cathedral, where they were shown the celebrated relics of Charlemagne and where Napoleon may have had some inspiration for his plans concerning the coronation. Josephine found time to send a letter to Hortense, urging her to write at once to Napoleon who seemed annoyed at not having heard from her:

Tell him of the hope which you cherish to see me at the time of your confinement. I cannot bear to think of being away from you at such a time. . . . So speak of it to Bonaparte, who loves you as if you were his own child, and thereby heightens my devotion to him.[17]

Leaving Aix on 11 September, Napoleon and Josephine made the romantic voyage up the Rhine, visiting Cologne, Bonn, Coblenz, and Mainz. Here they parted company, Napoleon continuing his tour of inspection and Josephine returning to France. At Nancy an elaborate reception, complete with triumphal arch, decorations, transparencies, and illuminations, greeted her. Pushing on, she was back in Paris in time for the birth of Hortense's second son, Prince Napoléon-Louis, on 11 October. This was domestic happiness, indeed, yet grandiose public plans quickly overshadowed such lesser excitements. For the first time in its history France was about to witness the dazzling spectacle of an imperial coronation.

❖ 16 ❖

Coronation

FOR as masterly a showman as Napoleon the prospect of an imperial coronation was an exhilarating challenge. All his versatile energies, therefore, were now thrown into the complicated preparations. While still on his Rhineland tour he had written with typical vigour to Pope Pius VII, respectfully desiring him to come to France in order 'to give, in preeminent measure, a religious character to the anointing and crowning of the First Emperor of the French'.[1] Crisp instructions were sent concurrently to Napoleon's uncle, Cardinal Fesch, now French ambassador at Rome, requiring him to accompany the Pope to France. The route was to be over the Mont Cenis Pass. 'I desire the Pope to arrive by the 18th Brumaire [9 November],' Napoleon explained succinctly, for all the world as if he were detailing the movements of a French regiment. 'If he is beyond the Alps before the 12th Brumaire I shall be satisfied.'[2] Plans for the ceremonial were pushed with very little regard for the convenience of the ageing Pontiff. Speed, above all, was essential. In order that there should be no delay in establishing an order of service, Napoleon sent to the arch-chancellor, Cambacérès, from Mainz a French translation derived from the Roman *Pontifical* of the ceremonies prescribed for coronation, asking Cambacérès to propose whatever modifications would seem suitable for French usage.

Reluctant at first, the sixty-four-year-old Pius VII finally agreed to come. Earlier he had exchanged one or two letters with Josephine, having sent her a papal ring in return for a surplice she had made for him. On another occasion he had sent her his apostolic blessing. Though his relations with Josephine may thus have been cordial, they were hardly close.

At all events, they had not reached the point where he could be sure of her name. Pius VII found it adequate to refer to the wife of Napoleon as Victoria. '*Dilectae in Christo Filiae Victoriae Bonaparte*' he wrote in one letter, and *Carissimae in Christo Filiae Nostrae Victoriae Gallorum Imperatrici*,' he wrote in another.[3]

The likelihood of delay soon developed. Napoleon was indignant to learn from Talleyrand that the Pope might not arrive until 2 December instead of the November date originally set. This was annoying, but when one deals with the papacy one cannot be utterly inflexible. 'I am willing to wait until 2 December in order to meet every delay,' Napoleon wrote sternly to Cardinal Fesch, 'but if the Pope hasn't arrived by that time the coronation will take place without him.'[4] As it turned out, Pius VII had left Rome three days before Napoleon wrote his letter, departing amid an emotional farewell from his flock and passing through weeping crowds who loudly wondered whether they would ever see him again. The Pope was accompanied by an imposing cortège. Thirty coaches and wagons were needed to transport the six cardinals, the ten bishops, and more than a hundred other officials. Crossing the Alps in November was no easy business; the strains of the journey, indeed, brought death to the eldest cardinal in the party.

At Paris the perennial bickerings of the Bonaparte family continued, for the several members grew daily more indignant at the unique historical role that Josephine was to play in the coronation. One other queen of France, Marie de Medicis, had been anointed and crowned, as Napoleon now intended that Josephine should be, but none had ever held the title of empress. The Emperor had little patience with the jealousies of his brothers and sisters. 'My wife is a good woman,' he told his secretary, Roederer, at Saint-Cloud, 'who does them [the family] no harm. She is willing to play the empress up to a point, and to have diamonds and fine clothes – the trifles of her age! I have never loved her blindly, yet if I have made her an empress it is out of justice. I am above all a just man. If I had been thrown into prison instead of ascending a throne, she would have shared my misfortune. It is right for her to share my grandeur.'⁵

The family remained stubborn and hostile. Joseph and Louis had been informed that their role in the coronation would be to appear as 'Grand Dignitaries of the Empire', and not as 'Princes' – a subtle distinction which to them appeared humiliating. If they were required to serve thus, they said, then their wives could not possibly be expected to carry Josephine's train. After a week's deadlock Napoleon ended the impasse by conceding to his two brothers the right to participate in the coronation as 'Princes'. Their wives, and also Napoleon's three sisters, Elisa, Caroline, and Pauline, could appear as 'Princesses', and by a baffling distinction they were told that their duty would be to 'hold up the robe' (*soutenir le manteau*) and not 'carry the train' (*porter le queue*) of the Empress. And with this promise the ladies for the time being were mollified. Not so formidable *Madame Mère* (Letizia Bonaparte), whose resentment was such that she chose to miss the coronation entirely and stay in Rome with her son, Lucien. This behaviour did not prevent the painter David later from putting her in a proud and central position in his historic canvas. Little wonder that with all these disagreements a visitor calling upon Josephine shortly before the great day found her in tears.

Napoleon's original plans to celebrate the coronation on 9 November – the anniversary of the coup of Brumaire – had to be postponed until 2 December. By this time the ancient royal palace of Fontainebleau, in whose environs Josephine had lived with Madame Renaudin and the Marquis de Beauharnais in those long-distant years following the breach with her first husband, had been refurbished as an imperial residence. Here Pius VII would be entertained on his first arrival. This plan involved tricky problems of protocol if Napoleon was to avoid taking second place to the Pope. The Emperor solved the difficulty by arranging to meet the Pontiff as if by accident in the royal forest near the palace. On the appointed day, therefore, the master of France, clad in simple green hunting costume, halted the papal cortège and dismounted to meet his elderly guest, who for his part descended diffidently in his white robes and silken shoes amid a sea of mud. After the mutual greetings an imperial carriage was quickly brought forward between the two men. Each thus entered the carriage simultaneously by a spearate door, Napoleon having seen to it that he entered from the right side and thus gained the seat of honour. Having won this advantage, it was simple enough for him to keep it on all similar occasions during the papal visit.

Josephine's duty, which she performed gracefully, was to receive Pius VII on the steps of the palace of Fontainebleau. This was on 25 November. Three days later the papal party was escorted to Paris, where elaborate quarters had been prepared at the Tuileries in the Pavillon de Flore, overlooking the Seine. An antechamber, dining-room, salon, chapel, throne room, bedchamber, study, and bathroom were arranged for the Pope. Fifty-six rooms were reserved for his suite on the floors above. They were well looked after. Although Pius VII had the appetite of a Christian ascetic, the same was not true of his staff. The record shows that staggering sums were expended daily on the elaborate foods consumed by his ravenous entourage.

The first plans, which were to have the coronation in the chapel of the Invalides, were quickly put aside in favour of the much grander setting of Notre Dame. To help with the planning, the painter Isabey was ordered to prepare seven elaborate drawings, each with more than a hundred figures, showing the various stages of the ceremony. Despairing of completing all this in the eight days that were allotted to him, Isabey chose instead to ransack the shops of Paris, buying up every toy figure that he could find. These he dressed in papal, imperial, and other costumes, placing them in a large model of the interior of the cathedral. With these figures Napoleon and his officials were able to perfect every elaborate detail of their plans.

Much had to be done if the general setting was to be worthy of the occasion, for like all religious edifices, Notre Dame and its environs had suffered much from neglect during the Revolution. Some old buildings on the south side of the cathedral were now demolished. The streets in the neighbourhood and the quays along the Seine were swept and sanded. A covered way, hung with fine Gobelin tapestries, was built from the archbishop's palace, which was to be used for the preliminary robings, to the great west entrance. Here, in front of the badly dilapidated doors, a huge, four-arched gothic porch of painted wood was erected. On it were thirty-six statues representing the principal towns of France. On one side was a statue of Clovis and on the other, of Charlemagne, each sceptre in hand. A long mast, rising between the twin towers, carried the *oriflamme* – the ancient banner of Saint Denis – high aloft.

Within the cathedral the transformation was equally elaborate. David was commissioned to redesign the interior as if for a vast theatrical spectacle. The choir screen and two subsidiary altars were removed, and sloping tiers of wooded seats covered with silk and velvet were built on either side of the nave. The whole interior was carpeted and the walls hung with gold-fringed crimson cloths, also of silk and velvet. On every pillar were elaborate candelabra with clusters of banners and winged victories in gilt. Twenty-four huge crystal chandeliers were hung from the lofty roof-vaults. On a platform to the left of the high altar a canopied throne bearing the papal arms was erected for Pius VII. Directly facing the high altar on a dais of four steps (conveniently and economically salvaged from the recent funeral of the archbishop of Paris) were placed the two chairs of state where Napoleon and Josephine were to sit during the first part of the ceremonies. Towards the west end of the nave, and placed so as to obscure the main entrance, was built a towering dais of twenty-four steps. Surmounting this stood a miniature triumphal arch of eight gilded columns, within which was placed the great throne of Napoleon, with Josephine's one step below it.

To make up still further for the indignities of the revolutionary period, Napoleon had seen to it that the cathedral was now presented with a rich collection of sacred vessels and processional crosses, some enamelled and encrusted with precious stones. He likewise gave vestments of precious lace and returned those sacred relics, once part of the treasury of the Sainte-Chapelle, which had been sent in 1791 to the church of Saint-Denis and later had been displayed in the 'cabinet of curiosities' in the National Library.

A coronation implied regalia. The royal treasure of the kings of France had been dispersed during the Revolution. Though Napoleon liked to think of himself as the successor of Charlemagne, he could have little hope that the Hapsburg emperor would permit the famous relics of Charlemagne to be taken either from Aix-la-Chapelle or from Nuremberg. Though one ancient weapon, purporting to be the sword of Charlemagne, was actually brought from Aix-la-Chapelle, the other parts of the regalia – the orb, the sceptre, the 'hand of justice', the ceremonial chains, the imperial rings, and the vessels for anointment – were either gathered from diverse sources or newly made. A crown of golden laurel leaves to be worn by Napoleon as he entered the cathedral was made by Paris jewellers, who also provided Josephine with her diadem, crown, and jewelled belt. In the days preceding the coronation, crowds were able to admire these articles in the windows of Biennais, the court jeweller.

All things considered, the cost of making the regalia was surprisingly moderate. The jewellers charged only 8,000 francs for Napoleon's crown of golden laurel leaves, 3,500 francs for his sceptre, and 1,350 for his orb. Josephine's diadem, crown, and belt were made at a cost of 15,000 francs. These, however, were trivial sums compared to the main expenditures. Josephine's magnificent robes of state cost nearly 75,000 francs. The imperial coach, specially built for the occasion, cost 114,000 francs, and 140 Spanish horses were bought at a cost of more than 1,300 francs apiece. The more than two thousand diamonds and brilliants that the jewellers assembled for Josephine's adornment were valued at close to 900,000 francs. A great jewel such as the famous 'Regent' (once the Pitt Diamond), which Napoleon wore in the pommel of his sword, has to be described as priceless. The official totals assumed by the Treasury of the Crown in 1804 came to about 3,000,000 francs, and those assumed by the Treasury of the State to 1,500,000 francs. This supposedly official sum was revised upward in 1813 to give a total figure of 8,500,000 francs for the complete cost of the imperial coronation. It is possible to make a rough estimate that would have the franc of that time equal the U.S. dollar of our own day. We may note, too, that the coronation of George IV of England in 1820 is reported to have cost some £250,000, which again by rough estimate could be converted to six million dollars. But to ask what the total cost of Napoleon's coronation was, in terms of the burdens actually imposed upon French taxpayers or in terms of what a coronation *should* cost, is to put questions that defy any precise answer.

Josephine, so much the passive participant in these splendid preparations, scored one dramatic victory. Seeing that her marriage with Napoleon was childless and that apparently nothing could end the rancour of his family, she could never altogether rid herself of the gnawing fear that her marriage would some day end either in a divorce or an annulment. The re-establishment of the Roman Catholic Church in France had cast a dangerous shadow over her civil marriage of 1796. Therefore, while the Pope was at Fontainebleau, Josephine had a private conversation with him during which she frankly told him of her 'secret' – that the bonds uniting the imperial pair were simply those of the civil ceremony. She begged the Pope to use his influence with Napoleon to change this state of affairs. Pius VII, who apparently had not realized the facts of the situation, assured Josephine that even at this late date he would insist, as a condition of his taking part in the coronation, on a prior religious marriage between the imperial couple.

The Pope at once carried out his promise, telling Napoleon that without such a legitimization he would refuse to take part in the coronation. However reluctantly, Napoleon was obliged to agree, and so, on the afternoon of 1 December, a private ceremony took place in the little chapel of the Tuileries. Cardinal Fesch officiated as grand almoner of France, Talleyrand and Berthier attended as witnesses (though they both subsequently sought to deny it), and thus, nearly nine years after the civil ceremony in the mayor's office of the second *arrondissement*, the religious marriage was solemnized. Taking no chances, Josephine two days later asked for, and obtained, a certificate of legality from Cardinal Fesch.

On the second day of December in the year 1804, Josephine was crowned and anointed Empress of the French. It was a freezing, wintry morning with overcast skies, flurries of snow in the air, and traces of white on the icy streets. The elaborate schedule made it necessary for some of the ladies of the palace to have their hair dressed for the great occasion long before daylight. As early as six o'clock the military contingents began to march to their appointed positions. At seven, the first guests were admitted to the freezing interior of Notre Dame. At this same hour of half-dawn the great officials set out on foot from the Palais de Justice, moving with slow dignity through the streets in their ceremonial robes and reaching their places by eight o'clock. Then the senators, the councillors of state, the members of the legislative body, and the tribunate began their march. They moved through sand-sprinkled streets on either side of which the houses were decorated with red, white, and blue bunting, tapestries, bunches of artificial flowers, and freshly cut green branches. Nine o'clock was the stipulated hour for the setting out of the diplomatic corps, as it was for the departure of the German princes who had come to the coronation and who had been given a sumptuous breakfast by Marshal Murat, governor of Paris.

At this same hour of nine, Pope Pius VII, clad in white, descended the steps of the Pavillon de Flore with his retinue and took his place in a state carriage drawn by eight grey horses. On its roof was a large papal tiara. By custom the carriage was preceded through the streets by a papal chamberlain riding astride a humble mule and carrying a large wooden cross. The strange presence of this unglamorous beast amid such a splendid pageant provoked considerable jocular comment from the less than devout Paris crowds who were, notwithstanding, soon moved to awed silence by the dignified and benign appearance of the Pope. His entrance into Notre Dame was spectacular; first was borne the apostolic cross, escorted by seven acolytes carrying golden candlesticks, then came one hundred bishops and archbishops, then the Pope, wearing his tiara and escorted by seven cardinals. As Pius proceeded to the papal throne near the high altar he was greeted by the singing of the *Tu es Petrus*. Once enthroned, he could settle down to a wait of nearly two hours in the bone-chilling cold of the cathedral for the arrival of the imperial couple.

Although Napoleon and Josephine were supposed to leave the Tuileries at ten, delays occurred. Thiard, the new chamberlain of the palace, has given a vivid picture of a half-dressed Napoleon rushing about his chambers in these last frantic minutes of preparation:

Had it not been for the solemnity of the occasion, I would have had difficulty in keeping my composure. Barefooted, he was already wearing white velvet pantaloons scattered over with golden bees, a lace ruff in the style of Henry IV, and over this his tunic of the mounted chasseurs – the only dressing-gown he ever had.[6]

Napoleon's costume for the procession before the coronation was the so-called *petit habillement*: silk stockings and breeches, half-boots of white velvet with gold embroidery and golden buckles, a jacket of crimson velvet, a short velvet cloak lined with white satin and fastened on one shoulder with a diamond clasp, and a black velvet cap having two aigrettes fastened by a diamond clasp. The general effect of this costume and of the costumes of the other men was that of the *style troubadour*, a style in which the plumed velvet caps, the short velvet cloaks, the sashes, doublets, swords, and diamond buckles all gave more suggestion of the Renaissance court of a Francis I than the military splendours of the new Napoleonic era born of the French Revolution.

Josephine wore a dress and train of silver brocade scattered with golden bees. Though her shoulders and neck were bare, her arms were covered by long sleeves. The tight-fitting dress, which had a delicate lace ruff with golden spangles fastened at the back, was in the new mode which had no waist except for a thin golden ribbon encrusted with precious stones. Her bracelets, clasps, and necklace were all of gold, set with jewels and with the antique cameos of which she was so fond. Her graceful diadem held four rows of pearls interlaced with diamond leaves; it rested upon her chestnut hair, which the *coiffeurs* had transformed into a mass of tiny curls so skilfully that, according to Madame de Rémusat, Josephine gave the impression of being twenty-five. As the splendid pair were about to leave, Napoleon, unable to contain himself, turned to his brother and exclaimed, 'Ah, Joseph, if only father could see us now!'[7]

The imperial procession made its delayed departure from the Tuileries at ten-thirty, to the sound of cannon. The coach, specially designed for the occasion and drawn by eight splendid horses, was generously designed with large glass windows so as to give a good view of its occupants. Joseph and Louis were also to ride in the imperial coach, and in the confusion of departure Napoleon and Josephine seated themselves on the wrong side and at the last moment had to make an embarrassing rearrangement. Twenty squadrons of cavalry escorted them through streets lined with troops. Arriving at the archiepiscopal palace, they changed to their coronation robes. Thus, when all preparations were completed, it was within a quarter of an hour of noon.

For the actual coronation Napoleon and Josephine appeared in robes which suggested the splendours of imperial Rome. The Emperor wore a long satin gown embroidered with gold, reaching to his ankles and held by a silken sash. Over this he wore the imperial mantle of crimson velvet, lavishly strewn with golden bees and bordered with an intricate pattern of olive, laurel, and oak leaves. Lined with ermine, it weighed over eighty pounds, so that four bearers, Joseph, Louis, Lebrun, and Cambacérès, were required to carry it. In the splendid profile that appears in David's painting the finely chiselled features of the Emperor, surmounted by the laurel crown, suggest some exquisite antique cameo. Throughout the ceremony, save for the actual moment of coronation, Napoleon wore on his head the simple golden ring of laurel leaves. Josephine's robe, likewise of crimson velvet and heavily sewn with golden bees, replaced the purple mantle that she had worn in the procession through the streets. This robe was carried (albeit reluctantly) by five princesses: Josephine's daughter, Napoleon's three sisters, and Julie Clary, the wife of Joseph.

While Napoleon clearly wished a religious sanction for his marriage, he had no intention of making the acquisition of an imperial crown dependent upon the will of the Papacy. He would be anointed, but he would not be crowned, by the Pope. Nor would he make his confession and take communion at the Mass that followed the coronation ceremony and was an essential part of it. Pius VII, for his part, would not be present while Napoleon was taking the constitutional oath to respect the laws of the Concordat, for these guaranteed liberty of worship and recognized as irrevocable the government's sale of former Church lands. All these compromises had been agreed upon in advance, so that the stories of sudden surprises sprung during the ceremony simply are not true.

As Napoleon and Josephine entered Notre Dame, the blaze of lights from the candelabra and the crystal chandeliers, the rich colour of the hangings, the splendid costumes of the guests crowded in the tiers of seats, and the flash of jewels and decorations combined to make a spectacle of almost unbelievable brilliance. Against this setting the congregation saw a solemn procession moving forward to the music of an orchestra of 460 pieces. Pius VII and his retinue stood waiting in the chancel to receive the imperial couple. First came the ceremonial officers, then Marshal Murat carrying the imperial crown. Josephine followed, escorted by her chamberlains and the five princesses. Then came the 'regalia of Charlemagne', followed by Napoleon, wearing the wreath of golden laurel, and carrying in one hand a silver sceptre capped by an eagle, and in the other a rod tipped with the hand of justice. As he and Josephine received holy water from a cardinal, the Pope approached the altar and began the *Veni Creator*. Napoleon then divested himself of his crown, sceptre, sword, ring, hand of justice, and imperial robe, all of which were placed on the high altar. Josephine's robe, ring, and crown were placed beside them.

The Pope charged Napoleon in Latin to see that law, justice, and peace would prevail among his people, to which Napoleon gave his pledge with the single word, *Profiteor* ('I promise'). Then, after the litany, Napoleon and Josephine were conducted to the altar where, kneeling, each was anointed with the triple unction on the head and on both hands. In the course of the Mass that followed, Napoleon and Josephine proceeded again to the high altar and knelt while the Pope blessed the regalia and passed them one by one to the Emperor. When Pius VII had bestowed all save the crowns, Napoleon took his and placed it upon his own head. Josephine then knelt before him with clasped hands in the position immortalized in David's painting. Taking her crown from the altar, Napoleon held it briefly over his own head, then placed it upon the head of the Empress. When, a year later, David planned the canvas depicting this scene he wisely put aside his first sketch, which had shown Napoleon with his left hand upon his sword-hilt, very awkwardly and ostentatiously crowning himself with his right while the Pope drooped forlornly behind him. Too much is too much, and so the painting as the world knows it was redesigned to have Josephine kneeling in the very centre of the canvas. After the event it seemed proper, too, to make other alterations. Napoleon had so dominated the proceedings that Pius VII ran the risk of losing all importance. Napoleon therefore ordered David to emphasize the Pope's role by painting Pius VII with his right hand slightly raised as if in the act of benediction. A careful observer will note, too, that Hortense and the three sisters of Napoleon are all depicted standing proudly erect, well away from Josephine's train, which is held by ladies-in-waiting. Thus art inaccurately records what had been the subject of so much argument and discontent during the preliminaries of the coronation.

Once anointed and crowned, the imperial pair proceeded slowly in solemn procession to the western end of the nave where they were to ascend the twenty-four steps to the great throne. This stage of the proceedings was marred by an altercation among the five princesses as to the proper method of carrying the Empress's robe – an altercation ended by brusque, angry orders from the Emperor. Other difficulties arose, for the great weight of his robes and the clumsy handling on the part of his attendants almost caused Napoleon to fall backwards as he began the ascent of the dais. Once safely enthroned, he was joined by Josephine and by the princes, princesses, great dignitaries, and court officials grouped in a splendid tableau below him. Then, mounting to the top of the dais, Pius VII raised his hands aloft and blessed the pair: '*In hoc solio confirmare vos Deus, et in regno aeterno secum regnare faciat Christus*' – 'May God confirm you upon this throne, and may Christ cause you to reign with Him in His eternal kingdom.' Kissing Napoleon upon the cheek, Pius then intoned the famous words that Leo III had used a thousand years before when crowning Charlemagne at Rome in the ancient basilica of St Peter: '*Vivat Imperator in aeternum*' – 'May the Emperor live for ever!'

After this acclamation the assembly returned to the choir for the completion of the Mass. At its conclusion the Pope retired to the sacristy to avoid the embarrassment of being present while Napoleon took the constitutional oath, administered to him by the presiding officers of the legislative bodies. By three o'clock in the afternoon the elaborate ceremony was over, which, considering that many had started out before dawn, was long enough. By the time the imperial cortège reached the Tuileries, night had fallen and Paris was illuminated.

On this evening of their most splendid day, Napoleon and Josephine dined modestly tête-à-tête in the Tuileries. After the meal the Emperor chatted gaily with the ladies of the court, who still were wearing the elegant costumes of the day. Through the great windows of the palace they looked out on a veritable fairyland – the illuminated gardens of the Tuileries. The *grande allée* was lined with brightly shining columns, reflecting the light from thousands of coloured lamps that hung from the branches of the trees, sparkling in the night. In the distance, high above what is now the Place de la Concorde and where only ten years before one could have descried the black tip of the guillotine, shone symbolically in the night an immense white star.

In addition to becoming Empress, Josephine was also to become Queen. The sequel to the coronation in Paris was a coronation at Milan, for the leaders of the Italian Republic that Napoleon had created as a successor to the old Cisalpine Republic were canny enough to see that monarchy was now the fashionable pattern of the hour. Early in 1805, therefore, a delegation of the principal citizens of Lombardy was received by Napoleon in the throne room of the Tuileries. Here these delegates informed him of their recently passed 'Constitutional Statute', which asked Napoleon to become their king. Napoleon's first plan had been to make his brother king of Lombardy, but the ever suspicious Joseph was unwilling to accept this crown at the expense of having to forfeit his rights of succession, such as they were, in France. Hence Napoleon now accepted, was proclaimed ruler of the Kingdom of Italy, and announced that he would guarantee the freedom of the kingdom and go to Milan to be crowned.

Josephine consequently found herself involved in further elaborate plans and preparations. A letter to her mother in Martinique gave the news. Pius VII, she wrote, was about to leave and would celebrate Easter at Lyons. She and her husband were also about to depart. On 2 April the imperial party left Paris, reaching Lyons eight days later, where for a week they were busy with ceremonies and public affairs of all kinds. Then, in what must still have been wintry weather, they made the arduous crossing of the Mont Cenis Pass on muleback, reaching Turin by the 24th. Here they had a formal meeting with Pius VII and his party, now returning to Rome. On 8 May Napoleon made his impressive entry into Milan, welcomed by the firing of cannon and the pealing of church bells. He made his residence at the Monza Palace, directly across from the gleaming marble cathedral where his second coronation was to take place.

This coronation was a splendid ceremony, echoing the earlier rituals at Paris. There were the same cheering crowds, the same splendid décor within the cathedral, the same brilliant uniforms and dresses, the same regalia. On the high altar of the cathedral rested the ancient iron crown of Lombardy. Pius VII did not officiate, his duties being performed by Cardinal Caprara, archbishop of Milan. Another difference was that Josephine attended, not as a participant, but as a spectator. She watched the elaborate ritual of the Mass, and she watched her husband place the old iron crown on his head, exclaiming as he did so, '*Dio me l'ha data, guai a chi la toccherà.*' ('God has given me this; woe to him who would touch it!')

On the following day a programme of games and races, resembling those of antiquity, was presented in a huge circus. In sharp contrast, and as if in tribute to the new age, a balloon ascent followed. The wife of the celebrated aeronaut, Gainerin, rose aloft, scattering flowers upon Napoleon and Josephine. 'In one day and in a single spectacle,' reported the *Moniteur*, 'the Italians combined what to the ancients was most spectacular and what to modern science was most daring, in the presence of a hero who surpasses both the ancients and the moderns.'[8]

The royal pair attended a brilliant fête at La Scala. On 7 June Eugène, who earlier had been made arch-chancellor of France, was proclaimed viceroy of Italy. Shortly afterwards, Napoleon left Josephine to go on an inspection tour that took him through all the chief fortified cities of northern Italy. At Genoa he slept in the bed once occupied by the Hapsburg emperor, Charles V. While Josephine paid a visit to the lovely Italian lakes, Napoleon wrote to her from Brescia as follows:

I have received your letter, my good little Josephine, and I learn with pleasure that bathing is doing you good. I advised you to do this a week ago. Lake Como will be good for you. The weather here is very warm . . . Tomorrow I shall have 40,000 troops on the battlefield of Castiglione. I shall be at Verona on Saturday and at Mantua on Monday. Adieu, my dear. Be sensible, gay, and happy. Such is my will.[9]

At the end of June the pair were together in Genoa, the ancient republic that now was destined to be incorporated into

France. A brilliant evening in the finest traditions of Italian showmanship was prepared for them at the harbour front. Before an enormous crowd Napoleon and Josephine embarked upon a barge designed as a floating temple, which then was rowed out to the middle of the bay. Four huge rafts, covered with trees, flowers, statuary, and even fountains, were moved alongside them. From this vantage point they could see that the whole town was illuminated, with magnificent fireworks bursting over the huge assembly of boats moving about on the water.

When Napoleon and Josephine reached Turin they received news of impending threats from the newly forming European coalition. It was necessary, therefore, to return at once to Paris. Travelling incognito and at top speed, the Emperor made the journey over the Mont Cenis Pass and to Fontainebleau in the astonishing time of eighty-five hours. Josephine followed. The splendours and triumphs of the Italian journey would soon give place to still another period of war.

❖ 17 ❖

War Once More

CORONATION in Paris and coronation in Milan gave Josephine an unprecedented position in the new framework of French society. From the summer of 1805 to the summer of 1807 she proceeded to enjoy the fruits of her triumph. Even more than in the past she lived under the shadow of war, yet this was war so spectacular and so victorious that its tragic aspects affected her but little. As empress, Josephine took her part in the elaborate ceremonials of the Tuileries and Saint-Cloud; she also busied herself with the improvement and adornment of Malmaison; she concerned herself with the matrimonial affairs of Hortense and Eugène; she took the waters at Plombières; and she pestered Napoleon again and again to let her accompany him on his campaigns. At times he would relent, but only so far as to permit her to go with him on the first stages of his travels and to maintain a kind of informal court during her stay at Strasbourg, Mainz, or Munich. *Inter arma silent uxores.*

In this summer of 1805 Napoleon had not yet freed himself from the project of a cross-Channel invasion of the British Isles – on the contrary, it seemed for the first time that the long preparations at Boulogne might actually lead to success. Only the disastrous failure of Admiral Villeneuve to provide Napoleon with the naval support which he had planned led the Emperor late in August to turn from the Channel and fling his armies against the Austrians and the Russians.

Josephine, meanwhile, was little concerned with questions of high politics. Arriving in Paris from Milan in mid-July, she bade farewell to her husband as he went off hopefully for a last inspection of the Channel ports. She greatly missed Eugène, now viceroy of Italy, whom she had just visited. The long journey from Milan had been tiring, and so she wrote from Saint-Cloud to Hortense in melancholy tones. 'My life proceeds sadly,' she complained, 'always distant from the person whom I love.'[1] Still, there were compensations, for this was the month for her annual pilgrimage to Plombières. The prospect was pleasing, even though the ceremonies en route were by now becoming somewhat burdensome. Napoleon had explicitly ordered that no detail be neglected and thus, although her party passed through Toul after nightfall in the pouring rain and at full gallop, the entire town was illuminated. When she reached Nancy at the grim hour of three o'clock in the morning a brigade of soldiers paid her military honours, while the mayor and town council greeted her with music and addresses of welcome. Here she took a few hours' rest and then set forth on the road again. Another full day's travel brought her to Plombières.

Even in this rustic retreat amid the pine forests of the Vosges a new note of splendour had been introduced. A company of the Third Infantry of the Line had been sent from Nancy to guard the Empress. On her arrival Josephine passed beneath an archway of green leaves in order to accept the inevitable address of welcome and, later, to watch the equally inevitable fireworks and illuminations. Her household consisted of an 'esquire of honour', a prefect of the palace, a controller, two ladies-in-waiting, five ladies-of-the-bedchamber, some footmen, coachmen, and stablemen. The costs of travelling amounted to 37,483 francs, and the costs of her one month's stay amounted to 134,482 francs. Clearly, an empress does not live in rustic simplicity.

Josephine did not altogether shed her cares amid her new glories. She wrote to Eugène saying that Napoleon was pleased with him as viceroy, but that he would wish Eugène to be firmer in his handling of Italian dissidents. Concerning Napoleon's family in Paris she told the old story of their hostility. 'If only they were well-disposed to us,' she wrote, 'they would have no better friends than ourselves.' To the son who had once written to her sternly from Egypt on the subject of her behaviour in Paris she reported that she was getting on well with Napoleon and did everything that she could to please him:

No more jealousy, my dear Eugène, I can truthfully tell you. Hence he is happier, and I am, too. I can say nothing of political news: it is all a mystery into which the Emperor never permits me to enter.[2]

Josephine heard from Napoleon while he was still at the great camp of Boulogne. His letter reveals him as a busy, yet warm-hearted and indeed devoted, husband.

I seldom have news of you. You forget your loved ones, and that is not good. I did not realize that the waters of Plombières have the same effect as the River Lethe.

It seems to me that in drinking these waters of Plombières you should say, *Ah, Bonaparte! If I die, who is there who will love you?* But things are far from that, aren't they? All passes – beauty, cleverness, affection, the sun itself; but that which will have no end is the good that I wish, the happiness – [illegible] – the favour of my Josephine. But I shall no longer be so tender if you make jokes about me.[3]

Towards the end of August, after making gifts to the poor as befitted an empress, Josephine left Plombières. After facing the now inescapable round of official receptions en route, by the close of the month she was back at Malmaison.

By this time it was clear to Napoleon that the Channel coast offered him no more promise of victories. Admiral Villeneuve, returning with his fleet from the West Indies, had put in at Cadiz instead of sailing for Brest as instructed. 'This is certainly treason,' the outraged Napoleon wrote. 'Villeneuve is a wretch who should be ignominiously dismissed.... He would sacrifice everything to save his skin.'[4] In August, two months before the decisive battle of Trafalgar, the Emperor abandoned his invasion plans and prepared for the lightning advance east of the Rhine which would bring the mass of his forces against the Austrians and the Russians. The great campaigns of Austerlitz, Jena, and Friedland were beginning.

Leaving the Tuileries late in September, Josephine accompanied her husband as far as Strasbourg. After several days of receptions, complimentary visits, and the like he pushed forward into Germany. Although Josephine would gladly have accompanied Napoleon, he willed otherwise. It became her duty, therefore, to keep up the busy round of receptions, balls, theatres, operas, and concerts. Strasbourg for a time seemed the crossroads of Europe, with delegation after delegation from Paris passing through, the men often accompanied by their ladies. Many of the princely rulers of Germany, now deeply impressed by the power of imperial France, likewise found Strasbourg a valuable centre for their affairs. Josephine played her role. She summoned, for example, the composer Spontini from Paris so that the society of Strasbourg could hear performances of *La Vestale* and his new religious composition, *O Salutaris*. She made many expenditures: plants for her gardens at Malmaison, animals for her zoo, art objects, and bric-à-brac. Josephine even presided when a Masonic lodge, the *Orient de Strasbourg*, held an initiation. This may have been a particular honour paid to the Empress; on the other hand it was not unknown in eighteenth-century France for some ladies to enter Freemasonic lodges. Napoleon was frequently honoured in Masonic circles, and one lodge in Paris was known as *Sainte Joséphine*.

Brief, soldierly notes came regularly from Josephine's warrior-husband. 'The weather is terrible,' he told her in one. 'It rains so much that I have to change my coat twice a day.'[5] On 19 October Napoleon received the surrender of the Austrian commander, Mack, at Ulm. By a brilliant encirclement and with practically no losses he had shattered an Austrian army of eighty thousand men and taken at least thirty thousand prisoners – a number which in his exultant letter to his wife he expanded to seventy thousand. Josephine's recognition of this victory consisted in attending a *Te Deum* in the cathedral and giving a fête for the ladies of Strasbourg. Napoleon meanwhile was driving forward through Augsburg and Munich until on 14 November he reached Vienna. Amid the press of war he did not forget Josephine. Though his letters had been brief, we can count at least thirteen in the six weeks following his departure from Strasbourg.

In one of these letters Napoleon urged Josephine to bear the burden of their separation more cheerfully:

I see with regret that you are very unhappy. I have been given details which make clear all the tenderness which you have for me. But you must have more courage and more trust. I had already cautioned you that I would be unable to write for six days. . . . You must be gay, amuse yourself, and hope that before the end of the month we shall see one another. I am advancing against the Russians. In a few days I shall have crossed the Inn.[6]

Towards the end of November Josephine was authorized to leave Strasbourg for Munich, her route taking her through Stuttgart, Ulm, and Augsburg. She had heard, so she informed Eugène in Milan, that the elector of Bavaria was preparing a fête for her. Of more personal concern to her were the rumours now circulating in Germany that Talleyrand on Napoleon's instructions was negotiating a marriage between Eugène and the Princess Augusta, daughter of the Bavarian elector. The plan was supposedly most secret and still conjectural, so Josephine asserted in a subsequent letter to Hortense:

Assuredly, if it were really a question of the marriage of your brother you are the first person whom I would tell. I was indeed told while in Strasbourg that the German papers had spoken of it. I recall that at this time everyone believed in the marriage, and I found myself the only one not in the secret. You know very well, my dear, that the Emperor, who has never spoken to me about this, would not marry off Eugène without my knowledge.[7]

The letter is less than candid, for Talleyrand had already told Josephine what was afoot. Secret or not the proposed marriage was soon to be a fact. Meanwhile such matters were overshadowed by the news of one of Napoleon's greatest victories, the battle of Austerlitz on 2 December.

The Emperor wrote three times to Josephine in order to tell her of this spectacular triumph over the Austrians and the Russians. Exhausted as he must have been, he sent her word on the day following the battle as follows:

Austerlitz, 3 December 1805

I have sent Lebrun to you from the field of battle. I have beaten the Russian and Austrian armies commanded by the two emperors. I am somewhat fatigued, as I have bivouacked for a week in open air, on nights that are quite chilly. Tonight I sleep in the château of Prince Kaunitz, where I shall rest for two or three hours. The Russian army is not only beaten, it is destroyed. *Je t'embrasse.*[8]

On the 5th he wrote again:

I have concluded a truce. The Russians are going home. The Battle of Austerlitz is the finest of all that I have fought; 45 flags, more than 150 cannon, the standards of the Russian Guard, 20 generals, 30,000 prisoners, more than 30,000 slain: what a horrible spectacle!

The Emperor Alexander is in despair. He is going to Russia. Yesterday I saw the Emperor of Austria at my bivouack; we chatted for two hours: we have agreed to make peace quickly.[9]

And on 8 December came still another letter, telling of the heavy Russian losses.

Josephine meanwhile was on the road to Munich, unaware of these great triumphs. She arrived on 15 December, soon to receive a further letter from her husband, written while he was preparing the definitive treaty with Austria and sounding a note unhappily different from that of its predecessors:

Great Empress [it began in sardonic tones], not a letter from you since your departure from Strasbourg. You have gone from Baden to Stuttgart and to Munich without writing a word. This is not very kind, nor is it very tender . . . Deign, from the height of your grandeur, to concern yourself a little with your slaves.[10]

On the following day he wrote again:

It is a very long time since I have had news of you. Do the elegant fêtes at Baden, Stuttgart, and Munich make you forget the poor soldiers who live covered with mud, rain, and blood?[11]

His reproaches were soon lost in the speedy march of events. On 27 December Napoleon made the Treaty of Pressburg with Austria, exacting a heavy indemnity and forcing the Hapsburgs to give up the last of their Italian lands, to turn over the Tyrol to Bavaria, and to recognize the rulers of Bavaria and Württemberg as kings. The days of the Holy Roman Empire were numbered, and Josephine's husband had, in fact, usurped the central position in Europe for so long held by the ancient line of the Hapsburgs. On the last day of the year and elated with his great triumphs, Napoleon – the new Charlemagne – rejoined his wife at Munich.

As the year 1806 opened, Josephine's principal concern was the marriage of Eugène to Augusta Amelia, eldest daughter of the ruler who, thanks to Napoleon, was now king of Bavaria. Napoleon's intentions were simple: for political reasons he wished to associate his dynasty with the venerable house of Wittelsbach. The first article of the proposed marriage contract – which had been drawn up early in January, unknown to Eugène and before he had caught so much as a glimpse of his intended bride – stipulated that as viceroy of Italy Eugène was to be called 'Imperial Highness' and 'Son of France'. He would take precedence over Napoleon's brothers, Joseph and Louis, he would sit at the Emperor's right hand, and be listed before the brothers in the *Almanach Impérial*. All was not plain sailing in this scheme, for Augusta Amelia, who most inconveniently was already betrothed to the hereditary prince of Baden, showed some unwillingness to obey her father's new orders. It was also important for France to remain on good terms with Baden and find a substitute bride for the hereditary prince. All these matters Talleyrand took in hand so quickly and expertly as to produce a double victory for the Beauharnais over the Bonapartes. Eugène's position in the imperial hierarchy was substantially advanced, and he would marry Augusta Amelia. The bride ultimately found for the disappointed prince of Baden was none other than Stephanie de Beauharnais, niece of Josephine and granddaughter of Aunt Fanny. When actually this second marriage took place in the following April, Napoleon outraged his brothers and sisters by generously referring to Stephanie in imperial terms as 'my daughter'.

The Emperor, meanwhile, had informed Eugène of the plans that were under way:

My Cousin [he wrote, the style of address indicating that Eugène was not yet an 'Imperial Highness'], I have arrived at Munich. I have arranged your marriage with the Princess Augusta. News has been published. This morning the Princess paid me a visit. She is very pretty. You will find her portrait on a teacup which I am sending you, but really she looks much better than that.[12]

Another letter in typical Napoleonic fashion gave Eugène his marching orders:

Twelve hours after the receipt of this letter you will set out with all speed for Munich . . . It is not necessary to bring much of a suite. Start promptly and incognito, as much to avoid danger as to avoid delays . . . One hour after receiving this, send me a courier to tell me the day when you expect to arrive.[13]

All went as planned. Eugène made the breathless journey from Padua in less than four days. On Napoleon's instructions he cut off his huge cavalry moustaches, which might, so the Emperor feared, be displeasing to his bride. The marriage contract was formally signed and the civil ceremony performed on 13 January 1806; the religious ceremony came on the following day. Splendid jewels had been ordered from Paris by Napoleon, who likewise issued strict instructions to all the Bonaparte brothers and sisters that each should send the bridal couple a present worth not less than fifteen or more than twenty thousand francs. Josephine was well pleased with this marriage, as she was quick to tell Hortense, who had been forbidden by her ever-suspicious husband to go to Munich:

I know all the regrets you must have had [Josephine added] at not being able to come and join us at Munich. I am not surprised at the sorrow which your husband's letter has caused you; but I realize that you do not have the strength to resist his firm demands.[14]

Back in Paris by the end of January, Josephine's next concern was the marriage of her niece, Stephanie de Beauharnais, to Prince Charles of Baden. This marriage, too, was a calculated affair of state, for Napoleon had now formally adopted Stephanie as his daughter. The civil ceremony and the signing of the marriage contract took place in the Gallery of Diana, while the religious ceremony followed in the chapel of the Tuileries. Great pomp and magnificent presents marked the occasion, while at night, as at the time of the coronation, Paris shone with brilliant illuminations.

These and other actions of Napoleon were all of a sort. He

was in process of creating the Grand Empire – a magnificent area of client states fringing a greatly enlarged France. To govern these territories he began to make generous use of his family. Brother Louis, married to Hortense, was soon to be king of Holland. Brother Joseph was to be king of Naples and then of Spain. Brother Jérôme was forced to give up his American wife, to remarry, and become ruler of the newly created kingdom of Westphalia. Murat, married to Napoleon's sister Caroline, was named grand duke of Berg and later king of Naples. Pauline, now Princess Borghese, received the Italian principality of Guastalla, while Elisa was granted the tiny state of Piombino. On the Beauharnais side Josephine was to see her daughter become queen of Holland. Her son was now viceroy of Italy and son-in-law to the king of Bavaria. Her niece, Stephanie, was married to the heir to the grand duchy of Baden. Rarely if ever has a family been so rapidly established in such widespread splendour.

For his Beauharnais kin Napoleon showed a genuine affection. Time and again he wrote to Hortense during his campaigns, and he was quick to protest when he did not hear from her. Eugène he treated with mingled affection and pride, tempered by an occasional soldierly reproof. For Eugène's wife, Augusta, he soon developed the warmest feelings. Here, for example, is the letter which the childless Napoleon wrote to Augusta a few days after her wedding, while on his way to Paris:

My daughter, the letter you have sent me is as agreeable as you are. The kind feelings I have towards you will be sure to increase every day; I know this from the pleasure which I take in recalling your fine qualities and from the need which I feel to have you reassure me that you are satisfied with everyone and made happy by your husband. Among all my concerns none are dearer to me than those which will guarantee the happiness of my children. Believe, Augusta, that I love you as a father and that I expect from you all the tenderness of a daughter. Protect yourself during your journey, as well as in the new climate when you arrive, taking as much rest as is convenient. You have done much moving about for a month, and you must realize that I do not wish you to become ill.

I end, my daughter, by giving you my paternal blessing.[15]

A letter to Eugène written four months later is a document extraordinarily revealing of Napoleon as a husband and a father. The eager Eugène had plunged so ardently into his work as viceroy that the Emperor, watching him closely, felt obliged to sound a few warnings:

My son, you work too hard; your life is too monotonous. This is good as far as you are concerned, for work to you is a means of refreshment; but you have a young wife who is pregnant. I think you should arrange to spend your evenings with her, and organize some social life. Why not go to the theatre once a week *en grande loge*? I think you should also have an establishment so that you can hunt at least once a week; I will gladly put a sum in the budget for this purpose. You must have more gaiety in your home; it is necessary for your wife's happiness and for your own health. Your work can be done in less time. I lead the life you do, but I have an older wife who does not need me to amuse her, and also I have more responsibilities; even so, it is true that I take more diversions and amusements than you do. A young wife needs to be entertained, above all in her present condition. You were once fond of pleasure; you must return to your old tastes.[16]

If only these happy marriage arrangements, which meant so much to Josephine, and the splendid triumphs of the spring of 1806 could have remained permanent! Yet, as the summer continued, dark shadows appeared. Russia had not made peace. England still ruled the ocean. Prussia, who had kept out of the Third Coalition, was now most bitter and resentful at the great changes taking place in Germany. True, the beautiful young Queen Louise of Prussia had written most warmly to Josephine in 1805, addressing her as 'my sister' and sending her fine gifts of porcelain from the royal factories:

I can only hope that this product of our factories meets your approval, Madame, and that above all this modest souvenir will have value in your eyes because of the feeling of friendship I offer you and with which I am, *Madame ma soeur*, your Imperial Majesty's good sister,

Louise[17]

Such good will was soon swept aside as Josephine found herself once again in a world of war. In August Prussia made preparations to join with Russia in a campaign against France. Napoleon decided to strike hard. In September he heard from Marshal Berthier in Germany. 'The Prussians no longer disguise their intention of making war on us,' Berthier wrote. 'Their armies are assembling on those points of Prussian territory which are near our advance posts.'[18] By this time Napoleon's plans were completed. Accompanied by Josephine he left on the day following Berthier's warning. Three days later they were at Mainz, where once again Josephine was to be left alone while Napoleon paid his court to the God of War. He would not see her for ten months.

Busy as Napoleon was with the campaign in which he would defeat the Prussians at Jena, fight the savage battles of Eylau and Friedland with the Russians, and at last settle accounts with both powers in the Treaties of Tilsit, he kept regularly in touch with his wife. At least seven letters went to Josephine in October, nine in November, and nine in December. Josephine, too, kept up her side of the exchange. 'I have received several letters from you,' the Emperor told her on 23 October, and on six subsequent occasions he acknowledged her further missives.[19] What Josephine wrote we can only infer. Quite clearly she was restless at Mainz, despite the pleasure she took in making gifts of chains, watches, necklaces, pearls, and snuff-boxes to her acquaintances in the old imperial capital – gifts for which the Parisian jewellers later submitted bills totalling 54,685 francs.

'I do not know why you weep,' Bonaparte told Josephine in one letter. 'Talleyrand has arrived and tells me that you do nothing but cry,' he wrote in another. 'But why? You have your daughter, your grandchildren, and good news [from me]; these are reasons for being contented and happy.'[20] In still another letter from Berlin, influenced perhaps by the efforts of Queen Louise to moderate his treatment of Prussia, he comforted Josephine and gave her some of his views on women:

I have received your letter, in which you seem angry at the bad things I say about women. It is true that I hate intriguing women above all else. I am accustomed to women who are good, gentle, and conciliatory; those are the sort I like. If such ones have spoiled me, it's not my fault, but yours . . . I like women who are good, simple, and sweet – because only such ones resemble you.[21]

Josephine, nevertheless, could not banish the boredom of Mainz, nor could she drive away her unhappiness. She pestered her husband to let her join him.

Napoleon tried to cheer his wife. 'I see with satisfaction that my views please you,' he wrote, answering her letter. 'You are wrong to think that I am only flattering you; I spoke of you simply as I see you.'[22] Arriving at Posen in December, he sought to allay Josephine's fears about the Polish ladies:

All these Polish ladies try to be French, but there is only one woman for me. Would you know her? I could easily describe her for you, but I would have to be so flattering that you would not recognize her; yet in truth my heart could say nothing but good about her. The nights are long here, alone.[23]

In another letter:

You say that you are not jealous. I have long noted that quick-tempered people always insist that they are not quick-tempered; those who are afraid often say that they are not; you, therefore, are convicted of jealousy. I am delighted![24]

In still another:

You must try to be calm. I have already told you that I am in Poland and that when winter quarters are established you can come; you must therefore wait for some days. . . . You beautiful women recognize no barriers at all; what you want must be. As for myself, I declare I am the most enslaved of men; my master has no human sympathies – this master is simply the nature of things.[25]

Throughout November and December 1806, Napoleon resisted as best he could Josephine's constant petitions to join him. Postponement, flattery, cajolery, and expressions of affection, along with blunt statements concerning the dangers and hardships of travel, were his weapons. 'Everything goes well,' he wrote from Berlin early in November, 'I only lack the pleasure of seeing you, but I hope that the time for this won't be too far distant.' Three weeks later he tried to reassure her: 'I shall decide in a few days,' he wrote, 'whether to summon you here or send you to Paris.' When, however, he had made the difficult journey into Poland his tone changed. 'You must wait a few days more,' he instructed Josephine from Posen on 9 December. A week later came the news that he was leaving for Warsaw. 'I shall be back in two weeks,' he wrote, 'I hope then to summon you.'[26] Unhappily, the stay at Warsaw was prolonged. If he could have returned to Berlin, so he explained, then perhaps Josephine might have joined him. His affairs, however, were pressing, and the soldier was required once again to move northward against the enemy.

On 28 December Napoleon defeated the Russians at Pultusk.

I can only write you a word [he informed Josephine at five o'clock on the following morning]. I am in a wretched farm-house. I have beaten the Russians, taken 30 cannon, their baggage train, and 6,000 prisoners. But the weather is terrible. It is raining, and we are in mud up to our knees.[27]

Such letters began to destroy Josephine's hopes. 'I am of the opinion you should return to Paris,' Napoleon wrote gingerly to her from Warsaw on the third day of the new year. 'Go to the Tuileries,' came the sterner message on 7 January, 'hold receptions and carry on the same life to which you were accustomed when I was there; such is my will.' The plaintive letters from Josephine continued to arrive, for on the morrow came the Emperor's decisive word:

The weather is too bad, the roads are unsure and atrocious, the distances are too great for me to permit you to come here where my business keeps me. It would take you a month to get here. You would arrive ill; possibly you would have to return at once; it would be folly. Your stay in Mainz is too depressing; Paris calls you; go there, such is my will. I am more put out than you, for I would have loved to share the long nights of this season with you; but one must obey circumstances.[28]

Reluctantly Josephine adjusted herself to the increasing evidence that her visit to Poland was impossible.

They tell me that you cry constantly [Napoleon wrote]. Fie! how ugly that seems! Your letter of 7 January grieves me. Be worthy of me, and show more character. Undertake the appropriate social duties at Paris, and, above all, be content. I am well and I love you very much, but if you cry all the time I shall think you are without courage and without character. I don't like faint-hearted people; an empress must have courage![29]

The struggle of words went on throughout January. 'I wish you to be gay, content with your lot,' Napoleon told her, 'and I wish you to obey, not moaning and weeping but with gaiety of heart, and a little happiness.' This was on 18 January. On the 23rd he wrote again:

I have received your letter of 15 January. It is impossible for me to permit women to make a journey such as this, with roads that are bad, unsafe, and muddy. . . . I laughed at what you said about taking a husband in order to be with him. I had thought, in my ignorance, that the wife was made for her husband, and the husband for country, family, and glory. Pardon my ignorance; one is always learning from our fine ladies.[30]

Soon came the news of the savage Battle of Eylau (8 February 1807), where the losses on both sides were appalling, and only a last minute Russian withdrawal enabled a badly shaken Napoleon to claim a victory. 'Don't be downcast,' Napoleon wrote to Josephine three days after the battle. 'All this will soon be over, and the happiness of seeing you will end all my fatigue.' On the next day he had a little more to say, 'My dear, I am still at Eylau. This countryside is covered with dead and wounded. It isn't the prettiest side of war: people suffer, and the spirit is oppressed to see so many victims.'[31]

Long before receiving this Josephine had accepted the inevitable. Leaving Mainz on 27 January, and being greeted en route by receptions at Strasbourg, Lunéville, and Nancy, she arrived in Paris on the last day of the month.

Napoleon's reasons for not having Josephine visit him in Poland did not arise entirely from matters of diplomacy, strategy, or travel. Two events occurring within a few days of each other and a third some months later powerfully affected the entire future course of his relations with his wife. At Pultusk, on the last day of the year 1806, he received news of the birth of a son, Léon, to Eléanore de la Plaigne, the divorced wife of a French cavalry captain. After two months of their marriage the captain had been imprisoned for forgery, and this Eléanore, a friend of Napoleon's sister, Caroline Murat, had been taken into her household as *lectrice*, or companion. Murat, it appears, had an affair with Eléanore and then in a fashion made standard over the centuries as a prerogative of royalty had early in 1806 passed her over to Napoleon for one of his transitory affairs. For these rendezvous she was ushered into the Tuileries where the Emperor on occasion worked late in his study. His busy day being regulated to the last minute, the following anecdote is at least credible. Beside the imperial couch was a clock, and Eléanore, whose pleasure in these meetings was less than total, found it possible on one occasion to reach forth and advance the hands stealthily by half an hour. Shortly afterwards the Emperor's eye caught a glimpse of the time, whereupon, uttering an astonished, 'So soon?' he returned forthwith to his desk and his papers.[32]

What gives this affair with Eléanore its importance is that Napoleon, learning that her child had been born on 13 December and having consulted his calendar, could make some strong claim to paternity – provided always that Murat's claims were not stronger. The infant, it was soon declared, bore a striking resemblance to the Emperor. Napoleon's present interest in Eléanore was not one of affection. Though she was well provided for, and her child was quickly and richly endowed from the imperial treasury, he refused to see her again. The significance lay elsewhere. Napoleon's marriage with Josephine had been childless; for years the problem of the succession had harassed him; yet thoughts of divorce and marriage were marred by the uncertainty as to whether he, rather than Josephine, was to blame for the lack of an heir. If he were to blame, remarriage would not help. If, however, Napoleon was truly the father of Léon, then divorce and remarriage took on a powerful new significance. Such was the ominous shadow soon to fall on the happiness of Josephine.

Precisely at the time when Napoleon heard the news of Eléanore and Léon, chance again affected his life. Leaving Pultusk for Warsaw, he stopped to change horses at the little post-station of Bronie. Here a small crowd of Poles had gathered to observe the conqueror of Europe. Among them was a young, dignified, blonde Polish lady of striking appearance, an ardent patriot who requested Duroc to present her to the prospective liberator of her country. She was Maria Walewska, the eighteen-year-old wife of a seventy-year-old twice-widowed Polish nobleman, and she was destined to be a burning flame in the life of Napoleon.

The Countess Walewska was no adventuress; on the contrary, she was modest, devoutly religious, and ardently patriotic. At a ball to which she was soon invited by the Emperor, which the Polish patriots finally prevailed upon her to attend, she rebuffed Napoleon's advances, as she did the insistent letters he wrote her. Her eventual yielding, after repeated refusals, came about only when her complacent husband had agreed to a separation, and when a delegation of some of Poland's leading political figures had lectured her about her duty to her country. She followed Napoleon to the East Prussian château of Finckenstein in the spring of 1807. Early in 1808 he prevailed upon her to come to Paris, and in the next year during the Austrian campaign she met him at Vienna where she was installed in an elegant mansion near Schoenbrunn. On 4 May 1810 she bore Napoleon a son, Alexandre-Florian-Joseph, who with his mother visited Napoleon at Elba in 1814 and much later, as Count Walewski, played a considerable role in the political life of the Second Empire.

This affair with Maria Walewska was not what set the Emperor's thoughts along the path of divorce from Josephine, for the possibility was already in his mind. The young Polish countess swept Napoleon off his feet with a directness that in his case had nothing to do with questions of high policy. A woman strikingly different from the actresses, the singers, and the anonymous beauties who tiptoed late at night along the corridors of the imperial residences, she brought an immediate transformation into the hard life of the soldier. The fine castle of Finckenstein with its blazing log fires was another world from the draughty, miserable farm-houses and the mud of the

Polish winter campaign. 'I have just established my head-quarters in a fine château in the style of Bessières,' Napoleon wrote to Josephine in April with deceptive innocence. 'There are many fireplaces, which is very pleasant seeing that I rise often during the night. I love to see a fire.'[33]

Maria Walewska's presence at Finckenstein was sufficient reason for Napoleon to require Josephine to remain in Paris – as the Empress soon began to suspect. Her letters in the spring of 1807 were marked with jealousy and complaint. Time and again Josephine had found that no matter how outrageous and scandalous her behaviour, only her presence and her charm were needed to win Napoleon back. Nothing ever had been unforgivable. Now her husband was a thousand miles away; she had not seen him for six months; she was forty-four, she wept constantly, and she was nervously upset; clearly her agonizing doubt was whether she could still maintain her spell over him.

Bonaparte tried to allay her doubts by jests and evasion. 'Put no faith in the evil rumours which may be spread about,' he wrote. 'Never doubt my feelings towards you, and have no uneasiness.'[34] In May he tried again:

I have received your letter. I don't understand what you say about women who are corresponding with me. I love only my little Josephine, kindly, sulky, and capricious, who can quarrel as gracefully as she does everything else; she is always adorable – except when she is suspicious; then she becomes a regular devil. But let's get back to these women. If I should occupy myself with one of them, I assure you it would have to be a genuine rosebud. Do those you speak about come in this class?[35]

While Napoleon thus interrupted his battles on the dreary plains of East Prussia with dalliance before the roaring fireplaces of *Schloss* Finckenstein, Josephine kept up the conventional routine of Paris, Malmaison, and Saint-Cloud. Within a few days of her arrival at the Tuileries she held a formidable reception for the senate, the legislature, the tribunate, the chapter of Notre Dame, and the prefect of the Seine – these notables all presenting her with addresses of welcome. She went to the Opéra in the rue de Richelieu, Napoleon having reminded her to attend in state, occupying the *grandes loges*, and not in the informal fashion she preferred. Nor should she attend the smaller theatres of which she was so fond. Her casual activities, indeed, though nothing like her reckless behaviour in the days of the Directory, were such as to reach the ears of her husband and led to stern warnings. 'I don't wish you ever to receive T[hiard],' Napoleon wrote, 'he is a bad subject, and you will hurt me if you don't obey.'[36] A few weeks later came another warning:

I hear, my dear, that the malicious talk which went on in your salon at Mainz is being renewed. Make it stop. I shall take it badly if you can't provide a remedy. You are letting yourself be hurt by the remarks of people who should be consoling you.[37]

In March he cautioned Josephine against any idea of travel during the summer:

You mustn't think of travelling this summer. You can't make the round of inns and encampments. I would like, as much as you, to see you and to live quietly. I could do other things than fight, but duty comes before all else. All my life I have sacrificed everything – tranquillity, my own desires, my happiness – to my destiny.

Good-bye, my dear. See little of this Madame P * * *; she is a woman of poor associations – too common and utterly worthless.[38]

Such communications hardly enlivened the days of Josephine. She kept in touch, to be sure, with her mother at Martinique. She found some comfort in writing to her children, telling them how good a correspondent her husband was. In point of fact, one can count thirty-five letters from Napoleon to her in the four-month period ending in her return from Mainz to Paris, and fifty-one letters in the ensuing six months of their separation – roughly two or three a week. 'The last week has passed very rapidly and very agreeably,' she wrote Hortense in March. 'I spent it at Malmaison, in the midst of the work going on there, and this employment has restored my health.'[39] Yet the tone of unhappiness, so evident in her letters to Napoleon, likewise appears in those to Hortense and Eugène, 'My health is fairly good, but my heart is very sad at the long absence of the Emperor.' Or, again, to Hortense, 'Sometimes

I get two letters a day from him; it is a great comfort, but it doesn't replace him.'[40] To Eugène went the same message, 'I get frequent letters from the Emperor. His health is always good, but his absence makes me very sad, and if this keeps on I don't know how I shall have the courage to bear it.' Still later she wrote: 'I expect to go immediately to Saint-Cloud; I need to for my health; I have been suffering from migraine, which I attribute to the season, or even more to the sorrow at being parted from those I love.'[41]

These, however, were transient sorrows. The great blow came suddenly when Hortense's idolized elder child, Napoléon-Charles, died at The Hague on 5 May after suffering six days with the croup. Hortense was prostrate. She was reported to have been paralysed for six hours, and for days afterwards lived and moved in a complete stupor. Josephine, too, was almost overcome with grief. She wrote at once to Napoleon in such agonized terms as to cause him to write back begging her to moderate her sorrow:

I wish I could be near you [he wrote at once] so that you could be moderate and understanding in your grief. You are lucky never to have lost a child; but this is one of the conditions and penalties going with our human misery. If only I could learn that you have become sensible, and that you are well! Would you wish to increase my sorrow?[42]

Again and again the soldier, to whom death was a common-place, wrote to Josephine and Hortense sternly urging them to moderate their grief. A letter to Hortense, written from Finckenstein on 20 May, went as follows:

My daughter, all that I hear from The Hague informs me that you are not being sensible; however legitimate your grief, it must have limits. Do not injure your health; seek some distractions, and realize that life is strewn with so many dangers, and is the source of so many ills that death is not the greatest of them.[43]

Josephine arranged to meet Hortense at the castle of Laeken, near Brussels. At this convenient rendezvous (for neither could travel further without the express permission of the Emperor) the two women found some solace for their grief.

Death struck once again during the summer. Josephine's mother, who had lived almost in solitude at Trois-Îlets, rejecting her doctors and seeing only her confessors, died on 2 June in her seventy-first year. She was given the funeral of a princess of the blood. Napoleon ordered the news to be kept temporarily from Josephine, fearing the effect upon her, already so deeply upset at the loss of her young grandson.

The death of Napoléon-Charles was the third ominous development for Josephine. He had always been much closer to the Emperor's heart than had Hortense's second child and thus his death, together with the implications of the birth of the infant Léon some months before, cruelly brought into focus the question of the divorce. While the summer of 1807 was to be a time of splendid achievement for Napoleon, it was not so for Josephine. Napoleon won the great victory of Friedland over the Russians in June and dictated a crushing peace treaty to Frederick William III of Prussia in July at Tilsit. While there the French Emperor embraced Tsar Alexander I of Russia on the famous raft in the middle of the River Niemen, and signed with him a treaty of alliance, recognizing Napoleon's new order in Europe. Few triumphs could have been greater. Yet for the Empress, awaiting in Paris her victorious husband's return and acting as guardian to Hortense's second infant, Napoléon-Louis, while his distraught mother took the waters at Bagnières, anything but victory was in store.

On 21 July 1807 after an absence from the capital of ten months – the longest such absence in his career – Napoleon returned to Saint-Cloud.

❧ 18 ❧

On Being an Empress

As empress, Josephine found herself subject to a life of ritual, the product of much conscious planning and some improvisation. Superb as an organizer, Napoleon saw no reason why in her official appearances Josephine's every move should not be guided by an etiquette as elaborate as any that the queens of France had accepted in the past. Whatever private life she could still claim for herself had to be fitted within the inexorable limits of this imposing imperial structure. Josephine did not always find it easy to conform.

The stage setting was provided by the palaces of the Tuileries, Saint-Cloud, and Fontainebleau, as well as by Malmaison and, less frequently, the Élysée, and Rambouillet. Travelling abroad, Josephine held court at Strasbourg where the ancient episcopal palace, magnificently reconstructed in the eighteenth century by the Rohan family, had now been taken over as an imperial residence and refurbished at a cost of 178,000 francs by the architect Fontaine. She also held court at Mainz, and she appeared as an honoured guest and relative through marriage in Baden, Württemberg, and the Italian kingdom. On occasion she still found happy seclusion at Plombières. Since funds for all her purposes came from the public treasury, she managed with no difficulty to run her expenditures far beyond the amounts stipulated for any given year. While complaints and even expressions of anger came at regular intervals from her indignant husband, he none the less paid the ever-recurring bills for the dresses, shawls, hats, and shoes, the silks, the feathers, the jewels, the perfumes, and the bric-à-brac Josephine could never long resist buying. The members of her elaborate retinue, from the bejewelled ladies of her court circles to the humblest menials of her kitchen, were subject to a far more effective control. They were appointed, instructed, classified, and paid by means of the administrative machinery that Napoleon devised and regularly scrutinized.

Some parts of the imperial ritual had taken shape during the awkward days of the Consulate when Bonaparte and Josephine held their receptions and soirées at the Luxembourg and the Tuileries. Their duties were made easier by the *savoir-faire* of those former nobles who turned in growing numbers to the new master of France. Talleyrand, despite his unfortunate wife, brought back much of the elegance of a past age. Josephine surrounded herself with ladies who, like her, had been members of the society of the *ancien régime*. Most of her responsibilities were, to be sure, conventional for her position: the receptions for ambassadors, the reviews of troops, the attendance at commemorative Masses, the state dinners, the galas at the Opéra – these were the polite rituals with which every court in Europe was familiar.

All such social activities, however much indebted to tradition, bore the peculiar flavour of the Napoleonic court. Even on the most formal occasions, the Emperor himself was capable of a savage bluntness, not to say rudeness, of manner. Many of his most distinguished marshals were men who had risen from the ranks; superbly self-assured, they saw no reason in their splendid new surroundings to divorce themselves from the rough, barracks atmosphere of their past. Napoleon also carried the burden of the Bonaparte family, for whom elegance was a relatively new concept and whose repeated and outrageous squabbles and scandals amply fitted the description, 'a veritable dog-kennel', once applied to them.

It was Napoleon's nature to leave little to chance or to the result of informal growth. Hence, as a result of laborious studies made by a special commission, a substantial quarto, *Étiquette du Palais impérial*, was prepared. The studies took final shape only after Napoleon himself had plunged actively into the discussions and had converted the general proposals into precise rules. These rules stipulated in characteristic Napoleonic detail the arrangement and use of the various rooms in the imperial residences, the number and precise duties of the imperial dignitaries and attendants together with the exact spots where they were to be stationed, the rights of *entrée* applying to all categories of guests, the rituals for all occasions – in short, a prescription for every minute detail of the imperial day whether Napoleon and Josephine were in residence at Paris or travelling abroad. Chapter II, for example, which is headed, 'On the Arrangement of Apartments and on the Rights of Entry into Each One of Them', has forty-eight precisely detailed paragraphs. Chapter V, 'On the Meals of Their Majesties', has forty-three paragraphs. Chapter XII, 'Court Mourning', covers every detail and every contingency. It says much for Josephine that she was able somehow to accept and carry out these stifling routines with skill, sympathy, invariable elegance, and at least outward pleasure.

On state occasions Josephine was attended by the same grand officers of the crown as was her husband: the grand almoner, the grand marshal of the palace, the grand hunter, the grand equerry, the grand chamberlain, and the grand master of ceremonies. Talleyrand, for example, as grand chamberlain still made the presentations to Josephine at the imperial receptions, even as he had done under the Consulate. Within her own section of the palace a particular arrangement of rooms and an elaborately organized staff was provided. The apartments of the Empress were divided into two groups. The first, the Apartment of Honour, served the more public purposes. It comprised an antechamber, a first salon, a second salon, a salon of the Empress, a dining-room, and a concert room. The second suite, the Interior Apartment, comprised the bedroom, the library, the dressing-room, the boudoir, and the bathroom of the Empress. While these arrangements applied most closely to the Tuileries, they were also carried out with modifications at other imperial palaces. A guest at Malmaison, for example, on entering the main foyer would find to his left a suite of rooms primarily serving the Emperor, and to his right he would enter the two salons and then the music room of the Empress.

At the Tuileries a first and second salon were needed within Josephine's Apartment of Honour so that careful distinction could be made concerning the social claims of the guests. Princesses of the imperial family and those ladies attached to their service, ladies of honour, ladies of the wardrobe, ladies of the palace, and wives of the grand officers of the Empire were all given the precious right of first entry and conducted within. So likewise were their male counterparts, the imperial princes, the grand officers of the Empire, and Napoleon's principal gentlemen of service.

The list of those who were to attend the Empress was substantial. Her almoner, a priest-confessor, was Ferdinand de Rohan, a bishop and member of one of the greatest families of France. Her principal lady of honour was the former Duchess de La Rochefoucauld – a distant relative of her first husband. Her first lady of the wardrobe was Madame Lavalette, a Beauharnais and Josephine's niece. The roster included seventeen ladies of the palace (some of them the wives of Napoleon's marshals), a number of ladies in waiting, various ladies of the wardrobe, ladies of the bedchamber, and a *lectrice*, or reader-companion. The male list included, in addition to the almoner, a first chamberlain, another whose duty it was to present ambassadors to her, and four 'ordinary' chamberlains. She had three equerries and a private secretary. Lower in the scale were a number of ushers (*huissiers*) who stood guard with halberds at the entrances to the two salons and decided according to the rank of the visitors whether one or both wings of the door should be flung open. There were four personal *valets de chambre*, two trusted footmen (one of whom was always present in her antechamber), and two pages, one preceding her and the other carrying Josephine's train whenever she left her apartments. These officials, many of whose duties were largely ornamental, served in addition to the large body of menials necessary for routine operations.

Such numbers tended to grow. By 1807 the number of ladies of the palace had risen from seventeen to thirty. A list for the year 1809 shows six ushers, seven *valets de chambre*, twenty-six footmen, three equerries, five minor civil officers, and forty-three men in the stables. These were the people directly serving the Empress; they acted in addition to the large staff necessary to maintain the grounds and buildings of the various imperial residences.

The rules for conduct within the apartments of the Empress were almost oriental in their rigidity. Entrance to the second salon was, as we have seen, closely restricted. Here, amid magnificent Beauvais tapestries, were chairs for the imperial princesses and, for the lesser ranking ladies of quality, stools with crossed legs. A chamberlain, dressed in red velvet embroidered with gold, did the honours and received the guests. More secluded even than the second salon was the salon of the Empress – furnished with Gobelin tapestries, with armchairs for the Emperor and Empress, and with side chairs and stools for the others. Here are examples of the rules governing this rigidly organized world:

xl. When Her Majesty is present in her Interior Apartment the chamberlain of the day may traverse the Apartment of Honour in order to take his orders; he must scratch lightly on the door of the bedroom, where one of the ladies of Her Majesty must always be in attendance and seek permission to introduce into her presence the chamberlain of the day.

xlii. The Empress never receives any man in her Interior Apartment unless he is one who is in her service.

xliii. Hairdressers and tradesmen must be introduced through a back corridor into the Interior Apartment of Her Majesty; they cannot go through the Apartment of Honour.

xlvi. When Her Majesty has risen, the ladies in attendance will admit the *valets de chambre* through the back corridors or passages in order to make her bed, and the scrub-men in order to clean the bedchamber in their presence.

Equally elaborate rules applied to travel. When the Empress went abroad in France, even without the presence of her husband, she was to be received with full military honours. In a garrison town the cavalry were to meet her half a league away and escort her with trumpets sounding. Half the garrison was to be paraded, the other half would line the routes. On her arrival the troops would present arms, officers would salute, flags dip, drums beat, and the artillery fire three salvoes. Her residence was to be guarded by a battalion of infantry flying its standard and commanded by a colonel. A squadron of cavalry, likewise commanded by a colonel, must also be present. Before her door two mounted sentinels were to be constantly on guard with drawn sabres. If, perchance, the Empress should go on board a naval vessel, it must fly the imperial standard, all its guns must be fired and the assembled crew must cheer seven times, 'Vive l'Empereur!' At the boundary of each department the Empress must be met by the prefect; at each district, by the sub-prefect; at each commune, by the mayor. All town bells were to peal, and if the Empress should pass a church, then the incumbent priest with all his assistant clergy, fully robed, must be at the church door. On great occasions Josephine was to ride in a state coach with eight horses, the servants all wearing the green imperial livery. Returning to Paris from a prolonged trip, she must be greeted with cannon and bells, following which all official bodies must appear in her throne room to present their homage. Such were the magnificent externals of Josephine's life in imperial France.

More intimately, Josephine's daily routine afforded her a large measure of aristocratic indolence interrupted by the recurrent demands of her imperial position. Awakened around eight o'clock by her ladies, she would breakfast leisurely in bed, play with her dogs, and then begin an elaborate toilette lasting from two to three hours. Josephine gave much time to the selection of dresses and appurtenances, and much time also to cosmetics and the bath, for like most creole ladies she was a fanatic for cleanliness. There were daily visits from the coiffeurs – splendid figures in embroidered coats and with swords at their side. There were also fortnightly visits from the court chiropodist, a German Jew named Tobias Koen, far less splendid in his valet's costume than the coiffeurs, yet also sporting his ceremonial sword.

These morning hours would be enlivened by pleasant conversation with the ladies of the bedchamber – all of them selected by Josephine for their charm and affinity of mind. She would on occasion be visited by her doctor, at first Dr Leclerc, a friend of Napoleon's physician, Corvisart, and a member of the medical faculty in Paris. After 1808 she was attended by Dr Horeau, likewise a friend and pupil of Corvisart. Her health, save for occasional headaches and crises of nerves, seems to have been good.

Luncheon, invariably at eleven, was a formal affair, served in considerable style in the yellow salon at the Tuileries. The Emperor was rarely present, choosing instead like many a modern businessman to take his food quickly at his desk. Josephine, therefore, employed these occasions to entertain the ladies of her service, the wives of distinguished figures in the capital, and those who qualified simply by being her friends. Although men were never invited to such luncheons, the Emperor occasionally would join the guests briefly for coffee.

The afternoons were variously occupied. If Josephine drove in the Bois de Boulogne, at that time a semi-wild hunting preserve, she would be accompanied by her equerry, by an officer, a trumpeter, and fourteen cavalrymen. She could not conveniently walk in the gardens of the Tuileries, for they were open to the public. More commonly, therefore, her afternoons were spend indoors in conversation, mingled with music, cards, and embroidering. Josephine had a librarian, the *abbé* Nicolas Halna, but few books; his duties actually were more those of a tutor. Josephine's imperial position required her to have a sure knowledge of ranks, titles, genealogies, and family history – a knowledge going far beyond that common to the fashionable society of the *ancien régime*. For such information, which the *abbé* Halna was admirably equipped to impart, Josephine proved an apt student. In striking contrast to the situation more than twenty-five years before, when others had laboured greatly to acquaint the young wife of Alexander de Beauharnais with the elements of literature and Roman history, she now impressed the court with the quickness of her responses.

Josephine wrote many letters and notes. In addition to her family correspondence she was besieged by people asking favours of the always sympathetic Empress. She worked tirelessly for her friends and relatives, seeking posts and pensions for them in a way that today might seem flagrant, but which then was the normal custom. Her letters by the hundreds still lurk in the archives of the ministries, testifying to her interest in her friends. This interest may sometimes have been less than genuine, as Carnot had discovered when he was minister of war under the Consulate. 'My dear Carnot,' Josephine told him by way of excuse, when he expostulated at the number of her requests, 'don't pay any attention to my recommendations or my notes. People get them from me by pestering me, and I give them indiscriminately to all and sundry.'[1] For this reason, understandably enough, Josephine's epistolary tasks never ended.

Save on state occasions, the Empress commonly dined tête-à-tête with her husband. Still, dinner could be an elaborate affair, for the Emperor wished his wife to be dressed always in her most elegant attire and to be served in full style. The hour of dinner remained uncertain, for the Emperor's work invariably came first. He, and he alone, would decide when to descend from his study or, perhaps, not to descend at all. By long custom, on the other hand, Sunday dinner was a family affair to which all Bonapartes, in semi-bourgeois style, could come. After 1806, when Louis, Jérôme, Joseph, and Murat were installed in their ruling posts throughout the Empire, they and their wives were seldom present, yet the privilege remained. Music, cards, billiards, and conversation – from which the Emperor frequently excused himself – occupied the evenings. From these the occasional visits to the theatre, concerts, and the opera provided, surely, a welcome diversion.

Bonaparte recalled at St Helena that he and Josephine, like good bourgeois folk, shared the same conjugal bed up till 1805, when, as he put it, 'political events obliged me to change my customary ways, for I found I had to work by night as well as by day'.[2] Whether or not he can be a hero, no man can be a stranger to his valet, and so we may read with interest the information recorded by Constant about such intimate matters:

When first Napoleon came to live at Saint-Cloud, he always slept in his wife's bed. Later on etiquette caused him to break this rule, and thus conjugal affection cooled somewhat. Indeed, the First Consul at last occupied apartments at some distance from those of Madame Bonaparte. In order to go to her, he had to walk down a long servants' passage, with rooms on either side occupied by members of the household, servants and others. When he intended to spend the night with his wife, he first of all undressed in his own rooms, and then went forth in a dressing-gown with a handkerchief tied around his head. Torch in hand, I walked in front.[3]

Josephine gave to the court of Napoleonic France a distinctive charm that history still remembers. Conversely, and perhaps ungratefully, history has given her a reputation for reckless, monumental extravagance. Inventories of her personal wardrobe, her jewels, and her bric-à-brac mount to seemingly enormous totals, and the precise calculation has been made, almost as if by way of epitaph, that Josephine died owing her numerous creditors nearly three million francs. Was Josephine one of the great spendthrifts of history? The answer, like much else in the past, is not to be found in a simple, unqualified affirmative.

Josephine was the product of her times. Her 'simple' childhood in Martinique was to a very large degree a life marked by self-indulgence, a life surrounded on every side by servile flattery and obedience. In the Europe to which she soon went, an ostentatious pattern of expenditures was as characteristic of the eighteenth-century aristocracy as it was to be of the industrial plutocracy of the nineteenth. Extravagance was even more a characteristic of the European monarchies. In comparison with the vast building works of a Louis XIV at Versailles, the dissipations of Louis XV, and the reckless gambling losses of a Marie Antoinette, Josephine's building expenditures at Malmaison seem genuinely modest and her personal expenditures almost forgivable. As to her endless gifts, they reflect, if not a sensible head, without any question a warm heart.

Taine's classic *Ancien Régime* has familiarized readers with the fantastic extravagances of the French monarchy before the French Revolution. The operation of the royal household of Louis XVI was estimated to have cost at least one-tenth of the public revenues. If Josephine and Napoleon played their imperial roles on the half-dozen separate stages of the Tuileries, Saint-Cloud, Fontainebleau, Malmaison, the Élysée, and

Rambouillet, we are reminded that Louis XVI was committed to the extravagant support of at least sixteen palaces and châteaux, including the hopeless extravagance of Versailles with its endless rooms and its canals extending to the farthest limits of the horizon. Louis paid seven and a half million livres a year for the support of his royal guards; he spent about a million annually on hunting, and half a million for liveries alone. Two millions were spent in 1778 for the purchase of furniture, while in that same year Louis owed 800,000 livres to his wine merchants. Marie Antoinette was notorious for her extravagances: 400,000 livres, Taine says, for one 'fairy evening' at Versailles and gambling debts in one year of 487,000 livres. Madame Du Barry had a diamond collar made for her dog. Such expenditures, it must be said at once, were fantastic and outrageous; they were one clear contribution to the fall of the French monarchy. It would be nonsensical, therefore, to use them in any sense as a valid yardstick against which to measure the extravagance of Josephine. Yet they may help to provide some sense of proportion and to give Josephine her due.

The wife of the Emperor never tired in her love for fine dresses, elegant jewels, soft fabrics, and shawls. She selected these with considerable taste and wore them with rare distinction. History has recorded that she was as generous in pouring gifts upon others as she was in acquiring fine treasures for herself – albeit this generosity was impulsive and indiscriminate. Napoleon, moreover, wished his wife to dazzle his court with her splendour. He instructed Barbé-Marbois, for instance, to select the finest jewels for Josephine when she was to make a tour through the Netherlands, and in 1809 he gave her a jewelled set (diadem, collar, comb, plaque for her belt, earrings, and bracelet) worth more than 100,000 francs.

No one would care to say that Napoleon paid his domestic accounts gracefully, for the memories of his mother's frugal household never left him. Milliners and dressmakers affected him as a red rag does a bull. On one occasion at Malmaison when the Emperor found an unknown stout woman waiting in the anteroom to Josephine's apartments, he turned on her in a fury. 'Who are you?' 'I am called Despeaux.' 'What do you do?' 'I am a milliner, Sire.' Whereupon the Emperor called loudly for his grand marshal, Duroc, and, failing him, for General Savary. The latter had suffered grievously from his own wife's millinery bills, and so on his arrival the astonished stranger found herself escorted unceremoniously and at top speed between two gendarmes down the long avenue of Malmaison.[4] At St Helena, nevertheless, looking back through the gentle haze of the years, the Emperor seems to have had few major complaints on the subject of his wife's reputation for reckless spending.

The general costs of Josephine's household were handled by what was known as the Treasury of the Crown. Her personal expenditures, where the real source of extravagance lay, were provided for under two headings: the *Cassette* and the *Toilette*. The former took care of the relatively modest sum of about 120,000 francs a year, provided by the Emperor and disbursed with great accuracy by an expert civil servant, Ballouhey. His accounts were invariably in order. Thus the *Cassette* made it possible for Josephine to contribute systematically, as an Empress was expected, to numerous good causes seeking her support. It also made possible special gifts to individuals in great need, as it did the provision of an astonishing variety of pensions, large and small.

Josephine's charities were endless. She paid 500 francs to a former nurse of Louise XVI. She found a pension for the mulatto nurse of her childhood. She provided for her relatives. She even provided for the support of that same Madame de Longpré who years before had turned Josephine's first husband against her. She would dribble away small sums to large numbers of people. In the month of September, 1808, a list shows 124 persons being given a total of 4,000 francs – an average of about 30 francs apiece. She gave money to painters, sculptors, and musicians, yet seldom, it seems, to men of letters. On the whole the *Cassette* was meticulously administered by Ballouhey with never a surplus or deficit at the year's end, and so, if this and this alone had been the point at issue, Napoleon would have had little about which to complain.

The trouble came with Josephine's personal expenditures and her charities which were somewhat illogically included in the general fund known as the *Toilette*. Here, between 1804 and 1809, she was allotted 360,000 francs a year. Invariably she spent about double this amount, thereby producing a heavy annual deficit. In addition she had other large debts that had accumulated in the years of the Consulate and had never been paid. The record shows that between 1805 and 1810 Napoleon had to authorize the successive payment of debts that in total came to 3,200,000 francs. And it must be noted that the ever-watchful Emperor, deeply convinced that there was not a tradesman alive who did not cheat Josephine, had insisted upon an average twenty per cent reduction before paying. These debts of Josephine were paid, not by a complaisant husband, but by an emperor whose name has become a legend for hard-driving efficiency and precise economy in all matters, great and small. They were paid by a man who would notice a discrepancy in the accounts of a humble storekeeper at Calais, or who would refuse to pay the incidental costs for coffee drunk by the servants at Malmaison. The spell of Josephine upon him, one cannot doubt, was enormous.

Putting together the sums in Josephine's formal budgets and the somewhat larger amount applied annually to Josephine's debts, one is safe in estimating her annual expenditures at well over a million francs (or by a very rough transposition, dollars). Where did the money go? Much went, we know, to charity. Much went in gifts that by no stretch of the imagination could be called charity. The account books show that in the five years running from September 1804 to December 1809, Josephine gave away nearly 924,000 francs, though some small parts of these 'gifts' were actually payments for services rendered. It may be worth while to attempt a comparison. In the roughly comparable period of four years and eight months from April 1810 to December 1814, Josephine's successor, the Empress Marie Louise, similarly gave away some 565,000 francs – and Marie Louise was a timid, awkward girl, to whom history has denied any significant reputation for extravagance.

If some of Josephine's expenditures went to maintain what could be called the dignity of the imperial presence, and if some expenditures (for example, the art objects bought for Malmaison) were shared with her husband, much money, we can be sure, Josephine spent directly on herself. There has been preserved an inventory headed, 'Diamonds of the Crown, 15 May 1811.' The total comes to about twelve and a half million francs. Of this amount, the 'Diamonds in the use of the Emperor' (including the celebrated Pitt Diamond in his sword pommel) were valued at seven and a half millions; the 'Diamonds in the use of the Empress' were valued at about four millions. The remainder – worth over one million francs – seem to be very largely jewels that Josephine had bought. To ask whether the possession of over twelve million francs' worth of precious stones by an emperor and empress is to be defined as extravagance is to raise questions, semantic and otherwise, beyond the scope of a biographer.

Every wardrobe and chest at the Tuileries and Malmaison must have been crammed with Josephine's clothing. An inventory of 1809 shows 673 dresses of velvet or satin, 33 dresses of cashmere, and 202 dresses for the summer. She had acquired 520 pairs of shoes in that year, with 265 pairs carried over from the year before. The list includes 980 pairs of gloves, 252 hats, and 60 cashmere shawls. There are 158 pairs of white silk stockings, 32 of rose-coloured and 18 flesh-coloured pairs. There are 498 chemises and two pairs of flesh-coloured pantaloons for riding. Extravagant in what she bought, Josephine was equally extravagant in what she gave away. She bought boxes, gold chains, perfumes, sweetmeats, pieces of materials, and mechanical toys (a monkey that played the violin, for example, and a flowering tree full of singing birds). It was impossible for her to see a tradesman without buying something from him, and on such occasions prices were rarely mentioned. It is not surprising therefore that Madame de Rémusat should report that Josephine's rooms were always crowded with those who had something to sell. Josephine loved to have her picture painted, so that she could give copies to her friends. She changed her lingerie thrice daily, so Madame de Rémusat tells us, and she never put on a pair of stockings that she had worn before.

Against this torrent of generosity and self-indulgence, the occasional efforts of the Emperor could do little. At a meeting of the administrative council of the household in February 1806, Napoleon had ruled that no member of the Empress's household was to receive any furniture, paintings, jewels or other goods supplied by merchants or individuals. All were to be sent to the *intendant* of the palace. If the Emperor had hoped in this way to stop such purchases he hoped, surely, in vain.

The verdict might well be that Josephine was vastly extravagant as a woman, yet not spectacularly so as an empress. Josephine's spending was not in the grand manner that marks the Marquise de Pompadour, Madame Du Barry, or the mad King Ludwig of Bavaria. It was not a gambling or a palace-building mania, but, rather, a kind of bourgeois extravagance to the *n*th degree – of a sort that leads one to crowd things endlessly into closets, into drawers, and into little boxes. Josephine's extravagances fell far short of being truly sensational. Between 1807 and 1810 the French budget ran between 720 and 750 million francs annually. That for 1811 was fixed at about one billion, that for 1812 was a little larger, and that for 1813 a little larger still. In 1807 the allotment for army and navy came to 427 million francs – well over half the total. Josephine's personal spending of a million francs a year, huge enough in an individual sense, does not place her in the company of those who have helped significantly to bring their country to bankruptcy and disaster.

The widely quoted statement that Josephine died leaving debts of nearly three million francs, while literally true, is not the whole picture and is less than fair to her reputation. Shortly after her death, Eugène and Hortense undertook to divide their inheritance, and for this purpose authorized an elaborate inventory of all Josephine's property, real and personal. In rounded numbers the inventory set the following value upon her possessions: classical antiquities and other sculptures, 230,000 francs; furniture, books, and musical instruments,

140,000 francs; paintings, drawings, and engravings, 990,000 francs; jewels, other precious objects, and real estate, 9,700,000 francs. When debts of nearly three millions were deducted from this total of eleven millions, the balance remaining for Eugène and Hortense amounted to over eight million francs. Few 'spendthrifts' have done better for their children.

❧ 19 ❧

'Malmaison, c'est Joséphine'

'*Malmaison, c'est Joséphine*'. Josephine's absorption with this estate reveals sides of her nature not always apparent in the formal words of her correspondence or in the conventional patterns of her official behaviour. Here she shared with Napoleon in a never-ceasing programme of renovation and transformation. Here she could relax with her family, engage in music, conversation, and charades, plan the elaboration of her gardens and flower-beds, and enrich her collection of paintings and other art treasures. Here, surely, was another world having little in common with the overpowering rituals dominating the palaces of the Bourbons – a world displaying Josephine at her gracious best.

The rebuilding of Malmaison produced an essentially modest château – a Sans-Souci or a Petit-Trianon. The dilapidated farm-house, with its tall casement windows and high-pitched roofs, directly expressed the architectural style of the seventeenth century. The remodelling undertaken by Josephine and Napoleon was in the neo-classical manner of the late eighteenth century, touched somewhat by the heavier splendours of *le style Empire*. The entrance hall, used for some elaborate functions and dinners, was of white marble, with tiled floors, graceful columns, and full-length windows overlooking the park. The Emperor's suite reflected both the style of the times and his own tireless energy. The architects Percier and Fontaine were obliged to redecorate his council chamber in ten days, because Napoleon would not tolerate a longer interruption. Hence they hung striped cloths simulating a military tent and had them supported by pikes, fasces, and standards, interspersing *trompe l'œil* paintings of ancient armour and weapons. The library was heavy with its dark mahogany bookcases, its tall columns, and the Pompeian frescoes of the vaulted ceilings. The observant amateur English artist, Bertie Greatheed, who was conducted through Malmaison in 1803, reported a curious detail: Bonaparte was always given one particular chair to sit in, so he was told, 'because he has the trick of cutting and hacking the elbows all to pieces'. Yet, he went on, 'the whole looks snug and gives the idea that the mistress is a comfortable woman'.[1]

Josephine's rooms were lighter and more elegant than her husband's, with magnificent furniture provided by the best cabinet-makers in France and with some antique paintings on stucco sent to her by her brother-in-law, Joseph, king of Naples. Portraits of Josephine and her children hung on the walls, as well as paintings by Girodet and Gérard in the newly emerging pre-romantic style on subjects derived from Ossian. Now vanished but visible in contemporary drawings, the specially built gallery housed Josephine's remarkable collection of paintings. The building completely lacked any grand staircase of the type so dear to the baroque tradition. The upper floor, reached by an austerely utilitarian stairway closed off from the downstairs entrance, was devoted largely to sleeping quarters. Here the very handsome chamber of the Empress, with its canopied bed surmounted by an imperial eagle, quite outshone the quarters of the Emperor, for whom an iron campbed sufficed.

Malmaison derived its great charm from the intimate association of the interior salons with the enchanting setting of the grounds. From Napoleon's study window a toy drawbridge led across a dry moat to the lawns. From the entrance salon one could pass through the high French casement windows to a terrace, to the right of which rose the cedar of Marengo, planted in 1801 by Josephine's orders. Across the lawns were the pools upon which glided the stately swans of Malmaison. From time to time more property was acquired. In 1809, when Josephine was negotiating for the purchase of land from a rather obnoxious neighbour, Napoleon wrote to his wife from Germany as follows:

I have received your letter of the 16th, and I gather that you are well. The old woman's house is worth only 120,000 francs. They never will get more for it. However, I leave you free to do what you wish, since it amuses you. But, once you have bought it, don't have it pulled down simply to construct some rocky crags.[2]

The planning of the grounds – only a poor fragment of which remains today – was strongly influenced by the romantic English school of landscape design. In one part stood an antique temple with eight Ionic columns; in another was a statue of St Francis by the Renaissance sculptor, Germain Pilon, set in a grotto containing a funeral relief by Girardon. This was planned, as the architect, Lenoir, explained, 'so that there would be a tomb in the park following the rules governing the design of an English garden'. Beside a small pond were two marble columns brought from the ancient château of Richelieu in Poitou. From this same source came two fourteen-foot red marble obelisks with gilt hieroglyphics, which were placed on the terrace. Statues for the façade facing the entrance court were obtained from the old royal park at Marly near Versailles. A fine statue of Neptune by Puget formed part of an elaborate fountain. Most striking, and indicative of the changing currents of taste, was the façade of a Gothic chapel of the Carmelite order, thirty-six feet high with remarkable sculptures, which had been dismantled and brought all the way from Metz to be installed on the top of a little rise.

Amid all this variety Napoleon as well as Josephine found refuge from the complexities of public life. The Emperor would walk, talk, work in his library, watch theatricals, and listen to the concerts that Josephine organized. He would inform himself on the mysterious subject of women's dress, engage in vigorous games of prisoners' base, play at bowls, and in general spend some of his happiest and most relaxed hours. For Josephine, Malmaison was, in simple terms, an earthly paradise.

Reared in a luxuriant tropical environment, Josephine had a passion for flowers; when given the opportunity at Malmaison she indulged this passion to the full. Admirers have written of '*Joséphine botaniste*' and 'Josephine, patroness of agriculture' – pleasant tributes, but in the technical sense clearly inaccurate. Not scientific interest, surely, but genuine aesthetic pleasure led Josephine into this most delightful aspect of her activities.

The collection of flowers and plants began to take shape almost as soon as Josephine acquired Malmaison. Her family sent her seeds of various kinds from the West Indies. The exotic voyages of the eighteenth century had resulted in the bringing back of strange new plant specimens to Europe, many of which found a welcome home in the *Jardin des Plantes* in Paris and the royal gardens at Kew in England. As early as July 1801, Bonaparte wrote to his wife saying that he had received some plants from London for her, and in that same year Josephine was engaged in some correspondence with the French plenipotentiary at London to see if the king of England could be persuaded to send her some plants from '*son beau jardin de Kew*'.

When the great German naturalist, Alexander von Humboldt, returned from America in 1804 with thousands of specimens, one of his associates was the French botanist, Aimé Bonpland, who was destined to play a large role at Malmaison. Humboldt's expedition provided Josephine with many plants, among them mimosa, heliotropes, cassias, and lobelias. Bonpland was in touch with Sir Joseph Banks, president of the Royal Society of England, with whom he exchanged specimens, as he did with the horticulturists at Kew and those at the University of Glasgow. Ambassadors and travellers abroad were encouraged to send home rare specimens, with the result that gifts came in from countries all over Europe, as well as from points as far distant as Morocco, Guiana, Mexico, and the Cape of Good Hope. During the campaign of 1809 Napoleon sent Josephine eight hundred plants and a great variety of seeds from Schoenbrunn, and other donations followed.

Between 1804 and 1814 it has been stated that 184 new species flowered for the first time at Malmaison. Its gardeners were responsible for introducing to France many plants, shrubs, and trees that are now commonplace: eucalyptus, hibiscus, phlox, cactuses, rhododendrons, dahlias, double jacinthas, and rare tulips. As in other respects Josephine was prodigal, willingly spending as much as three thousand francs on a rare bulb and constantly expanding the area devoted to cultivation.

The pink climbing rose, the *Souvenir de la Malmaison*, that is so often associated with Josephine was not developed until 1840. Roses did not at first much interest her, nor were they very popular in eighteenth-century France, coming after tulips, hyacinths, and carnations in general interest. On the advice of some of Josephine's botanists, many specimens of roses were nevertheless assembled in a kind of experimental garden where ultimately nearly two hundred varieties could be seen. Yet a rose garden in the true sense did not exist until later, and the famous rose paintings, so closely linked with her memory, were not prepared until after her death.

Josephine's first head gardener was an Englishman, Howatson, whom Napoleon strongly disliked because of his policy, hardly surprising, of planning informal English gardens everywhere. He was quickly replaced by a French expert, Morel, who, alas, turned out to be equally unsatisfactory. Moreover, he was disposed to go even further afield than Howatson for his models. Morel, it developed, had written not only *The Art of Gardens According to Nature*, but also *The Art of Constructing Gardens According to the Chinese*. Disagreements continued, for Josephine protested against the desires of her husband and of the architect, Fontaine, both of whom preferred gardens laid out, like the Tuileries, in formal, classical style. Following Morel, the distinguished botanist, Mirbel, acted as supervisor of gardens. He too created problems. He became the *bête noire* of Napoleon, largely because of his ineradicable tendency to spend more than his master had authorized. One year's planting came to double what had been stipulated. The great greenhouse, which was supposed to cost 40,000 francs, actually cost 192,000 francs. Mirbel, moreover, chose to live in considerable state; he had his private quarters at Malmaison, and he drove abroad with his own horses and cabriolet. In the Emperor's view this was too much. When dismissal came, Mirbel quickly found a botanist's paradise as *intendant* of properties to Louis Bonaparte, now king of Holland. One suspects that he obtained this post because of an appeal by Josephine to Hortense.

The biggest hot-house at Malmaison was an impressive structure generally comparable to those at Kew and Schoenbrunn and in addition possessing features that must have been unique. In the centre of the huge glass edifice was a salon having an open portico looking forth on the great masses of flowers. Illustrations show that this portico was held up by two columns of coloured marble, twelve feet high, with gilded bases and capitals. The salon, which had a ceiling of Pompeian designs, was said to have been in exquisite taste, with rich rugs, statuary, vases, and handsome furniture all decorated in the antique style.

Josephine, for whom technical scholarship was a distant world, was clever enough to take into her service distinguished figures in the world of botany. Under her sponsorship and with her financial help their contributions were substantial. Her interest was genuine, if we may believe the observant Bertie Greatheed, who gives us the following in one breathless sentence: 'Bonaparte always sleeps with his wife: in her dressing-room were four or five books on botany: the only ones I saw in the house.'[3] Josephine had impressive precedents in making her passion for the natural beauty of flowers and gardens a reason for the encouragement of botanical publications. Catherine the Great of Russia had sponsored the *Flora Rosica* of Pallas in 1784, and the Hapsburgs had similarly sponsored the famous *Descriptions des plantes les plus rares des jardins de Schoenbrunn* in 1797. Mirbel, Ventenat, and Bonpland provided worthy equivalents.

Charles-François Brisseau de Mirbel served as chief botanist and librarian between 1803 and 1806. He carried on a wide correspondence, drew up a manuscript catalogue, now lost, of the plants at Malmaison, and was responsible for the enlargement of Josephine's collection. Mirbel also engaged another botanist, Félix Delahaye, who had been to the South Seas; through him many rare plants were acquired.

A more famous name was that of Etienne Pierre Ventenat, a distinguished botanist who was employed by Josephine to prepare scientific descriptions of the various plants that Mirbel had secured and who was given the title, 'Botanist to Her Majesty'. In 1803 and 1804 appeared the two folio volumes, *Jardin de la Malmaison*, in which Ventenat gave detailed descriptions of more than two hundred plants. Surely Josephine was entitled to his eloquent dedication:

You have gathered around you the rarest plants growing on French soil. Some, indeed, which never before had left the deserts of Arabia or the burning sands of Egypt have been domesticated through your care. Now, regularly classified, they offer to us as we inspect them in the beautiful gardens of Malmaison an impressive reminder of the conquests of your illustrious husband and a most pleasant evidence of the studies you have pursued in your leisure hours. . . . Deign to accept the tribute of a work undertaken at your orders.[4]

Aimé Bonpland, who had accompanied Alexander von Humboldt on his great scientific journey through South America, became in 1809 a kind of *intendant* or supervisor, making new acquisitions, buying scientific works for the library, and sending valuable plants to various parts of France. Napoleon disliked him, as he did most of Josephine's botanists, and dismissed him abruptly in October for the crime of having moved a shrub without having first obtained the imperial authorization. Josephine, nevertheless, managed to get him back and retained him after her divorce for important work at Malmaison and later at her estate of Navarre. In 1813 Bonpland published his *Descriptions des plantes rares cultivées à Malmaison*, with sixty-four colour plates by Redouté, a continuation of the two folios prepared by Ventenat and Redouté ten years before and a work of genuine scientific and artistic importance.

This account of the progress of botanical studies in France leads directly to Josephine's association with the distinguished Franco-Belgian painter, Pierre-Joseph Redouté. This 'Raphael of the flowers', who had been trained in the studios of the brilliant Dutch floral artist, Van Spaendonck, earlier had been flower painter and drawing master to Marie Antoinette. According to a touching tradition, in 1792 he was summoned to the prison of the Temple by the royal family to watch and to paint the momentary blossoming of a cactus they had long treasured. Redouté could be called a veritable Talleyrand of the arts, for in addition to serving Marie Antoinette he served Josephine and subsequently various members of the restored Bourbon dynasty. Under the Revolution Redouté had continued to develop his remarkable artistic skill and to acquire through his work at the Museum of Natural History an acute knowledge of the structure of plants. In 1801 he began work on the illustrations for the new edition of Duhamel du Monceau's classic *Traité des arbres et des arbustes*, a magnificently illustrated set of seven folio volumes not completed until 1819. The first volume of this '*Nouveau Duhamel*' was dedicated to Madame Bonaparte, the next four to the Empress Josephine.

Redouté's first service to Josephine was to help with the interior decorations of Malmaison. He was paid 7,200 francs for a series of water-colours on vellum to be placed in Josephine's bedroom. Redouté also was paid 4,500 francs for decorations in the principal greenhouse. In the course of his work he developed his own techniques for reproducing plates in colour, notably in the two volumes of the *Jardin de la Malmaison*. What gives these plates their incomparable quality is the combination of meticulous exactness in detail with a true artist's feeling for colour and form. Redouté added to his fame by the illustrations for the eight volumes of *Liliaceae* which appeared between 1812 and 1816. Josephine contributed generously to the publication of these volumes: her initial subscriptions amounted to more than 20,000 francs, and she spent nearly 25,000 francs more in purchasing many of Redouté's original drawings. Josephine never saw his most famous work, *Les Roses*, which appeared between 1817 and 1824 in thirty parts and six plates each. At this time the Napoleonic legend was taking shape, and those who associated the memories of Josephine with the greatness of imperial France, could find in the beauty of Redouté's plates some symbol of what they believed Josephine to have been.

Malmaison also boasted of a zoo, or menagerie. Josephine found it easy to encourage a custom whereby ships' captains returning from distant lands brought gifts for the wife of the new master of France. As a consequence hardly a ship touched French shores that did not bring some beast, bird, or reptile for Josephine. A list of animals brought into Le Havre in June 1803 by the ships *Portefaix* and *Porteuse* includes an antelope, a gnu, a zebra, a falcon, five parrots, various other tropical birds, and seventeen assorted tortoises. Josephine spent five hundred francs to transport a chamois from Switzerland, and nearly three hundred francs to transport a seal from the coast. Eagles, gazelles, monkeys, kangaroos, ostriches, flying squirrels, Swiss cows (for which Swiss cowherds and milkmaids were suitably attired and housed) added to her collection. The zoo was hardly scientific. It boasted a female orang-outang that slept in camisole and chemise, ate with a knife and fork, and knew how to curtsey. At the Ministry of Foreign Affairs in the rue du Bac Talleyrand had been given a small monkey by Denon, the famous archaeologist. This remarkable animal had learned to seal dispatches with wax. One might guess that the simian diplomat may well have made trouble for the ministry, for when Josephine asked to have the monkey as a gift for her menagerie, Talleyrand promptly obliged.

The only suggestion of any scientific interest in this astonishing hodgepodge lies in Josephine's flock of five hundred prize merino sheep. This flock, which was handled under expert direction, was an annual source of young rams for French farmers and gives Josephine her slight claim to be regarded as a patroness of agriculture.

One of the most tantalizing aspects of Josephine's interest in the arts lies in her famous gallery of paintings, now dispersed. Out of what was clearly an undisciplined passion for collecting grew a truly extraordinary collection, which, according to the *Catalogue* printed in Paris in 1811, included most of the famous names in the history of continental European painting from Hans Memling to David.* Had it been preserved intact it

*Catalogue des tableaux de sa majesté l'impératrice Joséphine dans la galerie et appartements de son palais de Malmaison, Paris, 4°, 1811.

could have counted as one of the great European collections. These paintings, to be sure, did not please the ever-articulate Bertie Greatheed. 'The works of art,' he wrote smugly, 'convince me that Bonaparte does not know one bit about the matter. There are very few of any merit, and they are placed at haphazard, whenever they happen to suit as furniture, among indifferent, bad, and execrable.'[5] Whatever truth there may have been in Greatheed's criticism of their arrangement, his general estimate of the paintings was shockingly unfair.

One of the early dispatches that Napoleon sent back from Italy in 1796 had announced the forwarding of a spectacular list of art treasures as the spoils of war. In this list occur the names of Coreggio, Michelangelo, Leonardo, Titian, Raphael, and Veronese. Some of these paintings ultimately found a place in Josephine's collection at Malmaison. Throughout the years the flow of such treasures continued. Generals and administrators, knowing her interest, were quick to send works of art to her, chiefly from Italy and Belgium. After the battle of Jena, General Lagrange sent Josephine fifty paintings that a French military patrol had found stored in a forest cottage. They were from the gallery of the elector of Hesse Cassel and included four small paintings by Claude Lorrain and a 'Descent From the Cross' by Rembrandt.

Though occasionally Josephine would commission a purchase, the records do not show any very large sums spent in this way. In 1806, for example, she bought Metsu's 'Weighers of Gold' at Bruges for 1,800 francs. The exception would be contemporary works by genre painters and portraitists, for Josephine was always eager to have paintings of herself. The miniaturists also were regularly kept busy. Louis-Bertin Pérant, then much in vogue, was her favourite; since he received a total of 28,580 francs for miniatures probably costing about 500 francs apiece, he can be estimated to be responsible for at least fifty of these charming items. The total of other miniatures mounted into the hundreds.

Josephine owned paintings by most of the great Renaissance artists, among them Giovanni Bellini, Ghirlandaio, Andrea del Sarto, Giorgione, and Perugino. The *Catalogue* of 1811 shows three Raphaels, four small Leonardos, four Titians, and two canvases by Veronese. She owned paintings by Murillo, Van Dyke, Holbein, and Dürer. She had three Rembrandts and three Rubens. The names of the Flemish and Dutch painters constitute a veritable roster of famous artists of the seventeenth and eighteenth centuries: among them were Cuijp, Dow, De Hooch, Jordaens, Metsu, Ostade, Teniers, Ruysdael, and Ter Borch. The seventeenth-century Paul Potter, painter of cows, sheep, and quiet landscapes, was a great favourite, Josephine having at least sixteen examples of his work, among them 'La Vache qui Pisse'. Some of the Dutch and Flemish canvases had been bought by Josephine during her tour in 1803, others came from the museum at Cassel. The impressive French list included works by Champaigne, Claude Lorrain, Poussin, Greuze, Nattier, Gérard, Vernet, Regnault, and David. Among the many portraits of contemporaries was a crayon drawing of Napoleon at Malmaison by Isabey. Redouté's eight water-colours on vellum are also listed.

Josephine's collection had an extraordinarily wide scope, yet rather than having a true catholicity of taste or valuing most highly the Raphaels, the Leonardos, the Titians, the Rembrandts, the Poussins, and the Ruysdaels of her collection, she seems to have been chiefly devoted to the placid cows and the bucolic settings of Paul Potter and to the sentimentalized scenes of the *style troubadour*. She was not seriously and technically interested in the work of such great contemporaries as David, Gérard, Gros, Girodet, and Ingres, even though Gros was an old acquaintance whom she had presented to Bonaparte in 1796, and Gérard painted her at least eight times. Redouté, to be sure, she knew well and she could have chosen no greater painter of flowers. Her miniaturists were among the best of the epoch. She had much sympathy for Prud'hon, the great precursor of Delacroix and Géricault, whose painting of her reclining in the park at Malmaison is one of the best known of all the Josephine portraits. Yet the true direction of her taste is seen in her fondness for examples of the *style troubadour* – the fashion then current that found its subjects in the romantic idealizing of a medieval past. Duperreux's 'View of the Valley of Roncevaux and the Tomb of Roland', Forbin's 'Ossian Chanting His Poems', and Richard Fleuri's 'Farewell of Charles VII to Agnes Sorel', are characteristic examples of her preference. No less than seven of Fleuri's paintings, purchased at a cost of 7,000 francs apiece, were hung at Malmaison.

Josephine had the hoarding instincts of a collector but followed no rational plan. Her taste extended into many fields. She was very fond of small sculptures, cameos, medallions, and ivory carvings, buying much from Paris dealers. The list also includes larger sculptures, busts by Chaudet, Bosio, and Chinard, as well as statues by the ultra-fashionable Canova. There is a record of her paying 70,000 francs for Italian mosaics. She also bought ceramics and porcelains, Etruscan vases, ancient armour, and miscellaneous objects from Pompeii and Herculaneum.

The rooms at Malmaison soon proved inadequate for Josephine's impressive collection. Hence her architects constructed in 1809 a gallery nearly a hundred feet long, opening from her music room. Now totally disappeared, it can be seen today only as a tantalizing glimpse in a contemporary painting of the music room. The gallery had some striking features, combining skylights (an innovation first employed at the Louvre in 1803) with a generally gothic décor. It was most comfortably equipped. Two large carved and gilded armchairs with footstools (presumably for the Emperor and the Empress) were upholstered in green velvet; thirty smaller cross-legged chairs were covered in red morocco; the hangings were of white silk. Twelve console tables displayed Josephine's varied assortment of art objects. One is hardly surprised, therefore, that the total bills for this splendid setting came to 189,138 francs.

Napoleon rather than Josephine was responsible for the collection of books in the library. She bought occasional works on painting and botany and she subsidized the great folios produced by her botanical experts. In general, however, her expenditures in this realm were negligible; the accounts show as little as 125 francs spent by her in one year and 1,300 francs in another. Napoleon's own substantial collection has vanished, and the handsomely bound volumes at Malmaison today have been assembled from other sources, including the library of Marie Louise.

Ever since the days of the refurnishing at the rue Chantereine Josephine had been a generous patron of the Paris cabinet makers. A console of hers from the Tuileries is now in the Louvre. At Malmaison one can still see the magnificent dressing case of inlaid woods, having a miniature of the Emperor by Vigneux and silver-gilt fittings, mounted with ivory, tortoiseshell, mother-of-pearl, and crystal. Felix Rémond made it at Paris in 1806; he submitted a bill for 6,000 francs; and the Emperor, apparently not thinking the bill excessive, ordered it to be paid.

Among the curiosities of Malmaison was an elegant boat or barge, eighteen feet long, presented to Josephine by the prefect of police in the name of the city of Paris. The barge was put in the near-by stream, but since its length prevented it from turning, it proved useless and had to be moored near by in a small pond. Josephine, evidently intrigued, then ordered a small craft half the size to be made by her builder, Magin. The little boat, for which the builder was still asking payment in 1818, was ornamented with fine paintings, had cushions of horsehair fringed with gold lace, an embroidered flag, and a waterproof cover. One can only hope that Josephine enjoyed it.

In 1815 Alexander I of Russia paid what for those times was the enormous sum of 940,000 francs for the paintings at Malmaison that had once belonged to the elector of Hesse Cassel. In 1829 Hortense sold thirty more paintings to St Petersburg for 180,000 francs. Some paintings were sold by the heirs to the Louvre; others went to individual buyers; Eugène took many works with him to Munich; Hortense kept some at Arenenberg. A further sale, the catalogue of which may be seen in the British Museum, took place at Malmaison on 24 March 1819. In contrast to the magnificent haul made by Alexander, this catalogue included the typical and heterogeneous remainders of an estate, interesting chiefly because of their associations with Josephine. Only three pictures were listed.

The sale included many antique busts and statues – Juno, Diana, Antinous, Alexander Severus, and Augustus. The catalogue offered Etruscan vases, granite columns, mosaic-topped tables, cases, boxes, dresses, shawls, collars, laces, and feathers. Among the strangest items were a mummy's hand, a mummy's head, an entire mummy (male), and another (female) – last reminders of the Egyptian expedition of 1798.

The process of dispersal continued. Letters written by Napoleon to Josephine in the first days of the Italian campaign of 1796 were found in a closet by a valet and sold to a Polish nobleman. A French traveller at Calcutta noted in 1821 the series of water-colours on vellum that Redouté had painted for Josephine's bedroom. Visitors to the Hermitage at St Petersburg could in time enjoy paintings once at Malmaison. Some of Josephine's silver is now in a ski lodge in the Canadian Laurentians. Other treasures were sold in Brazil. Malmaison itself suffered a sorry dilapidation, followed by an equally sorry pseudo-restoration at the hands of Napoleon III. Only in the twentieth century has a splendid rehabilitation made it possible to recapture the tangible evidence of the Malmaison and the Josephine that once were.

❧ 20 ❧

Divorce

THE divorce that struck Josephine like the lash of a whip at the close of the year 1809 could not have been a startlingly unexpected development. It hurt, nevertheless, and hurt deeply. The childless marriage had raised more than once the gnawing possibility of such an outcome, yet this prospect seemed less likely when again and again Josephine gratefully recognized Napoleon's husbandly affection for her. The marriage, undertaken so casually in 1796, had brought both passionate delight and moments of profound despondency to her husband. Yet it had weathered every storm and had created unquestioned happiness for both partners. The turbulent beginnings, when the ardours of the young general had aroused so curiously mixed a response from his wife, had been followed by her reckless association (no doubt for money as much as for love) with the ineffable Captain Hippolyte Charles. These disordered years of the Directory had revealed Josephine at her attractive worst, and it is understandable that Napoleon's sense of outrage at his wife's foolish behaviour while he campaigned in Italy should have been exceeded only by his anger at her even more outrageous conduct while he was in Egypt. At this latter point he had written to his brother Joseph, telling him of his desire to get a house and bury himself in the country. On the eve of Brumaire there can be little doubt that Josephine's marriage stood on a most precarious foundation.

After Brumaire Josephine had seen the light. She then began to play the role of wife of the first consul with every mark of bourgeois respectability. It would have been most dangerous for her to do otherwise. She accepted the solid position her husband had created for her, and amid surroundings of growing splendour she found some security against the never-ceasing opposition of the Bonaparte clan. At the close of the year 1799 Josephine had left her somewhat gaudy surroundings in the old rue Chantereine for the new life of the palace – at the Luxembourg, at the Tuileries, at the Élysée, at Saint-Cloud, at Fontainebleau, and at Malmaison. Within a few years after her coronation, the brilliance of the Empress had dimmed the memories of her reckless widowhood and the unsavoury episodes of her first married years.

Josephine revealed herself as an affectionate, gracefully mannered, and warm-hearted wife – the principal ornament of the imperial court. Here, in contrast to the scandalous goings-on of a Caroline Murat or of a Pauline Bonaparte, she set a tone of elegant respectability. The uncertain marriage had at last grown to be an accepted, comfortable accommodation – good for both parties. Napoleon realized this. Amid all the bitterness of his exile at St Helena he more than once found time to speak nostalgic words about this woman whom he had married and made an empress.

The recurrent minor infidelities of the Emperor had begun during the Egyptian campaign. These accompaniments of the soldier's life were in part a protest against Josephine's indefensible behaviour at Paris. They continued to flourish in a fashion the conventional morality of the times easily accepted. Few people would have thought that an occasional rustle of skirts in the back corridors of the Tuileries, indicating the fleeting passage of an actress from the theatre or a singer from the opera, could raise any threat at all to the solidity of the imperial marriage. Whatever insecurity Josephine may have felt when she realized that such affairs were going on was a personal sorrow about which she could do little save to make momentary, tearful protests to her husband. If she had any larger concern as to her future, it was most surely allayed when on the very eve of the coronation Cardinal Fesch had performed the secret nuptial service at the chapel of the Tuileries. In the eyes of the Church, the marriage then became secure. But was it?

The threat to the marriage did not come from the rather colourful record of Josephine's past, nor did it come from the bright eyes of any current rival. Most certainly it did not come from the feminine extravagances that so often irked the tidy mind of her husband. These were matters he could manage to keep from getting out of hand. There is, indeed, in his later comments a suggestion of grudging admiration for Josephine's expensive elegance – an elegance that, after all, flattered his own position and that the budget of France could well afford. 'Josephine,' Napoleon told Caulaincourt during the retreat from Russia in 1812, 'was always begging me for things, and could even cry me into granting what I ought to have refused her.'[1]

The threat to the marriage came rather from the inescapable realization of the needs of public policy. There was, first, the ever-present problem of the succession. Secondly, there was need for a family connexion with one of the historic European dynasties. Napoleon was childless; his own brothers aroused little enthusiasm in him; and the right of 'adoptive succession' he had assumed at the time of the coronation carried the possible inheritance no further than to the children of Hortense and Eugène. The latter, to be sure, he had made viceroy of Italy and 'Son of France'. But then in 1807 Hortense's first son, another great favourite of Napoleon's, had tragically died. Although there were two other brothers, Napoléon-Louis, born in 1804, and Charles-Louis-Napoléon, born in 1808, their future was uncertain. It was likewise uncertain whether Eugène could stand up in face of the manifest and relentless hostility of the Bonapartes. And so the difficulties remained.

If it was Napoleon, and not Josephine, who was responsible for the failure of their union to produce an heir, as she more than once whispered to her ladies, then divorce and remarriage would be of no help. That is why the news of the birth of the infant Léon to Eléanore de la Plaigne, which reached the Emperor in Poland on the last day of 1806, was so momentous. If Napoleon had been a father once, he could be so again; to do this he must now find himself a wife younger than Josephine.

Chance is never absent from human affairs. Nothing in the logic of events could explain why at the very moment when Eléanore de la Plaigne had so conveniently demonstrated

Napoleon's capacities as a sire, the imperative need for a close alliance with one of the great European dynasties should have so deeply concerned the Emperor and his advisers. In 1806 Napoleon's diplomacy had been at work on a grand scale. He had destroyed the Holy Roman Empire. He had created the Confederation of the Rhine. He was in process of still further reorganization in Italy. He was about to create a new Poland. As arbiter of the Continent he wished to take his place among the crowned heads of Europe, not as an upstart adventurer but as one of them. The right marriage could do this for him.

Such ideas, which automatically presumed divorce, were as much present in the minds of the advisers of Napoleon as in his own. Talleyrand, Fouché, and Napoleon's own brother-in-law, Joachim Murat, were the most insistent; Fouché was bold enough to tell Josephine in July 1807 that a divorce was essential to the welfare of France. His notion was that reasons of state required Napoleon to seek the hand of a Russian grand duchess. Talleyrand, much less bluntly, whispered similar views.

Josephine reported these alarming prospects to her children. Though the hostility of Napoleon's brothers and sisters was an old story, she never tired of repeating it:

Prince Murat enjoys great favour [she wrote to Eugène in September 1807]. I have certain proof that while the Emperor was with the army he [Murat] used every effort to push him into a divorce. . . . It is clear that he wishes to succeed him.

Josephine then spoke candidly to her son about her problems:

As for myself, you know that I aspire for nothing but his love. If they should succeed in separating me from him, it is not the loss of rank that I should regret. . . . Sooner or later he would discover that all those who surround him think rather of themselves than of him, and he would know how he has been deceived.

However, my dear Eugène, I have nothing to complain of in him, and I am happy to count on his justice and his affection. As for you, my dear son, keep on behaving with the same zeal for the Emperor as you have done up till now; you will command general respect, and even the greatest favour cannot guarantee you this.[2]

Eugène's reply was touching evidence of the devoted, warm-hearted, yet sober attachment he had for his mother. Urging Josephine not to be upset by hostile tongues, he went on:

There is much talk of divorce; I have heard of it both from Paris and Munich, but I am reassured by your conversation with the Emperor, if it was such as you have described it. You must always speak frankly to his Majesty; to do otherwise would be to love him no more.

Eugène was realist enough to know that divorce was now an active possibility.

If the Emperor still pesters you on the subject of children, say it is not for him to keep on reproaching you over such matters. If he thinks that his own happiness, and that of France, require him to have some, let him not look abroad.

He must treat you well, give you an adequate settlement, and let you live in Italy with your children. The Emperor then will be able to make the marriage which his policy and his happiness demand. We shall remain no less attached to him, for there is no need for his sentiments towards us to change, even though circumstances should have obliged him to separate from our family. If the Emperor wishes to have children who are truly his, there is no other way. . . .

You must not fear either events or wicked persons. Don't pester the Emperor; and do make an effort to regulate your private expenses. Don't be so friendly with those about you, or you will soon be their dupe. Pardon me, dear Mother. I am eager to speak prudently to you, and give you good advice, because I have need of it also myself.[3]

Rumours of impending divorce continued to spread throughout 1807. Metternich, now Austrian ambassador in Paris, reported such rumours to his government. Napoleon grew furious at the blatant way in which Fouché, minister of police and a pillar of his administration, persistently ventured opinions concerning Napoleon's private life. 'I cannot,' the Emperor exploded, 'have confidence in a minister who one day is rummaging in my bed, and another day in my portfolio.'[4] In November Napoleon sent a stern letter to Fouché: 'For two weeks I have been hearing of foolishness from you. It is time for this to stop, and for you to cease meddling, directly or indirectly, in a matter which does not concern you in any possible way.'⁵ Fouché, strangely enough, kept on talking, and it took another letter from Italy at the end of November and still another to Maret, one of Napoleon's most trusted ministers of state, to bring the uncharacteristically loquacious minister of police to silence.

Despite all attempts to repress rumours, it was clear by the end of 1807 that plans for divorce and remarriage were beginning to assume reality. When Josephine asked to accompany Napoleon to Italy he refused, saying that the journey would be too hard for her. One suspects that he was somewhat awkward in her presence. High questions of state were involved in the search for a new bride, and, while a Russian or Austrian marriage was the most likely, many other possibilities existed. As early as August the methodical Napoleon had obtained a list of the eligible princesses to be found among great continental families, classified according to age, religion, and country. The complete list totalled seventeen, with members ranging in age from the scarcely thirteen-year-old Anna Pavlovna of Russia to Sophia Frederika of Saxe-Coburg who was twenty-nine. Little question existed but that the nineteen-year-old Catharina Pavlovna, sister of Alexander I of Russia, and the sixteen-year-old Marie Louise, daughter of Francis I of Austria, were the two most likely possibilities.

Throughout 1808 the tense situation continued.

You can easily guess that I have had much cause for unhappiness [Josephine wrote to Eugène in February after the Emperor's return from Italy], and I still have; the rumours circulating during the Emperor's absence haven't stopped on his return, and at this very moment there are more gossips than ever. . . . Well, I entrust myself to Providence and the Emperor's will; my only defence is my conduct which I shall try to make blameless. . . .

How unhappy do thrones make people, dear Eugène! I would resign mine tomorrow without any regret. For me the affection of the Emperor is everything. If I should lose that I would have few regrets about anything else. . . .⁶

Napoleon was too busy with other, urgent matters to bring

the question of divorce to a head. For part of the year 1808 he was at Bayonne, where for a brief spell Josephine was permitted to be with him. Here he concerned himself with the tangled affairs of Spain. In the early autumn he made the long trip to Erfurt, in Thuringia, where he renewed his alliance and friendship with Tsar Alexander. Following that, he went for a second time to Spain where, though he could as yet hardly foresee it, disaster was brewing for him. On the few occasions when he could find time to see Josephine he was a model of affection and devotion – as Eugène quickly was told. 'For six months,' she exulted, 'he has never been less than perfect towards me.'[7] Clearly, if the divorce was to come, as Josephine now more than ever feared, she would have the consolation of knowing that it would be the consequence of questions of high policy and not of the drying up of Napoleon's affections. During his second absence in Spain he sent Josephine fourteen letters in nine weeks – letters that were short and, understandably enough in view of his worries, perfunctory – yet he did not forget the woman whom once he had loved so ardently.

The year 1809 was decisive in the life of Josephine. She received Count Girardin late in February when he brought her news of Napoleon in Spain, and in reply she poured out the ominous information that Talleyrand and Fouché were planning what to do if Napoleon should be killed. Murat, so the reports went, would probably succeed the Emperor. Efforts were being made, Josephine told Girardin, to get Napoleon to divorce her. This could hardly have been news, but when Josephine went on further to say that Fouché was spreading the rumour that Napoleon had made one of the ladies of the household pregnant and that Josephine was intending eventually to claim this child of 'Madame XXX' as her own in order to try to save her crown, Girardin was too embarrassed to answer.

Dispatches were brought to Napoleon at the Élysée on the evening of 12 April 1809 with the news that Austria for the fourth time had taken the plunge and had opened hostilities against the French. 'They have crossed the Inn River,' Napoleon said. 'This means war.'[8] When Josephine during dinner asked to accompany him, he somewhat unexpectedly agreed. He went to his study, dictated half a dozen dispatches, read a report from Milan, talked to Fouché, and retired at midnight. He was awakened at two. At three o'clock his travelling carriage stood waiting in the darkness. At four fifteen Josephine, attended by only one maid, climbed in and five minutes later, the Emperor having arrived, they set off. It was to be their last journey together. Two days later, at dawn, they reached Strasbourg, where an exhausted Josephine sought rest and a tireless Napoleon set off shortly after midday to direct in person the historic campaign of Wagram against Austria.

As she had been required to do on earlier occasions, Josephine kept solitary state at Strasbourg, writing to her children, receiving Metternich in an audience as he returned from Paris to Vienna, and generally pursuing the empty life of a woman who awaits the news of her husband's exploits on the field of battle. In June, following a long established custom, she left for Plombières for a two months' stay. By mid-August she was back at Malmaison.

Napoleon's letters to his wife during this summer of battle shed little light on the fate of their marriage. Brief notes about his campaigns, a few exultant references to his victories, polite solicitude concerning his wife – there was little more, save a touch of brusqueness.

I haven't had a letter from you in several days [he wrote at the end of August]; the pleasures of Malmaison with its fine greenhouses and lovely gardens cause the absent to be forgotten; that's the rule, they say, among people such as you. Everyone tells me of your good health; I trust they are right.

Tomorrow I go for two days to Hungary with Eugène. My health is fairly good. Adieu, my dear,

Yours, Napoleon[9]

This brusqueness was perhaps related to the consciousness of his own devious behaviour. The Countess Walewska had arrived at Schoenbrunn in June, and Napoleon, victorious on 6 July in the bloody battle of Wagram, did not leave that lovely palace until mid-October, when peace was signed. By then he knew, and Josephine also knew, that the Countess Walewska was pregnant by him. Reason enough here, surely, for the reserved tone of his letters to Josephine. Yet he could – and did – dissimulate. 'I shall make a celebration,' he wrote from Munich to Josephine, en route to Paris, 'when we are renunited and I impatiently await this moment.'[10]

Napoleon reached Fontainebleau on 26 October, and Josephine hastened breathlessly from Malmaison to be with him. In the library the Emperor greeted her with shattering coldness. 'Ah, madame,' he said, 'here you are! You have done well to come, for I was about to leave for Saint-Cloud,' and with that he made as if to leave.[11] When Josephine wept, he melted to the extent of embracing her and arranging for them to dine together. Josephine dressed in her most elegant attire for the evening, but the cruel blow came later when she found that by the Emperor's orders the door connecting their two apartments was locked.

For more than two weeks Napoleon stayed at Fontainebleau, hunting and entertaining in imperial state, while a numbed Josephine moved like a ghost beside him in the mechanical performance of her duties. By mid-November they were back in Paris. Soon after, Napoleon wrote to Eugène in Italy, instructing him to come at once. It was clear that the climax of the domestic drama could not be far away.

Josephine broke down when Madame Junot and her little daughter, Josephine's namesake, paid a friendly visit:

I have felt [she sobbed] as if a deadly poison were creeping through my veins when I have looked upon the fresh and rosy cheeks of a beautiful child, the joy of its mother, but above all, the hope of its father! And I! struck with barrenness, shall be driven in disgrace from the bed of him who has given me a crown! Yet God is my witness that I love him more than my life, and much more than that throne which he has given me.[12]

She told Lavalette that Fouché had urged her for the good of France to divorce Napoleon. Did Lavalette, she asked, think that Fouché was really sent by the Emperor? Lavalette's answer, unhappily, seemed to be in the affirmative, yet both Josephine and her consultant agreed that she should wait for the initiative to come from the Emperor. 'Her grief,' the visitor recalled simply, 'was genuine and profound.'

Whatever the crisis, Josephine would have to face it in the presence of an exalted company. The close of the Austrian campaign had brought an extraordinary swarm of royalty to Paris: the rulers of Saxony, Westphalia, Württemberg, and Bavaria, the king and queen of Holland, the king and queen of Naples, the queen of Spain, and most of the ruling princes of the Confederation of the Rhine. This under other auspices could have been the period of Josephine's greatest triumph; it became instead a time of gnawing fear, of humiliation, and of personal sorrow.

Napoleon and Josephine dined tête-à-tête on Thursday 30 November in the Emperor's suite at the Tuileries. The hasty meal lasted just ten minutes; it proceeded in complete silence, and Josephine could only with difficulty keep back her tears. At its end the servants were quickly dismissed, and then Napoleon bluntly, but not unkindly, told Josephine of his decision: for reasons of state, which she should try to accept bravely, their marriage must come to an end. Count Bausset, who, as prefect of the palace, was in attendance in the next room, heard loud sobs through the door and then suddenly the Emperor appeared, most agitated in manner, and commanded Bausset to come in and help him. Josephine was lying on the floor, uttering hysterical cries. Napoleon held a torch, while Bausset tried to pick up the Empress with the intention of carrying her down the narrow private staircase that led to her apartments below. This failing, the Emperor called in the doorkeeper to hold the torch, and the two men then began the awkward descent, Bausset holding the Empress by the shoulders and Napoleon holding her by the legs. By all outward signs Josephine was unconscious. On the steep stairs Bausset's court sword became entangled between his legs and he nearly fell. Instinctively he tightened his hold on the Empress who, still with her eyes closed, whispered hoarsely to him: 'You are holding me too tight!' The tragedy, it seems, was something less than complete.[13]

The journey safely accomplished, Josephine was placed full length on a sofa. Amid great commotion the ladies in attendance were summoned, as was Napoleon's physician, Dr Corvisart, and Queen Hortense. The Emperor gave every sign of being deeply moved; almost apologetically he explained the situation to Bausset, a man, surely, in whom he was not accustomed to confide, saying that 'divorce has become a rigorous duty for me'. When the distraught Hortense told the Emperor that she and Eugène would now be obliged to follow their mother into exile, Napoleon was appalled. 'You would leave me thus?' he exclaimed, and shook with sobs. In the end Dr Corvisart's restoratives did their work, emotions subsided, and the painful bit of melodrama was over.

A few days later Josephine was able to attend the great reception at the Hôtel de Ville that marked the anniversary of the coronation and celebrated the signing of peace with Austria. She also found courage to be present at the huge banquet and reception at the Tuileries that night in honour of the visiting royalties. Yet the strain must have been acute for her, and she begged to be excused from the elaborate court that was held three days later.

Happily for Josephine, Eugène arrived from Italy on 7 December, and was thus able by his presence to give her the assistance upon which she had always counted. On the day after Eugène's coming, mother and son saw Napoleon in a formal interview. The Emperor said he would treat Josephine and her children most generously. Josephine was now sufficiently in command of herself to raise the question of a settlement for Eugène. She would do her duty, she said, but Eugène must be well treated. At this her son spoke up to say that under no circumstances would he make a bargain for himself out of his mother's suffering. It was agreed that there should soon be a formal gathering of the family in the Tuileries at which both the Emperor and Empress would make their views and desires clear. A document would then be signed and sent to the Senate, whose duty it would be to issue a formal *Senatus Consultum* recognizing the dissolution of the civil marriage.

The first official steps to terminate the marriage were taken on the evening of 14 December 1809 amid a blaze of splendour. The Bonaparte family, in full court dress of silks and jewels, faced the Emperor and the Empress in the throne room of the Tuileries. Louis, king of Holland, with his wife, Hortense, was there; Jérôme, king of Westphalia, with his wife, Catherine; Joachim Murat, king of Naples, whose queen was Napoleon's sister, Caroline; Pauline, Princess Borghese; and Eugène, viceroy of Italy. Talleyrand was there as vice-grand elector, Cambacérès was in attendance as arch-chancellor of the Empire, and Regnault de Saint-Jean d'Angely as secretary of state to the imperial family. Josephine, armed only with the support of her son and daughter, and doubtless conscious of the conflicting feelings of her husband, faced an icy Bonaparte family in what, after a contest of more than thirteen years, was the moment of their triumph.

Showing evident signs of emotion, Napoleon read a statement declaring that his only motive was the good of the state; that it was of concern to all his people that he should leave an heir for the throne on which Providence had placed him; and that he was sacrificing the dearest affections of his heart. He referred to Josephine as 'the one who has adorned fifteen years of my life', whose memory 'will always be engraved on my heart', who will retain her title of Empress, and for whom Napoleon will always be 'her best and dearest friend'.[14]

Josephine then undertook to read her reply – a statement prepared by Napoleon and passed to her by Talleyrand. 'With the permission of our august and dear husband,' it began, 'I declare that having no further hope of children who would satisfy the needs of his policy and the interest of France, I am pleased to offer him the greatest proof of attachment and devotion that could be given. . . .' At this point Josephine's voice choked with sobs. With an imploring gesture she passed the paper to Regnault, who solemnly read the document, ending with Josephine's declaration that she would now 'consent to end a marriage which henceforth is an obstacle to the well-being of France'.[15]

A statement had been prepared by Cambacérès in which both

parties agreed to the civil dissolution of their marriage. This was now formally signed and witnessed by the family. The Council of State, already assembled, received this document at ten p.m. and on the strength of it drafted a *Senatus Consultum* to be acted upon by the Senate itself. On 15 December the Senate met. Eugène then addressed it, explaining the motives of his mother and asking for the ratification of the *Senatus Consultum* intended to give legal sanction to the dissolution of the civil marriage of 1796. Approval was hardly to be doubted. '*Omnia animalia dicentia amen*,' Talleyrand commented.[16] He was not quite right, for the decision was less than unanimous. When the secret vote came, the results showed 76 in favour of dissolution, 7 against, and 4 blanks.

Thus the civil marriage had been dissolved – or had it? The Civil Code said that divorce could be obtained only for adultery, excesses, cruelty, or grave injuries. Moreover, a decree of 1806 exempted members of the imperial family from even these procedures, stipulating that the Emperor alone could grant or refuse a *séparation de corps*. Article 277 of the Civil Code said that mutual consent could not be invoked as a basis for divorce if a woman had reached the age of forty-five, and Josephine was now forty-six. Article 297, moreover, declared that in the case of a divorce by mutual consent neither party could contract another marriage for three years. In the Napoleonic scheme of things these were hardly more than quibbles. Article I of the *Senatus Consultum* of 16 December stated flatly and unequivocally, 'The marriage contracted between the Emperor Napoleon and the Empress Josephine is dissolved.'[17] Few in France or elsewhere would have cared to argue differently.

On that same day, in pouring rain, Josephine made a forlorn departure for Malmaison. Though she was still an empress, no pomp accompanied her going. She left in a closed carriage, followed by several others piled high with hat boxes, dresses, odds and ends of furniture, a parrot in a cage, and two of her favourite mongrels, each with its litter of puppies.

The annulment of Josephine's civil marriage left unsolved

the problem of her religious marriage. Since no civil legislation could affect the validity of this ceremony, the Church itself would now have to agree to the separation of those whom it had once joined together. Fouché, delighted at the Senate's action, had told Napoleon that 'only the sanctimonious, the trouble-makers, and the women between forty and fifty will not approve'.[18] Though this may indeed have been largely true, it did not affect the point at issue. How could the Church now be brought to agree to a religious annulment?

For Napoleon few problems were insoluble. Pope Pius VII was clearly out of the picture. Outraged at the French confiscation of his last temporal possessions in Italy, he had excommunicated Napoleon and was held a prisoner by the French at Savona, in northern Italy. His cooperation was impossible. But with respect to the Church in France, with its long tradition of action independent of Rome, the matter was quite different. There was always Napoleon's Uncle Fesch, once Corsican priest, then war contractor, and now cardinal and archbishop of Lyons. He had performed the secret ceremony of 1804. What could be more proper than to approach him and those high clergy in the capital known collectively as the Officiality of Paris?

Cambacérès, a skilled lawyer, submitted his arguments on 2 December. Proceeding on a narrowly legal basis he held that the religious ceremony was null for three reasons: witnesses were not present, the priest of the parish was not present, and the consent of the Emperor (to his own marriage!) had not formally been obtained. The Officiality of Paris astutely sidestepped an immediate decision by referring the question to a specifically created diocesan tribunal composed of three cardinals, an archbishop, and three bishops. Statements were taken. Cardinal Fesch explained that he had officiated under instructions from the Pope, thinking that these would suffice. He had been so satisfied at the time as to the validity of the nuptial benediction that he had given Josephine a certificate of legality. He was now prepared to agree that the procedure had been faulty. Both Talleyrand and Berthier, in flat contradiction to what seems to have been the contemporary evidence of 1804, declared that they were not present.

In the light of this testimony the decision of the diocesan tribunal could be foreseen. On 9 January, less than a month after the tensely unhappy evening in the Tuileries, the tribunal ruled that the marriage of Napoleon and Josephine 'must be regarded as badly and illegally undertaken, and null *quo ad foedus*, lacking the presence of the proper priest and of witnesses as stipulated by the Council of Trent. . . .' Napoleon and Josephine could therefore cease to regard each other as husband and wife. 'They are free from this marriage,' the ruling went, 'with the right to contract another.'[19] Apparently, in the eyes of the Holy Church, Josephine had been living in a state of concubinage. This sweeping decision was confirmed by a formal report from the Officiality of Paris on 12 January and publicly proclaimed in the *Moniteur* two days later. And so, in what surely must have been record time, the annulment, both civil and religious, was completed.

Josephine's new status had been fixed in part by the *Senatus Consultum* of December. It was now clarified in further arrangements made by Napoleon. Josephine was to keep the title and rank of Empress-Queen. She was to have Malmaison in full ownership – a substantial gift, seeing that the income from its farms and woodland more than met the routine operating costs. She was to have the Élysée Palace for her lifetime as a city residence. The *Senatus Consultum* provided that Josephine was to get two million francs annually from the Treasury of the State. To this, in view of Josephine's continuing debts, Napoleon belatedly added another million annually from the Treasury of the Crown. For the second time in her life Josephine was a free woman.

Josephine was soon made aware of the steps by which Napoleon was taking to himself a new wife. These matters are more a part of the history of Europe than they are of the life of Josephine, yet, curiously enough, she was brought into them. In essence the process was one by which the prospects of a Russian bride steadily receded in the face of the more promising

Austrian candidate. An 'extraordinary council' of grand dignitaries and ministers was held at the Tuileries on 28 January 1810 at that point of time when Josephine was seeking to adapt herself to the now lonely life of Malmaison. At this meeting only three voices spoke up in favour of a Russian marriage. Several weighty voices, including those of Eugène and Talleyrand, spoke in behalf of the Austrian alliance. Other alternatives were briefly considered. Yet such diverse opinions could not seriously affect the decision; for Napoleon, working closely with Metternich, had to all intents and purposes now made up his mind.

Even Josephine was prepared to give what help she could to the rising star of Marie Louise. When Madame Metternich paid a courtesy visit in these first difficult days, Eugène and Hortense offered assurance that they were 'Austrian in their souls'. Then, when Josephine joined them, she took pains to re-emphasize her children's pledge, declaring that since Napoleon was clearly determined to marry again, a wedding with Marie Louise was closest to her heart. She would do all she could to further it, and once it was accomplished she would work heart and soul to see that the Emperor and his new bride would be mutually happy. This report the Austrian ambassador quickly passed along to Vienna.

The way was soon cleared for the Austrian marriage. Early in February an inconclusive reply to Napoleon's tentative overture came in from Russia, whereupon, thanking Alexander politely, Napoleon immediately ordered the information to be sent to Vienna that he desired to arrange a marriage with Marie Louise. A contract was prepared, and Berthier drove off post-haste as a special ambassador to Vienna, bearing magnificent gifts.

On 11 March 1810 a marriage by proxy was celebrated in the Augustine Church at Vienna, and immediately afterwards Marie Louise, now turned eighteen and instructed by her father to submit herself in every respect to her new husband's will, set out for the rendezvous with the Emperor, whom she had never seen. An impatient Napoleon, twenty-two years older than his bride, met Marie Louise in the forest of Compiègne. Enchanted with his first sight of the buxom princess, the Emperor drove with her to the near-by château and escorted her up to her apartments. Attendants and courtiers, assembled below, waited ceremoniously for the imperial couple to reappear – but they waited in vain. Assured by Fesch that the proxy marriage met all canonical requirements, Napoleon delayed not a moment in asserting his rights as a husband.

At Paris, when the religious service was celebrated in the Chapel of the Tuileries, the ceremonial, word for word, was that used in the marriage of Louis XVI and Marie Antoinette. By contrast to this splendid occasion, the civil ceremony uniting Bonaparte and Josephine in 1796 and even the hastily arranged religious ceremony of 1804 must have seemed to Napoleon trivial indeed. Within three months of the parting with Josephine, Napoleon had found himself an exalted bride. He had assured himself of a vast horde of Hapsburg relatives, and he was confident that Marie Louise would soon provide him with an heir.

❧ 21 ❧

Seclusion

JOSEPHINE was now mistress of Malmaison in her own right. The gloomy weather of December added melancholy to the all too familiar surroundings where every room and every vista reminded her of happier days. Though she gave the outward appearance of being a desperately forlorn woman, she could in all conscience find little to complain of in Napoleon's attentions. Within a day of her departure from the Tuileries he wrote solicitously, saying that he had heard of her unhappiness and urging her to be brave. On the day following he turned up at Malmaison for a brief visit, and on that same evening he wrote to her again from Paris:

My dear, today I found you weaker than you should have been. You have shown courage in the past, you must find courage now to support you. Don't give way to gloomy melancholy; you must try to be resigned, and above all take care of your health, which is so dear to me. . . . You must never doubt my constant and tender friendship, and you would greatly misunderstand all my feelings towards you if you imagine that I can be happy if you aren't happy, or content if you cannot find rest.

Adieu, my dear, sleep well. Know that I wish this.[1]

Other letters came almost daily – brief, to be sure, yet kindly, and all urging her to accept philosophically the solution that was now inescapable. On Christmas Day Josephine, Eugène, and Hortense dined with Napoleon at the Trianon, responding to an invitation that the Emperor had brought in person the preceding day. Since the king of Württemberg was there, for a few hours Josephine was exposed to a little of the splendour with which she had long been familiar. The meeting led, indeed, to the proposal that Josephine should receive the rulers of Württemberg and Bavaria at Malmaison. She did so, yet these meetings were only a temporary distraction. When Josephine received her old friend of Directory days, the former Thérèse Tallien, now Madame de Caraman-Chimay, whom Napoleon had once forbidden her to receive, the two women were deeply moved and embraced amid a torrent of tears.

There was, too, the distraction of Napoleon's Austrian marriage, concerning which, as we have seen, Josephine expressed favourable views to Madame Metternich. It was an ironical situation that the dispossessed partner should have worked on behalf of her successor, all the more so since at one stage of the proceedings Metternich suggested to his wife that Josephine be used to convey delicately to Napoleon the receptive attitude of the Austrian court. Josephine, who had spent a lifetime in doing favours for others, now apparently acted so as to have some claim upon the gratitude of those who regarded the Austrian marriage as a triumph for French diplomacy.

Yet, as the month of January dragged along, Josephine's unhappiness continued. She found some relief in knowing that an attentive Napoleon, not content with the financial settlement to which he had formally agreed, would do even more. He would give her 100,000 francs for extraordinary expenses at Malmaison. 'You can,' he explained, knowing her weakness, 'plant whatever you want.' He would also, with some proviso, pay bills for jewellery – 'when they have been audited by the officials, for I don't wish thefts on the part of the jewellers.' Josephine would find, moreover, in the safe at Malmaison between 500,000 and 600,000 francs. 'You can take this,' he volunteered, 'to provide for your silver and linens.'[2] This was generosity indeed, yet a restless Josephine soon found that life at Malmaison palled; once more she was eager to be on the move. If only she could make occasional visits to the Élysée Palace she might happily recapture something of the excitement of Paris. The palace was hers, and Napoleon had thoughtfully arranged to put it in shape. 'I have tried to straighten out your affairs here,' he wrote from the Tuileries, 'and have ordered everything to be taken to the Élysée.'[3] Two days later he wrote, 'I shall be glad to know that you are at the

Élysée, and happy to be able to see you more often, for you know how much I love you.'[4]

On 3 February, therefore, Josephine arrived at the Élysée, where Eugène was awaiting her, and there for a time she had the pleasure of her devoted son's company. Some days after he had left for his post in Italy she sent him alarming news: 'We have had a fire, two days ago in the apartment you occupied. . . . Apparently it was smouldering while you were there, and I am no longer surprised that you should have complained of smoke. The fire had eaten into a beam which passed through the chimney. Everything in the apartment was destroyed.'[5] The stay at the Élysée could be, of course, only a temporary interlude in the life that Josephine was now expected to lead. Early in March she returned to Malmaison.

By this time, as the plans for the Austrian marriage were coming to a head, Napoleon might well have felt that both the Élysée Palace and Malmaison were too near to the centre of excitement. On 11 March (the very day on which the proxy marriage took place in Vienna), he arranged for the issuing of letters patent converting the Norman château and estate of Navarre, situated about three miles from Évreux and some sixty miles north-west of Paris, into a duchy, to be bestowed upon Josephine. This news he at once conveyed to Josephine, explaining further that on her death the duchy would pass to whichever son of Eugène she should have selected. 'I send you a copy of these details,' the happy Josephine wrote at once to Eugène. 'It is very sweet to see that the Emperor thinks of me, and that his feelings are always the same. You will be as happy as I am.'[6]

Napoleon's motives were not alone those of thoughtfulness and generosity. This is clear from another letter of the same day in which Josephine received her precise marching orders:

My dear, I hope that you will be pleased with what I have done about Navarre. You will have new evidence of my desire to be kind to you. Arrange to take possession of Navarre; you should go on 25 March and spend the month of April there.[7]

The purpose was obvious. Navarre was an imposing gift, for

it had guaranteed revenues of two million francs annually; and yet at the same time the gift represented for Josephine a temporary decree of exile. This she was not long in discovering.

What Josephine found on arriving at the château of Navarre in the bleak March weather of Normandy was enough to make her heart sink. Although the formal greetings of the officials at Évreux reminded her that she was still an empress, the château itself caused her a painful shock. Her new home can be reconstructed only in imagination, for it was gutted by fire in 1834 and levelled to the ground two years later. The château had been erected by a nephew of the great Turenne in 1686, at a time when the ornateness of the baroque style had not yet been tempered by the elegance of the eighteenth century. The building was designed in the form of a huge cube, two stories high, with its symmetry re-emphasized by rectangular terraces on all four sides, fenced in by balustrades and having elaborate flights of granite steps leading to four imposing entrances. Dominating the cube was a huge dome, sheathed in lead, on the flattened top of which the owner had intended to erect a colossal statue of his uncle, the great Marshal Turenne. This hope, however, had never been realized. Whether or not the building was fortunate to have escaped this crowning magnificence one can only conjecture. It clearly did not impress the Norman peasantry, to whom the strange cube with its flattened dome suggested an inverted cooking pot, hence the name – *la marmite* – they irreverently bestowed upon it.

Within the building four vestibules led from the entrances to a huge, circular, central salon which rose to the full height of the building and was lit by windows in the great dome. The only space, consequently, for private living quarters was found in the awkward triangular areas cut off in each corner of the cube by the walls of the circular salon. The château had long stood empty, and only within a few days of Josephine's arrival had furnishings been rushed in. The cold was glacial, much of the panelling was rotten, the building reeked of dampness, and even in midwinter the great salon was completely without means of heating.

Outside, the formal park was broken up by a spectacular

network of ponds, waterfalls, and canals, making in the summer an enchanting vista of Chinese kiosks, temples of love, and gardens of Hebe. It was still winter, however, and the chill watery areas on every hand, which seemed to serve only as reservoirs for countless streams of water trickling down from the surrounding slopes, intensified the general bleakness. Josephine told Hortense all her troubles:

I was saddened by the welcome I received. The residents of Évreux showed much eagerness at my arrival, but the organized ceremonies somewhat resembled condolences. Doubtless they were sorry that I no longer amounted to anything – but I am putting aside these mournful ideas. The Emperor is happy . . . and this thought is a great consolation to me.

For her immediate surroundings Josephine had little good to say:

Everything here has to be done over. The château is not habitable. The people I have brought with me have only one little room each, and the doors and windows won't close. My quarters are also small and inconvenient. The woodwork is in bad condition. The park is magnificent; it is a valley between two hillsides covered with woods of the greatest beauty; but there is too much water. . . .[8]

Not only were the surroundings acutely uncomfortable, but Josephine had the unhappy experience of seeing many of the members of her old household drift away. Her former entourage had now been sharply reduced. A few faithful companions, to be sure, remained, Madame d'Arberg and Madame Gazzani chief among them. Napoleon, moreover, had seen to it that Josephine had the necessary minimum of chamberlains and equerries – young men, usually, and not too well known to her. Nevertheless, this ensemble was a far cry from the happy company of Malmaison. Of an evening Josephine, once so fond of gossip and gaiety, found relaxation in playing *tric-trac* with the bishop of Évreux, a kindly neighbour who came regularly for cards. 'He is a very pleasant man,' Josephine reported to Hortense in simple words which convey much, 'despite his seventy-five years.'[9]

Hortense could not be with her mother in these trying weeks, for she herself was in the midst of a domestic crisis of the first magnitude. At the time of Napoleon's remarriage Hortense had returned briefly to her tormented and morose husband, King Louis. In April she made a last attempt at reconciliation by going to Amsterdam, but unhappily Louis' conduct towards her, as before, made life unbearable. Josephine shared in these sorrows only through an exchange of correspondence. By the beginning of June Hortense's health was in danger of breaking, and so she left Holland abruptly for Plombières, where on many previous occasions she had found with Josephine happiness and relaxation. King Louis, whose relations with Napoleon likewise had reached the breaking point, abdicated in July. 'You must have received a courier from Holland to tell you of the king's latest act of folly.' Napoleon wrote to Hortense. 'My will is to unite Holland with France. I will send you a copy of the letter you should transmit to the Regency, if you have not already done so ... You are set free by this step that the king has taken. You can now live tranquilly in Paris. . . .'[10]

During these difficult domestic days, when Josephine keenly felt her daughter's sorrows, she quite naturally counted the hours until she could return to the happier surroundings of Malmaison. Now that the imperial marriage celebrations and ceremonies were safely over, Josephine learned through Eugène that Napoleon would agree to her departure at the end of April, and would also assure her of much-needed funds for the repair of the château. This good news provided an exchange of letters in which the relationship between the two at that time is strikingly displayed:

I have received through my son [Josephine began in business-like fashion] the assurance that Your Majesty consents to my return to Malmaison, and that you agree to let me have the advances which I have requested in order to make the château of Navarre habitable. This double favour, Sire, largely dispels the uncertainty, indeed, the fear, which the long silence of Your Majesty had caused me.

Having given the Emperor a brief sketch of her immediate plans for travel, Josephine then spoke intimately of herself:

I have made a great sacrifice, Sire, and every day I realize even more its extent. However, this sacrifice will be what it must be: it is conclusive on my part. Your Majesty will not find your good fortune troubled by any expression of my regrets.

I shall never cease my prayers for Your Majesty's happiness; perhaps, even, I shall pray to see you again. But let Your Majesty be convinced that I shall always respect your new situation – I shall respect it in silence; confiding in the feelings you once bore towards me I shall put them to no further proof. I shall put my trust in your justice and your good heart.

I limit myself to asking one favour, which is that you will deign sometime to find the means to reassure me and those about me that I will always have a little place in your memory and a large place in your esteem and your affection. This, whatever it may be, will moderate my sorrow without compromising – and this matters most of all to me – the happiness of Your Majesty.[11]

'A little place in your memory and a large place in your esteem and your affection.' To this Napoleon replied almost immediately.

My dear, I have received your letter of 19 April; it is badly put. I am always the same; my feelings do not change. I don't know what Eugène could have told you. I haven't written because you haven't; and I have tried to do that which would suit you.

By all means go to Malmaison and be happy there; I too shall be glad to get news of you and to send you news of myself. I shall say no more until you have compared this letter with yours; after that I leave you to judge whether you or I may be the better friend.

Adieu, my dear. Keep well, and be fair, both to yourself and to me.[12]

Josephine replied with emotion:

A thousand, thousand tender thanks for not having forgotten me! My son has just brought your letter. How eagerly I read it, and yet how long it took, for there was not a word which did not cause me to weep; but these tears were so sweet. I know my heart to its depth and I know what it will always be; some sentiments are life itself, and end only when life ends.

I am in despair that my letter of the 19th displeased you. I don't recall all its phrases, but I know what unhappy feelings inspired it – it was the sorrow of having no news from you.

I wrote to you when I left Malmaison and on how many occasions since have I wished to write! But I knew the reasons for your silence, and I feared to write a letter that would be demanding. Yours has been like balm to me. Be happy – as happy as you deserve to be! My whole heart is speaking to you. You have just provided me with my share of happiness – a share which I deeply appreciate. For me nothing can equal a place in your memory.

Farewell, my dear. I thank you as tenderly as I shall always love you.[13]

This exchange of letters represents, surely, the emotional *dénouement* for Josephine in the ordeal of separation. As for Napoleon, married less than a fortnight before to his eighteen-year-old Austrian bride, and now on the eve of an imperial tour through Belgium, it was a brief moment of deep feeling soon swallowed up in the inevitable onrushing course of events. A letter from Compiègne on 29 April gave his plans for a visit to Antwerp and told Josephine simply that he had no objection to her taking the waters at Aix. 'My feelings for you never change,' he ended simply and somewhat austerely, 'and I greatly desire to know that you are happy and contented.'[14]

Josephine's thoughts were all on her departure from Navarre, but as the spring quickly advanced and the gardeners undertook their tasks, the outdoor setting became a thing of beauty. A kinsman, Maurice de Tascher, visited Josephine early in May and has described his walk with her through the Garden of Hebe, where he saw roses and lilacs in bloom, running streams, and lawns so perfectly kept that 'art troubled the charms of nature'. She also showed him the Garden of Love, an enchanting combination of cascades, pools, statuary, and 'elegant perspectives'. Josephine seemed altogether worthy of the setting. That evening the young visitor wrote in his diary: 'Yes, still beautiful and seductive; despite her forty-five years, one would have taken her this morning for the elder sister of the Graces.'[15] Josephine's eloquent guest was the same Maurice de Tascher who two years later was to die 'of exhaustion and grief' in a Königsberg hospital after leading his younger brother, badly wounded and also doomed to die, two hundred leagues on horseback through the snows of Russia.

From the summer of 1810 onwards, when the scars of divorce began to heal, Josephine's life adjusted itself to the restrained tempo that henceforth it would follow to the end. The Grand Empire was at its height, yet Josephine, though still an empress, had little part in its splendour. While Napoleon bestrode Europe like a colossus, administering territories that extended from Ragusa to Lübeck and from Madrid to Warsaw, Josephine concerned herself with the petty domestic tasks of moving back from Navarre to Malmaison or planning an idle summer excursion to the waters of Aix-les-Bains.

In June Napoleon paid Josephine a brief visit. Arriving at Malmaison at ten in the morning and accompanied by Bessières, he strode into the foyer of the château, demanding urgently of the footman, 'Where is Josephine, isn't she up yet?' The servant quickly pointed out the Empress walking in the garden, and Napoleon ran towards Josephine, and she to him. 'They embraced,' so says the diary kept by the observant footman, Piout, 'and one could see the tears of joy flowing down the cheeks of one as much as of the other.'[16] Their meeting lasted for an hour and a half. Afterwards Josephine wrote to Hortense:

I have had a day of happiness. The Emperor came to see me. His presence made me happy, even though it renewed my sorrows. . . . While he was with me I was strong enough to keep back the tears which were ready to flow, but after he left I could no longer restrain them and I felt very miserable. He was good and kindly to me, as he usually is, and I hope that he read in my heart all the tenderness and devotion I have for him. I spoke to him of your position and he is of the opinion that you should not return to Holland. . . .[17]

An idyllic summer in the pleasant surroundings of Aix-les-Bains, to which Josephine had travelled incognito as the Countess of Arberg, soon went by. Eugène found time to visit his mother as he returned to his duties in Italy. Hortense, tense and unhappy after the breach with her husband, visited Josephine twice. The entourage of the Empress included several of her ladies and five chamberlains. One of these latter, the youthful Lancelot-Théodore, Count Turpin de Crissé, has been elevated by some of Josephine's biographers to be her lover. The role seems highly improbable. Twenty years her junior, Lancelot-Théodore had emigrated as a boy during the Revolution and after his return had developed some talent as an artist. Hortense recommended him to her mother, and at least three of his Italian landscapes hung in her gallery at Malmaison. The evidence for an 'affair' comes almost entirely from an uncorroborated passage in the *Memoirs* of the Countess of Kielmansegge, a most dubious source indeed, and from the *Memoirs* of Mademoiselle Ducrest, a work long known to be an almost complete fabrication. The young Count Turpin de Crissé was undoubtedly a man of charm who brightened the summer's company. He painted some enchanting water-colours of Josephine's excursions, and it is a bound copy of these sketches at Malmaison, still containing a few faded flowers, that seems to have aroused the imagination of the scandalmongers. Josephine's letters, and the general tenor of her life in these months give little substance to such speculations.

Although happy during the summer, whether taking the waters at Aix or making excursions to Geneva, Lausanne, Berne, Biel, and the Swiss mountains, Josephine was still deeply concerned about her children and her own future. She tried also to keep in touch with the Emperor, who was good enough occasionally to respond. Hearing once of a sudden summer storm that almost swamped the small boat in which Josephine's party was being rowed across a mountain lake, he wrote to her in charming mock-concern: 'For a native of the Islands of the Ocean,' he protested, 'to be drowned in a lake would have been a fatality indeed!'[18]

As the summer months quickly slipped by, Josephine's next moves were uncertain. One temptation was to go to Milan where Eugène's wife, Augusta, was expecting another baby. For such a trip imperial permission would be necessary. Another temptation was to purchase a small estate in Switzerland. Josephine therefore wrote in September to Napoleon, outlining the alternatives:

May I return to Paris, or must I stay here? Assuredly, I would prefer to be near you, especially if I could hope to see you, but if this is not permissible what would be my role all winter? . . .

I am charging the Queen [Hortense] to discuss my interests with you, and to enter into all the details about which I cannot write. She will tell you how dear you are to me, and say that there is no sacrifice too much for me to make if it will add to your happiness. If you require me to stay, I shall rent or buy a little country place on the shore of the lake. I wish only to know if it would be suitable for me to get one near Lausanne or Vevey if I can find what suits my taste. I shall also go to Italy to see my children. I expect to spend part of the autumn travelling about in Switzerland, for I have much need of distraction, and I can find it only by changing my abode. I shall return again, perhaps, next summer to the waters at Aix which have done me so much good. This will mean a year of absence, but a year which I could bear because of the hope of seeing you at last, and because my conduct would have won your approval. . . . Oh, I beg you, don't refuse to guide me; advise your poor Josephine; it will be a proof of your affection and will console her for all her sacrifice.[19]

Napoleon was too concerned with other matters to give Josephine much guidance. He had already written to tell her briefly and exultantly that Marie Louise was four months pregnant. 'She is doing well,' he added, 'and is much attached to me.'[20] While Josephine awaited a further letter from Napoleon that would clarify her plans, a curious warning came from Madame de Rémusat, long an attendant and friend of Josephine, but now a close friend of Talleyrand and as such moving with him in secretly royalist circles. The time had not yet come, Madame de Rémusat told Josephine, for a rapprochement with Marie Louise, who had a tendency to be jealous. What would Josephine find to do in Paris? Both Malmaison and Navarre would be too near the idle gossip of Paris, and hence Josephine would soon have to go away. Far better for her to spend the winter in Italy with Eugène. This advice seemed to Josephine to be a veiled hint at possible permanent exile, as she soon told Eugène. A letter now came from Napoleon. 'Go see your son this winter,' he said, 'and then return to the waters at Aix next year or spend the spring at Navarre. I would urge you to go to Navarre at once if I did not fear that you would be bored. My opinion is that you should consider for the winter only Milan or Navarre; after that I am ready to approve whatever you do; I don't wish in any way to hamper you.'[21]

Josephine now made a decision that flew in the face of the evident desires of Napoleon that she keep away, and grasped instead the alternative he had reluctantly included at the end of his letter. She informed Hortense at Paris that she had decided to go now to Navarre, for travel to Italy seemed too arduous, and a six months' stay too long. She was pleased to hear from Hortense of Napoleon's continued concern over her happiness. 'I have made the greatest of sacrifices – the affection of my heart – for him,' she wrote. 'You will find me much changed, my dear daughter: I have lost all the good the waters did me. For a month I have lost weight. I feel great need for rest. . . .'[22]

Before leaving she made arrangements for the purchase of the small estate of Prégny-la-Tour, near Geneva. The cost was 165,000 francs – a sum to which Napoleon did not object. By mid-November she was back at Malmaison.

Steadily the life of Josephine reduced itself to the routines and trivialities of a middle age that had no major purpose. Letters came from Napoleon expressing the polite hope that she would be happy at Malmaison and Navarre. Letters went from Josephine to Eugène and Hortense rejoicing in the birth of a son to Eugène's wife, Augusta, at Milan, or expressing concern that the settlement due to Hortense after her separation from Louis had not been fixed. Recommendations went forth urging jobs and sinecures for Josephine's friends. There was excitement in March on the news of the birth of a son to Napoleon – the king of Rome. Josephine wrote to the Emperor at once, for he replied promptly to her within two days of his son's birth:

My dear, I have received your letter, and I thank you. My son is big and is thriving. I hope that he will do well. He has my chest, mouth, and eyes. I hope he will fulfil his destiny.

I am always most happy with Eugène; he never has caused me any sorrow.[23]

Late in 1811 came a characteristically stern note from Napoleon, reminiscent of the earlier times when he had fumed over Josephine's ever confused finances. After a few polite nothings he burst forth as follows:

Put some order into your affairs. Spend only 1,500,000 francs yearly and put aside a similar amount. In ten years you will have a reserve of fifteen millions for your grandchildren; it is pleasant to be able to give them something and be useful to them. Instead, I hear that you are running into debt, and that is bad. Look after your affairs and stop giving to everyone who asks for something. If you wish to please me, behave so that I will know that you have a large surplus. Imagine my bad opinion of you if I should find you indebted, with an annual income of three millions. . . .[24]

The letter stung. Josephine told Eugène about it, saying that the rumours of her debts were much exaggerated, but that she would try to set her house in order. Napoleon, apparently, was not satisfied with mere promises. He found time during an inspection tour in the Rhineland to send a long letter to his minister of finances on 1 November, telling him that Josephine's *intendant* would receive no more money until there was proof that her debts were paid. Josephine's finances, Napoleon said, were still reported to be very disordered, and he went on to make unfavourable comparisons with Marie Louise, who, he boasted, did without new clothes and accepted privations in order to be out of debt and be able to balance her books every week. Action was soon taken, for the *intendant* was able to report that with what Josephine had in cash and with what she could get from the sale of timber on her estates, her debts could be paid within a year and that by 1813, all going well, there would be a surplus of over a million. The Emperor was still unconvinced. He was so stern in his warnings that his finance minister, Mollien, told him Josephine had several times been in tears. This was too much. 'You mustn't make her weep,' the Emperor said anxiously, and when he wrote again to Josephine he explained that his sole purpose was to make sure that Josephine would have money later on for her grandchildren. 'Never doubt my affection for you, and don't be unhappy about these matters,' the master of Europe concluded, not unkindly.[25]

As the year 1812 opened, Josephine wrote triumphantly to Eugène with news almost too good to be true:

I have put off writing to you, dear Eugène, in order to be able to assure you positively of something that will please you – my affairs are in order and all my debts paid. Such is my new year's gift for you, and I know your affection towards me well enough to be sure that you will be delighted.[26]

One is tempted to believe, charitably, that Josephine was at least making an attempt to straighten out her tangled financial affairs, whether or not she was actually as successful as she claimed.

Josephine entered the year 1812 in the shadow of tremendous events. 'The Emperor,' she wrote to Eugène in February, 'seems to have forgotten me,' as well he might, for he was now ever more deeply involved in a growing antagonism with Russia that was to lead to the great campaign of 1812 and to his ultimate disaster.[27] He had time to arrange that Josephine exchange the Élysée Palace for the castle of Laeken, outside Brussels – an exchange that pleased the Emperor since it gave him a fine town residence. Josephine accepted the arrangement though, as it happened, she never saw Laeken. She knew little, indeed, of events in France. 'I am a stranger to everything,' she told Eugène.[28]

During the spring Napoleon's relations with Tsar Alexander went from bad to worse. Late in April the Russian ambassador, Kurakin, visited the Tuileries and submitted an ultimatum to Napoleon. War, to all intents and purposes, had begun. At six in the morning of 9 May Napoleon left Saint-Cloud to launch his great campaign against Russia. Whereas in the past it had been Josephine who travelled with Napoleon, now Marie Louise accompanied him, travelling as far as Dresden where the presence of the Austrian emperor and the kings of Saxony and Prussia gave brilliance to the last of such imperial occasions. Then Napoleon pushed on without Marie Louise, elaborating the plans to bring his huge, conglomerate armies of more than half a million men into battle against the Russians.

He had not forgotten Josephine. At Gumbinnen, in the farthest corner of East Prussia, a letter arrived from her asking permission to visit Eugène's wife and children in Milan. 'I see no objection to your going to Milan to be with the vicereine,' Napoleon wrote in evident haste, 'You would do well to travel incognito. It will be hot. My health is good. Eugène is doing very well. Never doubt my interest and my affection.'[29] Four days later he hopefully crossed the Niemen River.

Josephine set out for Milan where, during those weeks while the Grand Army toiled eastward across the Russian plains, she enjoyed the delights of family reunion. By September she was at Aix-les-Bains, finding to her surprise that several of the Bonaparte family were also present. Almost at the moment of her arrival Napoleon was fighting the bloody battle of Borodino, that hideous, one-day September encounter in which 28,000 French and 35,000 Russians were left wounded or dead.

Amid the placid charms of Aix Josephine soon received the letter which her son wrote her on the day after Borodino, while the long rows of fallen were still unburied:

My dear mother, I am writing to you from the field of battle. I am well. The Emperor has won a great victory over the Russians. We fought for thirteen hours. I commanded the left wing. We have all done our duty, and hope that the Emperor will be satisfied.

I cannot thank you enough for the attentions and kindness you have shown to my little family. You are adored in Milan, as you are everywhere. People have written charming things about you and you have turned the head of everyone you have approached.[30]

From Aix Josephine moved on in October to Prégny, the little estate on the shores of Lake Geneva she had purchased in the preceding year. Life for a time became almost gay, with dances, visits of courtesy from local officials, and pleasant excursions along the lake. Napoleon, meanwhile, was on the eve of disaster. On 19 October, almost the same day on which Josephine departed from Prégny for Paris, he left Moscow and embarked on the retreat that was to destroy what was left of the 600,000 men he had once commanded.

When Josephine reached Malmaison on 25 October, the period of her travels was over. Even more than previously she was a stranger to the climactic events of the time – a lone woman on the fringe of momentous happenings. Though she was curious enough to wish to see Marie Louise it does not seem that she succeeded. According to the memoirs of Madame Avrillon she did contrive to see the infant king of Rome, meeting him at the little summer palace, known as the Bagatelle, on the outskirts of Paris near the Porte de Chaillot, where Madame de Montesquieu took him daily to play. Josephine wept, kissed the child, and arranged with the portraitist, Madame Thibaut, to have a copy made of a painting in the possession of the Emperor for the very large price of 10,000 francs. Josephine also received the Countess Walewska, who visited Malmaison with her son, and watched Josephine tempt the infant Alexander Walewski, son of an imperial father, with cakes and playthings.

These were indeed momentous days, a period in which the ill-fated General Malet tried to raise a revolt in Paris against the Emperor, only to be seized, tried, and shot. Others, too, were abandoning their allegiance to the imperial cause, not the least of them being Talleyrand – that Prince of Weathercocks who with unfailing virtuosity timed to a nicety the moment for making the transition from one régime to its successor. In these days some have written of 'the conspiracy of Malmaison', implying that the little household of Josephine had now become a centre of treason to the imperial cause. To write thus is to do an injustice to Josephine and to ignore the clear evidence of letter after letter which she sent to her devoted son in Italy, now back from the Russian campaign and absorbed in his viceregal duties. Certainly the majority of those around her – nobles of the old régime, many of them former *émigrés* now reinstated – were at heart better disposed to the royalist cause than they could ever be to a Napoleonic empire of failing strength. Madame de Rémusat, close friend of Talleyrand, Madame d'Audenarde, Madame de la Rochefoucauld,

Madame d'Arberg, and Madame de Viel-Castel together made up what has been called a veritable Faubourg Saint-Germain. Yet they were hardly a conspiratorial group. In his daily visits to Madame de Rémusat, Talleyrand began to drop his hints of an imminent Napoleonic downfall. The men associated with Josephine's household: Viel-Castel, Pourtalès, Turpin de Crissé, Dalberg, Vitrolles, Semallé, and Roux Laborie, were all ready to assume their place in a Bourbon restoration, and some, indeed played small parts in the last-minute manoeuvres that brought it about. To say more is to give them an importance which they do not deserve.

As for Josephine, the simple statement must suffice that she was apparently ignorant of these intrigues and took no part in them; she kept her loyalty to the Emperor until the day of his abdication; and she concerned herself in these darkening times with maintaining her ties with Hortense and Eugène. Little else remained for her to do.

❧ 22 ❧

Finale

IF 1812 had been a year of ominous portent for France, 1813 and 1814 were years of disaster. As Napoleon gathered another great army to meet the coalition massing against him in Saxony and Bohemia, Josephine was so far removed from events as hardly to know their nature, and certainly not to realize their catastrophic significance. While Hortense made the accustomed summer visit to Aix-les-Bains, Josephine happily took care of the two grandchildren at Malmaison. As autumn approached, Napoleon's shattering defeat at Leipzig in October announced the beginning of the end. His father-in-law, Emperor Francis I, had turned against him and thrown the full forces of Austria into battle opposing France. Bernadotte, marshal of France, husband of the Désirée who had once loved Napoleon, and now crown prince of Sweden, had brought his adopted country into the coalition and seriously coveted for himself the very throne that Napoleon occupied. In Italy Joachim Murat, king of Naples and brother-in-law of Napoleon, was likewise contemplating abandoning the Emperor and making an approach to the coalition. Loyalties were giving way like rotted timbers in an overloaded bridge. Spain was already gone, and Wellington's armies now crossed the passes of the Pyrenees into France. Russian armies had overrun the Grand Duchy of Warsaw; Prussia had become a pillar of the great coalition; and members of the Confederation of the Rhine were turning one by one against Napoleon. 'They have betrayed me, yes, all of them,' the Emperor was to write bitterly within a year to Josephine.[1]

Only Eugène, it seemed, as viceroy of Italy, held firm in his loyalty to the Emperor. When his father-in-law, the king of Bavaria, told him in October that Bavaria was about to join the coalition and suggested that Eugène do likewise, he indignantly spurned the proposal. Josephine had reason to be proud, so she told her son more than once, of his constancy. This attitude, clearly revealed in her letters to Eugène, throws a warm and favourable light upon her attitude to Napoleon in these hours of his greatest trial. Unfortunately, as the year ended and the coalition crossed the Rhine at Basel and began the invasion of France, Napoleon was too closely involved in the brilliant but unavailing battles of January, February, and March – the 'Campaign of France' – to have any clear picture of Eugène's actions. He received conflicting reports about his stepson, judged him wrongly, and so imposed upon both Eugène and Josephine an altogether unfair burden of criticism and reproach.

The unhappy episode, which placed an additional strain on the last months of Josephine's life, had almost trivial beginnings. Eugène's wife, Augusta, was about to have her third child, and the husband, understandably, had tried to arrange with the Austrian commander in Italy for his wife's safety in the event that she should have to be left behind in Milan. Reports of this overture to Austria aroused Napoleon's suspicions, all the more since he had learned that Joachim Murat was in process of going over to the enemy. In January Napoleon instructed Eugène under no circumstances to begin the withdrawal of his forces until he learned that Murat had formally joined the allies. Wishing apparently to modify his instructions, Napoleon then took the curiously unmilitary step of writing to Josephine asking her to convey to Eugène instructions to withdraw northwards to the Alps, leaving only covering forces in Mantua and the other fortresses. His letter, so Josephine told Eugène, ended with the words 'France above all! France needs all her children.'[2]

Eugène, however, still awaited formal word of Murat's action and until this came was unwilling to disengage. He therefore stood fast in Italy. Writing to his mother he hotly rejected any imputations upon his patriotism, and in his anger wrote similarly to the Emperor. Napoleon's next solution consisted of ordering poor Augusta, momentarily expecting her baby, to make the long journey to Paris. This would involve a trip over the Alps clearly impossible to a woman in her condition. The command caused Eugène to be even more outraged, and produced in addition an astonishing letter of refusal from Augusta to Napoleon:

Without any doubt [she wrote boldly to the Emperor] I know my duty and my husband's towards Your Majesty. We have given ample proof, and we have never failed. . . . It is sad to be obliged to say that for recompense we have been plunged into sorrow and mortification which nevertheless we have borne silently and patiently. . . . What have I done to deserve so curt an order for departure? When I married I never thought things would come to this. . . . In spite of all I shall obey your orders. I shall leave Milan if the enemy force me to; but my duty and my affection make it a law for me not to leave my husband. Since you require me to risk my life, I wish at least to have the consolation of finishing my days in the arms of the one who has all my affection and causes all my happiness. . . . In spite of the sorrow Your Majesty causes us, I shall never cease to rejoice in his happiness and wish for that of the Empress.[3]

Eugène, deeply moved on learning of his wife's courage and devotion, wrote exultantly to her, swearing that it would be impossible for any letter to do more than hers had done. If Napoleon, as we may suspect, was touched, he managed to conceal his feelings. He wrote gruffly to Eugène, calling the letters from him and his wife 'extravagant', and declaring that they must have lost their heads. 'I paid you no compliments for your loyalty,' he added, 'because you only did your duty.'[4] To Augusta he wrote that he was touched by the sympathy of her heart and the vivacity of her spirit. 'I only thought,' he explained lamely, 'that with your disposition you would have a difficult confinement in a country which is a theatre of war and in the midst of enemies. It would be better for your safety to come to Paris.'[5]

Nothing upset Josephine so easily as an imputation against Eugène. She had been deeply shocked, and the happy outcome of this flare-up only intensified, if that were possible, her devotion to him. In the difficult weeks that were ahead of her this devotion gave her strength and helped to carry her through the tragic crisis of the Emperor's downfall.

The Campaign of France, in which Napoleon won victory after victory against a coalition that somehow never ceased to advance, ended at the gates of Paris. By the last week of March the allies were within striking distance of the capital. Most unwisely Napoleon left his brother Joseph in command and went himself to Fontainebleau. Josephine, who had spent these anxious weeks at Malmaison, was very close to the path of the allied advance. 'I'm tormented by the position you are in,' she wrote to Eugène in Italy on 24 March, 'and by our own. However, they have been speaking since yesterday at Paris of an English courier coming from London who has told everyone that he brings England's signature to a peace treaty. God grant that this news is true. France never had greater need for peace.'[6] The rumour was false, yet the end was very near.

For greater safety, Josephine left Malmaison on 29 March for the long trip to the château of Navarre, journeying with her diamonds and pearls sewn in her skirts and her other jewellery packed in strong boxes. The cortège was considerable, for Josephine had assembled all her carriages, and since post-horses could not be counted upon en route she took all the horses from the Malmaison stables. The journey was adventuresome, for no one knew what enemy patrols might be encountered. The party spent the night at Mantes and then, pushing on, reached Navarre on the evening of the 30th, the very day of the surrender of Paris. Hortense arrived breathless from Versailles with her two sons, having defied an order from Marie Louise, whom Napoleon had made regent, to go to Blois. En route the party had the excitement of seeing one lone Cossack, who emerged momentarily from the forest of Rambouillet and then disappeared back into it. Soon, however, with the surrender of Paris, the arrival of the allied monarchs in the capital, and the proclamation of a provisional government under Talleyrand, the physical dangers threatening Josephine and Hortense disappeared.

Despite the plaintive note in Josephine's letters, the tragedy of these days was most assuredly not hers, but rather that of

Napoleon, who had seen his armies defeated, his Empire crumble, his marshals one by one desert him, and his Hapsburg empress disappear into the west. On 2 April the senate had declared Napoleon and his family deposed from the throne. At Fontainebleau he soon saw that he could offer little further resistance, and thus on 6 April he signed in profound gloom the famous Act of Abdication, renouncing for himself and his heirs the crowns of France and Italy. 'Once more,' recorded the faithful Caulaincourt who was with him, 'he spoke of the Empress and his son, and of the Viceroy and the Empress Josephine, whose interests he asked me to bear in mind.'[7] The allies then quickly drafted a definitive treaty, which was received by Napoleon late on 12 April. He deferred his decision concerning this ultimate step and talked instead of his companions. 'Eugène,' he asserted during his reminiscences to Caulaincourt on this sad evening, 'is the only one of my family who has never given me a single cause for dissatisfaction. His mother made me very happy. Those are the sweetest recollections of my life.'[8] During the night he attempted suicide by taking poison, but was revived. 'You are to tell Josephine,' he instructed Caulaincourt who attended him as he hoped unavailingly for death, 'that she has been very much in my thoughts.'[9]

In the morning, recovered from his ordeal, Napoleon put his signature to the Treaty of Fontainebleau. Henceforth he would be sovereign of the island of Elba and the Bonaparte family would be most comfortably provided for. As for the Beauharnais, Hortense and her children were to be granted 400,000 francs annually – a sum less only than the 500,000 francs granted to Joseph and Jérôme and more than what was stipulated for the other Bonapartes. Eugène was promised a suitable establishment outside France (later fixed as the duchy of Leuchtenberg, in Bavaria). Josephine, with a guaranteed annual revenue of 1,000,000 francs was the most generously treated of all these. On the 20th Napoleon bade farewell to his Guard at Fontainebleau in what has been known ever since as the *Cour des Adieux*. He travelled incognito through France, took ship, and on 4 May went ashore at Porto-Ferrajo to assume sovereignty of the minuscule principality of Elba.

As Napoleon's career on the grand stage of events thus seemed to be coming to an end, Josephine's life also moved into the shadows. At Navarre her entourage was royalist to the core, though Josephine kept herself apart from this newly developing trend. In the little group of her immediate companions, Madame Gazzani was Belgian, Princess Giedroyc was Polish, and the two Van Berchems were Swiss. Madame de Rémusat, once so zealous in Josephine's support, was now busy distributing to all and sundry the white cockade of the Bourbons. Thus, even before Napoleon had reached Elba the times, truly enough, had changed.

At Navarre Josephine was concerned with the immediate question of the safety of her beloved Malmaison. 'I do not need to urge you to take care of Malmaison,' she wrote to her superintendent, Bonpland, 'I count on your zeal and your attachment to me. If you can arrange for a protective guard, be sure to have the officer dine with you and provide food for his soldiers.'[10] Other detailed instructions followed. A few days later she sent to a friend, the Countess Cafarelli, news from Navarre: 'We are brokenhearted at what is happening, above all at the ingratitude of the French. The papers are full of the most dreadful attacks; if you haven't read them don't do so, for they would make you ill.'[11]

Josephine's indignation at the new order did not prevent her from appealing to one of its principal architects, Talleyrand, now head of the provisional government. A powerful instinct for survival led her to write to him for some assurance concerning the settlement that had been made for her at the time of her divorce:

I learn [she wrote to Talleyrand on 8 April] that the fate of the Emperor and his family is about to be fixed. Mine was settled four years ago by the Senate. The settlement then allotted to me was my sole support in the retreat where I have lived. I wait for the Senate to act anew, and I place my interests and those of my children in your hands. Counsel me in these circumstances, and I shall follow your advice with confidence.[12]

What Talleyrand replied is unknown. By this time the terms of the Treaty of Fontainebleau were completed, and Josephine discovered that while they were still generous (a million francs for her annually), they did not approach the three millions she had been granted in 1810. She had no alternative but to accept.

More striking than this correspondence is the famous letter of 9 April, which Josephine wrote to Eugène who was still at his post in Italy. Fighting by this time had ceased and Napoleon's abdication was nearly a reality:

What a week I have spent, my dear Eugène! How I have suffered at the way in which they have treated the Emperor! What attacks in the newspapers, what ingratitude on the part of those upon whom he showered his favours! But there is nothing more to hope for. All is finished; he is abdicating.

As for you, you are free, and absolved from any oath of fidelity; anything more that you could do for his cause would be useless; act for your family.[13]

'Act for your family.' Would it have been better, as one scholar writes, if Josephine had never written this letter, or if, having received it, Eugène had at once burned it? In the course of the nineteenth century the most ardent Bonapartists, Frédéric Masson in the lead, would use this letter to demonstrate what they chose to consider the black ingratitude of one unworthy of the affection and the dignities that Napoleon had showered upon her. Such a conclusion, surely, is unfair. The all too fragmentary correspondence of the preceding months shows that she warmly supported Eugène when he stood his ground in defending Napoleon's cause. She praised her son's constancy to the Emperor, and she urged him to continue in it. She took pride in Eugène's loyalty, and in a very precise sense it seems proper to say that his loyalty was hers also. Now she had seen Napoleon's marshals turn against him; there was treason in his very family. That a woman of fifty, alone and uncertain of the future, should have kept up a mock-heroic fight for a lost cause would be asking too much. The man whom she had supported up to, and indeed after, the day of his abdication had chosen to put Josephine aside and marry another. 'Act for your family' was advice that in all reasonableness she could now give to a son whose devotion had been demonstrated beyond all doubt.

Even so, a letter which came a few days after she had written to Eugène – a letter penned by Napoleon on 16 April as he waited at Fontainebleau in those unhappy days following the signature of the treaty – must have caused her deep emotion. This last known letter of Napoleon to Josephine concludes the joint story of their two lives:

I wrote to you on the eighth of this month (it was Friday) and perhaps you never received my letter. There was still fighting and possibly it was intercepted; now communications are re-established. I have made my decision and I have no doubt that this letter will reach you.

I shall never repeat what I then told you; I complained then of my situation; now I congratulate myself; my mind and my heart are free of an enormous burden; my fall is great, but at least, according to what they say, it serves a useful purpose.

In my retirement I shall substitute the pen for the sword. The narrative of my reign will be surprising; people have only seen me in profile, and I shall show myself full-face. What things are there for me to make known! What men there are about whom they have wrong opinions! I have showered benefits on thousands of wretches! What did they do, in the end, for me?

They have betrayed me, yes, all of them. I except only our dear Eugène, so worthy of you and of me. May he be happy under a king who can appreciate the instincts of nature and of honour!

Adieu, my dear Josephine. Resign yourself, as I am doing, and never lose the memory of one who has never forgotten you, and never will forget you.[14]

By mid-April 1814, Josephine made her last return to Malmaison. The complaints of loss of weight that appear in her letters are confirmed in the last portraits and by the comments of contemporaries. Although she may not fully have realized it, she was becoming seriously ill. Nevertheless, the social demands coming from the new group of arrivals at Paris were soon felt at Malmaison. Josephine had learned through Madame Cochelet, lady-in-waiting to Hortense, that many of the distinguished Russians in Paris, including the great Alexander himself, were eager to pay her visits. She had warm messages from Metternich, from the Duke de Berry, nephew of Louis XVIII, and from members of the provisional government. All were one in their desire to greet her cordially, and not to count her among the Bonapartes whom they had succeeded in overthrowing.

Such attention to Josephine raises interesting problems. Why should so unpolitical a figure command such great interest? Curiosity, both about the Empress and about Malmaison, had something to do with it. In the case of Tsar Alexander, a great ladies' man, there was also the desire to meet the romantic figure who had risen so high and her daughter, the former queen of Holland. For other leaders of the coalition it might have been simply an anti-Napoleonic gesture, in so far as Josephine had been separated from the Emperor. In the case of the Bourbons, shrewd calculations of political expediency were involved. *La bonne Joséphine* had her following, as pamphlets sold on the streets of Paris soon were to show. The temper of France was uncertain, Bonapartism was not dead, and what better way could there be to rally support than by showing respect to a woman who had been a product of the *ancien régime*, a victim of the Revolution, and for a decade the most glittering ornament of imperial France?

Alexander I came to Malmaison on the day after Josephine's arrival, first having ascertained politely through an aide whether his visit would be acceptable. Hortense made her appearance during the visit and found her mother walking in the garden with the tsar. Alexander was all charm, and Josephine responded warmly. Yet Hortense, still not accustomed to the new state of affairs, greeted him with much reserve. Following this first Russian visit Alexander wrote to Josephine as follows:

It is with the keenest regret that I noticed your Majesty had some anxieties; but I have every reason to hope that you will convince yourself they have no foundation. Though I do not wish to exploit the permission you have been kind enough to accord me, Madame, I look forward to presenting my respects to you on Friday at your dinner hour.[15]

Alexander came again, and still again. Josephine was quick to order new clothes from Paris and to prepare at Malmaison to give elegant dinners for her guests. Perhaps, at long last, a new age would be dawning for her. Although the burden must have been most tiring, she received the king of Prussia, the grand duke of Baden, the prince of Bavaria, the prince of Mecklenburg, visitors from England, and a sprinkling of Russian grand dukes.

To Josephine's inexpressible delight, Eugène arrived on 9 May from Italy, having taken his wife and children, including the month-old daughter who had been born in Mantua, to visit Augusta's family at Munich. Eugène was in high favour with the Bourbon court, for was he not, after all, the son of that Viscount de Beauharnais who had lost his life under the Terror, and might he not under the restored monarchy in France serve his country as once his father had done, and under his father's ancient title?

A few days later Josephine went with a family party to Hortense's estate outside Paris at Saint-Leu, where once again Tsar Alexander was present, exuding kindness and cordiality. On this occasion Josephine, true to her fondness for flimsy dresses, had worn a costume that in the tricky spring air caused her to contract a chill from whose effects she never really recovered. That afternoon, while the rest of the party drove through the forest of Montmorency, Josephine remained indoors. She told Madame Cochelet that she felt exhausted and depressed, in part through thinking of the lonely figure of Napoleon on his tiny island of Elba, in part through fearing that the promises of an endowment for her children would never be realized.

In these days a striking figure from a distant past likewise visited Malmaison. Madame de Staël, who again and again had aroused Napoleon's ire and had long been an exile from France, returned from England and quickly paid her respects to Josephine. The interview was difficult, for Germaine as always was bursting with questions that, it is said, she had been preparing ever since 1810. She flung these at the gentle Josephine in the picture gallery until at last the Empress, 'very agitated, very much moved', was constrained to dismiss her insatiable inquisitor.

A dinner for the king of Prussia and his two sons was followed by a dinner on 24 May for Alexander and the Russian grand dukes. Ill as she was, Josephine could do no less than follow the dinner by opening the ball with the tsar. She then walked out in the evening air through the gardens with him, and this walk was the beginning of the end. Two days later, when she was very hoarse, her personal physician was sufficiently concerned to begin applying plasters to her throat. On the 28th the fever was aggravated, and the doctors, now deeply concerned with the condition of Josephine's throat, prophesied a long illness.

Clearly, Josephine's condition was grave. Plans were made for the members of the family to share watches at her bedside. They were hardly needed, for on the morning of Sunday 29 May 1814 Josephine was dying. While Hortense and Eugène were away at Mass, the Abbé Bertrand, tutor to Hortense's children, administered the last sacraments. At noon, in the bedroom which overlooked the park and the great cedar of Marengo, and in the presence of her children, Josephine died.* She was twenty-five days short of reaching her fifty-first birthday.

Josephine's obsequies were marked, as had been so many aspects of her life, with unusual elements. Royal etiquette, to be sure, stipulated that Eugène and Hortense, the two living beings closest to her, should leave Malmaison for the château of Saint-Leu within hours of her death and be represented during the days of public mourning and at her funeral only by Hortense's two small sons, the one six and the other ten. Fate had brought it about that her first husband should lie in an unmarked grave in Paris, and that her second, to all intents a captive on the island of Elba, should learn only by chance of her death. The fortune of politics determined that the new Bourbon régime in France, nervous of its position on returning

* Josephine's complaints of a loss of weight and exhaustion, together with the doctors' anticipation of a long illness, suggest some malignancy. The autopsy, conducted by the chief anatomist of the Faculty of Medicine, reported an extreme inflammation of the whole trachea with a large gangrenous spot on the larynx. Both the bronchial tubes and the lungs were choked with blood. All other organs were completely healthy.

to a country where popular allegiance might still be uncertain, dared pay only timid respect to the dead Empress. And it was, surely, an irony of the gods that led those who prepared Josephine's death certificate to increase the calculated error that she had made about her age at the time of her civil marriage to Napoleon in 1796. She had then reduced the gap between their ages by four years; in death the gap still remained, and the date of her birth was still wrongly recorded, so as to make her forty-five.

Josephine's body lay in state for three days in a chamber hung with black and lit by candles. The roads from Paris were crowded with people wishing to pay their respects; twenty thousand passed by the bier of the daughter of Martinique. Louis XVIII sent a letter of condolence, and Alexander I went in person to Saint-Leu to convey his regrets to Hortense and Eugène and to announce to Hortense that Louis XVIII had been pleased to grant her the title of Duchess of Saint-Leu.

The funeral took place on 2 June. The coffin was carried from Malmaison to the parish church of Rueil between long lines of troops. These could hardly be French soldiers, whose allegiance to Napoleon had ended only two weeks before and whose position was uncertain. The route was guarded therefore by the militia of the canton and by Russian guard regiments in full-dress uniform. Many mourners of high rank, representatives of the tsar and the king of France, the ladies and gentlemen of Josephine's entourage, and a considerable crowd of the curious followed the coffin.

The funeral sermon was preached by the archbishop of Tours, loyal servant of the new régime, pious remembrancer of the old. He delighted members of Josephine's family by his eloquent testimony of her charm, her sympathy, and her generosity. Unable to omit all reference to Napoleon, he likewise delighted the Bourbons by avoiding explicit use of his name, speaking of Napoleon only as 'one who did not claim for himself the immortal honour of restoring the Bourbons to the throne of their ancestors, yet by his very first actions gave people to believe that he would'.[16] The archbishop paid generous tribute to the many efforts Josephine had made to help the *émigrés* and to find positions for those royalists who had returned from exile to the service of their country. Louis XVIII is said to have breathed a sigh of relief and gratitude at the dexterity with which the archbishop had thus kept the balance between France's Bonapartist and Bourbon sympathies.

The truest tribute to Josephine was paid elsewhere. Paris was flooded with pamphlet literature about her. Though some of it was scurrilous, and some of it was anti-Bourbon and nothing more, by far the greater part hailed *la bonne Joséphine* – Frenchwoman, wife, and companion of the great Emperor. In this way the first nostalgic surge of admiration for the exile at Elba arose, and the first step was taken in the creation of that great romantic fiction of the nineteenth century, the Napoleonic legend. Far better for Josephine's fame that she should have died in this hour, than to have lived to endure the inevitable pettiness of life in an age to which she would have been a stranger. Far better that she should have left behind as her contribution to the legend the romantic record of her kindliness and grace.

It appears that no one, not even Hortense or Eugène, acted quickly to send Napoleon the news of Josephine's death. A valet returning from Elba to France found a newspaper at Genoa with the story and sent it to the Emperor. Much later, at St Helena, Napoleon was to speak often of his wife, including candid appraisal of her weaknesses and husbandly amusement at her foibles with an evident and deep devotion.[17] His inner thoughts at Elba are unknown. 'At the news of this death,' one very close to him has recorded, 'he appeared profoundly afflicted; he shut himself up within, and would see no one but his grand marshal.'[18]

Long thoughts he must have had of Josephine – intimate memories going back from the unhappy present through years of imperial splendour to the fevered times of the Revolution. Through these two decades – as dramatic a twenty years as history can provide – the all too human life of the creole of Martinique had run like a fine thread, tarnished as any life may be, then mingling with the splendid golden cord of an imperial France, woven into its substance and inseparably a part of it.

Genealogical Tables

I TASCHER DE LA PAGERIE

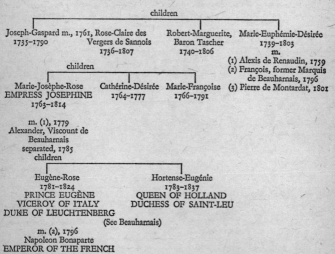

Gaspard-Joseph m., 1734, Françoise Boureau de la Chevalerie

children

Joseph-Gaspard m., 1761, Rose-Claire des   Robert-Marguerite,   Marie-Euphémie-Désirée
1735–1790   Vergers de Sannois   Baron Tascher   1739–1803
      1736–1807   1740–1806   m.

                        (1) Alexis de Renaudin, 1759
children   (2) François, former Marquis
                          de Beauharnais, 1796

Marie-Josèphe-Rose   Cathérine-Désirée   Marie-Françoise   (3) Pierre de Montardat, 1801
EMPRESS JOSEPHINE   1764–1777   1766–1791
1763–1814

m. (1), 1779
Alexander, Viscount de
Beauharnais
separated, 1785
children

Eugène-Rose   Hortense-Eugénie
1781–1824   1783–1837
PRINCE EUGÈNE   QUEEN OF HOLLAND
VICEROY OF ITALY   DUCHESS OF SAINT-LEU
DUKE OF LEUCHTENBERG
           (See Beauharnais)

m. (2), 1796
Napoleon Bonaparte
EMPEROR OF THE FRENCH
divorced, 1810

2 BEAUHARNAIS

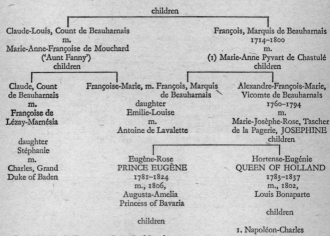

Claude, Count de Beauharnais

children

Claude-Louis, Count de Beauharnais
m.
Marie-Anne-Françoise de Mouchard
('Aunt Fanny')
children

François, Marquis de Beauharnais
1714–1800
m.
(1) Marie-Anne Pyvart de Chastulé
children

Claude, Count
de Beauharnais
m.
Françoise de
Lézay-Marnésia

Françoise-Marie, m. François, Marquis
de Beauharnais
daughter
Emilie-Louise
m.
Antoine de Lavalette

Alexandre-François-Marie,
Vicomte de Beauharnais
1760–1794
m.
Marie-Josèphe-Rose, Tascher
de la Pagerie, JOSEPHINE
children

daughter
Stéphanie
m.
Charles, Grand
Duke of Baden

Eugène-Rose
PRINCE EUGÈNE
1781–1824
m., 1806,
Augusta-Amelia
Princess of Bavaria

Hortense-Eugénie
QUEEN OF HOLLAND
1783–1837
m., 1802,
Louis Bonaparte

children

1. Joséphine-Maximilienne, m. Oscar I of Sweden
   1807–1877
2. Eugénie-Hortense-Auguste, m. Frederick William of
   1808–1847   Hohenzollern-Hechingen
3. Auguste-Charles-Eugène, m. Maria II of Portugal
   1810–1839
4. Amélie-Auguste-Eugénie, m. Pedro I, Emperor of Brazil
   1812–1873
5. Theodoline-Louise-Eugénie, m. William of Württemberg
   1814–1857
6. Maximilien-Eugène-Auguste, m. Grand Duchess Marie,
   1817–1839   d. of Nicholas I of Russia

children

1. Napoléon-Charles
   1802–1807
2. Napoléon-Louis
   1804–1831
3. Charles-Louis-Napoléon
   NAPOLEON III
   1808–1873

3 BONAPARTE

Carlo Maria Buonaparte m, 1764, Letizia Ramolino
1746–1785   1750–1836

children

Joseph
1768–1844
KING OF NAPLES
KING OF SPAIN
m.
Julie Clary

NAPOLEON
1769–1821
EMPEROR OF
THE FRENCH
m., 1796,
(1) JOSEPHINE DE
BEAUHARNAIS
divorced 1810
m., 1810,
(2) Marie Louise
of Austria
son
Napoleon Francis
KING OF ROME
1811–1832
had further children by:
(3) Eléanore Denuelle
de la Plaigne:
Léon Denuelle
1806–1881
(4) Countess Maria
Walewska:
Alexandre-Florian,
Count Walewski
1810–1868

Lucien
1775–1840
m.
(1) Christine Boyer
(2) Marie Jouberthon

Maria Anna Elisa
1777–1820
m.
Prince Baciocchi

Louis
1778–1846
KING OF HOLLAND
m.
Hortense Beauharnais
children
Napoléon Charles
1802–1807
Napoléon Louis
1804–1831
Charles Louis Napoléon
1808–1873
NAPOLEON III

Paula Maria
(Pauline)
1780–1825
m.
Prince Borghese

Maria Annunziata
(Caroline)
1782–1839
QUEEN OF NAPLES
m.
Joachim Murat
KING OF NAPLES

Jérôme
1784–1860
KING OF WESTPHALIA
m.
(1) Elizabeth Patterson
(2) Princess Catherine
of Württemberg

Bibliographical Essay

THE enormous literature on the Empress Josephine includes more than fifty biographies in several languages. In writing seriously about her a major difficulty is posed by the unreliable memoirs, the anecdotal trivia, and the garbled or manufactured letters that crowd the post-Napoleonic period. It is almost a rule that the better the story about Josephine the more unreliable its source will be. Within a year of her death a dozen pamphlets about her had appeared in Paris; one, for example, purported to contain her last will and testament. Spurious memoirs and letters, supposedly by Josephine, were printed in 1820, provoking a quick protest from her son, Eugène de Beauharnais. In 1828, nevertheless, the publishers outdid themselves by issuing an equally spurious three-volume set of her so-called memoirs. The memoirs of Madame Ducrest, a lady-in-waiting to Josephine, which appeared in 1828, and those of Mademoiselle Avrillon, her *première femme de chambre*, which appeared in 1833, are typical examples of another sort of half-imaginative literature, as much the creation of the publishers as of their reputed authors. Josephine, it is clear, did not have the least interest during her retirement at Malmaison in writing her own memoirs. Though fluent and sympathetic in conversation, she had no part in that age of the Restoration in Europe when memoir-writing seemed to become a compulsive necessity and was without question a most lucrative source of funds. Not until 1857, when the biography by Joseph Aubenas appeared, could her life begin to be placed on some kind of respectable documentary foundation.

Substantial difficulties have existed, too, with the published correspondence. Scholars can now tabulate more than two hundred and fifty letters written by Napoleon to Josephine. While over two hundred of her personal letters (apart from the recommendations with which she tirelessly bombarded the ministries) are known, most of them are letters to her children. Not a single letter from Josephine to her first husband, Alexander de Beauharnais, has survived; and those extant written by her to Napoleon can be counted on the fingers of one hand. The task of collecting the evidence has been made harder by editors, among them Josephine's daughter, Queen Hortense, and Josephine's grandson, Napoleon III, who amended or scissored out from Napoleon's letters passages that might cast a shadow upon past glories or offend against mid-nineteenth-century propriety.

If Josephine has remained silent, her biographers have not. The first important documents appeared unexpectedly in 1824. A young Englishman, Charles Tennant, having made the Grand Tour, published his impressions in a two-volume work which bore the remarkable title, *A Tour Through Parts of the Netherlands, Holland, Germany, Switzerland, Savoy and France, in the Year 1821, Including a Description of the Rhine Voyage in the Middle of Autumn, and the Stupendous Scenery of the Alps in the Depth of Winter, by Charles Tennant, Esq. Also Containing, in an Appendix, Fac Simile Copies of Eight Letters in the Hand Writing of Napoleon Bonaparte to his Wife Josephine*. These eight Napoleonic letters mark a new biographical beginning. Tennant explained that he had bought them from 'a Polish nobleman who attached himself and all his fortunes to Bonaparte, whose confidence he enjoyed in several diplomatic negotiations'. The mysterious nobleman told Tennant that a servant had found the letters in a cupboard at Malmaison a few days after Josephine's death, and had sold them to him. Tennant's published facsimiles were so skilfully done, both as to calligraphy and paper, that they have been known to be offered for sale as genuine Napoleonic autographs. Although Tennant's letters showed Bonaparte in an extraordinarily human and vivid light, at the time they attracted little attention.

Eight further letters from Bonaparte to Josephine were included in a multi-volume potpourri, *Mémoires d'une contemporaine*, published in 1827, 'La Contemporaine' being the pseudonym of Ezelina van Aylde-Jonghe. These had a derivation curiously like that of the Tennant letters. They had been stolen by a *valet de chambre* at Malmaison, sold to the Duchess of Courland, lent by her to Madame Genlis, and copied by her for the editor, Ladvocat, who published them. Both these groups of letters gave dramatic evidence of the young Bonaparte's ardent infatuation for Josephine and suggested that her life might be written as one of the great romances of history.

The next important publication seemed to weaken this possibility. In 1833 appeared at Paris the two volumes, *Lettres de Napoléon à Joséphine pendant la première campagne d'Italie, le Consulat et l'Empire: et lettres de Joséphine à Napoléon et à sa fille*. Published under the sponsorship of Queen Hortense, the volumes contained over two hundred letters from Napoleon to Josephine, seventy letters from Josephine to Hortense, but only two from Josephine to her husband. The ardent letters that Tennant had published in 1824 were emphatically not included, and it is now clear that many in this 1833 collection had undergone rigorous pruning. Although three of Napoleon's early love letters to Josephine were printed by François Gilbert de Coston in his heavily documented *Biographie des premières années de Napoléon Bonaparte* (2 vols., Paris, 1840), in general little notice seems to have been taken of them.

Napoleonic studies were soon furthered by the march of events. In December 1848 Louis-Napoléon Bonaparte, grandson of Josephine and at the same time nephew of Napoleon, was elected president of the Second French Republic. Soon emperor, he was eager to recapture the glories of his great predecessor. Hence, in 1854, the decision was made to set up a commission that would assemble and edit the correspondence of Napoleon I. By 1858 the first volume of what ultimately was to be a sumptuous thirty-two volume official collection was published. It is here that Charles Tennant, silent since 1824, reappears.

In May 1858 one of the editorial commissioners, Prosper Mérimée, received the visit of a handsome English lady accompanied by her husband, a Mr Tennant, 'of a respectable age', a former M.P. He had in his possession eight letters of Bonaparte, seven of them to Josephine, and would, he said, be prepared to sell them for eight thousand francs. On investigating the letters, Mérimée had no doubts of their authenticity; yet he had other qualms. 'They are,' he reported to Marshal Vaillant, minister of war and president of the commission, 'very burning love letters, written during the first Italian campaign. It is a question of hardly anything but kisses, in places the names of which are not found in the *Dictionary of the French Academy*.'*

What Vaillant replied to Mérimée, or how anxiously the nine members of the commission may have scrutinized these letters, or what was the fate of the originals, we do not know, but the policy of the commission had already been determined. Tennant's letters were not included and, as it turned out, all but two of the ninety-three letters from Napoleon to Josephine eventually printed in the official *Correspondance* were those previously available in the Hortense edition of 1833.

The industry of individual scholars was able to make good what governmental documentation failed to provide. Joseph Aubenas, who had lived for several years as an official in Martinique, made use of important island sources and also had access to papers in the Tascher de la Pagerie family, these including some early letters

*PROSPER MÉRIMÉE, *Correspondance générale*, 2ᵉ série, t. II, *1856–1858* (Paris, 1955), pp. 515–16.

from Josephine to her parents that shed much light on the troubles of her first marriage. His two volumes, *Histoire de l'impératrice Joséphine* (Paris, 1857), stand out as the only substantial study of Josephine before we come to the last decade of the nineteenth century.

The name of Frédéric Masson first appears in 1895 when he published two articles on Josephine in the *Revue de Paris*. Masson was an extraordinary character. A republican by family tradition, he had held a state scholarship as a young student in the 1860s because of his father's death on the streets of Paris during the June days of the Revolution of 1848. Masson, nevertheless, became an ardent and almost mystically dedicated Bonapartist. Those who wish to savour fully the Bonapartism of this perpetual secretary of the French Academy should read his prefaces, most especially that to *Napoléon et les femmes* (1894), in which Masson tells of how as a boy he had listened to the stories of old Napoleonic veterans and had been allowed by them to touch the very scars of their ancient wounds. Masson saw no incongruity in comparing Napoleon to the Son of Man and in capitalizing, during moments of deep emotion, the pronouns with which he referred to him.

The profound devotion which Masson had to the name of Napoleon left little room for any corresponding affection for the name of Beauharnais, and so along with his studies of the Bonaparte family he felt impelled to re-examine the career of Josephine in order to determine whether she was worthy of the place which tradition and family piety had come to assign to her. After a quarter of a century of labour and the publication of four searching volumes of biography – *Joséphine de Beauharnais* (1898); *Madame Bonaparte* (1920); *Joséphine impératrice et reine* (1899); *Joséphine répudiée* (1900) – he found, in the simplest possible summary, that she was not. A lifetime devoted to the history of Bonaparte family, a lifetime which resulted in writing some thirty-five volumes, made it possible for Masson to accumulate an extraordinary collection of manuscript materials and a staggeringly encyclopaedic knowledge of the printed sources. It is, parenthetically, another curiosity of Masson that in all his volumes he invariably refused to cite these sources which, one must concede, were impressive enough. The *Fonds Masson* in the Bibliothèque Thiers at Paris – the old home of Thiers in the Place Saint-Georges – consists of 586 cartons, portfolios, registers, and bundles of material assembled by Masson, much of it bearing directly upon Josephine and for the most part incorporated in his various studies. No student can possibly ignore

Masson's scholarly work; yet few today would accept the entire validity of his approach or of his conclusions.

Contemporaneously with Masson's writing the Martinique historian, René Pichevin, published his *Impératrice Joséphine* at Paris in 1909. Like Aubenas, he had access to a good many family papers, some of them unknown to Masson, and he used these to make a strong defence of Josephine. His title is misleading, for the work goes only to the time of Josephine's return to France from Martinique in 1790. Hector Fleischmann's *Joséphine infidèle* (Paris, 1910) must be listed, if only because it qualifies as being easily the most savage of all the attacks directed against her. Joseph Turquan's *La Générale Bonaparte* (Paris, 1895) and his *Impératrice Joséphine* (Paris, 1896) are only somewhat less hostile.

Since Masson's death in 1923 scholars have continued their labours. Edouard Driault's biography (Paris, 1928) is the sympathetic work of a good Napoleonic scholar. The elaborate biography of the Marquis de Sainte-Croix de la Roncière, *Joséphine impératrice des français* (Paris, 1934), though showing a wide local knowledge of Martinique and having splendid illustrations, reproduces with astonishing lack of critical judgement some of the most flagrant forgeries of the 1820s. In contrast to this, the two volumes of Jean Hanoteau on the Beauharnais family, *Joséphine avant Bonaparte: Le Ménage Beauharnais* (Paris, 1935), and *Les Beauharnais et l'empereur* (Paris, 1936), are models of accurate scholarship and permit us to question in many respects the very hostile interpretations of Masson. In his first volume Hanoteau used the highly revealing letters of Alexander de Beauharnais preserved in the Tascher de la Pagerie archives at the château of Petit-Fresnoy and in the Bibliothèque Thiers to demonstrate, as Masson had not been able to do, the heavy burdens that Alexander imposed upon his wife. In the second volume he printed seventy-three letters from Josephine to Eugène preserved in the Leuchtenberg Archives at Munich, adding very substantially to the seventy-two letters of Josephine in the 1833 collection authorized by Hortense. These significantly enlarge our knowledge of Josephine's later years and particularly of the period of Napoleon's downfall. André Gavoty's *Les Amoureux de l'impératrice Joséphine* (Paris, 1961), on the other hand, though embellished with the outward appearance of scholarship, seems to proceed on the assumption that if a story of scandal about Josephine has once appeared in print it must be true. The most workmanlike biography of Josephine in English, devoid of any attempt at fine writing, still remains Philip W. Sergeant's *The*

Empress Josephine, Napoleon's Enchantress first appearing in Hutchinson's Library of Standard Lives (New York, 1909). The recent biography of Hubert Cole, *Joséphine* (New York, 1962), appeared after the manuscript of this volume had been completed.

With three exceptions, no attempt is made here to include any of the enormous literature dealing directly with Napoleon. Arthur Lévy's *Napoléon intime* (Paris, 1898) brings one very close to the great Emperor. Louis Garros's *Itinéraire de Napoléon Bonaparte* (Paris, 1947) is an invaluable day-by-day record of Napoleon's movements, almost as useful for a study of Josephine as it is for a study of the Emperor. And the first of the seven volumes of Friedrich Kircheisen's monumental *Napoleon I, sein Leben und seine Zeit* (Munich, 1911) contains in chapter XVIII a sensible, sympathetic, and balanced judgement upon Josephine by one of the very greatest Napoleonic scholars.

For nearly a century the only edition of Napoleon's letters to Josephine was that authorized by Queen Hortense in 1833. Léon Cerf, *Lettres de Napoléon à Joséphine* (Paris, 1929), brought this material into up-to-date form by including the letters previously omitted or garbled. This work is now superseded by Jacques Bourgeat, *Napoléon: lettres à Joséphine* (Paris, 1941) which gives 254 letters, in many cases establishing the full text of documents previously printed. Bourgeat is the most convenient edition to use, though unfortunately a few of the later letters are wrongly dated. Jean Savant, *Napoléon et Joséphine. Première édition intégrale, avec de nombreux inédits, des lettres de Napoléon à Joséphine* (Paris, 1955), raises the total of Napoleon's letters to 265. He includes many facsimiles and corrects Bourgeat's mistakes in dating. Savant, unfortunately, does not limit himself to his editorial duties but carries on a ceaseless attack upon the character and morals of Josephine as he also does in his *Napoléon et Joséphine, leur roman* (Paris, 1960). Incomplete English translations of the letters, made from earlier editions and of mediocre quality, have been published by J. S. C. Abbott (New York, 1856), H. F. Hall (London, 1901), and H. W. Bunn (New York, 1931).

Scholarship has steadily enlarged our knowledge of the circle within which Josephine moved and thus has enriched the picture we have of her. Constance Wright's *Daughter to Napoleon* (New York, 1961) gives a graceful account of Hortense de Beauharnais. Research of another sort has evaluated Josephine's association with the arts, particularly as seen in the galleries, the furnishings, and the gardens of Malmaison. References to these materials will be included in subsequent appropriate paragraphs. Such works, in contrast to the imitative and repetitive biographies of which seemingly there is no end, give stature and respectability to the field of Josephine studies.

For the background at Martinique the following, in addition to the biographies of Aubenas and Pichevin, are useful: Cabuzel A. Banbuck, *Histoire politique, économique et sociale de la Martinique sous l'ancien régime* (Paris, 1935); S. Daney, *Histoire de la Martinique* (4 vols., Fort-Royal, 1846–7), especially vol. IV; and Gabriel Hanotaux and Alfred Martineau, *Histoire des colonies françaises* (6 vols., Paris, 1929–33), vol. I. Jean Baptiste Thibault de Chanvallon, *Voyage à la Martinique* (Paris, 1763), has a most valuable contemporary appreciation of creole life. J. Gabriel, *Essai biographique sur Madame Tascher de la Pagerie* (Paris, 1856), describes Josephine's mother. Anecdotes about Josephine's girlhood will be found in: Louise Cochelet, *Mémoires* (4 vols., Paris, 1836–8); Marie Anne Lenormand, *Mémoires historiques et secrètes* (2 vols., Paris, 1818–22); Jean Gabriel de Montgaillard, *Souvenirs* (Paris, 1895); and Claude Augustin de Tercier, *Mémoires politiques et militaires* (Paris, 1891). An account of Aimée du Buc de Rivery, as fantastic as the author's title, is given in Lesley Blanch, *The Wilder Shores of Love* (New York, 1954).

The most important source for Josephine's life to the time of the Revolution, is the correspondence of Alexander de Beauharnais printed in Jean Hanoteau's *Le Ménage Beauharnais* (Paris, 1935). Theodore Iung, *Bonaparte et son temps, 1769–1799, d'après des documents inédits* (2 vols., Paris, 1881), prints in vol. I Josephine's marriage certificate and the baptismal certificates of Eugène and Hortense. The original documents concerning the separation are in AN, Y, 13,975, printed in Caroline d'Arjuzon, *Joséphine contre Beauharnais* (Paris, 1906). For the social circle of Fanny de Beauharnais see: F. K. Turgeon, 'Fanny de Beauharnais. Biographical Notes and a Bibliography', *Modern Philology*, August, 1932; Alfred Marquiset, *Les Bas-bleus du premier Empire* (Paris, 1913); M. Foucaux [Mary Summer], *Quelques salons de Paris au dix-huitième siècle* (Paris, n.d.). See also: Louis Joseph de Bouillé, *Souvenirs et fragments* (3 vols., Paris, 1906–11), vol. I; and H. Lemery, *La Révolution française à la Martinique* (Paris, 1936).

For life in Paris under the Terror see: Jean Robiquet, *La Vie quotidienne au temps de la Révolution* (Paris, 1938). For details concerning Josephine see: A. Reh, *Deux lettres inédites d'Eugène de*

Beauharnais et de Jérôme Bonaparte, collegiens (Strasbourg, 1937); Arthur Chuquet, 'Deux signalements de Joséphine', *Feuilles d'Histoire, année 1909*, I, 245–6; II, 62–3; Louis Bigard, 'Joséphine de Beauharnais à Croissy', *Revue des études napoléoniennes*, March–April 1926; Eugène de Beauharnais, *Mémoires et correspondance* (10 vols., Paris, 1858–60), vol. I; Queen Hortense, *Mémoires* (3 vols., Paris, 1927), vol. I.

Documents concerning the imprisonment of Josephine and Alexander are in AN, F⁷4591; AN, F II, 294; AN, W429. For the imprisonment see: *Almanach des prisons, ou anecdotes sur la régime intérieure de la Conciergerie, du Luxembourg, etc., et sur différens prisonniers . . .* (Paris [1794]); Charles A. Dauban, *Les Prisons de Paris sous la Révolution* (Paris, 1870); Paul Pisani, *La Maison des Carmes (1610–1875)* (Paris, 1891); Alexandre Sorel, *Le Couvent des Carmes et la Séminaire de Saint-Sulpice pendant la Terreur* (Paris, 1864).

Life in Paris under the Directory is described in: Alphonse Aulard, *Paris pendant la réaction thermidorienne* (5 vols., Paris, 1898–1902), documents; Meade Minnigerode, *The Magnificent Comedy* (New York, 1931); and Henri d'Alméras, *Barras et son temps* (Paris, 1930). A good deal of information can be derived from: Joseph Bonaparte, *Mémoires et correspondance* (10 vols., Paris, 1854–8), vol. I; Jean Nicolas Bouilly, *Mes Récapitulations* (2 vols., Paris, 1836–7), vol. II; and from the memoirs of Hortense and Eugène where the story of Alexander de Beauharnais's sword gets strong confirmation. The so-called *Mémoires de Barras* (4 vols., Paris, 1895–6), though vivid, are a savagely hostile compilation concocted by Barras and others at a much later date. Some interesting details of Paris by an English visitor are given in Helen Maria Williams, *A Tour in Switzerland* (London, 1898). Copies of a few letters from Josephine to her mother in this period are in BN, *Nouv. acq. fr.*, 9324. A copy of the marriage contract and of the marriage register is in the Bibliothèque Thiers, *Fonds Masson*, 28, also printed in the *Revue des études napoléoniennes* for April 1936.

For further details, chiefly concerning the marriage and Josephine's home on the rue Chantereine see: Gustave Bord and Louis Bigard, *La Maison du 'dix-huit brumaire'* (Paris, 1930); G. Lenôtre [pseud. of Louis Gosselin], *Paris révolutionnaire: vieilles maisons, vieux papiers*. 1ᵉʳ série (Paris, 1905); Henri Clouzot, 'Un soir de ventôse an iv à l'hôtel de Mondragon', *Revue des études napoléoniennes*, July 1935; Georges Mauguin, *L'Impératrice Joséphine: anecdotes et curiosités* (Paris, 1954).

Information about Josephine's first married years comes indirectly from Napoleon's letters to her. The following memoirs are useful: Laura, Duchess d'Abrantès, *Autobiography and Recollections* (4 vols., Eng. trans., New York, 1893); Antoine V. Arnault, *Souvenirs d'un sexagénaire* (4 vols., Paris, 1833); François Y. Besnard, *Souvenirs d'un nonagénaire* (2 vols., Paris, 1880); Louis Antoine de Bourrienne, *Memoirs of Napoleon* (4 vols., Eng. trans., London, 1885), vol. I; Stanislas de Girardin, *Mémoires, journal, et souvenirs* (2 vols., Paris, 1829); Louis-Jérôme Gohier, *Mémoires* (2 vols., Paris, 1824), vol. I; Antoine R. Hamelin, 'Douze ans de ma vie', *Revue de Paris*, Nov. 1, 15, 1926; Auguste-Frédéric de Marmont, *Mémoires du duc de Raguse* (9 vols., Paris, 1857), vol. I; André François de Miot de Melito, *Mémoires* (3 vols., Paris, 1858), vols. I, II. The unpublished diary of Carrion de Nisas is in the Bibliothèque Thiers, *Fonds Masson*, 223. For Hippolyte Charles see Louis Hastier, 'Joséphine et le capitaine Charles,' *Revue des deux-mondes*, January 1949, and the same author's *Le Grand amour de Joséphine* (Paris, 1955). Berthier's reports to Josephine on Bonaparte are given by Arthur Chuquet in his *Episodes et portraits, deuxième série* (Paris, 1910), and by Paul Bonnefons in the publication, *Souvenirs et mémoires*, I (1898), 61–71. For other details of these years see: A. Philippe, 'La Citoyenne Bonaparte à Epinal', *La Révolution dans les Vosges, 2e année* (1908–9); P. J. Verhaegen, "Le Comte de Mérode et Joséphine Bonaparte', *Revue générale*, April 1899; André Gavoty, 'Le Beau-frère de couleur de l'impératrice Joséphine', *Revue des deux-mondes*, January 1956; E. Giannini, *Giuseppina Buonaparte a Lucca nel 1796, narrazione d'un contemporaneo* (Lucca, 1890). Bonaparte's affair in Egypt with Marguerite Fourès is described by Frédéric Masson in his *Napoléon et les femmes* (Paris, 1904). Seven letters from Josephine to Barras running from September 1796 to April 1799 were first published by Alberto Lumbroso in his *Miscellanea Napoleonica, série V* (Rome, 1898). The most complete account of the coup of Brumaire is in Albert Vandal's classic *Avènement de Bonaparte* (2 vols., Paris, 1907–8).

The general pattern of life under the Consulate is described in Henri d'Almeras, *La Vie parisienne sous le Consulat et l'Empire* (Paris [1909]); Gilbert Stenger, *La Société française pendant le Consulat* (6 vols., Paris, 1903–8); G. Lenôtre [pseud. of Louis Gosselin], *Les Tuileries* (Paris, 1933). The vivid *Mémoires de Constant, premier valet de chambre de l'empereur* (10 vols., Paris, 1830), with various subsequent editions and translations, was put together by several hacks for the booksellers, Lavocat, from the notes of Louis Constant Wairy, and has much information beginning in 1799. In addition to the diaries of Paul and Eyre, mentioned in Chapter XIV, see Alexander M. Broadley, ed., *The Journal of a British Chaplain in Paris . . . the Revd. Dawson Warren, M.A.* (London, 1913), and Johann F. Reichardt, *Un Hiver à Paris sous le Consulat, 1802–1803* (Paris, 1896). Additional memoirs of some use are: Claude François Méneval, *Mémoires* (3 vols., Paris, 1849), and Henriette, Marquise de la Tour du Pin Gouvernet, *Journal d'une femme de cinquante ans* (Paris, 1913).

The ceremonial of the coronation and the establishment of an imperial court can be studied in: *Procès-verbal de la cérémonie du sacre et du couronnement de Ll. MM. L'empereur Napoléon et l'impératrice Joséphine* (Paris, 1805); *Livre du sacre de l'empereur Napoléon*, edited by Frédéric Masson (Paris, 1908); *Etiquette du palais impérial* (Paris, Imprimerie impériale, 1808); *Liste des dames de la maison de S. M. l'impératrice et reine et celles des princesses* (Paris, 1807); Arthur L. Imbert de Saint-Armand, *La Cour de l'impératrice Joséphine* (Paris, n.d.); Frédéric Masson, *Napoleon and his Coronation* (Eng. trans., London, 1911).

C. Pfister, 'Les Passages de Napoléon I et de Joséphine dans le département de la Meurthe', *Mémoires de l'Académie Stanislas*, X (1913), 8–94, gives vivid details about the various imperial journeys through Lorraine from 1798 to 1809. Further details of this period are given in: *Passage à Lyon de leurs majestés Napoléon Ier empereur des français et roi d'Italie et de l'impératrice Joséphine en 1805* (Lyons, 1806); C. dell' Acqua, *L'Imperatore dei Francesi Napoleone I e l'augusta sua consorte Giuseppina nel Maggio 1805 in Pavia* (Milan, 1905); Frédéric Masson, *Napoléon chez lui: la journée de l'empereur aux Tuileries* (Paris, 1894); Emile Marco de Sainte Hilaire, *Mémoires d'un page de la cour impériale (1804–1815)* (Paris, 1848). Further memoirs for the imperial period are: Claire Elisabeth de Rémusat, *Mémoires, 1802–1808* (3 vols., Paris, 1879–80); Mlle Avrillon [pseudonym of Catharinet de Villemarest] *Mémoires de Mlle Avrillon, première femme de chambre de l'impératrice, sur la vie privée de Joséphine, sa famille et sa cour* (2 vols., Paris, 1835); Louis-François de Bausset, *Mémoires anecdotiques sur l'intérieur du palais et sur quelques événements de l'Empire depuis 1805 jusqu'au 1er mai 1814 pour servir à l'histoire de Napoléon* (2 vols., Paris, 1827).

Descriptions of Malmaison and its life are contained in the following: Joseph Bilkiet, *Malmaison. Les appartements de Joséphine* (Paris, 1951); Jean Bourguignon, *Malmaison, Compiègne, Fontaine-bleau* (Paris, 1946); Adolphe M. de Lescure, *Le Château de Malmaison*, *histoire, description, catalogue des objets exposés sur les auspices de S.M. l'impératrice* (Paris, 1867). For the gardens see: Charles Leger, *Redouté et son temps* (Paris, 1945); R. Bouvier and E. Maynial, *Aimé Bonpland* (Paris, 1950); André Leroy, *Les Roses de Redouté et de l'impératrice Joséphine* (Sceaux, 1950); Paul Maynard, *L'Imperatrice Joséphine, bienfaitrice de l'horticulture et de l'agriculture . . .* (n.p., 1952); Georges Mauguin, 'Une Impératrice botaniste', *Revue des études napoléoniennes*, October 1933; Aimé Bonpland, *Déscription des plantes rares cultivées à Malmaison et à Navarre* (Paris, 1813).

On Josephine as a collector, and her expenses see: *Catalogue des tableaux de Sa Majesté l'impératrice Joséphine dans la galerie et appartements de son palais de Malmaison* (Paris, de l'imprimerie de Didot jeune, 1811); Pierre Schommer, 'L'Impératrice Joséphine et ses tableaux', *Revue de l'Institut Napoléon*, October 1962; *Ibid.*, 'Musée de Malmaison: Quatre acquisitions', *Revue des Arts, Musées de France*, 1957, No. 5; *Ibid.*, 'Malmaison, hier, aujourd'hui, demain', *Revue de l'Institut Napoléon*, October 1958; G. Ledoux-Lebard, 'Les Canots de Joséphine à Malmaison,' *Revue de l'Institut Napoléon*, January 1957; *Ibid.*, 'La Liquidation des objets d'art provenant de la succession de l'impératrice Joséphine à Malmaison', *Archives de l'art français, Nouv. Pér. tome XXII* (1959); Serge Grandjean, 'Les Collections de l'impératrice Joséphine à Malmaison et leur dispersion', *Revue des Arts, Musées de France*, 1959, Nos. 4–5; *Ibid.*, 'Un Meuble précieux de Joséphine', *Revue de l'Institut Napoléon*, January 1956; Camille Roehard, *Dans les coulisses de l'histoire: Les livres de comptes des impératrices Joséphine et Marie-Louise conservés à la bibliothèque publique de Gray* (Gray, 1927); Alphonse Maze-Sencier, *Les Fournisseurs de Napoléon et des deux impératrices* (Paris, 1893); A. P. de Mirimonde, 'Les Dépenses d'art des impératrices Joséphine et Marie-Louise', *Gazette des Beaux Arts* (1958), pp. 89–108, 137–54; André Gavoty, 'Mésaventures d'un fonctionnaire impérial', *Revue des deux-mondes*, 1 February 1958.

The most substantial treatment of the divorce is in Henri Welschinger, *Le Divorce de Napoléon* (Paris, 1889). An official Catholic account by the Abbé Louis Grégoire, *Le 'Divorce' de Napoléon et de l'impératrice Joséphine, Étude du dossier canonique* (Paris, 1957), disagrees with Welschinger on many points and claims that the officiality of the Paris diocese acted properly according to Gallican law in recognizing that the Senate had already annulled the civil marriage. René Pichevin has a brief pamphlet, *Le Mariage de l'empereur* (Paris, n.d.), arguing that the whole proceedings were illegal and improper. Frédéric Masson also describes the divorce at considerable length in his *Quatre conférences sur Joséphine* (Paris, 1924). In addition to vivid accounts of the crisis in the memoirs of Bausset, Constant, and Madame de Rémusat, previously cited, see also Antoine Marie de Lavalette, *Mémoires et souvenirs* (2 vols., Paris, 1831), vol. II. There is much concerning the Austrian marriage in Prince Metternich's *Mémoires, documents et écrits divers* (5 vols., Paris, 1880–2), vols. I, II. Max Billiard, *Le Fils de Napoléon Ier* (Paris, 1909) gives an account of Léon Denuelle.

For Josephine's life in seclusion the following are useful: Georgette Ducrest, *Mémoires sur l'impératrice Joséphine, la cour de Navarre et la Malmaison . . .* (Paris, 1906); Auguste Charlotte de Kielmansegge, *Mémoires de la comtesse de Kielmansegge sur Napoléon Ier* (2 vols., Paris, 1928), vol. I; Nicholas Rogue, *Souvenirs et journal d'un bourgeois d'Évreux (1740–1830)* (Évreux, 1850); Maurice de Tascher, *Journal de campagne d'un cousin de l'impératrice (1806–1813)* (Paris, 1933); Prince Charles de Clary-et-Aldringen, *Souvenirs . . . Trois mois à Paris en 1810* (Paris, 1914); Jacques Hérissay, *Joséphine à Navarre, 1810–1814* (Évreux, 1955); S. Robert, *Les séjours de l'impératrice Joséphine en Suisse, Genève, Neuchâtel, Berne, 1810 et 1812* (Neuchâtel, Paris, n.d.); Jean Bourguignon, ed., *L'Album du voyage de l'impératrice Joséphine en 1810 à travers la Suisse et la Savoie. Avec les trente-trois sépais exécutés au cours du voyage par le comte de Turpin de Crissé, chambellan de l'impératrice* (Paris, 1935); Maurice Collignon, *Napoléon Ier dans l'Eure . . . Joséphine à Navarre, le voyage de Napoléon en 1810* (Louviers, 1910); André Gavoty, 'Joséphine et Lancelot-Théodore Turpin de Crissé', *Revue des deux-mondes*, October 1956. E. P. Brouwet, 'Malmaison et Navarre de 1809 à 1812; Journal de Piout', *Revue des études napoléoniennes*, May–June 1926.

Josephine's *acte de décès*, wrongly giving the date of her birth as 24 June 1768 is printed in *Revue des études napoléoniennes*, May–June 1924. The report of her autopsy is printed in Frédéric Masson, *Joséphine répudiée* (Paris, 1900), p. 361n. Jean Bourguignon, *Les Adieux de Malmaison* (Paris, 1930), has a brief account of Napoleon's visit to Malmaison after Waterloo. Guy Ledoux-Lebard's meticulous account of the funeral monument erected by Eugène and Hortense to Josephine's memory in 1825 in the church at Rueil, 'Le Tombeau de l'impératrice Joséphine à Rueil', is in *Bulletin de la Société de l'Histoire de l'Art français* (1956). The entire July 1964 issue of the *Revue de l'Institut Napoléon* is devoted to scholarly articles on Josephine.

Notes

The following abbreviations are used for works frequently cited:

AN	Archives Nationales, Paris.
Abrantès:	Abrantès, Duchess of, *Autobiography and Recollections* (4 vols., Eng. trans., New York, 1893).
Aubenas:	Aubenas, J., *Histoire de l'impératrice Joséphine* (2 vols., Paris, 1857).
BN, *Nouv. acq. fr.*:	Bibliothèque Nationale, Paris. *Nouvelles acquisitions françaises*.
Bourgeat:	Bourgeat, J., *Napoléon, lettres à Joséphine* (Paris, 1941).
Bourrienne:	Bourrienne, L. A. F. de, *Memoirs of Napoleon* (4 vols., Eng. trans., London, 1885).
Corr.:	*Correspondance de Napoléon Ier publiée par ordre de l'empereur Napoléon III* (32 vols., Paris, 1853–69).
Hanoteau, *Ménage*:	Hanoteau, J., *Le Ménage Beauharnais: Joséphine avant Napoléon* (Paris, 1935).
Hanoteau, *Empereur*:	Hanoteau, J., *Les Beauharnais et l'empereur: lettres de l'impératrice Joséphine et de la reine Hortense au prince Eugène* (Paris, 1936).
LNJ:	*Lettres de Napoléon à Joséphine . . . et lettres de Joséphine à Napoléon et à sa fille* (2 vols., Paris, 1833).
Masson, JB:	Masson, F., *Joséphine de Beauharnais, 1763–1796* (Paris, 1898).
Masson, MB:	Masson, F., *Madame Bonaparte, 1796–1804* (Paris, 1920).
Masson, JIR:	Masson, F., *Joséphine, impératrice et reine, 1804–1809* (Paris, 1899).
Masson, JR:	Masson, F., *Joséphine répudiée, 1809–1814* (Paris, 1900).
Masson, NSF:	Masson, F., *Napoléon et sa famille* (13 vols., Paris, 1897–1914).
Pichevin:	Pichevin, R., *L'Impératrice Joséphine* (Paris, 1909).

Savant: Savant, J., ed., *Napoléon et Joséphine. Première édition intégrale . . . des lettres de Napoléon à Joséphine* (Paris, 1955).

2. BIRD OF THE ISLANDS

1. Pichevin, p. 64.
2. *Ibid.*, p. 44.
3. J. B. T. de Chanvallon, *Voyage à la Martinique* (Paris, 1763), p. 38.
4. J. G. M. de Montgaillard, *Souvenirs* (Paris, 1895), p. 277.
5. C. A. de Tercier, *Mémoires politiques et militaires* (Paris, 1891), p. 15.
6. L. Cochelet, *Mémoires sur la reine Hortense* (Paris, 1836-8), I, 374-6; M. A. Lenormand, *Mémoires historiques et secrets* (Paris, 1818-22), I, 56.

3. A MARRIAGE IS ARRANGED

1. Hanoteau, *Ménage*, p. 28.
2. Aubenas, I, 92-3.
3. Masson, JB, p. 104.
4. *Ibid.*
5. Hanoteau, *Ménage*, p. 49.
6. *Ibid.*, p. 50.
7. *Ibid.*
8. *Ibid.*, p. 52.
9. *Ibid.*, p. 51.
10. Masson, JB, pp. 108-9.
11. Pichevin, pp. 97, 98.
12. Hanoteau, *Ménage*, p. 46.
13. *Ibid.*, pp. 54-5.
14. *Ibid.*, pp. 56-7.
15. *Ibid.*, pp. 57-9.
16. *Ibid.*, p. 66.
17. *Ibid.*, p. 67, n. 1.
18. *Ibid.*, pp. 75-7.
19. *Ibid.*, p. 78.
20. *Ibid.*
21. BN, *Nouv. acq. fr.*, 4689, fols. 8-22. Summarized in Pichevin, pp. 112-5.
22. Act of marriage in A. Mentienne, "Les Registres paroissiaux de Noisy-le-Grand", *Bulletin de la Société de l'Histoire de Paris* (1894), pp. 126-7.

4. STORM AND STRESS

1. Hanoteau, *Ménage*, p. 85.
2. *Ibid.*, p. 88.
3. *Ibid.*, p. 89.
4. *Ibid.*, p. 90.
5. *Ibid.*, p. 96.
6. *Ibid.*, p. 107.
7. *Ibid.*, pp. 101-3.
8. *Ibid.*, p. 106.
9. *Ibid.*, pp. 112-3.
10. *Ibid.*, pp. 114-5.
11. *Ibid.*, pp. 137-8.
12. *Ibid.*, pp. 138-9.
13. *Ibid.*, p. 132.
14. *Ibid.*, pp. 123, 134, 135, 140.
15. *Ibid.*, p. 137.
16. *Ibid.*, p. 142.
17. *Ibid.*, pp. 145-6.

5. PARTING

1. Hanoteau, *Ménage*, pp. 150-1.
2. *Ibid.*, p. 151.
3. *Ibid.*, pp. 156-7.
4. *Ibid.*, p. 155.

5. *Ibid.*, pp. 155–6.
6. *Ibid.*, pp. 157–9.
7. *Ibid.*, pp. 159–60.
8. *Ibid.*, p. 162.
9. *Ibid.*, pp. 164–5.
10. *Ibid.*, p. 175.
11. *Ibid.*, p. 173.
12. *Ibid.*, p. 185.
13. Masson, JB, pp. 138–41, where it is wrongly dated, as are the extracts in Hanoteau, *Ménage*, pp. 167–9. Original in AN, Y, 13,975.
14. Hanoteau, *Ménage*, p. 218.
15. Masson, JB, pp. 141–3.
16. Hanoteau, *Ménage*, pp. 176–8.
17. *Ibid.*, p. 201.
18. AN, Y, 13,975. Printed in C. d'Arjuzon, *Joséphine contre Beauharnais* (Paris, 1906), pp. 6–12. Extracts in Hanoteau, *Ménage*, pp. 192–4.
19. L. J. A. de Bouillé, *Souvenirs et fragments* (Paris, 1906–11), I, 52–3.
20. Hanoteau, *Ménage*, pp. 196–7.
21. *Ibid.*, pp. 205–6.
22. BN, *Nouv. acq. fr.*, 4689, fols. 1–6. Printed in Arjuzon, *Joséphine contre Beauharnais*, pp. 13–19. Extracts in Hanoteau, *Ménage*, pp. 198–200.

6. FREEDOM

1. Hanoteau, *Ménage*, pp. 210–11.
2. Aubenas, I, 150–1.
3. Hanoteau, *Ménage*, pp. 222–5; Pichevin, pp. 206–15.

7. REVOLUTION AND TERROR

1. De Bouillé, *Souvenirs et fragments*, I, 53–4.
2. Hanoteau, *Ménage*, p. 231.
3. *Ibid.*, p. 236n.
4. Eugène de Beauharnais, *Mémoires du prince Eugène* (Paris, 1858), I, 29.
5. P. J. B. Buchez and P. C. Roux, *Histoire parlementaire de la Révolution française* (Paris, 1834–8), XXIX, 109.
6. A. Mathiez, *The French Revolution* (New York, 1928), p. 352.
7. Masson, JB, pp. 225–6.
8. *Ibid.*, pp. 218–20.
9. L. Bigard, 'Joséphine de Beauharnais a Croissy', *Revue des études napoléoniennes* (March–April, 1926), p. 112.
10. AN, F74591, fols. 35–6; Masson, JB, p. 228.
11. *Ibid.*, p. 232.
12. *Ibid.*
13. *Almanach des prisons ou anecdotes sur la régime intérieure de la Conciergerie, du Luxembourg, etc. . . .* (Paris [1794]). Reprinted in LNJ, II, 207–10.
14. Alexandre Sorel, *Le Couvent des Carmes et la séminaire de Saint-Sulpice pendant la Terreur* (2nd edn., Paris, 1864), p. 251.

8. LIFE, LIBERTY, AND THE PURSUIT OF HAPPINESS

1. Eugène de Beauharnais, *Mémoires*, I, 30.
2. C. A. Dauban, *Les Prisons*

de Paris sous la Révolution (Paris, 1870), p. 375.

3. H. d'Almeras, *Barras et son temps* (Paris, 1930), p. 276.

4. Corr., I, no. 44.

5. Joseph Bonaparte, *Mémoires et correspondance politique et militaire* (Paris, 1855), I, 142–3.

6. Masson, JB, pp. 246–7.

7. Aubenas, I, 267–8.

8. BN, *Nouv. acq. fr.*, 9324, fols. 382–4.

9. *Ibid.*, fols. 385–7.

10. *Ibid.*, fols. 388–91.

11. G. de Sainte-Croix de la Roncière, *Joséphine impératrice des français* (Paris, 1934), p. 98.

12. D'Almeras, *Barras et son temps*, pp. 205–6.

13. F. Y. Besnard, *Souvenirs d'un nonagénaire* (Paris, 1880), II, 146–7.

9. BONAPARTE

1. J. Kemble, *Napoleon Immortal* (London, 1959), p. 14.

2. F. Masson and G. Biagi, eds., *Napoléon inconnu: papiers inédits* (Paris, 1895), II, 286.

3. *Ibid.*, p. 277.

4. Quoted in Kemble, *Napoleon Immortal*, p. 71.

5. F. Masson, *Napoléon et les femmes* (Paris, 1904), p. 13.

6. Corr., I, no. 42.

7. *Ibid.*, no. 65.

8. Joseph Bonaparte, *Mémoires et correspondance*, I, 131.

9. A. Lévy, *Un Grand profiteur de guerre . . , G. J. Ouvrard* (Paris, 1929). p. 41.

10. Corr., I, no. 64.

11. Quoted in Kemble, *Napoleon Immortal*, p. 89.

12. Corr., I, no. 72.

13. G. Gourgaud, *Sainte-Hélène: Journal inédite de 1815 à 1818* (Paris 1899), II, 329.

14. H. G. de Bertrand, *Cahiers de Sainte-Hélène, janvier–mai, 1821* (Paris, 1949), p. 99.

15. Corr., I, no. 77.

16. Bourgeat, p. 6.

17. *Ibid.*, p. 9. Savant, p. 28, questions whether this is really an answer to Josephine's note.

18. *Ibid.* A photostat of the original is in the Houghton Library at Harvard University.

19. P. W. Sergeant, *The Empress Josephine* (London, 1909), p. 86.

20. A. F. L. Marmont, *Mémoires du duc de Raguse* (Paris, 1857), I, 93–5.

21. Queen Hortense (Hortense de Beauharnais), *Mémoires de la reine Hortense* (Paris, 1927), I, 42.

22. Bourrienne, II, 399.

23. Bourgeat, pp. 14–16.

24. Corr., I, no. 89.

25. Masson, *Napoléon et les femmes*, p. 17.

26. A. V. Arnault, *Souvenirs d'un sexagénaire* (Paris, 1833), III, 31.

10. 'PARTING IS SUCH SWEET SORROW'

1. Bourgeat, p. 20.

2. A. Decaux, *Letizia, mère de*

l'empereur (Paris, 1949), pp. 138–9.

3. Bourgeat, pp. 21–2.
4. *Ibid.*, pp. 22–4.
5. Corr., I, no. 257.
6. Marmont, *Mémoires du duc de Raguse*, I, 187–8.
7. Savant, p. 58.
8. Corr., I, no. 443.
9. Bourgeat, pp. 31–2.
10. A. Lumbroso, *Miscellanea Napoleonica*, Série V (Rome, 1898), p. 262.
11. Abrantès, I, 254.
12. A. Aulard, *Paris pendant la réaction thermidorienne et sous le Directoire* (Paris, 1898–1902), III, 180–1.
13. Bourgeat, pp. 29–30.
14. *Ibid.*, pp. 30–1.
15. Arnault, *Souvenirs d'un sexagénaire*, II, 286.
16. Bourgeat, p. 29.
17. *Souvenirs et mémoires, recueil mensuel de documents . . .* (Paris, 1898–9), I, 55. Masson, MB, p. 45, omits the parts indicating Josephine's desire to join her husband.
18. Bourgeat, pp. 33–4.
19. *Ibid.*, pp. 34–5.
20. *Ibid.*, p. 37.
21. Facsimile in F. G. de Coston, *Biographie des premières années de Napoléon Bonaparte* (Paris, 1840), I, 466.
22. Bourgeat, p. 39.
23. *Ibid.*, p. 42.
24. *Ibid.*, pp. 42–3.
25. Masson, MB, pp. 62–4.
26. *Souvenirs et mémoires, recueil mensuel de documents*, I, 58.

11. WIFE OF A HERO

1. A. R. Hamelin, 'Douze ans de ma vie,' *Revue de Paris*, Nov. 1, 1926, pp. 14–15.
2. Bourgeat, pp. 50–1.
3. Besnard, *Souvenirs d'un nonagénaire*, II, 144.
4. Aubenas, I, 348–9.
5. Masson, MB, p. 84.
6. *Souvenirs et mémoires, recueil mensuel de documents*, I, 61–77.
7. Bourgeat, p. 60.
8. Masson, MB, p. 98.
9. A. F. Miot de Melito, *Mémoires* (Paris, 1858), I, 159.
10. Bibliothèque Thiers, Paris, Fonds Masson, no. 223, I, 81.
11. G. Mauguin, *L'Impératrice Joséphine: anecdotes et curiosités* (Paris, 1954), p. 21.

12. JOSÉPHINE INFIDÈLE

1. F. M. Kircheisen, *Napoleon* (New York, 1932), p. 134.
2. *Ibid.*, p. 136.
3. S. C. Girardin, *Mémoires, journal, et souvenirs* (2nd edn, Paris, 1829), I, 143–5.
4. Bourrienne, II, 389; J. Christopher Herold, *Mistress to an Age* (New York, 1958), p. 181.
5. G. Lacour-Gayet, *Talleyrand (1754–1838)* (Paris, 1928–34), I, 272.
6. Masson, MB, p. 124.
7. L. Hastier, *Le Grand amour de Joséphine* (Paris, 1955), pp. 152–4.
8. *Ibid.*, p. 160.

9. Masson, MB, p. 131.

10. *Les Papiers sécrets du Seconde Empire*, No. 9 (Brussels, 1871), p. 8.

11. Lumbroso, *Miscellanea Napoleonica*, Série V, p. 252.

12. Masson, MB, p. 128.

13. *Ibid.*, pp. 130–1.

14. *Ibid.*, p. 131.

15. *Ibid.*, p. 132.

16. *Ibid.*, p. 135.

17. *Ibid.*, pp. 137–8.

18. *Ibid.*, pp. 142–3. Masson dates this wrongly.

19. J. E. Howard, ed., *The Rise to Power* (*Letters and Documents of Napoleon*, vol. I [New York, 1961]), pp. 258–9.

20. British Museum, Add. MS. 23003.

21. Masson, MB, pp. 139–40.

22. Bourrienne, I, 199.

23. Mauguin, *L'Impératrice Joséphine*, p. 36.

24. Miot de Melito, *Mémoires*, I, 228.

25. J. N. Bouilly, *Mes récapitulations* (Paris, 1836–1837), II, 162–76.

26. Hastier, *Le Grand amour de Joséphine*, p. 184.

13. MISTRESS OF THE TUILERIES

1. L. J. Gohier, *Mémoires* (Paris, 1824), I, 198–9.

2. Abrantès, I, 268.

3. Bourgeat, p. 71. Facsimile in Gohier, *Mémoires*, II, frontispiece.

4. Walter Geer, *Napoleon and Josephine* (New York, 1924), p. 94.

5. Masson, MB, p. 197.

6. Bourrienne, I, 399.

7. G. Lenôtre, *Les Tuileries* (Paris, 1933), pp. 156–7.

14. THE CONSULATE

1. L. Constant, *Mémoires de Constant, premier valet de chambre de l'empereur* (Paris, 1830), II, 153–4.

2. Masson, MB, p. 248.

3. *Ibid.*, p. 252.

4. Bibliothèque Thiers, Paris, Fonds Masson, no. 28.

5. *Ibid.*

6. Savant, p. 153. Omitted in Bourgeat.

7. Savant, pp. 155–7. Omitted in Bourgeat.

8. Bourgeat, p. 77.

9. Corr., VI, no. 4938.

10. Masson, MB, pp. 336–7.

11. Bourgeat, p. 78. Should be *an IX*.

12. S. C. de Girardin, *Mémoires, journal, et souvenirs* (2nd edn., Paris, 1829), I, 199.

13. LNJ, II, 219–21. Should be 1802.

14. Masson, MB, 317.

15. (London, 1814), p. 87.

16. (Bath, 1803), p. 24.

17. BN, *nouv. acq. fr.*, 9324.

18. Bourgeat, pp. 78–80. Should be 1802.

19. *Ibid.*, p. 80. Should be 1802.

20. *Ibid.*, p. 82. Should be 1802.

21. Lacour-Gayet, *Talleyrand* (*1754–1838*), II, 91–2.
22. LNJ, II, 222–3.
23. Bourrienne, I, 341.
24. C. d'Arjuzon, *Mme Louis Bonaparte* (Paris, 1901), p. 78.
25. BN, *nouv. acq. fr.*, 9324, fols. 403–6.
26. Masson, MB, pp. 367–8.

15. STEPS TO A THRONE

1. Savant, p. 164. Not given in Bourgeat.
2. Claire Elisabeth de Rémusat, *Mémoires* (Paris, 1880), I, 300–1.
3. LNJ, II, 229–31. Should be March, 1804.
4. Rémusat, *Mémoires*, I, 313.
5. *Ibid.*, p. 315.
6. Masson, NSF, II, 375.
7. *Ibid.*, p. 401.
8. Bourgeat, pp. 89–90.
9. N. T. Dagher, *Napoléon textes inédites et variantes* (Geneva, 1955), pp. 15–16. Not in Savant or Bourgeat.
10. Bourgeat, p. 90.
11. *Ibid.*, p. 91.
12. Savant, pp. 173–6. Not in Bourgeat.
13. *Ibid.*, p. 176. Not in Bourgeat.
14. *Ibid.*, p. 178. Not in Bourgeat.
15. Bourrienne, II, 385.
16. S. Gay, *Le Salon de l'impératrice Joséphine à Aix-la-Chapelle* (n. p., n. d., pamphlet, BN), pp. 120–52.
17. LNJ, II, 233–4.

16. CORONATION

1. Corr., IX, no. 8020.
2. *Ibid.*, no. 8027.
3. Bibliothèque Thiers, Paris, Fonds Masson, no. 28.
4. Corr., X, no. 8161.
5. P. L. Roederer, *Journal* (Paris, 1909), p. 214.
6. A. T. M. de Thiard, *Souvenirs diplomatiques et militaires* (Paris, 1900), p. 5.
7. L. F. J. de Bausset, *Mémoires anecdotiques* (2nd edn, Paris, 1827), I, 24.
8. A. L. Imbert de Saint-Amand, *La Cour de l'impératrice Joséphine* (Paris, n. d.), p. 176.
9. Savant, p. 182. Not in Bourgeat.

17. WAR ONCE MORE

1. LNJ, II, 238–42.
2. Hanoteau, *Empereur*, pp. 5–9.
3. Bourgeat, p. 92.
4. Corr., XI, no. 9179.
5. Bourgeat, p. 97.
6. *Ibid.*, p. 99.
7. LNJ, II, 246–7.
8. Bourgeat, p. 103.
9. *Ibid.*, pp. 103–4.
10. *Ibid.*, p. 105. Date should be December 9.
11. *Ibid.*
12. Corr., XI, no. 9636.
13. *Ibid.*, no. 9638.
14. LNJ, II, 252.
15. Corr., XI, no. 9683.
16. *Ibid.*, XII, no. 10099.
17. Mauguin, *L'Impératrice Joséphine*, p. 83.

18. Corr., XI, no. 10841.
19. Bourgeat, p. 109.
20. *Ibid.*, pp. 107, 110.
21. *Ibid.*, p. 112.
22. *Ibid.*, p. 113.
23. *Ibid.*, p. 119.
24. *Ibid.*
25. *Ibid.*, p. 120.
26. *Ibid.*, pp. 112, 117, 121, 122.
27. *Ibid.*, p. 123.
28. *Ibid.*, pp. 125, 126.
29. *Ibid.*, pp. 127–8.
30. *Ibid.*, p. 128.
31. *Ibid.*, p. 132.
32. Masson, *Napoléon et les femmes*, p. 167.
33. Bourgeat, p. 141.
34. *Ibid.*, p. 138.
35. *Ibid.*, p. 145.
36. *Ibid.*, p. 129.
37. *Ibid.*, p. 137.
38. *Ibid.*, p. 140.
39. LNJ, II, 268–9.
40. Hanoteau, *Empereur*, pp. 37–8; LNJ, II, 266.
41. Hanoteau, *Empereur*, pp. 38, 42.
42. Bourgeat, p. 146.
43. *Ibid.*, p. 147.

18. ON BEING AN EMPRESS

1. S. J. Watson, *Carnot, 1753–1823* (London, 1954), p. 161.
2. To Montholon, quoted in Kemble, *Napoleon Immortal*, p. 128.
3. Constant, *Mémoires*, I, 158.
4. Masson, JIR, pp. 63–4.

19. 'MALMAISON, C'EST JOSÉPHINE'

1. B. Greatheed, *An Englishman in Paris* (London, 1953), p. 136.
2. Bourgeat, p. 182.
3. Greatheed, *An Englishman in Paris*, p. 136.
4. E. P. Ventenat, *Jardin de la Malmaison* (Paris, 1803), I, dedication.
5. Greatheed, *An Englishman in Paris*, p. 136.

20. DIVORCE

1. A. J. G. de Caulaincourt, *With Napoleon in Russia* (New York, 1935), p. 338.
2. Hanoteau, *Empereur*, pp. 48–9.
3. *Ibid.*, p. 49, n. 1.
4. H. G. de Bertrand, *Cahiers de Sainte-Hélène: Journal, 1818–1819* (Paris, 1959), p. 442.
5. Corr., XVI, no. 13329.
6. Hanoteau, *Empereur*, pp. 52–3.
7. *Ibid.*, p. 55.
8. Corr., XVIII, no. 15061.
9. Bourgeat, p. 181.
10. *Ibid.*, p. 183.
11. Bourgeat, p. 187.
12. Abrantès, IV, 126–7.
13. De Bausset, *Mémoires anecdotiques*, I, 370–3.
14. Masson, JR, p. 80.
15. *Ibid.*, pp. 81–2.
16. R. Pichevin, *Le Mariage de l'empereur* (Paris, n.d.), p. 19.
17. *Ibid.*, pp. 14–15.

18. L. Madelin, *Fouché* (Paris, 1900), II, 146.

19. Pichevin, *Le Mariage de l'empereur*, p. 16.

21. SECLUSION

1. Bourgeat, p. 192.
2. *Ibid.*, pp. 196–7.
3. *Ibid.*, p. 200. Not dated, but January 28, 1810.
4. *Ibid.*, p. 199.
5. Hanoteau, *Empereur*, pp. 69–70.
6. *Ibid.*, p. 71.
7. Bourgeat, p. 201.
8. LNJ, II, 298–300.
9. *Ibid.*, p. 301.
10. Queen Hortense, *Mémoires*, II, 97.
11. Bourgeat, pp. 202–3.
12. *Ibid.*, p. 203.
13. *Ibid.*, p. 204.
14. *Ibid.*, pp. 204–5.
15. Maurice de Tascher, *Le Journal de campagne d'un cousin de l'impératrice* (Paris, 1933), pp. 289–90.
16. G. Lenôtre, *Napoleon* (Paris, 1933), p. 159.
17. LNJ, II, 316–17.
18. Bourgeat, p. 208.
19. Hanoteau, *Empereur*, p. 78 n.
20. Bourgeat, p. 208.
21. *Ibid.*, pp. 209–11. Madame de Rémusat's letter is also given here.
22. LNJ, II, 331–6.
23. Bourgeat, p. 214.
24. Bourgeat, pp. 215–16. Wrongly given as 1813.

25. *Ibid.*, p. 216. Wrongly given as 1813.
26. Hanoteau, *Empereur*, pp. 94–5.
27. *Ibid.*, p. 96.
28. *Ibid.*, pp. 96–101.
29. Bourgeat, p. 215.
30. LNJ, II, 369 n.

22. FINALE

1. Bourgeat, p. 217.
2. Masson, JR, p. 310.
3. *Ibid.*, pp. 316–17.
4. *Ibid.*, pp. 318–19.
5. *Ibid.*, pp. 319–20.
6. Hanoteau, *Empereur*, p. 117.
7. A. J. G. de Caulaincourt, *No Peace with Napoleon!* (New York, 1936), p. 191.
8. *Ibid.*, p. 244.
9. *Ibid.*, p. 258.
10. Masson, JR, p. 330.
11. *Ibid.*, pp. 331–2.
12. Bibliothèque Thiers, Paris, Fonds Masson, no. 416 (copy).
13. Hanoteau, *Empereur*, p. 118.
14. Bourgeat, pp. 216–17.
15. Mauguin, *L'Impératrice Joséphine*, p. 87.
16. Masson, JR, p. 367.
17. Cf. E. A. de Las Cases, *Le Mémorial de Sainte-Hélène* (Paris, 1951), I, 226; Bertrand, *Cahiers de Sainte-Hélène: Journal, 1818–1819*, pp. 408–10.
18. Masson, JR, p. 371. Madame Bertrand, who with

her husband, Count Bertrand, accompanied Napoleon both to Elba and St Helena, claims to have been the one to give the Emperor the news of Josephine's death. See *The St Helena Journal of General Baron Gourgaud* (London, 1923), p. 293. The widely accepted story that Napoleon's dying exclamation at St Helena in 1821 was 'Joséphine' has no better authority than that of Count Montholon, whose memoirs were not published until 1846. He is a most unreliable witness to whom the servants at St Helena gave the nickname, 'the Liar'. The evidence favours Bertrand's version: 'Who retreats? – At the head of the army!' See R. Korngold, *The Last Years of Napoleon* (New York, 1959), p. 391.

Index

A.B. = Alexander de Beauharnais; J = Josephine; N = Napoleon